Personalized Learning Through Adaptive Systems and Intelligent Tutoring

Assia Benabid
University Hassan II, Morocco

Imane El Imadi
University of Hassan II, Morocco

Ghizlane Chemsi
University Hassan II, Morocco

IGI Global
Scientific Publishing
Publishing Tomorrow's Research Today

Vice President of Editorial Melissa Wagner
Director of Acquisitions Mikaela Felty
Director of Book Development Jocelynn Hessler
Production Manager Mike Brehm
Cover Design Jose Rosado

Published in the United States of America by
IGI Global Scientific Publishing
701 East Chocolate Avenue
Hershey, PA, 17033, USA
Tel: 717-533-8845
Fax: 717-533-7115
Website: https://www.igi-global.com E-mail: cust@igi-global.com

Library of Congress Cataloging-in-Publication Data

Names: Benabid, Assia, 1965- editor. | El Imadi, Imane, 1987- editor. | Chemsi, Ghizlane, 1980- editor.
Title: Personalized learning through adaptive systems and intelligent tutoring / Edited by Assia Benabid, Imane El Imadi, Ghizlane Chemsi.
Description: Hershey, PA : IGI Global Scientific Publishing, [2025] | Includes bibliographical references and index. | Summary: "Through a combination of theoretical insights, practical applications, and case studies, this book examines how these technologies can transform education into a more inclusive and effective experience. It also addresses important challenges such as data privacy and accessibility, ensuring that the benefits of personalized learning are available to all"-- Provided by publisher.
Identifiers: LCCN 2024059632 (print) | LCCN 2024444467 (ebook) | ISBN 9798337307404 (hardcover) | ISBN 9798337307411 (paperback) | ISBN 9798337307428 (ebook)
Subjects: LCSH: Individualized instruction. | Tutors and tutoring--Technological innovations. | Student-centered learning.
Classification: LCC LB1031 .P3734 2025 (print) | LCC LB1031 (ebook) | DDC 371.39/4--dc23/eng/20250213
LC record available at https://lccn.loc.gov/2024059632
LC ebook record available at https://lccn.loc.gov/2024444467

British Cataloguing in Publication Data
A Cataloguing in Publication record for this book is available from the British Library.

Table of Contents

Detailed Table of Contents

Smart education using Explainable Artificial Intelligence (XAI) aims to enhance the learning experience by integrating advanced AI technologies that are transparent, understandable, and interpretable. This approach fits together the strengths of AI with the requirement of clarity and trust in educational systems. The implementation of Explainable Artificial Intelligence (XAI) within smart educational platforms is becoming a remarkable revolution in how education is delivered, encountered, and monitored. This revolution impacts several aspects of the cycle of education, ranging from individualized learning to crafting policy. It provides transparency and accountability through XAI so that the learning materials created with AI will be fair and accessible to everyone. The shift to a flexible, data-driven, and student-centric education model is developing learners with the necessary skills to navigate shifting global landscapes.

The renovation of pedagogical activities aims not only to put an end to the monotony of learning but also to keep pace with the evolution of the digital era. This research has two objectives: first, it seeks to support the approach of assessing mind maps using AI technologies; second, it aims to analyze learners' motivation during the creation of mind maps based on a questionnaire that evaluates their situational motivation toward this pedagogical activity. This cross-sectional, analytical, and quantitative study was conducted with a sample of 300 second-year scientific baccalaureate students from the Settat Casablanca Academy (Morocco) during the 2024–2025 academic year. The measurement instrument used (SIMS) to assess situational motivation consists of four dimensions: intrinsic motivation, identified regulation, external regulation, and amotivation. The statistical analysis of the results reveals a significant increase in situational motivation during the creation of mind maps, indicating that the intervention has a positive impact.

Digital innovations are profoundly transforming teaching and learning methods. Research shows that integrating video microlearning quizzes as a pedagogical strategy promotes active student involvement and encourages them to adopt optimized learning approaches. The adoption of these technologies also generates a multitude of data that facilitates the evaluation of learners' behavioral engagement. This study aims to explore the impact of video microlearning quizzes on student engagement and motivation. Through a quantitative approach, the analysis of digital data from student activities provided insights into their degree of involvement and consequently their behavioral engagement. Additionally, a questionnaire based on the Situational Motivation Scale (SIMS) was administered at the end of the semester to analyze

A lack of standardized communication was identified among Intesive Care Unite (ICU) providers in a public hospital in southern Morocco. This quasi-experimental pre-post test study aimed to evaluate the effectiveness of personalized simulation-based learning using the SAED tool (French adaptation of SBAR) to enhance structured communication between nurses and physicians in intensive care. Eleven nurses participated in the study, which employed three data collection instruments: a sociodemographic questionnaire, a SAED knowledge assessment, and an evaluation of communication as perceived by the recipient. Data analysis through SPSS revealed significant improvements in participants' theoretical knowledge of the SAED tool and their performance in structured communication during telephone calls with physicians. The study demonstrates the effectiveness of this approach in enhancing ICU nurses' communication skills, suggesting potential benefits for patient safety and quality of care, although further research with larger samples is recommended to validate these findings.

Purpose: Personalized adaptive learning uses technology to adjust teaching strategies in real time, adapting to the characteristics, performance and evolution of each learner. This scoping review aims to explore and synthesize existing knowledge on the application of personalized, individualized, intelligent or responsive learning systems in the training of nursing and midwifery students. Methods: This review followed exploratory review methodology in accordance with PRISMA guidelines. Searches were conducted in the main international databases: Scopus, PubMed, ScienceDirect. Results: The included studies reported that Adaptive Learning improves students' academic performance and promotes engagement, with an increase in learner involvement. Likewise, it enables learning to be personalized by adjusting content to individual student needs. Conclusion: This study explored the use of personalized adaptive learning among midwifery and nursing students. Further research is needed to address technological challenges and enhance its implementation in education.

The chapter discusses personalized learning and adaptive systems, emphasizing their role in enhancing student engagement and equity. It highlights how these approaches tailor educational experiences to meet individual needs through real-time data analysis. Key features include continuous assessment, immediate feedback, and customized learning pathways that allow students to progress at their own pace, fostering motivation and ownership of their learning. Adaptive systems also address educational disparities by providing targeted support for underperforming students, ensuring equitable access to resources. By personalizing the learning experience, these technologies enable students to choose pathways that align with their interests and learning styles, promoting a sense of autonomy. Ultimately, the chapter argues that integrating adaptive systems into personalized learning frameworks is essential for creating an equitable educational environment where all students can thrive.

Nursing students face several difficulties in understanding the material of an emergency care course.This study describes the design and evaluation of a virtual learning environment (VLE) integrated into a flipped classroom approach to address these issues. Using the ADDIE model, the VLE incorporated adaptive learning mechanisms to personalize content based on student progress and performance. The pilot implementation involved 56 second-year nursing students in Casablanca, Morocco, who accessed online resources and participated in class activities. Results showed moderate resource usage, with peaks before assessments, and highlighted multiple-choice questions as the most utilized and appreciated resource. Students expressed overall satisfaction with the course design, resource variety, and user-friendliness. However, limited use of interactive tools like forums was observed, and no significant correlation was found between content usage frequency and exam scores. The study suggests that flipped classrooms and VLEs can effectively support nursing education.

This longitudinal study explores the integration of immersive virtual labs to bridge the gap between language input and effective output for first-year Master students

Preface

The landscape of education is undergoing a radical transformation, driven by the intersection of artificial intelligence, data analytics, and personalized learning methodologies. In this evolving context, adaptive systems and intelligent tutoring technologies have emerged as powerful tools that respond dynamically to individual learner needs, offering personalized paths through instructional content. This book, *Personalized Learning Through Adaptive Systems and Intelligent Tutoring*, is an exploration of these technologies—how they function, how they are being applied, and how they are shaping the future of learning across diverse educational settings.

As societies navigate the demands of a digital era, there is increasing recognition that traditional, one-size-fits-all approaches to education are no longer sufficient. Learners today bring with them varied backgrounds, abilities, learning styles, and goals. The promise of adaptive learning lies in its ability to meet learners where they are, providing customized support, feedback, and pacing to enhance understanding and engagement. Intelligent tutoring systems, powered by advances in AI and machine learning, are not just supporting this vision—they are redefining what is pedagogically possible.

In today's interconnected world, the need for scalable, flexible, and efficient learning solutions is more urgent than ever. The global challenges of accessibility, educational inequality, and the rapidly changing demands of the job market require innovations that can cater to a wide range of learners and contexts. Adaptive learning systems, powered by sophisticated algorithms, hold the potential to bridge these gaps by offering targeted instruction that adapts to the learner's unique needs. As such, these technologies do not just complement traditional teaching—they can radically change how knowledge is transferred and acquired. The ability of adaptive systems to continuously adjust to the needs of individual learners makes them an essential tool for fostering deeper engagement, improving educational outcomes, and preparing learners for the challenges of the future.

This book is intended for a broad and interdisciplinary audience. Researchers in the fields of educational technology, learning sciences, and AI will find a wealth of theoretical and empirical insights. Educators and instructional designers will discover practical frameworks and applications to inform their practice. Policymakers and educational leaders will benefit from an overview of the systemic implications and policy considerations tied to the implementation of these technologies. Developers and innovators will be able to draw inspiration from real-world use cases and best practices. This convergence of perspectives aims to foster a richer, more inclusive conversation around personalized learning.

Beyond the technological promise, this volume also addresses the critical issues that come with it. Questions of data privacy, algorithmic bias, accessibility, and ethical implementation are woven throughout the discussion. Adaptive learning must not only be efficient and effective—it must also be equitable and responsible. The contributions in this book reflect a commitment to this balanced view, acknowledging the power of innovation while remaining grounded in the human dimensions of learning.

As we stand at the intersection of cutting-edge technology and long-established educational principles, this book aims to chart a course for how personalized learning can be implemented in ways that are both innovative and deeply human-centered. The inclusion of diverse voices from different educational contexts offers a holistic view of the potential impact of adaptive learning, while also recognizing the challenges that must be overcome. These insights will provide educators, researchers, and policymakers with the tools to engage critically with emerging technologies, ensuring that they are used responsibly and effectively.

By compiling leading research, applied strategies, and visionary outlooks, this book aspires to serve both as a comprehensive introduction to adaptive systems and intelligent tutoring, and as a springboard for further inquiry and development. It contributes to the growing discourse on how education systems can leverage technology not simply to digitize instruction, but to transform it—making it more responsive, inclusive, and aligned with the needs of lifelong learners in an increasingly complex world.

Ultimately, *Personalized Learning Through Adaptive Systems and Intelligent Tutoring* advocates for a future in which all learners are empowered to succeed through learning experiences that adapt to them, rather than the other way around. We hope this volume inspires thoughtful reflection, meaningful dialogue, and bold action among those dedicated to the future of education.

Acknowledgments

We would like to express our deepest gratitude to everyone who supported us throughout the development of this book, ***Personalized Learning Through Adaptive Systems and Intelligent Tutoring***. The journey of writing and compiling this work has been both intellectually enriching and personally rewarding, and it would not have been possible without the encouragement and collaboration of many individuals.

A special thanks goes to *IGI Global* for their unwavering support, professionalism, and commitment to academic excellence. Their guidance throughout the publication process has been instrumental in transforming our vision into a reality and bringing this book to a global readership.

We also wish to acknowledge our colleagues, contributors, and research communities whose insights and feedback helped sharpen our ideas and deepen the quality of the work presented here. Their shared dedication to advancing educational technologies has been both motivating and affirming.

Lastly, we are grateful to our families, friends, and institutions for their patience, encouragement, and belief in our work. Their support made it possible for us to dedicate ourselves fully to this project.

Assia Benabid, Imane El Imadi, and Ghizlan Chemsi

Introduction

The rapid evolution of artificial intelligence and data-driven technologies has ushered in a new era of personalized learning—one that holds the potential to transform education at every level. Adaptive systems and intelligent tutoring platforms are no longer distant promises; they are becoming integral components of modern educational ecosystems. This book, ***Personalized Learning Through Adaptive Systems and Intelligent Tutoring***, provides a timely and comprehensive exploration of these innovations. Through theoretical frameworks, practical applications, and in-depth case studies, the authors illuminate how adaptive technologies can tailor instruction, foster engagement, and improve outcomes for diverse learners across contexts.

What sets this volume apart is its balanced approach. It not only celebrates the potential of intelligent tutoring and adaptive learning systems but also engages critically with the ethical, technical, and pedagogical challenges they present. Issues such as data privacy, accessibility, and equitable access are explored with depth and responsibility. This book will serve as an essential resource for educators, researchers, developers, and policymakers who are committed to building a future of education that is both technologically advanced and deeply human-centered. As you begin reading, prepare to be challenged, inspired, and equipped with new perspectives on what personalized learning can—and should—look like.

Chapter 1
Smart Education:
A Need of the Hour Using Explainable Artificial Intelligence (XAI)

Harshali Yogesh Patil
https://orcid.org/0000-0003-1228-8737
S.K. Somaiya College, Somaiya Vidyavihar University, India

Marielia Assumption
S.K. Somaiya College, Somaiya Vidyavihar University, India

G. B. Hema Latha
S.K. Somaiya College, Somaiya Vidyavihar University, India

ABSTRACT

Smart education using Explainable Artificial Intelligence (XAI) aims to enhance the learning experience by integrating advanced AI technologies that are transparent, understandable, and interpretable. This approach fits together the strengths of AI with the requirement of clarity and trust in educational systems. The implementation of Explainable Artificial Intelligence (XAI) within smart educational platforms is becoming a remarkable revolution in how education is delivered, encountered, and monitored. This revolution impacts several aspects of the cycle of education, ranging from individualized learning to crafting policy. It provides transparency and accountability through XAI so that the learning materials created with AI will be fair and accessible to everyone. The shift to a flexible, data-driven, and student-centric education model is developing learners with the necessary skills to navigate shifting global landscapes.

DOI: 10.4018/979-8-3373-0740-4.ch001

INTRODUCTION

Overview of XAI

Decision-making has transformed to more informed measures by using machine learning and artificial intelligence models in most organizations and industries. Over time, the developments of these technologies become more enhanced and complex, thereby challenging the understanding of humans about the process of AI solutions' decision-making. These challenges can be addressed using explainable AI. Explainability has been recognized as a crucial component for AI system adoption by 2020 in a variety of scenarios (Doshi-Velez & Kim, 2017; Lipton, 2018; Ribeiro, Singh, & Guestrin, 2016a). XAI is a systematic approach, and a collection of techniques designed to explain the results and outputs produced by AI and machine learning (ML) algorithms. This chapter will explore the concept of XAI, how it works and why it is needed. The traditional programming and Machine Learning (ML) types are showcased in figure 1.

Figure 1. Traditional Programming and Machine Learning types.

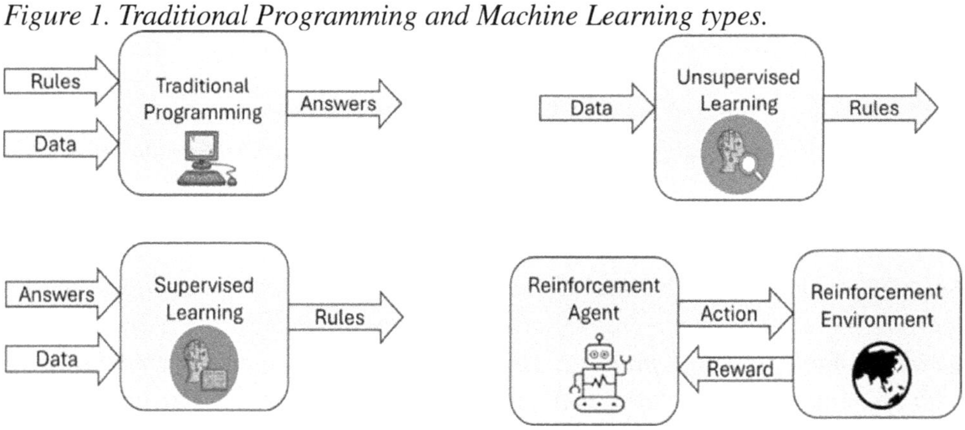

In ML models, accuracy and interpretability are the important parameters. Accuracy specifies how good the model is, whereas interpretability provides how the model can be represented. The goal of the ML model is to get good accuracy and high interpretability. But in some real-world use cases there is a trade-off between accuracy and interpretability. The highly interpretable algorithms such as classification rules, or linear regression, are often inaccurate. Whereas very accurate deep neural network algorithms are classic examples of black boxes. The graphical depiction of accuracy and interpretability of ML algorithms is shown in figure 2.

Machine Learning models are biased and unfair and that's one of the biggest challenges with the modelling. The models are trained on the data which are incomplete, biased and unrepresentative. These models learn from the biased and reflect results in the predictions as well, that leads to discrimination and unfair results. This compromises the fairness and neutrality of the models.

The roots of the explainable AI can be traced back to early days of machine learning research work, where transparency and interpretability was considered as the most important factor. This historical context has led to the development of a wide variety of explainable AI methods and approaches, that offers critical insights and benefits across various applications and domains (Adai & Barrada, 2018; Saeed & Omlin, 2023).

Figure 2. The trade-off between interpretability and accuracy of some relevant ML models (Morocho-Cayamcela et al, 2019)

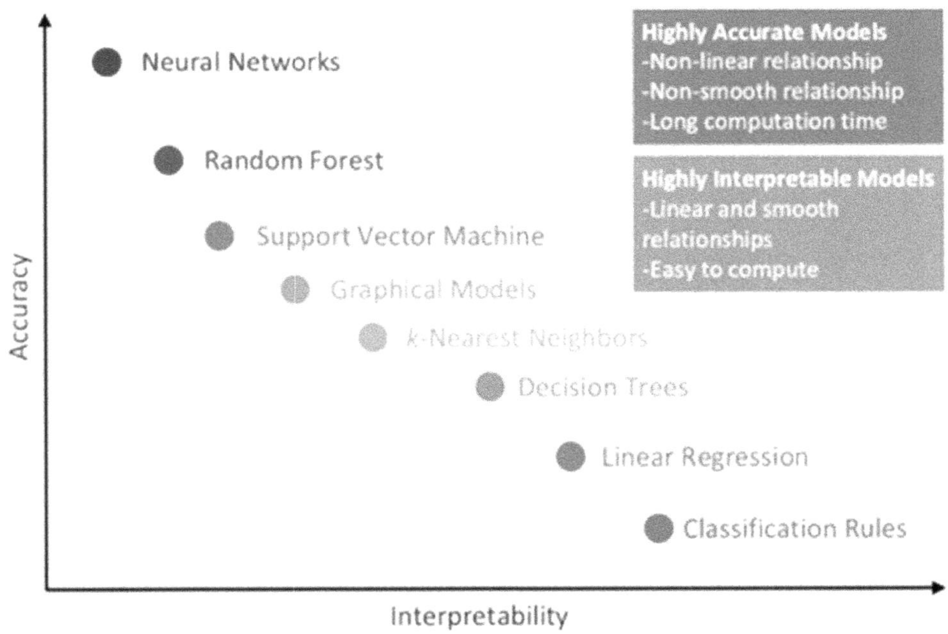

Explainable AI categorisation is based on model organization, techniques to provide understandable insights for the decision making process. The key categories of the XAI are model specific approaches, types of explanations, explanatory frameworks and evaluation of explanations. Generally, there are two options such as, to ensure that the trained machine learning algorithm can be interpreted or to derive human understandable explanations of a complex trained model. This is usually referred to as model based or post hoc post hoc methods, that can be further divided into black box approaches and white box approaches. Black box approaches mean nothing about the model is not known, it just uses the relationship between inputs and outputs. However, the white box approaches have access to the model internals (e.g. gradients or weights of a neural network). The XAI leads to the whole psychology area about what makes good explanations and which explanation types are the best for humans. Hence the response function is used to derive explanations. Figure 3 describes the categorization in XAI, where the method covers model agnostic and model specific types (Angelov et al, 2021). The model agnostic means the XAI algorithm can be applied on any kind of model such as random forest neural network or support vector machine model whereas on the other hand model specific types are only for neural networks. The model specific approach includes comparatively simple models like linear regression or decision trees. These models are inherently easier to explain. The complex models such as neural networks are interpreted after the model training is done. Some examples of such models are SHAP, LIME, and attention mechanisms.

Figure 3. Categorization in XAI.

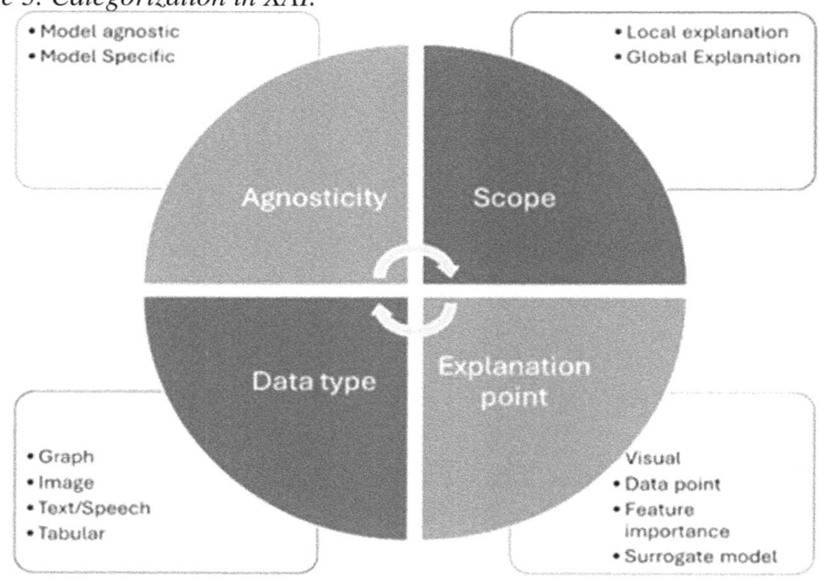

The XAI categorizes the methods into global and local approaches, this refers to explaining the whole model or just parts of the model. The decision boundary of a complex model can be highly non-linear for instance, consider a classification problem and the complex function can separate the two classes. Hence sometimes it just doesn't make sense to provide explanations for the global model. Global explanations provide an overview of the model's behaviour across the entire dataset, while local explanations focus on individual predictions. XAI use terminology feature importance to indicate how much each feature contributes to a model's predictions.

XAI categorised as explanatory frameworks to provide clear and understandable explanation of decisions made by AI models. The Rule-based Systems generate human-readable rules that describe the decision-making process whereas the counterfactual explanations provide evidence for decisions by demonstrating how small adjustments to input attributes could produce alternative results.

Evaluation of explanations in XAI is crucial to ensure that the provided insights are meaningful and trustworthy. The key evaluation criteria cover fidelity, which specifies how well the explanation exhibits the model's actual decision making. Stability indicates the consistency of explanations when data changes slightly or the model changes slightly. Assessment of how well user needs are met in terms of usefulness and clarity is referred to as metrics of evaluation.

XAI uses ethical considerations where decision understanding is crucial. Mostly it is used in critical applications like healthcare and finance, to address the bias, transparency and fairness.

In recent years, researchers and developers of artificial intelligence have given more importance to XAI models. Indeed, the introduction of highly interactive technologies that facilitate close collaboration with users has rendered explainability an essential. This aims to mitigate disbelief and the perception of unpredictability that AI can generate, particularly among amateurs. Likewise, XAI's potential as a significant resource has been recognized due to its ability to improve intelligent systems' usability and lessen the negative effects of black box systems (Carli & Calvaresi, 2024).

Smart Education

Smart education refers to a cutting-edge technology used for teaching and learning, which is used to enhance educational outcomes. The smart education research has undergone rapid advancements, aimed at the transformation of educational systems, thereby facilitating increased engagement and empowerment for students, educators, and administrators (Singh & Miah, 2020). The advancement of novel technologies facilitates learners in achieving greater efficacy, efficiency, flexibility, and comfort in their educational endeavours. Learners use intelligent devices to obtain digital resources via wireless networks and to engage in both individualized and coherent learning experiences. The concept of smart education has acquired keen interest, which encapsulates learning in the digital era (Zhu et al, 2016). Smart education embraces digital tools, personalized learning experiences, and data-driven insights to create a more effective and engaging environment for students. Smart education adopts a variety of technologies, like online learning platforms, interactive simulations, and artificial intelligence. With the help of technology advancement, educators can create tailored lessons. This facility helps the students/learners to achieve the learning outcomes. Adaptive learning software are available to identify the strengths and weaknesses of the learners in real time. The customized learning plan and resources will help the learners to maintain motivation and interest in learning.

Importance of explainability in educational AI applications

XAI has garnered significant scholarly interest in recent times, particularly as AI systems are increasingly integrated within diverse sectors, notably in the realm of education. Fostering trust and enhancing the effectiveness of AI systems within educational contexts necessitates a robust ability to interpret the processes underlying their decision-making (Chaushi et al, 2023). Explainability in the domain of XAI indicates clarifying the decisions made by AI systems. The idea of these AI systems is to reduce the "black box" nature found in many machine learning models, where the reasoning behind their results is unclear and not easily understood by humans. The key properties of the explainability are shown in figure 4. Explainability helps the stakeholders to understand how an AI system functions and can ensure informed decisions. Transparency deals with how clear and logical the model's operations and decisions are. Interpretability indicates the degree to which a human can understand the cause of a decision. Justification means providing evidence for a particular prediction or decision. Trust means improving the user's confidence and providing AI system reliability through the understandable outcomes.

Figure 4. Key components of explainability

Explainable AI in education is crucial for trust, effectiveness, accountability, personalized feedback, diagnostic insights, and parent engagement. Explainable AI is gaining scholarly attention as it becomes more integrated into various sectors. In education domain feedback plays a vital role in facilitating learning and motivation. Educators also use feedback to evaluate teaching strategies and support individual student needs. Data analysis is vital for educational institutions to improve performance and decision-making, benefiting administrators and managers(Khosravi et al., 2022; Drake & Walz,2018).

LITERATURE REVIEW

To boost model accuracy and instill confidence in educational systems, explainable AI (XAI) focuses on enhancing the transparency and understanding of AI decision-making processes. XAI employs an array of tools, including rule sets, logic-based systems, quantitative indicators, and visualizations, to clarify how AI models derive their decisions, the factors that influence these outcomes, and how such decisions may shift with the introduction of new information. This methodology effectively narrows the gap between sophisticated AI models and their interpretability, thereby increasing access to AI-driven insights for educators and students alike. While the XAI research outlines its mission to provide clear justifications for the decisions made by AI systems, it does not specifically highlight any research gaps or limitations in existing XAI approaches that could impede the progress toward developing transparent and comprehensible AI models (Wang, 2024).

Explainable AI, or XAI, increases the transparency and interpretability of AI decision-making while enhancing model accuracy to place trust in the overall education systems. XAI applies all the wide range of tools that include rules sets, logic-based systems, quantitative indicators, and visualizations to make clearer how AI models derive their decisions as well as what factors influence those outcomes and how such decisions might evolve with new information. The methodology successfully closes the significant gap between state-of-the-art AI models and their interpretability and is, therefore, making it possible for both educators and learners to increase accessibility of insights from AI. Although the XAI research sets out its objective as being able to clearly justify the decisions made by AI systems, there is no explicit identification of research gaps or limitations of existing approaches to XAI that may limit the advancement toward achieving explainable and intelligible AI(Singhal et al, 2024).

This research will improve the transparency of AI models used in LMS and EDM by studying XAI in the education sector. What is specifically appealing about XAI is how its main educational purposes revolve around explanation - but in the context of providing an accurate account based on learning needs. It underlines the requirement for interpretation explanations that are compatible with the learning intent and traces the growth of XAI methods in this context. The paper identifies gaps in research that show areas to be explored further and the need for a better adaptation of the methodologies of XAI into educational contexts. The study underlines the need for developing new methodologies of XAI with better interpretability and capabilities of decision-making in educational settings and thus stronger benefits of AI systems in learning for students. (Rachha & Seyam, 2023).

This study explores the role that XAI plays in education, especially as a critical use for clarity in decision-making within the educational sphere. XAI enables the facilitation of increased understanding between teachers and students and collaboration among man and machine by elaborating on thought processes that support AI-based recommendations and evaluations. Apart from this, the paper analyzes the application of XAI in various fields such as banking, health care, and transportations with examples of ways such applications will promote societal growth and industrial development. Of course, XAI has achieved great milestones; however, this domain is too young, with much left to explore to combat its existing problems and enhance its performance. From the discussions above, it can be surmised that continuous innovation is necessary in XAI for this to become clearer and more operational, especially in academic contexts to transform instruction methods and assist learners.(Liu, 2023).

The KONX approach aims to provide a dynamic knowledge network for predictive models in academic advising at higher education institutions using semantic web technologies. It introduces better querying of data and adaptability via a feedback mechanism to align multiple educational data sources. The case study, therefore, tests a prototype that underlines transparency and user confidence in AI systems for predicting student outcomes. However, it does not explore whether KONX's methodology is scalable to larger datasets or even applicable in any other environment but the experimental one as well as potential challenges associated with applicability of its results into real life. (Iatrellis et al, 2023).

Customizes the learning experience for each individual student who fosters the growth of tExplainable Artificial Intelligence (XAI) significantly enhances the critical thinking skills and adaptive systems of the students, even ensuring transparency. their analytical thinking ability and Solution oriented skills go along with the existing knowledge and cognitive abilities. The primary benefit of XAI in educational settings lies in its ability to clarify AI decisions, helping students find the reason over the AI's recommendations. This clarity brings deeper reflection and metacognitive awareness. Platforms like RiPPLE exemplify this approach, leveraging learning science and crowdsourced data to provide tailored activity suggestions. These recommendations ensure that students grasp the rationale behind their learning paths, aligning with their current knowledge levels. By utilizing XAI, adaptive learning environments not only address students' immediate educational needs but also lay the foundation for them to become independent and critical thinkers in the future. Therefore, XAI significantly enhances adaptive learning systems by fostering and supporting the development of critical thinking skills (Idrizi, 2024)

It means discussing how to introduce the XAI subject in the classroom in order to provide individualized learning, whereby students and AI systems can exchange explanations. The paper also describes the process by which students self-explain their thought processes in order to discover which knowledge and skills are deficient. Simultaneously, the AI system uses abstract representations of algorithms and its underlying mechanisms to explain its suggestions. In addition to developing students' metacognitive abilities, this mutual explanation process provides insightful information about the difficulties that students encounter when their knowledge or abilities are lacking. This method seeks to enhance learning outcomes by using self. To improve overall educational efficiency and better match educational interventions with the requirements of individual learners, the study highlights the potential advantages of adopting XAI technologies, also known as Educational explainable Artificial Intelligence technologies (Ogata et al, 2024)

By adapting analytic approach]with this analytical approach the critical role of Explainable AI (XAI) in enhancing model transparency and fostering human-AI collaboration in an era dominated by advanced AI technologies. It addresses the reality that XAI responds positively for higher accountability and trust-building through the explanation of AI system decisions. XAI makes it easier to explain how an AI system comes up with decisions and hence creates avenues for stakeholders to understand and rely on the outcome of automation more effectively. It introduces post-hoc explanation techniques as an important instrument in the radical improvement of the users' understanding and their trust in AI-developed solutions. It also speaks to the need for further research into more sophisticated post-hoc methods of interpretation of difficult complex processes such as neural networks, and the promise of models that are more interpretable, such as decision trees. In particular, it illustrates how XAI can change AI-driven decision-making by exploiting transparent models that potentially open up accountability and collaboration even more than in a world where algorithmic decisions are made more impossible and opaque. (Kumawat, 2024).

The article allows the incorporation of enriching knowledge and trust among learners in computer science education, explained with the back of a competency-based framework. The specific focus has been made on how students' individual attributes, such as their perceived success, engagement, and performance, impact their utilization and understanding of these explanations. Thus, it can be seen that the study calls for a far more effective method to meet learner's needs. Such a method would take into account the use of a variety of explanations, including local and counterfactual kinds, and textual and visual formats. It, therefore, stresses the importance of offering individualized explanations to the learner when they are needed to enhance effective learning in technologically advanced settings. At the same time, it underlines that research in explanation effectiveness has an academic gap concerning personal traits, and therefore further research should be conducted to make explanations adapt to different learners' needs and to develop better educational outcomes. (Felix et al, 2024).

This research examines the usage of explainable AI in applied analytics, particularly through a case study that will be based on predicting student performance on online courses. Due to the sheer volume of data online education has created, there is a rapid deployment of XAI,to identify the at-risk students, and provide tailored feedback.Nonetheless, grasping these models is vital for establishing trust and ensuring their efficacy. The research showcases how XAI methodologies can refine model diagnostics and tackle performance-related issues. Additionally, it underscores how various XAI techniques can enhance transparency and foster trust within educational contexts. By making machine learning models more comprehensible, stakeholders are better equipped to understand and utilize these tools for enhanced educational outcomes." (Liu & Khalil, 2024).

This research article introduces EXAIT, utilized in a public high school in Japan to recommend mathematics tests and provide justifications for these recommendations. These can be divided into three groups: RecoExp, interacting with the explanations; RecoCon, receiving only suggestions without any explanation; and RecoNone, not interacting at all. The Bayesian Knowledge Tracing approach was used in the design of the system for supporting students in summer assignments. As a matter of fact, from the analysis of the learning log files of 222 students, it was found that the RecoExp group, involving interaction with the explanations, performed much better than the others. The analysis illustrates how explainable AI can be used to facilitate self-directed learning and motivation for students. As such, although the research concludes the relevance of EXAIT, it does not bridge particular research gaps nor present challenges that can be considered for further study(Majumdar et al, 2023).

2. TRANSPARENCY AND TRUST IN AI SYSTEMS

The paramount requirement for transparency and trust cannot be overstated concerning the development and implementations of AI systems. Here's a more detailed look at these concepts and their relevance:

Transparency:

Transparency in AI refers to the level of clarity and transparency regarding the operation and logical procedure for decision making within an AI system. This includes several critical parts:

1. Explainability- A way in which the dissection of decisions made by an AI system has to be done, which includes rendering inaccessible algorithms understandable for users and stakeholders.
    1. Data Sources- Clearly stating all the data that feeds the AI, its origins, and how it is processed
    2. Model interpretability- How models work with the explanation of weights and features that are used in the prediction.
    3. Algorithmic Process: It involves the techniques and reasoning behind the algorithms that govern the underlying process.
    4. Decision-Making Pathways: Explaining how the AI system reaches its decisions or recommendations.

Trust

Trust in artificial intelligence systems is achieved through transparency, among other factors that are as vital.

1. Consistency: Making sure that AI system functions are dependable and correct even after a long period.
2. Ethical Standards: Establishing and maintaining standards that ensure the prevention of misuse of AI or unhealthy applications.
3. Security Measures: It is an unlawful access prevention mechanism, so that no unqualified access or manipulation while handling secured data.
4. Accountability: Clear definition of who should be held accountable based on the decisions of the logical AI system and identification of arising issues.

The need for clarity and trust cannot be overstated.

- User Confidence: By promoting transparency, users can gain a clearer understanding of AI systems, fostering trust and encouraging their effective utilisation.
- Regulatory Compliance: Numerous regions are instituting regulations that mandate transparency in AI to safeguard user rights and promote ethical practices.

- Error Detection and Correction: Transparency enables the identification of problems or inaccuracies within AI systems, which aids in enhancing performance and driving improvements.

3. THE IMPORTANCE OF EXPLAINABLE AI ENHANCING DECISION-MAKING, TRUST, AND ACCOUNTABILITY

1. Enhances the Decision-Making Insight

Understanding the Process: In the case of AI systems that explain the reasoning behind the conclusions or recommendations being made, users know better why it is also as important to understand what decisions are made

Knowability of Models: Feature importance scores, graphics, and even decision trees can better this process as they help to make complex models understandable by making it clear how different variables affect the outcome

2. Improve Accountability

Recognition of Mistakes: Artificial intelligence system making transparent decisions will allow for error and biases to be found and corrected. That's how accountancy will ensure that the system does work justly and as intended.

Clarifying Responsibility: Explainable AI will certainly clarify who owns the responsibilities of a decision made by the system, but that is more fundamental for handling concerns and making better performance.

3. Boosts User Trust

Informed Choices: The more the users understand the functioning of an AI system, the more they will trust it. More generally, for healthcare for example, if a patient understands how an AI diagnoses a disease based on symptoms and comes up with conclusions, he will be more likely to trust the AI diagnostic tool.

Connections for Empowerment: Clear language by AI methods would help improve relationships between the technologies themselves and the human stakeholders, explaining, in particular, their participation in the fight for fairness and transparency.

4. Encourages ethical and equitable use.

Bias Detection: The most important feature explaining to detect as well as correct the bias related to AI models is explainability. It considers the effect features have on decisions and appropriate changes can be made to remove unjust biases.

Regulatory Compliance: There are many regulations which demand some level of explainability from AI systems. Obeying these standards helps not only achieve compliance but also develop that trust between the user and regulatory authorities.

5. Enhances Education and Training

User Education: It improves education and training. Thus, while supplying informative responses at a user-education level, one educates the users about how well they can be interactive with the AI systems and aware of the limitations of those AI systems. It is particularly important in areas like finance and healthcare where the decision-making process holds a lot of importance.

Developer Understanding: What the developer should realize through explainability is providing such transparency about the performance and behavior of a model to aid further refinement of AI system.

Approaches to Enhance Explainability

1. Model-Agnostic Techniques: Methods such as LIME (Local Interpretable Model-agnostic Explanations) and SHAP (SHapley Additive exPlanations) facilitate the interpretation of predictions from complex models by simulating their behaviour with simpler, more understandable models.
2. Interpretable Algorithms: Utilising models that are inherently interpretable, like linear regression or decision trees, allows for clearer explanations of the decision-making process.
3. Visualization Tools: The use of visual representations, including heatmaps and partial dependence plots, can effectively demonstrate how different feature values influence predictions.
4. Feature Significance: Identifying and ranking the features that have the greatest impact on the model's output, often through scoring systems, enhances understanding.

How transparency can be implemented and its significance in the context of educational AI.

Basically, explainability is key to building and maintaining trust in AI systems. It can make AI contribute to responsible use while also enhancing the user's confidence in the technology, thus ensuring that the human-AI system adheres to ethical and regulatory requirements.

It also has to be transparent, educational, because when applied in the education sector, the technological tools must be seen as fair, efficient, and trustworthy In education they are fair, effective, and trusted by educators, students, and parents.

1. Overview of AI Tool Functionality

It discusses in detail the potential and capabilities of AI-based tools.

Algorithmic Transparency: Explain how the AI system is processing information and how it makes choices. In other words, for example if an AI technology provides customized learning resources, share the cues that drive these recommendations-be it through the performance metrics and student learning preference.

Model Interpretability: How does the model work? That is, how do specific components, such as a student's assessment scores or engagement, influence the prediction of this individual's learning needs or learning achievements?

2. Transparency in Data Utilization
    - Data Collection: The kind of data collected from students and teachers should clearly define types, such as academic record data; interaction logs; and feedback.
    - Data protection: Educate all stakeholders on the safeguards which ensure data will be secured and made anonymous in order to ensure privacy is not violated.
    - Data Objectives: This is a statement that explains why data is being collected, such as for improving educational outcomes, tailoring the learning experience, or reviewing the effectiveness of educational programs.
3. Mechanisms for Feedback and Accountability
    - User Input: Provide education staff, the learners, and their parents with an opportunity to voice thoughts on AI system proposals and decisions. This enables feedback to improve the system so that it meets the expectations of end-users.
    - Error Alertability User Process: Describe methodology whereby users can raise errors or issues about the outputs of the AI system, and explain how the system will be corrected or addressed with users.

- Oversight on Decisions: Human evaluation of any recommendations made by an AI. For instance, if an AI system determines a student needs to be intervened, the related teacher should be given an opportunity to review and verify the recommendation.

4. Bias and Fairness
   - Bias Test: Continuously test to detect and remove biases in the system so that its recommendation and support would not be biased. For example, check whether the system favors or disfavors certain student demographics.
   - Fairness Standards Develop and communicate the fairness standards for the AI system to follow in order to ensure that all students will be treated fairly.
5. Alignment with Educational Goals
   - Learning Objectives: Verify that AI-recommended practices and decisions align with learning objectives and curricula. For example, if an AI tool suggests some additional practice exercises for a student, it should ensure that the practice exercises are in relation to the current objectives for which the student is learning.
   - Effectiveness Review: Track and document the progress of AI interventions/ recommendations towards improvements in student outcomes and make such information available to relevant stakeholders.
6. Educator Training and Engagement
   - Training initiatives: Organizations should provide professional development training to teachers in the techniques of interpreting and using AI-generated insights effectively. Such engagement with the insights will fuel trust and confidence in the recommendations and decisions rendered by the AI system.
   - Collaborative design: In this method, teachers should be involved in designing and developing to ensure the inclusion of their needs and considerations in the decision-making process.
7. Compliance with Regulations
   - Regulatory Compliance: This should ensure that the AI system meets the set regulations and standards in terms of data privacy, ethical use, and educational equity.
   - Transparency updates: Reports or routine updates on the operation of the given AI system must include explanations relating to accuracy, fairness, and influence on educational outcomes.

Some of the greatest examples of transparent educational AI are the Adaptive Learning Platforms: DreamBox and Khan Academy, which clearly show how they alter the learning material according to the engagement and performance of students. Others include AI grading and assessment tools, which usually enlighten learners on how and what criteria and weight are given to one topic or another. Educational resources that appear in recommendation engines can elaborate on their reasoning for making recommendations-thus, for example, for particular areas that a student requires additional support.

Conclusion: Educative AI with transparent decision-making centrally involves clear explanations of decision processes, open communication on data usage, and established lines of feedback and oversight. As an outcome, this transparency will lead to the establishment of trusting relationships, most importantly, and it is an effortless way to ensure that ethically set practices are introduced in the AI tool used in the classroom.

Communicating AI decisions to stakeholders (educators, students, parents)

The success in AI decision communication towards educators, students, and parents is a prime way to making AI in education tools trusted, understood, and used appropriately. Here's how to accomplish this:

1. Customize Communication for Different Stakeholders

Educators: They are required to be well-rounded on the mechanisms by which AI makes its decision-making processes, including technical details and practical applications in the classroom. The educators need to know how AI suggestions can be integrated into their teaching techniques and how they would make sense of the data produced by the AI system.

Students: Explain in simple words how the AI tool supports them in their learning and monitors their performance. Explain how AI feedback or suggestions can better help them reach their learning objectives, what actions they will likely take based on such feedback or guidance.

Parents: Explain to their child exactly the role that AI tools play in their child's educational journey. Implore on the role that AI plays for the tracking of academic progress and recognition of individual learning needs, hence allowing properized learning experiences.

2. Establish Context and Justification

Context of the Decision: Explain the situation in which the AI is making a decision. For instance, if an AI system suggests additional practice exercises, explain what factors it has considered, such as previous performance trends or known learning patterns.

Justification: Clearly, justify the recommendations. For instance, if it is suggested by an AI system to amend a learning plan for a student, explain the rationale that supports the change and hence aligns with the academic goals of the student.

3. Incorporate Visuals and Real-World Examples

Visual Tools Use charts, graphs, and similar visual aids to explain data and AI decision-making processes. Visual elements can make complicated information easier to understand, making it easier to digest for more diversified audiences.

Practical Examples Come and share specific examples in which AI-decision making comes into action. For example, explain a case study where the AI system did not point out the difficulties in learning of a student and then show how that pinpointing leads to improved academic performance.

4. Discuss the Advantages and Challenges

Advantages: Discuss the benefits that their integration can make possible, such as tailoring learning to the student's needs, very swift response time, and focused help. Explain how these outcomes improve the results of the learning process.

Challenges: It should be clear what types of challenges AI systems create. Among these challenges, such things as an AI system's inability to guarantee total integrity of data, its need for human oversight, and potential infrequent errors or biases should be mentioned.

5, Provide Access to Comprehensive Information

Documentation: Detailed documentation or guides should be available explaining how the AI system works, including details of the algorithms, data sources, and decision-making processes. This type of information would help educators have a well-rounded understanding of the system.

FAQs and Support: Designate a 'frequently asked question' section or offer support resources that will enable all the stakeholders to get hold of frequent interrogations they will have as regards the AI system..

6.. Promote Feedback and Communication

Feedback Channels: Open up channels for stakeholders to give feedback on the decisions and performance of the AI system through surveys, feedback forms, or regular meetings.

Open Communication: The educators, students, and parents must have an open discussion concerning the AI system. For example, they should discuss probable enhancements and clarify all the misconceptions or myths prevailing within them.

7 . Safeguard Data Privacy and Security

Privacy Policies: This will include data privacy policies regarding how your students' and users' personal information will be protected, how you adhere to privacy laws, and data security measures.

Data Use: Clarify the way in which the AI system is using its data so that even it can be used for teaching purposes and further enhance learning achievements.

8. Educate and Assist Stakeholders

Training Programs: Training programs shall be designed and offered to educational institutions so that the teachers and resource persons can become well-equipped to understand and use the AI tools more effectively. Live demonstrations and hands-on activity with the AI system shall be made.

Support materials: They provide support as well as resource facilities to educators, students, and parents in order to remove any questions or issues that may prevail during involvement with the AI.

9. Highlight Achievements

Success Stories: Provide success stories and case studies which would reflect the positive impact the AI system has on the outcome achieved through learning. This will create the confidence and help them actually realize the tangible benefit of the technology.

Implementing these principles would be able to ensure that AI-related decisions are clearly communicated to educators, students, and parents and, through such efforts, build trust and collaboration. Such a move would help maximize the benefits of AI tools through solution of concerns and improvement in understanding their role in education.

Usability and accessibility

In the context of XAI, usability and accessibility therefore form a basis fundamental to the development of AI systems that are not only easy to understand but practical for a large spectrum of users who may have different needs and skills. The next section details some effective approaches in improving usability and accessibility for explainable AI.

Usability in Explainable AI

Usability pertains to the ease and efficiency with which users can engage with and comprehend an AI system. To improve usability, consider the following strategies:

User-Centric Design:

- Intuitive Interfaces- Clear, intuitive interfaces that communicate the information such that everything is easy to understand. In this respect, the interface of an AI should make it easy to understand through dashboards that convey insights to users in a digestible manner.
- Customizable Views: Provide a possibility that enables users to create their own views of explanations by allowing them to choose their individual preferences or needs. For instance, the system might present different visualization styles, levels of detail, or modes of presentation.

Clear Explanations:

- Simplify Complex Concepts:Break complex, difficult-to-understand processes and decisions made related to AI into even more accessible parts. Use non-technical language as much as possible.
- Use Visualizations: Use charts, graphs, and other visual tools to illustrate how the AI really reached that decision or prediction. Visual aids can be great illustrations of something that was conceived to be complicated.

Interactive Features:

- Interactive Explanations: Include interactive elements that allow a user to consider how changing inputs influence the decisions an AI makes. Consider providing sliders or input fields to let users modify variables and see which outputs have changed as a result.
- Feedback Mechanisms: Evolve features whereby the users can ask a question or clarify right within the system itself.

Accessibility in Explainable AI

Accessibility must be in AI systems to take on board people with the widest possible range of abilities and disabilities. The following provides some ways in which accessibility can be enhanced:

- Inclusive Design

Screen Readers: All the visual content and interactive elements should be accessible to screen readers. Textual descriptions should be present for pictures, graphs, and any other visual elements.

- Keyboard Access

Provide an accessible user interface that can be fully accessed with a keyboard. Keyboard shortcut should give users access to all interactive features.

- Colour and Contrast High Contrast Colour Scheme

Ensure the colour scheme has sufficient contrast so that either a user with or without a visual problem can read and see text and key elements that would stand out against the background.

- Colorblind-Friendly Design: Don't rely on color alone to convey your message. Use patterns or shape or text labels with color.
- Text and Font

Choices Variable Text Size: Give the user the ability to adjust the text size so he or she can accommodate any degree of visual loss.

ReadableConductive Fonts: Use clear easy-to-read fonts. Avoid fonts that are too detailed or ornate.

- Multimodal Communication:

Formats: Give information about diversity in formats, including text, audio, and video, which is considered to resonate with the preference and need of users. For example, ensure the video materials come with subtitles and transcripts to make the information clear to users.

Plain Language: Use simple language and avoid words at high level technical jargon that make information hard for users with varying levels of familiarity to understand

- Compliance with Standards:

Strict observance of accessibility standards set by accessibility guidelines such as WCAG.

- Testing for accessibility with the help of users with disabilities at regular intervals is highly necessary to identify and eliminate all barriers.
- User Feedback:

Collect Feedback from the Users: Acquire knowledge regarding challenges and scopes through opinions of users who have a disability.

- Improvement Continuously: Improve the system due to constant feedback from the user side for better accessibility and better use.

Implementation Strategies

1. Design workshops: Engage in workshops with different user groups during the design phase to ensure that usability and accessibility requirements are taken into account from the beginning.
2. Prototyping and Testing: Prototyping, followed by usability and accessibility reviews, is conducted in order to get as much feedback as possible and adjust accordingly before implementing it at full scale.
3. Training and Support: Take time to train the users to operate the AI system effectively, which shall be accompanied by its features of accessibility and best practices.

By focusing more on usability and accessibility, developers and organizations can create explainable AI systems, whether they are transparent and understandable to users of all capacities or abilities. This will make sure that the AI does not disrupt differences in various environments but meets the different needs of diverse audiences.

Designing user-friendly AI systems for education

The creeds of XAI have, thus mandated the need to develop tools that are at once good in satisfying educational goals and transparent, hence amenable to use by users such as instructors, learners, and parents.

Here’s a comprehensive guide to designing these systems:

1. Recognize User Requirements and Context

Stakeholder Analysis: Identify the various stakeholders-including educators, learners, and guardians-and comprehend their different requirements, hopes, and barriers in respect of AI tools.

Alignment with Education: The AI system must evolve to meet the objectives of teaching and curricula to be still relevant and effective for improving learning outcomes.

2. Create User-Friendly Interfaces

Clear and simple designs: Create clean, uncluttered interfaces. A design should not overwhelm the user with information; rather, it should promote navigation without creating barriers to access.

Uniform Design Elements: The use of uniform design elements, such as colours, typefaces, and icons, enables easy memorization by users.

3. Utilize Explainable AI Methods

Interactive Explanations Provide interaction that allows the user to try different inputs or actions and see how they affect the decisions of the AI. For example, students might vary parameters and see what changes in their performance ratings.

Visual representations: Graphs, charts, heat maps, etc., can be used to represent AI decisions. For example, in graph form, the same student will show improvement in his performance over time due to the interventions suggested by AI.

4. Ensure Accessibility

Promote Assistive Technologies: Develop accessible user interfaces that are compatible with assistive technologies.

Differentiated fonts and images: Enables users to adjust the font size, color scheme, contrast level, and other visual features according to their needs.

Multimodal Communication: Information to be given in more than one format as text, audio, and video catering to all kinds of learning styles and abilities.

5. Facilitate Effective Communication

Simple and Plain Language: use simple language and avoid technical words while referring to the decision of AI so that lay persons will be able to understand without possessing technical knowledge.

Provide Context: Explain not only the results but also the rationale for AI suggestions. For example, if an AI system recommends extra practice for a student, explain why-for example by reference to recent test performance.

6. Incorporate Feedback Mechanisms

Establish channels of feedback by which users can give their opinions about the explanations and suggestions of the AI system. Feedback channels may include feedback forms, surveys, or comments within the platform directly.

Iterative Improvement: Make continuous improvement in the AI system, if required, based on the solicited feedback to streamline it further in order to meet user needs and efficiency.

7. Integrate Training and Support

Educator, students and parent training: That way, educators, students, and parents would also be effectively utilizing the AI system with practical examples and hands-on activities.

Help Resources: Detail resourceful materials including user manuals, FAQs, and video tutorials, which help the user find his or her way with more effectiveness and comprehension of AI.

8. Design for Adaptability

Customizable Options: It should allow the user to change settings and preferences. In this way, the AI system can be tailored to meet individual needs. For example, instructors should be allowed to change the detail level of reports or the amount of feedback they receive.

Responsive Learning: Design the AI system to be responsive to variety by enabling personal support based on the level of personal progress and preference.

9. Prioritize Data Privacy and Protection

Transparent Data Policies: Should clearly state the organization's policies related to how student data is collected, used, and protected. This ensures adherence to laws dealing with data protection. It will give end-users peace of mind as they work on your website.

Strong Security Measures: This involves implementing strong security measures that will prevent unauthorized access and breaches in the user's data.

10. Encourage Collaborative Efforts

Collaboration Tools: Collaborative tools that allow the interaction of students, parents, and teachers should be supported. Examples of such tools include collaboration dashboards that can be shared for easy follow-up and discussion whenever AI flags such progress.

Community Engagement: Engage with the academic community and so, on feedback and co-developing and enhancing the AI system.

Examples of User-Centric AI in Education

Personalized Learning Platforms: Solutions like DreamBox and Knewton are developed to provide customized learning experiences in which educators can see explicitly how the learning path is adjusted to reflect the performance of students.

Interactive Tutoring Systems: Among others, an interesting group of tutoring systems is represented by the so-called ITS: Interactive Tutoring Systems. One example is provided by Carnegie Learning's MATHia, which entertains students with animated explanations and feedback, telling them how to correct their work and what they should do next.

Classroom data analysis tools: Analyze data by classroom and print out visualization reports to allow teachers to make informed decisions in their instructional practices.

Based on these findings, creating user-centric AI systems for educational purposes requires not just intuitive design but also simple explanations, accessibility, and efficient communication. A critical consequence would be that educational AI tools become a vital tool in the learning process, highly augmenting the learning experience while maintaining clarity and accessibility to everyone.

Explainable AI (XAI) systems for all including disability

Ensuring that Explainable AI (XAI) systems are accessible to all students, including those with disabilities, is essential for fostering equitable educational opportunities.

A thorough strategy for enhancing accessibility in XAI systems includes the following components:

1. Design for Varied Abilities

Screen reader compatibility: All the material, including all kinds of visualizations and interactive features, must be compatible with screen readers. Images, graphs, charts-and other non-textual elements-must have descriptive text.

Keyboard Navigation The system must be fully accessible with a keyboard. All interactive elements must also be accessible by keyboard and have discernible focus indication.

Voice Command: Include voice command capability in this system for all those users that may not effectively use the usual input devices. Voice commands should be able to activate all features of the AI system.

2. In Multiple Media

Text equivalents: All graphic material shall be available in a form that, taken separately from their accompaniment, would be accessible to most readers; charts and diagrams should be supported with a text version of or summary intended to have an equivalent meaning for readers.

Audio Descriptions would be included for visual materials, so that visually impaired students could be able to listen and understand graphs, pictures, and other visual information.

Includes: Transcripts of Audio and Video materials, Subtitling of video material for hearing impaired students.

3. Ensure Visual Accessibility

Color Contrast: Higher contrast schemes should be selected for better readability for students with low vision or color blindness. Ensure that text and important elements have meaning against the background.

Customizable visuals: Users should be able to change text size, style, and color schemes of their desires. Implement the features for students to customize the display so that they are easily readable and comfortable to read.

- Non-colour Indication Don't do everything with color. Ensure information is just as accessible to colour-blind users as anyone else by employing patterns, shapes, and labeling as distinction methods.

4. Establish Clear and Consistent Navigation

User-Friendly Navigation: It should be easy to understand and user-friendly, ensuring that all the navigational elements are explained as well as have their own labels.

Uniform Design: There should be uniform layout and design all over the AI system so that users can easily ascertain where to locate information and how to interact with different entities.

5. Facilitate Personalization and Adaptability

Customizable Features: It includes features that allow learners to personalize their experience to suit their specific needs. For instance, it allows the students to pick their point of explanation needed or vary the speed at which interactive elements are deployed.

Adjustable Preferences: Provide options to change settings according to accessibility by the user, such as text size, contrast, and audio feedback.

6. Ensure Accessible Explanations

For teaching, visual tools that allow educators to monitor and analyze student performance are indispensable in creating data-driven educational environments. A wide range of data visualization forms is used to present information in an easily interpretable format so educators can make informed decisions about instruction and support.

Here are some summary statements that outline key visual tools and provide good strategies for using them:

Clear Language: Explain in plain language and avoid using technical jargon. The material should be understandable for students with intellectual impairments or those with a second language.

Engaging Feedback: Add interactive features that allow learners to raise questions or seek further clarification. All such interactions, including those with people with disabilities, must be accessible to all.

7. Conduct Regular Testing and Gather Feedback

Accessibility Audits For ongoing accessibility audits, audiences with disabilities would always be consulted and assessed for identifying potential barriers. Assurance that automated as well as manual checks would be used to ensure compliance with the accessibility standards.

Consumer Intelligence: Positive and Negative Feedback from Students with Disabilities User insights in this case can be obtained by monitoring the experiences and problems arising for students with disabilities and formulating continuous improvements of the AI system, incorporating that collected information.

8. Comply with Accessibility Standards

WCAG Compliant: Therefore, your AI system should comply with the Web Content Accessibility Guidelines so that it adheres to one of the most distinguished standards of accessibility. This would include provision of text equivalent alternatives, compatibility using keyboards, and making content perceivable and usable.

Meets Legal Compliance: All legal standards and regulations, whether in the country of the United States by the Americans with Disabilities Act, ADA, or in other countries, must be complied with.

9. Provide Training and Support

Educator Training- Train educators on how best to use the AI system with students with disabilities. Provide resources and best practices in supporting diverse learning needs.

Student Support It should provide access support tools to the students who, for instance would give students guides on how to use features to ensure accessibility, as well as how to get assistance if their problem arises.

Examples of Accessible XAI in Education

- Adaptive Learning Platform: Features such as Blackboard and Canvas platforms that provide accessibility features, including screen reader compatibility, optional text options to customize, and high-contrast settings.
- Interactive Tools: There are several tools available, like Microsoft's Immersive Reader, that come loaded with tools to support the different styles of learning that students must have. These include text-to-speech, translation, and alternative text formatting.
- Accommodations Support for Assistive Technologies: The learning materials should be accessible on assistive technologies such as Braille displays, text-to-speech and speech recognition software.

Incorporating such factors in the design and deployment of XAI systems may promote inclusive education tools able to give all students an equal opportunity, irrespective of disability, to learn by flexible access to learning resources and assistance.

Accessible AI tools in education

There are many examples of accessible AI tools in education that not only express the principles of Explainable AI (XAI) but ensure decision-making processes can be understood, and features can be used by all and especially students with disabilities.

Here are some notable examples:

1)Microsoft Immersive Reader

Description: Immersive Reader is an AI-based tool created to enhance reading and comprehension for all students, particularly those with dyslexia and other reading impairments.

Features Include:

-Text-to-Speech: It reads written text aloud to allow the student to listen to the material.

-Customizable Text Options: Their text size, spacing, and font type need to be set up or made adjustable for clarity and easy readability.

-It underlines grammatical features and syllables to make easy to understand.

-Another tool about translation function allows the text to be translated into other languages; thus, this is applied to serve students of a different linguistic background.

Accessibility Support: It is designed to work with screen readers, offers customizable visual settings, and integrates with numerous Microsoft educational applications.

2)Google Classroom Enhanced by Read&Write

Description: Google Classroom serves as an educational platform that seamlessly integrates with Read&Write, a tool designed to assist learners with varying needs.

Features:

- Text-to-Speech: This converts printed text from reports, websites, and other written material into words, which can be heard.
  Speech Recognition: It can allow users to voice out what's in their minds instead of typing.
- Dictionary and Translation: Provides definitions and translations for a better understanding.
- Highlighting and Notes: This feature allows the students to highlight the important texts in the curriculum and mark annotations that will help the students while studying and revising.

Accessibility: Read&Write is designed to work with screen readers, provides options for text customization, and integrates smoothly with Google Classroom.

3. Kurzweil 3000

Overview: Kurzweil 3000 is an assistive technology designed to support students facing challenges in reading and writing.

Key Features:

- Text-to-Speech -TTS has the ability to convert written content into audio, further assisting in understanding.

Dictionaries: Visual and printed dictionaries of vocabulary-building.

-Highlighting and Annotation: Enables the student to mark up and comment on text so that s/he becomes more engaged with and understanding of the text.

-New reading choices: Users can adjust the speed of the screen and select any of the available many voices.

-Accessibility: Incorporates a range of accessibility features, including compatibility with screen readers and adjustable text settings.

4. DreamBox Learning

Overview: DreamBox Learning is an AI-driven adaptive math platform designed to deliver tailored educational experiences for students.

Key Features:

-Adaptive learning: The degree of difficulty or course path is changed by the learning method to the extent that each child performs and needs to be achieved.

-Visual and Interactive Tools: In addition to the visualization tools, use graphical and interactive materials to make mathematical processes interesting and easy to understand.

This report feature is a detailed report of student improvements and flaws.

Accessibility: Incorporates features that accommodate various learning styles, including visual supports and interactive components.

5. Microsoft Azure Cognitive Services

Overview: Microsoft Azure Cognitive Services provides a comprehensive array of AI tools and APIs that can be seamlessly integrated into educational applications to enhance accessibility.

Key Features:

-Computer Vision: Offers capabilities in image recognition and description, thereby making it possible to generate text descriptions of visual material.

-Speech services: These include speech to text and vice versa, thus improving the mode of communication to students who have speech or hearing problems.

-Language Understanding: This is targeted at coming up with applications that actually could understand the natural language and process it in order to enhance interaction between a user and educational resources.

Accessibility: Offers customization options to create educational tools that address a broad spectrum of needs and disabilities.

6. SageMath

Overview: SageMath is a free, open-source mathematics software system that encompasses a variety of tools and features aimed at enhancing learning and problem-solving in mathematics.

Key Features:

-Interactive Tutorials: It provides attractive and interactive tutorials to describe any type of concept of mathematics.
-Customization: the ability to change settings on the tool for better clarity and interaction.
Ingression: Serves well as other learning resources and tools are used collectively with it.

Accessibility: Supports various assistive technologies and offers customizable settings to improve user experience.

7. Axel.ai

Overview: Axel.ai is an artificial intelligence-driven platform tailored for the creation and management of educational materials.

Key Features:

-Content Development: Creating accessible and user-friendly content on instruction, automatically summarizing and translating them for its features.

- Access standards compliance. This will ensure that all the content produced meets adopted access standards. This also includes providing an alternative text for images and videos.
- Inclusive Design: Producing content rich in senses and accessible to diverse learning preferences and disabilities, the primary aim being an inclusive education for all.res for automated summarization and translation.

These examples demonstrate clearly how accessible AI tools can support different disabilities and learning requirements, while still being clear and transparent. In every case, the features ensure as much involvement by AI-driven educational technology as possible.

CHALLENGES AND FUTURE DIRECTIONS IN EXPLAINABLE AI (XAI) IN EDUCATION

The challenges and future directions in Explainable AI must thus be explained to ensure that these tools are effective, equitable, and trustworthy for an increasingly AI-based education institution.

Table 1. Challenges facing AI in Education.

Challenges	Issue	Consequences
Complexity of AI Models	Numerous AI models, particularly those based on deep learning, possess a high degree of complexity that complicates their interpretability. This intricacy can hinder the ability to offer clear and comprehensible justifications for their outputs	In the absence of transparent explanations, educators, students, and parents may find it difficult to trust or utilise AI tools effectively.
Data Privacy and Security	Educational AI systems frequently necessitate access to sensitive information, including personal data of students. Safeguarding this data while adhering to privacy regulations poses a significant challenge.	Insufficient data protection measures can result in privacy violations and a decline in trust towards AI systems.
Bias and Fairness	AI systems have the potential to reinforce or exacerbate existing biases present in educational datasets, which can lead to inequitable treatment of specific student groups. Addressing fairness and reducing bias is an essential challenge.	Bias in AI can create disparities in educational opportunities and outcomes for students from diverse backgrounds.
Scalability and Integration	Creating AI systems that are user-friendly and accessible to all students, including those with disabilities, necessitates thoughtful design and tailored solutions.	Neglecting usability and accessibility can diminish the effectiveness of AI tools and prevent certain students from fully engaging with these technologies.

continued on following page

Table 1. Continued

Challenges	Issue	Consequences
Educational Alignment	Challenge: For AI tools to be effective, they must be in sync with educational objectives, curricula, and teaching methodologies. Achieving this alignment requires continuous collaboration between AI developers and educators.	A lack of alignment can diminish the relevance and efficacy of AI tools in enhancing educational outcomes.
Stakeholder Trust and Acceptance	Establishing and sustaining trust among educators, students, and parents is essential for the successful adoption of AI tools. Concerns regarding AI decision-making and transparency can influence acceptance.	A deficit of trust may result in resistance to the use of AI tools, thereby undermining their potential advantages.

Table 2. Future Directions

Features	Direction	Goal
Advancing Explainability Techniques	Develop and refine techniques that make complex AI models more interpretable, such as model-agnostic methods, interpretable machine learning models, and visualization tools.	Improve the clarity and comprehensibility of AI explanations, making them more useful and actionable for educators and students
Enhancing Data Privacy and Security	Implement advanced data protection measures, such as differential privacy, secure multi-party computation, and encryption, to safeguard sensitive educational data.	Ensure that AI systems handle data responsibly and comply with privacy regulations while maintaining effectiveness
Addressing Bias and Promoting Fairness	Develop methods to detect, evaluate, and mitigate bias in AI systems, and ensure diverse and representative training data.	Create fair and equitable AI tools that provide all students with equal opportunities and support.
Improving Usability and Accessibility.	Design AI systems with inclusive features, such as customizable interfaces, adaptive learning options, and support for assistive technologies	Ensure that AI tools are accessible and user-friendly for all students, including those with disabilities.
Improving Usability and Accessibility	Design AI systems with inclusive features, such as customizable interfaces, adaptive learning options, and support for assistive technologies.	Ensure that AI tools are accessible and user-friendly for all students, including those with disabilities.
Facilitating Integration and Scalability	Develop frameworks and tools that simplify the integration of AI systems into educational environments and support scalability across different contexts.	Enable broader adoption and effective implementation of AI tools in diverse educational settings.
Aligning AI with Educational Goals	Foster collaboration between AI developers and educators to ensure that AI tools are aligned with curricular standards, teaching practices, and educational objectives.	Enhance the relevance and impact of AI tools in supporting teaching and learning.

continued on following page

Table 2. Continued

Features	Direction	Goal
Building Trust and Transparency	Engage in open communication with stakeholders about how AI systems work, their benefits, and limitations. Provide mechanisms for feedback and oversight.	Build and maintain trust in AI tools, ensuring that they are accepted and effectively utilized in educational settings.
Promoting Continuous Learning and Adaptation	Implement mechanisms for continuous learning and adaptation of AI systems based on user feedback and evolving educational needs.	Ensure that AI tools remain relevant and effective over time, adapting to changes in educational practices and technologies.

By addressing these challenges and pursuing these future directions, the field of XAI in education can advance to provide more transparent, equitable, and effective AI tools that enhance learning and support educational success for all students.

4. DATA PRIVACY AND SECURITY IN EDUCATIONAL AI

Data privacy and security

Data privacy and security are probably the most important concerns in deploying and using AI systems in education, from Explainable AI (XAI). Here is a comprehensive discussion on how to manage these issues and best practices in ensuring robust data privacy and security in educational AI systems.

1. Data Privacy Concerns

Figure 5. Data Privacy concerns

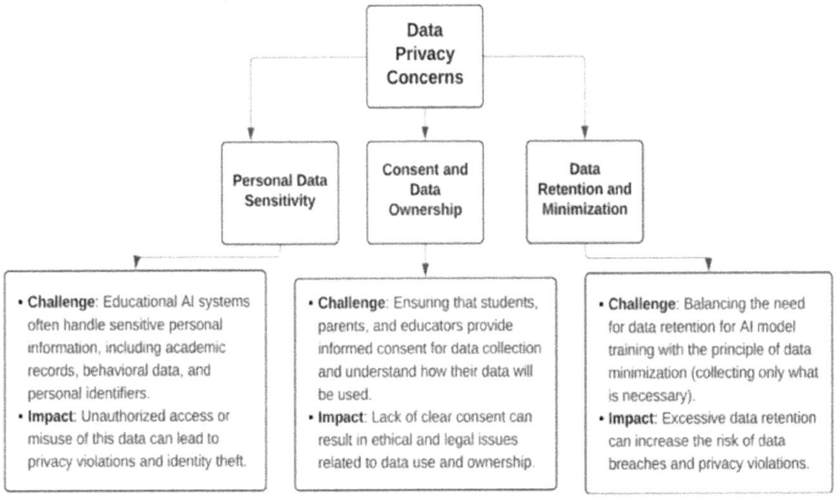

2. Data Security Measures

Figure 6. Data Security Measures

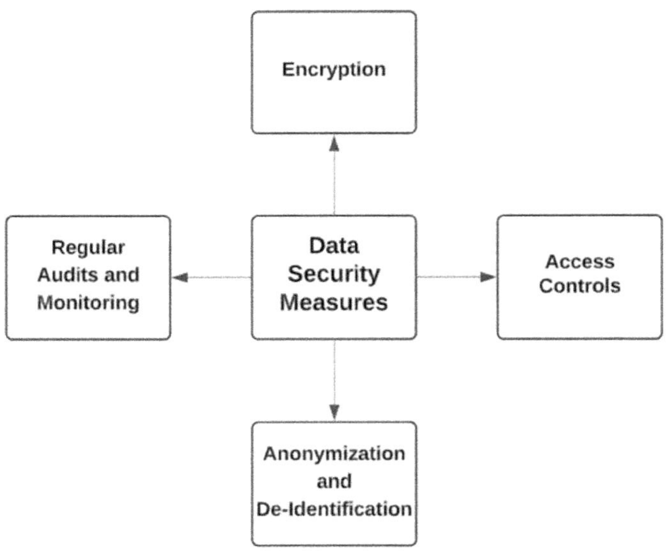

Table 3. Best practices for data privacy.

Encryption		
Challenge: Protecting data both at rest and in transit to prevent unauthorized access.	**Impact: Encryption ensures that data remains confidential and secure even if intercepted or accessed by unauthorized parties.**	**Implementation: Use robust encryption algorithms for data storage and transmission. Ensure end-to-end encryption for data exchanged between users and AI systems.**
Access Controls		
Challenge: Restricting access to sensitive data to authorized personnel only.	**Impact**: Proper access controls prevent unauthorized access and potential misuse of data.	**Implementation**: Implement role-based access controls (RBAC) and multi-factor authentication (MFA) to secure access to data and systems.
Anonymization and De-Identification		
Challenge: Protecting individual identities in datasets used for training and analysis.	**Impact**: Anonymization reduces the risk of personal data being linked back to individuals.	**Implementation**: Apply techniques such as anonymization, pseudonymization, and data masking to ensure that personal identifiers are not exposed.
Regular Audits and Monitoring		
Challenge: Ensuring ongoing compliance with data privacy and security practices.	**Impact**: Regular audits help identify vulnerabilities and ensure that security measures are effectively implemented.	**Implementation**: Conduct regular security audits, vulnerability assessments, and compliance checks. Use real-time monitoring tools to detect and respond to security incidents.

3. Best Practices for Data Privacy and Security

Table 4. Addressing emerging threats.

	Challenge	Impact	Implementation
Compliance with Regulations	Meeting the requirements of data protection legislation such as GDPR, FERPA, and COPPA.	Ensuring compliance allows educational AI systems to align with legal standards for data privacy and protection.	Keep abreast of relevant laws and implement strategies that promote compliance. Develop clear data privacy policies and acquire the necessary consents
Transparency and Explainability	Ensuring that data practices and the decision-making processes of AI are clear and comprehensible to users.	By fostering transparency, trust is established, enabling users to grasp how their data is utilized and safeguarded.	Offer straightforward descriptions of data collection, usage, and protection methods. Guarantee that AI systems provide rationales for their decisions in accordance with the principles of Explainable Artificial Intelligence
Secure Data Storage	Protecting data housed on servers and databases from unauthorized access.	Ensuring secure data storage mitigates the risk of data breaches and maintains the integrity of the information stored.	Employ secure servers and cloud storage options that incorporate robust access controls and encryption. Consistently update and patch systems to defend against potential vulnerabilities.
User Education and Awareness	It is essential to ensure that users, including students, educators, and parents, are informed about data privacy practices and their responsibilities in safeguarding their personal information	When users are well-informed, they are more capable of protecting their data and comprehending the management of their information.	Offer training sessions and resources that focus on best practices for data privacy. Instruct users on the significance of creating strong passwords, identifying phishing attempts, and interpreting privacy policies.

Addressing Emerging Threats

There are two ways to handle Treats

1) Adapting to New Risks

Continuing adaptation based on the changing face of security threats and vulnerabilities of AI systems. Emerging risk management can keep organizations away from breaches and safe with data. Continuous awareness of emergent security threats and control measures update. Collaboration with cybersecurity professionals to forge solutions towards newer security issues.

2) Ethical Consideration

Equilibrium between the pros AI and ethical issues related to data handling and privacy must be created. This will make sure ethical practice in the applications of AI, allowing responsibility to handle their user issues, even protecting the user's privacy. Create and enforce ethics in using AI. Consult stakeholders and engage them on the issues at hand regarding ethics and integrate ideas.

In conclusion, the best approach in dealing with data privacy and security within educational AI and explainable AI is a whole approach formed of solid technical safeguards and compliance to legal and ethical requirements, transparency, and incessant education for the users. These are best practices recommended by which educational institutions can ensure proper safety of sensitive information, establishment of trust among the involved stakeholders, and responsible and effective use of AI systems.

Integration with existing educational systems

Integrating Explainable AI (XAI) into existing educational systems

Incorporating XAI into an existing education system raises a set of challenges. These challenges are divided into technical, organizational, and pedagogical aspects. We must keep in mind that a proper and sound consideration of these factors will result in successful implementation and application of the XAI tools in education.

Here is a brief overview of these challenges:

1. Technical Challenges
   a) Compatibility with Legacy Systems

Introducing AI solutions into a preexisting framework would raise several challenges, particularly the compatibility of older systems. Most institutions are dependent on some legacy technologies or proprietary software, which makes it difficult to integrate modern AI tools. This disconnection can lead to increased costs and longer periods for implementation, which are among the obstacles that hinder the expected benefits of AI integration. Indeed, middleware or API development can offer an integration bridge between legacy systems and innovative ones, and a step-by-step strategy for integrating or modernizing the legacy also presents some viable alternatives to the solution of these problems.

b) Data Integration and Interoperability

One of the major issues with AI is merging data and ensuring interoperability: information coming from multiple sources forms the very cornerstone of the systems that AI embodies. Merging data from one's various systems is hard and labor-intensive work, usually leaving incomplete or wrong insights that reduce general effectiveness of applications of AI. Standardized data formats and protocols can simplify the sharing of information, and using accepted data integration platforms widely for data standards can make the flow of data much smoother.

c) Scalability Issues

For instance, scale and size as well as scope diversity of educational institutions can make it challenging about scaling issues. Meeting very small classrooms to comprehensive districts demand lots of extra scalability that sometimes are not supportive of the efficiency of AI solutions, and this has a tendency of portraying various performance issues to the user. It also requires to overcome this challenge by developing AI systems with scalable architectures that could handle the fluctuating workload. Cloud-based solutions obviously are advantageous as the scaling is dynamically possible, and thus institutions can adjust resources according to size and exact requirements.

2. Organizational Challenges
    a) Resistance to Change

The biggest problem that appears when trying to introduce AI technology into learning environments is the unwillingness to be changed. Teachers, school administrators, and other stakeholders show uneasiness in new tools, mainly due to a lack of knowledge or fear about interference with already established traditions. Such a tendency seriously can stand in the way of effective implementation and use of AI solutions. This challenge may be mitigated if adequate training and professional development are made available to the users, such that they understand and embrace the new technologies. Stakeholders may also be involved in the planning and decision-making phases to own the decision-making process and make the adoption of AI tools easier.

b) Cost and Resource Constraints

The implementation of XAI systems poses considerable challenges; most of which would be the significant financial resources and investment into technology, training, and continuous support. Budgetary constraints may limit an organization's capability to successfully embrace and leverage sophisticated AI tools, thereby potentializing their disadvantages. Such a challenge can be alleviated by researching different funding avenues such as grants and collaborative partnerships for securing the much-needed financial backing. Further, pilot programs may best start to demonstrate the advantage of XAI systems, making it easy for organizations to make these projects successful before going further with bigger implementation efforts.

c) Coordination Across Departments

Collaboration between IT, curriculum design, and administration departments usually ensures that AI tools are well-implemented in educational environments. When teamwork is inadequate, there is a disorganized way of applying these technologies, with a lack of consistency in their application, negating the overall effect of AI. A cross-departmental team and clear lines of communication are necessary. This strategy promotes alignment and encourages cooperation during the integration process, thus bringing about a more unified and effective deployment of AI tools within the institution.

3. Pedagogical Challenges
   a) . Alignment with Educational Goals

The effectiveness of the tools depends on how well they harmonize with the educational goals, curricula, and teaching methods. Failure to align them can make these tools ineffective or irrelevant in a learning environment, eroding any potential benefits. Educators should be engaged in design to especially focus AI systems towards supporting current curricula and teaching practice. Further, the involvement of educators in the design phase will guarantee that more relevant and useful tools are generated that may lead to a successful AI in education settings.

b) Balancing AI and Human Interaction

In order to effectively produce quality learning outcomes, AI-driven learning must be balanced with human interaction. Too much reliance on the use of AI has the effect of weakening the educator's role and undermining personalized support students need for their development. The challenge can, however, be addressed by using AI more as a supportive tool for teaching, rather than a substitute for it. Thus, designing such AI technologies that can give meaningful insights and improve the dynamics between teachers and students can help to bring about a better educational environment.

4. Ethical and Transparency Challenges

a) Ensuring Explainability

Clear and understandable explanations of AI decision-making processes lead to trust and more transparency regarding educational results. When AI systems fail to give explanations, it leads to mistrust and misuse of tools in the organizations and reduces their overall performance. To improve this, explainable AI (XAI) methods, which give clear insight into how and why AI decides, must be used in deployments. On the other hand, making it clear for all those involved in the work process, be it teachers, pupils, or parents, may help build confidence and promote responsible AI use in the education sector.

b) Addressing Privacy and Security

The educational data is fragile, and there must be data privacy and security in addition to the incorporation of AI systems. In case of instances of data privacy breaches or even inadequate security, there could be severe legal and ethical repercussions and even a loss of trust in the system. This challenge can be addressed by implementing data protection practices that are very strong and cover sensitive information through encryption and access controls. Another significant issue is observance over the relevant data protection regulations and stakeholder's involvement with developing privacy policies. Such cooperation can play an essential role in the safe operation of AI in the educational sector.

5. Training and Support Challenges
   a) Adequate Training for Educators

The efficient transfer of AI tools into the teaching methodologies of educators can be assured by effective training provided to the educators. Without proper training, utilization of AI tools would lead to being suboptimal and hence limit what is intended within the learning outcomes. An important challenge, therefore, that needs to be overcome is by formulating comprehensive programs for training through the provision of practical engagement with AI tools. Moreover, continuous support and assistance by the educators will also help them to better utilize AI technologies in effective ways for the improvement of teaching practices and therefore learning outcomes.

b) Technical Support and Maintenance

The challenge remains in ensuring that technical support and maintenance for AI systems are conducted in a manner to tackle the problems and updates. The aspect of supportlessness will cause some problem, and in the long run, reduce the effectiveness of AI tools. If one can establish a sound support system, with help desks and troubleshooting resources, planned regular maintenance and updates of AI systems may, in the long run, remain an effective solution.

Table 5. Future Directions

	Direction:	Goal:
Enhanced Integration Strategies	Develop more seamless integration strategies that account for diverse educational environments and technologies.	Create flexible, modular integration approaches that can be tailored to different contexts and needs.
Collaboration and Partnerships	Foster collaboration between AI developers, educational institutions, and policy makers to address integration challenges	Build partnerships that facilitate the development and deployment of AI tools that meet educational needs and standards
Adaptive and Scalable Solution	Design AI solutions that can adapt to different educational settings and scale effectively.	Ensure that AI tools can be used effectively in a wide range of educational contexts and environments

Overcoming such problems while exploring future directions will enable educational bodies to better embed the XAI system into their existing systems, improve the learning process, and guarantee that AI mechanisms are effective and ethical as well as in consonance with the objectives of education.

Future Trends and Advancements in Smart Education with Explainable AI (XAI)

As educational technology continues to advance, the incorporation of Explainable AI (XAI) is poised to significantly impact the realm of smart education. Below are some anticipated trends and developments that are likely to influence the future of smart education through the application of XAI:

1. Personalized Learning Experiences

Learning experiences become personalized on a large scale in education due to recent innovations in AI and XAI. XAI is going to be a tremendous feature applied by the AI systems in creating particular learning experiences with specific needs and preferences of each student. This method will help enhance the learning but also helps educators understand and further motivate the recommendations driven by AI in support of the unique path learned by each student. Curricula will also be changed dynamically based on actual, real-time student performance and review using AI technology. Since XAI can make sure that the curricular change is explainable, each of the educators and students will be able to understand the underlying reasons that prompted the changes, hence boosting trust in the learning and educating processes and increasing effectiveness of learning results.

a) Adaptive Learning systems

The ability of AI systems will continue to integrate explainable artificial intelligence (XAI) so that it can offer customized learning experiences tailored to the personal needs and preferences of individual learners. Educators will eventually be able to understand AI-generated recommendations much better and thus better assist each student through his or her unique learning journey.

b) Dynamic Curriculum Adjustments

Tools in AI will alter curricula in such a way as to align with the performance of students and feed. Explainable AI (XAI) will make it possible for awareness of the purpose for altering curriculum so that there can be understanding and trust among the teachers and students in regard to these changes

2. Enhanced Educational Analytics
    a) Data-Driven Insights

Artificial intelligence will be used to enhance better comprehension of student performance, student engagement, and learning patterns. Explainable AI can be used to add meaning and actionability to these insights so educators can make informed intervention decisions

b) Predictive Analytics for Student Success

Predictive analytics will identify potential academic strugglers and make specific recommendations regarding interventions likely to be helpful. Explainable AI, or XAI, will make prediction processes evident enough for educators to understand and have faith in the need for prompt intervention.

3. Intelligent Tutoring Systems
    a) AI-Enhanced Tutoring

Advanced intelligent tutoring systems will evolve towards more customized guidance support. Explainable AI, or XAI, will clearly explain exactly what is behind the tutoring suggestions and feedback, so that all the support provided is much more effective.

b) Interactive Learning Assistants

AI-Powered Learning Assistants shall be virtual assistants whose operations are powered by artificial intelligence: they can provide instant answers and resources to the student. The use of Explanable AI (XAI) will ensure that the recommendations and action made by the virtual assistant are clear and explained to the student.

4. Inclusive and Accessible Education
   a) Customized Learning Tools

Tailored Educational Resources in AI will design tailored educational resources that would cater for the great variety of learners' needs and disability. This will be explained with the understanding that Explainable AI will provide clear explanations and support for them as a means of improving accessibility and usability for all students.

b) Enhanced Support for Diverse Learners

Improved Assistance for Varied Learners in Artificial Intelligence will increasingly cater to students with diverse educational requirements, particularly those with cognitive or physical challenges.Explainable AI (XAI) will offer clear insights into the methods used for implementing accommodations, aiding both educators and students in comprehending the necessary modifications.

5. AI in Classroom Management
   a) Intelligent Classroom Environments

Artificial Intelligence Intelligent Classroom Environments: Manage classroom interactions. The student behavior will be tracked, and the collaborative activities will be enhanced. Explainable AI: Provide insight into the classroom management decisions for teachers to understand and be able to trust AI-driven recommendations.

b) Automated Administrative Tasks

The current tasks such as grading and scheduling will now be entrusted to Artificial Intelligence. Explainable AI would then convey the transparency related to decisions made by the automobile so that professors can evaluate and verify the work obtained through AI.

6. Ethical and Transparent AI Systems
    a) Enhanced Ethical Frameworks

There is going to be much more importance to the creation of ethical frameworks for the use of AI in education. XAI will thus play a significant role since it will show them clearly in their decision-making processes and ensures that there are considerations of ethical factors.

b) Accountability and Oversight

Accountability and monitoring of AI systems will become focus points within educational institutions. The role of Explainable AI (XAI) in support of such an initiative would be to provide transparent explanations about how AI makes its decisions, thereby helping improve general oversight and accountability.

7. Integration with Emerging Technologies
    a) AI and Augmented Reality (AR)

The integration of AI and AR is enhancing immersive educational experiences. Such clarity would allow the increased accessibility and efficiency of the technology for educators and learners through more understandable interactions between AI and AR components, explainable AI.

b) AI and Internet of Things (IoT)

Thus, the convergence of AI and IoT has led to developing intelligent classrooms and educational environments. Explainable AI will therefore clarify the processes involved in which IoT devices collect and use the data that is collected to improve transparency for teachers as well as learners while enhancing the education experience.

8. Collaborative and Social Learning
    a) AI-Driven Collaborative Tools

Artificial Intelligence will foster collaborative learning by leveraging tools that support group projects and peer-based collaboration. Explainable AI will provide added transparency into how management AI takes and executes recommendations within a class, hence helping students build trust and collaborate more effectively.

b) Social-Emotional Learning (SEL)

It would enhance SEL as it monitors and attends to the emotional and social needs of the students. This would ensure that SEL interventions provided are clear in their processes and reasoning, so educators and students know and embrace the aid given.

9. Continuous Improvement and Feedback
   a) Iterative Learning Models

AI systems will continue improving their capabilities with learning and user-performance metrBased feedback to help develop insights into processes for enhancements and ensure educationally fit development of AI.

b) Feedback Loops

Mechanism for two-way feedback processes between AI and human users: This is how information from feedback can be used to improve and optimize educational resources. XAI would make clear how integration of feedback into AI systems leads to continuous improvement toward attainment of educational goals.

Conclusion

More designed, inclusive, and transparent learning experiences will be brought about by XAI as an evolution of smart education. Addressing the current issues and building on the progress made in XAI would allow educational institutions to make good use of AI tools, enhance outcomes, and build trust among educators, students, and parents. Such developments tell a lot more about the possible alterations that AI will bring into education and how it ensures benefits for all learners without violating ethical standards.

Learning Analytics DashboardsVisual Tools for Monitoring and Analyzing Student Performance

Learning analytics dashboards serve as essential instruments for educators to track, assess, and understand student performance metrics. By offering visual depictions of intricate data, these dashboards assist educators in making data-driven decisions aimed at improving both teaching practices and student learning outcomes. Below is a summary of the nature of learning analytics dashboards, their primary characteristics, and strategies for their effective application in educational environments.

1. What Are Learning Analytics Dashboards?

In simple terms, learning analytics dashboards are interactive visual tools which aggregate, display, and analyse data related to student learning and performance. They apply diversified techniques of data visualization to present information in an easy-to-understand and user-friendly form for educators so that they can track progress, identify trends, and make data-driven decisions.

2. Key Features of Learning Analytics Dashboards

Figure 7. **Features of Learning Analytics Dashboards**

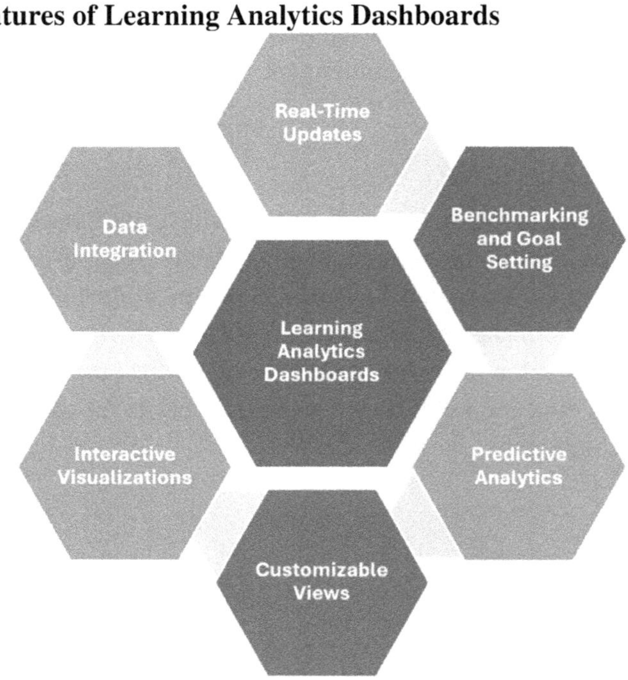

Table 6. Description and Benefits

Features	Description:	Benefit
Data Integration	Dashboards integrate data from multiple sources, such as student information systems, learning management systems (LMS), and assessment tools.	Provides a comprehensive view of student performance across different platforms and data points.
Real-Time Updates	Many dashboards offer real-time or near-real-time data updates.	Allows educators to monitor current performance and make timely interventions if needed.
Interactive Visualizations	Includes charts, graphs, heatmaps, and other visual representations	Makes complex data more understandable and actionable. Users can interact with visualizations to explore different aspects of the data.
Customizable Views	Users can often customize dashboards to focus on specific metrics or student groups.	Tailors the dashboard to meet individual needs and priorities, such as tracking progress in specific subjects or monitoring at-risk students.
Predictive Analytics	Some dashboards include predictive analytics features that forecast future performance based on historical data.	Helps in identifying students who may need additional support before issues become critical
Benchmarking and Goal Setting	Dashboards often allow for benchmarking against standards or goals.	Enables educators to set performance targets and measure progress towards achieving them

3. Effective Use of Learning Analytics Dashboards

Figure 8. **Effective Use of Learning Analytics Dashboards**

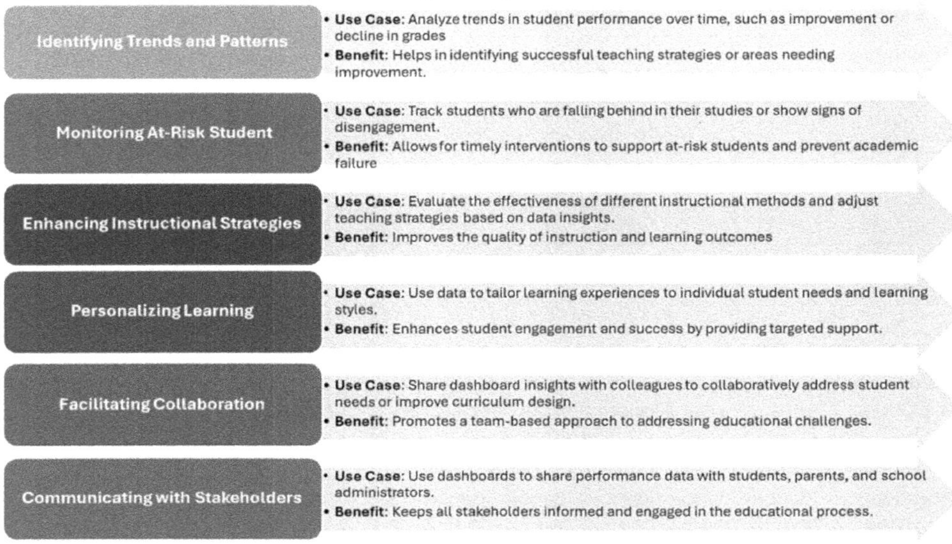

4. Best Practices for Implementing Learning Analytics Dashboards

Figure 9. Implementing Learning Analytics Dashboards

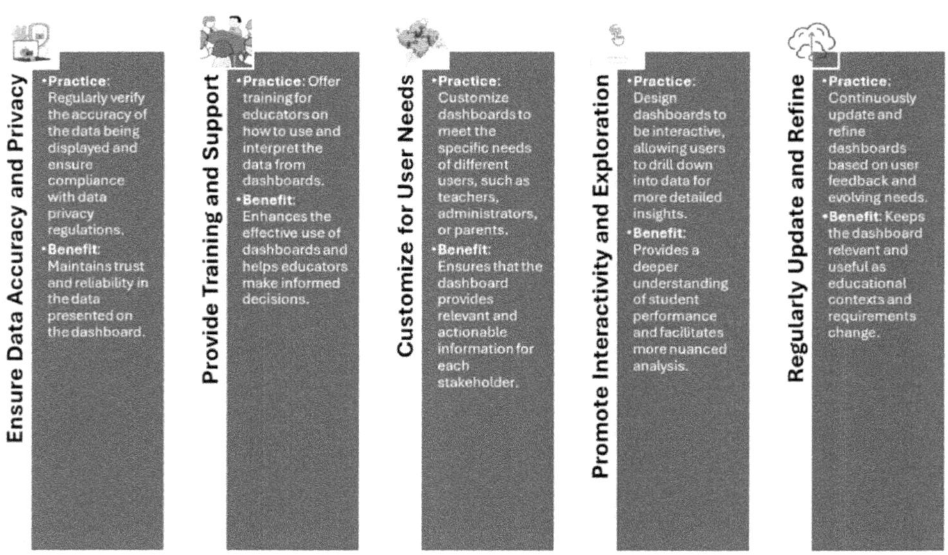

5. Future Trends in Learning Analytics Dashboards

Figure 10. **Trends in Learning Analytics Dashboards**

Visual Tools

For teaching, visual tools that allow educators to monitor and analyze student performance are indispensable in creating data-driven educational environments. A wide range of data visualization forms is used to present information in an easily interpretable format so educators can make informed decisions about instruction and support. Here are some summary statements that outline key visual tools and provide good strategies for using them:

Figure 11. key visual tools

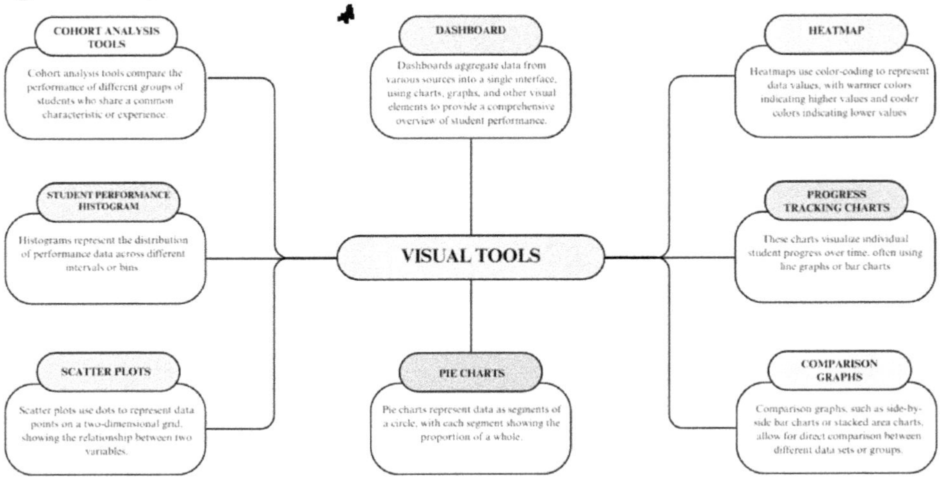

Figure 12. Dashboard Examples and Tools

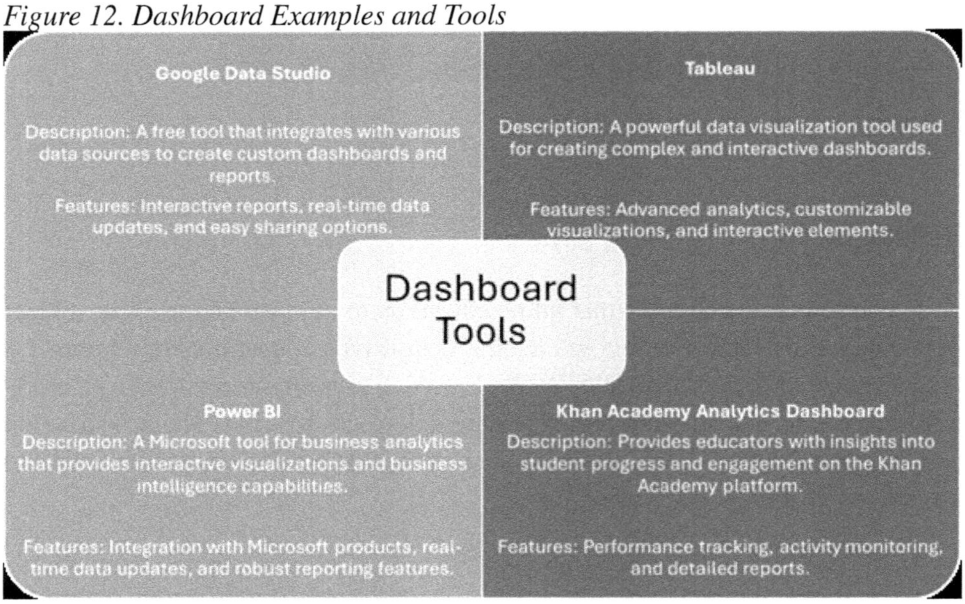

Conclusion

Visual tools for monitoring and analyzing student performance are essential for making data-driven decisions in education. They help educators understand complex data, track progress, identify trends, and provide targeted support to students. By leveraging these tools effectively, educators can enhance the learning experience, address individual needs, and improve overall educational outcomes.

In summary, learning analytics dashboards are transformative tools that help educators make data-driven decisions by providing clear, actionable insights into student performance. As technology advances, these dashboards will become more sophisticated, offering enhanced features and capabilities to further support effective teaching and personalized learning.

5. Assessment and Feedback:

Additionally, the integrity of teaching methods, educational resources, and educational technologies is made easier by extensible AI. Its adaptable and modular structure enables it to take advantage of new instructional ideas, disciplines, and technology.XAI in enriching adaptive training systems by promoting transparency to develop students' critical thinking skills. XAI within educational contexts demystifies AI decisions, allowing learners to understand the reasoning behind AI-driven guidance, promoting self-reflection and metacognitive awareness (Idrizi et al, 2023). AI programs, for instance, are able to track students' progress, evaluate how they use digital resources, and provide prompt, personalized feedback. This approach allows educational materials to be adjusted to align with every learner's study preferences and speeds, which may enhance both student engagement and achievement levels (Kayalı et al, 2024).

5A Automated grading systems and their explainability

More efficient procedures for evaluation and feedback must be established in educational environments in order to promote tailored instruction and enhance student learning outcomes. (Kayalı et al,2024)Extensible AI provides a comprehensive solution that supports the ongoing assessment of student performance by utilizing data-driven insights, automated assessments, and customized feedback.The progress of automated grading systems is being propelled the investigation of the various algorithms, an emphasis on interpretability and efficiency, and the establishment of a comprehensive evaluation framework. These elements collectively improve the capacity for effective assessment within the educational sector(Chen et al, 2024) With the help of real-time progress reports generated by this technology, teachers may adapt their pedagogy to better suit the diverse learning styles of their students as well as the ever-changing curriculum. Furthermore, creative teaching strategies, educational tools, and learning materials may be integrated with extendable AI. Faster and more consistent evaluation of student contributions in a variety of formats, such as essays and quizzes, is made possible by its modular and flexible technologies. Although these methods Figure: lighten the burden on teachers, they also bring up crucial issues related to equity.

Figure 13. Automatic grading system explainability

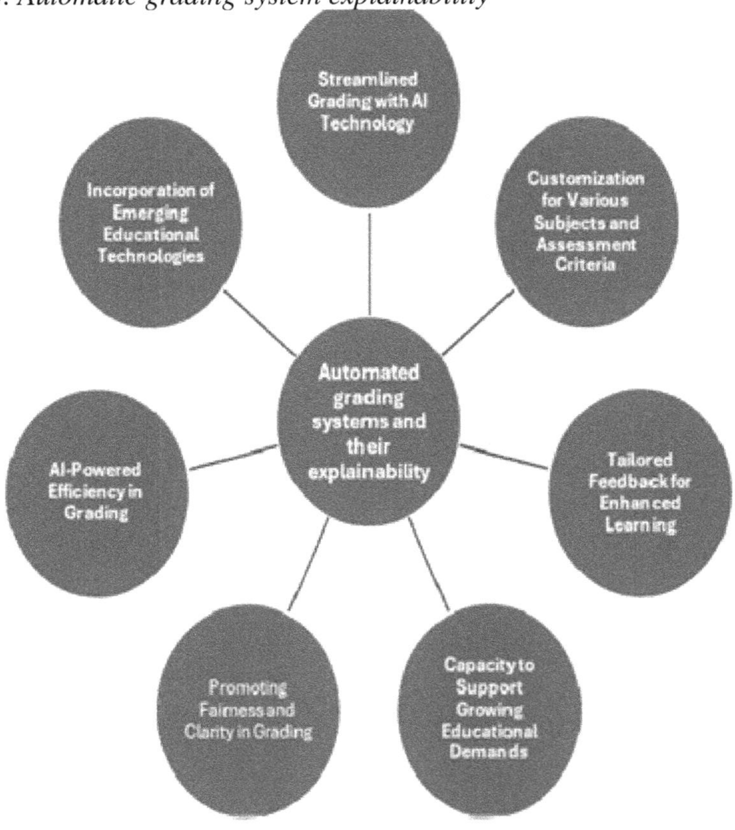

1. **AI-Powered Efficiency in Grading**:Extensible AI automates the grading process, drastically reducing the time educators spend on manual assessments. The system evaluates large volumes of assignments with speed and consistency, ensuring timely feedback for students.

2. **Streamlined Grading with AI Technology:**Extensible AI streamlines the grading process, significantly minimizing the time teachers dedicate to manual evaluations. The system processes a high volume of assignments swiftly and consistently, ensuring that students receive prompt feedback.
3. **Customization for Various Subjects and Assessment Criteria:** One can customize his automated grading according to the needs of varying subjects and assessment criteria with an extensible AI-based grading system. Educational requirements will change, and the AI techniques will be updated or extended to fit into the changed formats of assessments, ranging from quizzes to even more complex projects and straightforward essays.
4. **Capacity to Support Growing Educational Demands:** Even as the number of learners keeps increasing, extensible AI ensures that such systems scale up without compromising the accuracy and quality of the grading processes. This functionality is quite fundamental in large classrooms or online learning environments where traditional grading methods would be very cumbersome.
5. **Tailored Feedback for Enhanced Learning:** Grading systems can be made to provide more than just numeric scores through the extensible AI, giving differential feedback that will cater to the individual work of every student. Such an approach promotes deeper understanding through pointing out where a student needs to improve his or her skills..
6. **Incorporation of Emerging Educational Technologies**: n moving ed-techs, adaptable AI keeps abreast of new models, tools, and functionalities that can be added to the ed-tech system. This makes the automated grading systems abreast with innovations like NLP for essay evaluation
7. **Promoting Fairness and Clarity in Grading:** The deployability of extensible systems integrating explainable AI ensures that the grading processes are transparent. Therefore, by revealing why grades were assigned, these systems help foster a better understanding on the sides of the educators and learners and increase fairness as well as trust in the evaluation process.

5B. Skill gap analysis and targeted interventions

Skill gap analysis and targeted interventions for educators, students, and school administrators in the context of AI involve a series of approaches.

Skill Gap Analysis of Educators:

Identify Current Skills:Identify Existing Skills: Determine the knowledge of educators related to concepts of AI, AI tools, and AI applications relevant to their practice. Assess their existing skills in leveraging emerging tech platforms and data analytics instruments that are crucial to AI-augmented learning spaces.

Determine Required Skills: Modern learning environments require educators to have a wide range of skills to effectively teach and keep their learners engaged. To begin with, one needs to be technologically equipped, as technology-driven resources and learning spaces increasingly form part of classrooms. This includes the ability to navigate systems of adaptive learning technologies, online collaboration tools, and learning management systems. Adaptive teaching strategies should also, therefore, be critical. Educators should be able to assess the needs of different learners and vary the methods through which they teach to respond appropriately to those needs. Educators are also adept at stimulating learner engagement through interactive teaching techniques.

Targeted Interventions For Educators: Critical concepts and applications encompass AI literacy. It is necessary to incorporate AI tools in planning lessons and instruction. In addition, the application of their analysis and insights into using AI can also open up learning opportunities for one's self.

Gap Analysis: Evaluate the existing competencies against the necessary qualifications. Determine particular domains in which educators require additional growth Professional Development Workshops.

Peer Learning Communities: Facilitate collaboration among educators to share best practices and experiences with AI tools.establish mentorship or coaching programs to help educators adapt and refine their use of AI in teaching.

2. Skill Gap Analysis of Students & Targeted Interventions For Students.

Skill Gap Analysis of Students

Assess Existing Competencies: Evaluate students' knowledge of artificial intelligence and its relevance to their respective disciplines. Examine their proficiency in utilizing AI tools for research, analytical tasks, and problem resolution.

Determine Necessary Competencies: Comprehend the fundamentals of AI and its influence on their area of study. Attain proficiency in employing AI tools and applications for academic assignments and projects. Foster critical thinking and address ethical implications associated with AI.

Conduct a Gap Analysis: Identify the differences between students' current competencies and the skills necessary for their academic and professional achievements.

Targeted Interventions For Students.

AI Literacy Initiatives: Establish courses or workshops focused on the foundational concepts of AI and its applications across diverse sectors. Facilitate experimental experience with AI tools through engaging projects and the assignments.

Resource Availability: Ensure the connection of the AI tools and platforms for educational and research endeavors.

Career Counseling: Offer advice on how proficiency in AI can improve career opportunities and incorporate these skills into academic and professional development plans.

3. Skill Gap Analysis of Administrators & Targeted Interventions For Administrators

Skill Gap Analysis of Administrators

Assess Existing Competencies: Examine the understanding of administrators regarding the function of AI in educational management and decision-making processes. Evaluate their capacity to manage the incorporation of AI into educational frameworks and policies.

5 C. Real-world applications and their impact on educational outcomes

Real-world applications in education entail the incorporation of practical, real-life situations and challenges into the learning experience. This methodology mentioned Table: can profoundly influence educational results by improving student engagement, comprehension, and knowledge retention. Below are several real-world applications and their effects on educational outcomes:The practical application of education has been crucial in numerous real-world scenarios over the past 25 years, spanning a wide array of fields. These include power systems, subway operations, enology and wine production, computer security, collaborative learning, driver assistance technologies, website evaluation, self-training for drivers, access to medical imaging, the contextualization of interoperable open-source tools for businesses, database management, and strategic infrastructure projects in transportation, among others. (Brezillon et al, 2023)

Table 5. Real world Applications with explainability

Method Name	Functioning of Methods
Project-Based Learning (PBL):	Students engage in projects that tackle real-world issues or inquiries, frequently in partnership with community organizations or businesses. Examples of such projects include formulating a business strategy, designing an eco-friendly garden, or developing a marketing initiative for a local nonprofit.
Experiential Learning:	Acquiring knowledge through practical experiences, including internships, field excursions, and laboratory investigations. Illustrative instances encompass internships across diverse sectors, field research in environmental science, and hands-on experiments conducted in chemistry laboratories..
Case Studies:	Examining actual cases and situations to implement theoretical understanding in practical contexts. Illustrative instances encompass business students evaluating corporate strategies, medical students investigating patient cases, and law students reviewing legal precedent.
Service Learning:	Integrating community service with academic studies allows students to utilize their classroom knowledge to address the needs of the community. Illustrative examples include engineering students engaging in local infrastructure initiatives, education students providing tutoring in underprivileged schools, and health science students organizing community health fairs..
Simulationsand Role-Playing:	Employing simulations and role-playing activities to replicate real-life scenarios and enhance decision-making abilities. Illustrative examples encompass business simulations, medical training laboratories, and mock trials within legal education.
Problem-Based Learning (PrBL)	Students gain knowledge by tackling complex, open-ended problems that do not have a single correct answer. Examples include engineering students who are assigned to create innovative products, nursing students who develop patient care plans, and IT students who formulate cybersecurity strategies.

The Influence of Educational Outcomes: The influence of educational outcomes is significant, affecting both individual advancement and societal development. Students who attain high educational standards typically experience enhanced career prospects, increased earning potential, and greater personal growth(Kumawat et al, 2024) . On a larger scale, education promotes social mobility, mitigates inequality, and stimulates innovation within communities. It equips learners with essential skills infor navigating a rapidly changing world. Furthermore, favorable educational outcomes lead to healthier societies, as educated individuals are more likely to make informed choices, resulting in better public health and greater civic participation. Below are several impacts Table: of educational outcomes:

Table 6. Outcomes of using Real world Applications

Techniques	Educational outcomes
Enhanced Engagement and Motivation:	Practical applications enhance the relevance and appeal of learning, thereby boosting student motivation and engagement. When education is linked to real-world scenarios, students are more inclined to recognize its value and significance.
Enhanced Analytical Thinking :	Learners cultivate advanced knowledge through engagement with intricate, real-life challenges that necessitate analysis, synthesis, and evaluation. They acquire the ability to tackle issues from various perspectives and formulate creative solutions.
Enhanced Engagement and Motivation	The incorporation of real-world applications into the learning process renders education more pertinent and captivating, thereby boosting student motivation and engagement. When students can relate their education to actual life scenarios, they are more inclined to recognize its value and significance.
Improved Critical Thinking and Problem-Solving Skills:	Students enhance their higher-order thinking abilities by engaging with intricate, real-world challenges that necessitate analysis, synthesis, and evaluation. They acquire the skill to examine problems from various perspectives and cultivate creative solutions.
Better Retention and Understanding:	Learning within a contextual framework enhances students' comprehension and retention of information. Practical applications offer specific instances that render abstract ideas more concrete and accessible for understanding.
Development of Transferable Skills:	Students develop competencies that are directly relevant to the professional environment, including collaboration, effective communication, project management, and flexibility. These competencies improve their employability and prepare them for the challenges they will encounter in the real world.
Increased Collaboration and Social Skills:	Numerous practical learning experiences necessitate collaboration and teamwork, which aids students in cultivating social and interpersonal skills. They acquire the ability to work efficiently with varied groups, engage in negotiation, and address conflicts.s.
Greater Sense of Responsibility and Civic Engagement:	Numerous practical learning experiences necessitate collaboration and teamwork, which aids students in cultivating social and interpersonal skills. They acquire the ability to work efficiently with varied groups, engage in negotiation, and address conflicts

6. Student Engagement and Motivation:

The application of generative AI to improve student engagement and motivation represents a promising field of advancement.Fundamental concepts of artificial intelligence are presented, along with an explanation of their particular applications and significance within the realm of higher education.(Limonava et al,2023) Additionally, the potential of utilizing AI process and supporting tools to enhance student engagement is discussed, offering a comprehensive overview of the opportunities that exist(Nguyen et al, 2024)This technology has the capability to develop personalized and dynamic knowledge updating preferences, and motivations of each student. several methods Figure: through which generative AI can facilitate these

Figure 14. Types of student Engagement

1.Personalized Learning Experiences:GWith generative AI, contents can be tailored to the individual learning style and pace of each learner. Data generated from a student's interaction with a learning activity can be used by AI to adapt materials. In this case, it makes it easier, helps present data in more varied formats, video, doc, etc., or offer customized feedback..

2.Generative AI tools:quizzes, games, or virtual situations related to the topic can be made with generative AI tools. This kind of AI tool offers instant feedback and reinforcement, making students learn better than through traditional classroom learning. For instance, simulations created with AI can allow students to really absorb themselves in a historic situation or conduct a scientific experiment or explore a mathematical theory in a highly immersive way.

3. **Gamification and Reward Systems:** AI could design adaptive reward systems that react to student learning, thereby producing badges, levels or challenges in congruence with the educational journey. Limonava et al.(2023) Gamification turns a student's learning into a game-like experience. This makes students intrinsically motivated to participate and sustain their engagement.
4. **Adaptive Learning Systems:** ILEs adapt the content of the education delivery according to the learning advancement, preferences, and goals. Explainable Artificial Intelligence (XAI) explains the reasoning for adapting the content

of education delivered, which enhances the trust and understanding of the learner as well as the instructor about the system decision. This may range from reasons to propose a set of exercises based on performance metrics or the changes made to the learning trajectory.

5. **AI-Generated Feedback and Encouragement:** In AI-driven environments, learners and instructors often want to know why the system is doing what it is doing, such as suggesting a review topic or giving that specific kind of feedback. XAI provides transparency with explainability, providing clear and interpretable explanations. This degree of clarity enables users to control their learning process.
6. **Role-Playing and Scenario-Based Learning:** It has practical insights that determine why a particular learning activity has been either a success or a failure. Such can be shown by way of example through scenarios such as it makes it clear to the learner why they cannot understand a certain concept or why a particular educational strategy is more effective than another. XAI, in doing so, promotes reflective learning.

7.Creative Assignments: Generative AI possesses the capability to inspire students by aiding them in the development of original content, such as stories, artistic creations, or various projects. For instance, students can collaborate with AI to write essays or create visuals for their presentations. This partnership can enhance the enjoyment of assignments and foster creativity, resulting in heightened engagement.

8. **Natural Language Interactions:** AAI-based chatbots or virtual tutors may facilitate real-time interactions with students about the subject matter, responding to questions, further explaining, or provide more examples. Ongoing dialogue encourages them to seek more from learning than just traditional education.

9.Emotion and Sentiment Analysis: The generative AI has the scope to deduce how a student is feeling or interested in a particular point in time through text, voice, or facial expressions. Based on this interpretation, AI can adapt its methods in a manner that keeps the students interested, praise them, or advise them to try to change the way in which the learning is being delivered.

6A. Interactive learning environments powered by XAI

Interactive learning environments (ILEs) serve as innovative educational platforms that actively engage students through their dynamic, responsive, and adaptive characteristics. It uses the latest technologies of AI, data analytics, and HCI for personalizing learning experiences. Although the integrations improve quality education, they increase learners' depth of understanding about the mechanisms through which AI drives recommendations, feedback, and decisions.

Personalization and Adaptation: ILEs customize the content being learned based upon the learners' advancement, preference, or goals. XAI could provide explanations on why changes are actually made to create more trust and comprehension with the learner as well as the teacher for its choices; this may be in reasons for the recommendation of specific exercises as based upon certain performance metrics or the change in learning pathways that are in place.

Transparency in Decision-Making:In AI-enhanced environments, both learners and educators often desire insight into the rationale behind particular system actions, such as the recommendation of a review topic or the nature of the feedback provided. XAI enhances transparency by delivering clear and interpretable explanations. This level of transparency is essential for building trust and empowering users to take control of their educational experiences.

Feedback and Reflection: Explainable AI, as the name suggests, brings success or challenges of various learning activities. For instance, it can shed light on reasons why a student finds a topic particularly challenging, or why a particular method of teaching is effective. Thus, these insights with XAI really encourage reflective learning to let the students reflect as well on what they do well and what they need to improve on.

.**Interactive Explanations:** In Interactive Learning Environments (ILEs): Students can ask the ILEs to point out how the AI could be doing something and in this way interact more richly with the system. This can be, for instance, asking how a certain concept might be related to the students' learning goals or how a particular score was arrived at. To the degree that such questions can be clearly answered and understandably explained using Explainable AI, this promotes student engagement..

Teacher Support: Educators using ILEs will greatly benefit from XAI, which gives insights for educators to know patterns in the performances of students and where some students would need more support; thus, allowing the educator to pinpoint the root causes of the challenges being faced. XAI will facilitate informed decisions that teachers make regarding interventions, classroom management, and effective disposition of resources.

Ethical AI: Because AI is now commoditizing the learning structure and the unintended consequences of automation too often stand as the elephant in the room. XAI can alleviate these issues, speaking to students and faculty about the reasoning that is happening, in such a way to help them find and address potential biases, making education fairer and more ethical.

Examples of XAI-Powered Interactive Learning Environments

Adaptive Learning Systems: Coursera and Khan Academy are platforms that use artificial intelligence to personalize learning. Adding the sense-making ability of the explainable AI to these systems will further the strengths of these systems by giving a rationale to proposed resources and assessments.

Intelligent Tutoring Systems (ITS): Using XAI to explain exactly what the reasoning steps learners should pay special attention to, as recommended by the problem-solving action of ITSs such as Carnegie Learning's Cognitive Tutor, would give clear open dialogue between the learner and the AI tutor.

Virtual Laboratories: In the sciences and engineering, a virtual lab fortified with XAI might make explicit the reasoning that leads to simulated results in order to help better understand complex processes such as chemical reactions or physical dynamics.

In summary, the integration of XAI within ILEs has the potential to generate a more transparent, engaging, and reflective educational experience. Clarified further through its decision-making processes, XAI enables deeper interaction between learners and educators with AI, thus building trust, enhancing learning outcomes, and encouraging ethical AI practices in education.

6.B. The Role of Gamification in Student Engagement

Gamification, is the incorporation of design of games leaderboards, challenges the non-gaming contexts, plays a crucial role in enhancing student engagement, particularly within adaptive learning environments.. Its importance is underscored by the fact that formal lectures frequently experience a decline in student interest and high rates of absenteeism, which can adversely affect the educational journey and future career opportunities of students(Limonova et al, 2024)

1.Enhanced Engagement through Personalization: Adaptive learning technologies customize educational content to organize and preferences of individual learners. The addition of gamification further boosts motivation by providing incentives such as points or badges for achieving milestones, thereby sustaining student interest.

The function of XAI: By promoting transparency within the adaptive learning framework, XAI allows students to understand the reasoning behind the distribution of specific rewards or challenges, fostering trust in the system. When learners are aware of the logic guiding the adaptive features (such as the choice of more difficult or easier questions), they are more likely to feel motivated and confident in their educational experience.

2. **Feedback and Progress Monitoring:**In a gamified learning environment, as portrayed above, students learn from continuous feedback through scores, levels, and leaderboards. This kind of immediate feedback system lets learners know their progress and areas that need further improvement. XAI's role: XAI can further explain the feedback system. For instance, it would give a reason why something was assigned, some sense of how close a learner is to mastering some aspect of a skill, or it could contextualize the reasons leading to a particular score. All these improve motivation as students perceive the system to be fair and bespoke to own journeys.

3.Fostering Independent Learning: Independent Learning by Means of Gamification:Gamification gives students choice on what to choose or to work on for the next challenge or task. This approach promotes autonomy and a sense of responsibility for their learning experiences. The role of XAI: XAI could shed light on the impact of alternative learning choices, showing how one choice might shift the direction of learning in a significantly different way than another.

4. **Adaptive Difficulty and Tailored Rewards:**Adaptive difficulty in gamification is introduced in the problem set that is calibrated to match the ability of learners so they do not fall into a suboptimal learning zone. They should not be bored or feel too frustrated. Well-designed rewards may include access to new resources or popular badges customized for each student's needs. The role of XAI is to further explicate the reason behind adaptive difficulty and customized rewards so that the learners understand how the system is responding to their performance. For example, XAI could say that due to the demonstration of competence by a student on previously covered subjects, he has been assigned a more challenging task and, in doing so, he enhances his learning experience.
5. **Fostering Collaboration and Social Learning: S**ocial games can be serious games as well that contain a mix of challenges for groups, team activities, or competitive leaderboards. It is because of these elements that cooperation and social learning are facilitated but the learners are encouraged to learn from each other as well. Role of XAI: In Gamified systems, XAI can provide information regarding group dynamics such as how the contribution of a member is being calculated in that group or how problem-solving collaboratively benefits the group as a whole.

This makes the students realize that they are also a part of the team and, hence they begin to take an interest in the game.

Conclusion 6.C. Illustrations of AI-Enhanced Engagement Tools

In the AI-embracing engagement tool world, there is an indispensable role in developing transparency and trust by explaining the action-fixing processes that occur inside AI systems, particularly adaptive learning environments. Several examples of AI-enhanced engagement tools follow as illustrations of the principles of XAI

1. **Adaptive Learning Platforms Featuring Explainability:** Explainable Artificial Intelligence (XAI) is gaining acknowledgment for its essential contribution to the improvement of adaptive learning systems. By ensuring transparency in AI-based educational tools, XAI encourages critical thinking and self-reflection in students. This incorporation not only tailors learning experiences to individual needs but also elucidates the reasoning behind AI suggestions, thus enhancing engagement and comprehension(Idrizi et al., 2024).

Example: DreamBox Learning employs AI to customize mathematics lessons for students. Through the application of XAI, both educators and learners can comprehend the reasoning behind particular lesson suggestions or modifications in challenge levels.

2. **Chatbots and Online Tutors:** assist learners by delivering immediate feedback and responses to inquiries. XAI contributes to the transparency of these systems by elucidating the rationale for specific responses or recommendations.

Example: MATHia from Carnegie Learning combines virtual tutoring with AI capabilities. XAI methodologies could clarify why the system provides a certain hint or problem to a student, thereby enhancing trust in the AI's support.

3. **Learning Analytics Dashboards Incorporating XAI:** AI-driven dashboards evaluate student performance and engagement metrics to assist educators in making informed decisions. XAI can shed light on the processes behind these analyses.

Example: Knewton provides an adaptive learning platform equipped with comprehensive analytics dashboards for instructors. XAI could offer explanations for why certain students are identified as at-risk or why specific resources are suggested for intervention.

4. **Gamified Learning Platforms with Explainability:**Gamified educational platforms utilize AI to modify games or challenges according to the learner's progress. XAI can provide explanations for the presentation of certain challenges or the adjustments made to game difficulty based on learner interactions. For example, Kahoot! employs AI to engage students through adaptive quizzes. With the integration of XAI, both students and educators could comprehend the reasons behind the selection of specific questions or varying difficulty levels for different learners.XAI and integration of gamification into adaptive learning systems not only foster engagement but also give strength to the transparency and reliability of the educational experience. The understandability to students through XAI of what the system is actually doing leads to better motivation and a feeling of freedom through the gamified elements as fair and beneficial.
5. **AI-driven Writing Assistance Tools with XAI:**Writing support tools deliver immediate feedback to students regarding grammar, style, and content quality. The incorporation of XAI can enhance these tools by providing explanations for the AI's suggestions and corrections. For example, where Grammarly offers feedback on writing, XAI may help explain why a particular correction or recommendation was made. This integration of such tools will give users an insight into what the AI is considering when it's making decisions, which will lead to increased transparency, trust, and understanding in the learning process.

7.0. **Educator Support for career Development:** It definitely helps teachers by improving the professional development of educators through the personalization of insights into students' learning behaviors, which lets educators modify their teaching according to the special needs and behaviors of the students. XAI makes recommendations based on clear rationales to engender trust among educators and encourage them to use data-informed methods. Immediate feedback on teaching practices identify what needs improvement, and focused professional development initiatives ensure that training is addressed to specific needs. Additionally, XAI fosters collaborative learning networks through networking educators who face similar challenges, and recommends shared resources. Even after this support, virtual coaching can continue in order to help teachers better regulate classroom dynamics. Further, the ethical factors associated with the deployment of AI are taken into consideration; therefore, users are aware of the issues of privacy associated with data as well as bias. Lastly, incorporation of XAI into the learning environment will create a more supportive and more robust learning environment for both the instructor and the students .

Personalized Learning Insights:Through the analysis of a student's data set, the XAI tools will provide teachers with unique learning patterns to inform instruction to fit all students' learning differences.

Transparent Decision-Making:applies transparency to recommendations, which helps the teacher understand the rationale behind the proposed interventions or strategies thus furthering the chances of its adoption into school practice.

Feedback and Assessment: The teachers get instant feedback about the effectiveness of their teaching methods as well as the degrees of student's involvement. XAI can even analyze classroom interactions to provide suggestions for improvement from which data are collected.

Resource Optimization: By using the XAI, teachers will be able to find and combine better teaching resources aligned with the curriculum and teaching objectives, saving time and effort.

Enhanced Classroom Management:Using data analysis, XAI can offer techniques for better management of classroom activities as well as rising student engagement so that teachers can spend less time elsewhere other than their teaching work.

Ethical Considerations:XAI can potentially facilitate conversations that assist educators in dealing with issues related to data privacy and bias to ensure that technology becomes a facilitator of learning rather than an obstruction.

Professional Networking:AI can connect educators with their colleagues who have a similar interest or facing similar challenges, thus building a supportive network for exchanging best practices and resources.

7.1. AI as a Catalyst for Teacher Professional Development

Role of AI in Education is widely increasingly acknowledged as a vital resource for enhancing teacher professional development. Traditional methods of professional growth often fall short, as they tend to offer one-size-fits-all solutions that do not address the specific developmental needs of individual educators. In contrast, AI provides a tailored approach, allowing teachers to access personalized resources and receive immediate feedback, thereby improving student outcomes(Jamal et al, 2024)

AI-powered virtual coaching platforms also significantly contribute to professional development by providing ongoing feedback. These platforms evaluate recorded classroom sessions, delivering objective assessments of various teaching components, including pacing and student engagement. This continuous feedback loop fosters a culture of self-reflection, enabling educators effectiveness over time.

Ultimately, the incorporation of AI into professional development creates a supportive environment that promotes lifelong learning.

7.2. ClassRoom Management through AI Insights

Classroom management is one of the most important elements of the learning process; it impacts student engagement and success in learning significantly. The traditional approaches rely on instincts and experiences in educational methods, which can sometimes lead to inconsistency in certain matters. The AI in classroom management brings novel solutions adaptive and insightful into the needs and dynamics involved in every classroom. AI may improve classroom management through real-time data, tailored strategies, and proactive intervention.

All the various classroom dynamics, including, for example student behavior, engagement, or participation, can be detected and viewed by AI tools. In this regard, one may use AI-driven systems such as monitors of student behavior during lessons where eventually trends that may even appear to be disengagement or challenges in terms of behavior can be found. Such tools can then give educators insights into when the students are most focused and when they tend to become uninterested by analyzing data coming from classroom sensors or cameras.

That real-time information also allows instructors to make impromptu decisions on their end. Thus, if an AI tool indicates that the students are beginning to grow inattentive at a certain point in the lecture, a teacher can adjust their plans by having a small interactive activity that could redirect attention to that class. This immediate feedback loop creates an adaptive learning environment in which instructors may change their management tactics in real-time.

AI will enable the classroom management strategies to be tailored according to the needs of the students. AI can help identify specific instances requiring extra assistance and switch to alternative management strategies within classes if some students constantly cause disruptions. A specific example might be a student attending classes with constant disruptions: a student may suggest targeted interventions that include checking up on that student individually or changing seating for such a student.

7.3.Explainable AI in supporting teachers' instructional strategies

Explainable AI (XAI) is now increasingly recognized as an important component of the learning infrastructure, especially in supporting teachers with their teaching practices. With the ever-increasing utilization of artificial intelligence in school environments, the need for transparency and understanding of its operation becomes crucial. It helps teachers understand the logic used by an AI system to come up with certain recommendations so that they can make informed decisions about their pedagogical approaches.

Other than teaching improvement at the individual level, XAI promotes collaboration among teachers. The applications of AI may be able to collect data on teaching from multiple classrooms, thus high lighing best practice and areas of improvement in the classroom. XAI can let these insights be accessible and actionable to the teachers, so that knowledge diffusion is promoted and that encourages the sharing of know-how among teachers. For instance, in a particular class, if an AI system determines that interactive activities are more effective, then it can share its grounds as to why this is the case. This would be considered as such shared knowledge meant to encourage mutual cooperation in teaching faculties to find other strategies based on the insights obtained from data analysis. This collaborative model would thus be very helpful towards professional learning communities, as teachers can discuss the AI generated recommendations and, over time, all of them help "harden up" their instructional approach through this on-going process of professional development.

A crucial function of explainable AI (XAI):XAI enables teachers to be professionally developing continually. The educators can come to understand their instructional practices through engagement with AI tools and pinpoint specifically where they can improve. XAI provides feedback not only on successful strategies but also the reasoning for their effectiveness. This is a very essential reflective practice for professional development by providing the means with which to critically review teaching strategies and outcomes. In addition, XAI can steer teachers toward relevant professional development that will meet their discovered needs and therefore provide meaningful growth..

Promoting a Data-Driven Culture

The integration of XAI in teaching practice leads to a data-driven culture within educational institutions. With the realization of the reasons behind AI suggestions, more educators embrace data-informed decisions within their practice. This fosters constant analysis of student performance data. With the said analysis, teachers are able to identify trends and, thus, adapt their teaching interventions accordingly. To the extent that XAI encourages thought in support of evidence-based practice, it should make a significant difference to outcomes to a large extent because of the growth in teacher competency as they become more successful at using data to inform their practice.

CONCLUSION

Explainable AI is a very powerful tool for augmenting teachers' instructional practice. XAI allows the teacher to improve his or her practice by being transparent and clear about what insights AI has generated. Knowing why AI recommends something will also help establish trust among teachers to adopt personalized, data-driven ways of teaching. Furthermore, XAI fosters collaborative learning among educators and promotes continuous professional development towards developing a culture of reflection and growth.

REFERENCES

Adadi, A., & Berrada, M. (2018). Peeking inside the black-box: A survey on explainable artificial intelligence (XAI). *IEEE Access : Practical Innovations, Open Solutions*, *6*, 52138–52160. DOI: 10.1109/ACCESS.2018.2870052

Angelov, P. P., Soares, E. A., Jiang, R., Arnold, N. I., & Atkinson, P. M. (2021). Explainable artificial intelligence: An analytical review. *Wiley Interdisciplinary Reviews. Data Mining and Knowledge Discovery*, *11*(5), e1424. DOI: 10.1002/widm.1424

Brézillon, P. (2023). The Real-World Applications. In *Research on Modeling and Using Context Over 25 Years* (p. 5–18). Springer Nature Switzerland. DOI: 10.1007/978-3-031-39338-9_2

Carli, R., & Calvaresi, D. (2024). The Wildcard XAI: from a Necessity, to a Resource, to a Dangerous Decoy. In Calvaresi, D., (Eds.), Lecture Notes in Computer Science: Vol. 14847. *Explainable and Transparent AI and Multi-Agent Systems. EXTRAAMAS 2024*. Springer., DOI: 10.1007/978-3-031-70074-3_13

Chaushi, B. A., Selimi, B., Chaushi, A., & Apostolova, M. (2023, Jul). Explainable artificial intelligence in education: A comprehensive review. In *World Conference on Explainable Artificial Intelligence* (p. 48-71). Cham: Springer Nature Switzerland. DOI: 10.1007/978-3-031-44067-0_3

Chen, D., & Xu, F. (2024). Design and implementation of machine learning algorithms in automatic grading of students' assignments. *Journal of Electrical Systems*, *20*(3s), 899–919. DOI: 10.52783/jes.1388

Doshi-Velez, F., & Kim, B. (2017). Towards a rigorous science of interpretable machine learning. *arXiv preprint arXiv:1702.08608.*

Drake, B. M., & Walz, A. (2018). Evolving business intelligence and data analytics in higher education. *New Directions for Institutional Research*, *2018*(178), 39–52. DOI: 10.1002/ir.20266

Félix, E., Amadieu, F., & Broisin, J. (2024). Personal Characteristics and Explanations in Technology-Enhanced Environments: An Exploratory Study in Computer Science Education.

Iatrellis, O., Samaras, N., Dervenis, C., & Panagiotakopoulos, T. (2023, October). KONX: A Dynamic Approach for Explainable AI in Higher Education. In *Proceedings of the 7th International Conference on Algorithms, Computing and Systems* (p. 118-124). DOI: 10.1145/3631908.3631925

Idrizi, E. (2024, May). Exploring the Role of Explainable Artificial Intelligence (XAI) in Adaptive learning systems. In *Proceedings of the Cognitive Models and Artificial Intelligence Conference* (p. 100-105). DOI: 10.1145/3660853.3660877

Jamal, A. (2023). The role of Artificial Intelligence (AI) in teacher education: Opportunities & challenges. *International Journal of Research and Analytical Reviews, 10*(1), 140–146.

Kayalı, B., & Balat, Ş. (2024). Assessment, Evaluation, and Feedback in Online Education With Artificial Intelligence-Supported Tools. In *AI Algorithms and ChatGPT for Student Engagement in Online Learning* (p. 124–135). IGI Global. DOI: 10.4018/979-8-3693-4268-8.ch008

Khosravi, H., Shum, S. B., Chen, G., Conati, C., Tsai, Y., Kay, J., Knight, S., Martinez-Maldonado, R., Sadiq, S., & Gašević, D. (2022). Explainable Artificial Intelligence in education. *Computers and Education Artificial Intelligence*, *3*, 100074. DOI: 10.1016/j.caeai.2022.100074

Kumawat, K. (2024). Explainable AI: Interpretable models for transparent decision-making. *International Journal of Food and Nutritional Science*, *9*(3). DOI: 10.48047/IJFANS/09/03/30

Limonova, V., Santos, A., São Mamede, H., & Filipe, V. (2023). The research context of artificial intelligence and gamification to improve student engagement and attendance in higher education.

Lipton, Z. C. (2018). The mythos of model interpretability: In machine learning, the concept of interpretability is both important and slippery. *ACM Queue; Tomorrow's Computing Today*, *16*(3), 31–57. DOI: 10.1145/3236386.3241340

Liu, Q., & Khalil, M. (2024, May). Explainable AI in Learning Analytics: Improving Predictive Models and Advancing Transparency Trust. In *2024 IEEE Global Engineering Education Conference (EDUCON)* (p. 1-7). IEEE. DOI: 10.1109/EDUCON60312.2024.10578733

Liu, Y. (2023). Explainable artificial intelligence and its practical applications. *Applied and Computational Engineering*, *4*(1), 755–759. DOI: 10.54254/2755-2721/4/2023419

Majumdar, R., Takami, K., & Ogata, H. (2023, July). Learning with Explainable AI-Recommendations at School: Extracting Patterns of Self-Directed Learning from Learning Logs. In *2023 IEEE International Conference on Advanced Learning Technologies (ICALT)* (p. 245-249). IEEE. DOI: 10.1109/ICALT58122.2023.00078

Morocho-Cayamcela, M. E., Lee, H., & Lim, W. (2019). Machine learning for 5G/B5G mobile and wireless communications: Potential, limitations, and future directions. *IEEE Access : Practical Innovations, Open Solutions, 7*, 137184–137206. DOI: 10.1109/ACCESS.2019.2942390

Nguyen, A., Kremantzis, M., Essien, A., Petrounias, I., & Hosseini, S. (2024). Enhancing student engagement through artificial intelligence (AI): Understanding the basics, opportunities, and challenges. *Journal of University Teaching & Learning Practice, 21*(06). DOI: 10.53761/caraaq92

Ogata, H., Flanagan, B., Takami, K., Dai, Y., Nakamoto, R., & Takii, K. (2024). EXAIT: Educational eXplainable artificial intelligent tools for personalized learning. *Research and Practice in Technology Enhanced Learning*, 19.

Rachha, A., & Seyam, M. (2023). Explainable AI in education: Current trends, challenges, and opportunities. *SoutheastCon, 2023*, 232–239. DOI: 10.1109/SoutheastCon51012.2023.10115140

Ribeiro, M. T., Singh, S., & Guestrin, C. (2016). Model-agnostic interpretability of machine learning. *arXiv preprint arXiv:1606.05386.*

Saeed, W., & Omlin, C. (2023). Explainable AI (XAI): A systematic meta-survey of current challenges and future opportunities. *Knowledge-Based Systems, 263*, 110273. DOI: 10.1016/j.knosys.2023.110273

Singh, H., & Miah, S. J. (2020). Smart education literature: A theoretical analysis. *Education and Information Technologies, 25*(4), 3299–3328. DOI: 10.1007/s10639-020-10116-4

Singhal, A., Pratap, P., Dixit, K. K., & Kathuria, K. (2024, Mar). Advancements in Explainable AI: Bridging the Gap Between Model Complexity and Interpretability. In *2024 2nd International Conference on Disruptive Technologies (ICDT)* (pp. 675-680). IEEE.

Wang, F. H. (2024, Jun). On the Effect of Explainable AI on Programming Learning: A Case Study of using Gradient Integration Technology. In *CS & IT Conference Proceedings* (Vol. 14, No. 12). CS & IT Conference Proceedings. DOI: 10.5121/csit.2024.141202

Zhu, Z. T., Yu, M. H., & Riezebos, P. (2016). A research framework of smart education. *Smart learning environments, 3*, 1-17.

Chapter 2
The Impact of AI-Assisted Mind Map-Based Learning Assessment on Motivation

Safa Boukhari
https://orcid.org/0009-0004-7887-3431
University Hassan II, Morocco

Mohamed Radid
University Hassan II, Morocco

Aziz Naciri
University Hassan II, Morocco

Ghizlane Chemsi
University Hassan II, Morocco

Mounir Sadiq
University Hassan II, Morocco

ABSTRACT

The renovation of pedagogical activities aims not only to put an end to the monotony of learning but also to keep pace with the evolution of the digital era. This research has two objectives: first, it seeks to support the approach of assessing mind maps using AI technologies; second, it aims to analyze learners' motivation during the creation of mind maps based on a questionnaire that evaluates their situational motivation toward this pedagogical activity. This cross-sectional, analytical, and quantitative

DOI: 10.4018/979-8-3373-0740-4.ch002

study was conducted with a sample of 300 second-year scientific baccalaureate students from the Settat Casablanca Academy (Morocco) during the 2024–2025 academic year. The measurement instrument used (SIMS) to assess situational motivation consists of four dimensions: intrinsic motivation, identified regulation, external regulation, and amotivation. The statistical analysis of the results reveals a significant increase in situational motivation during the creation of mind maps, indicating that the intervention has a positive impact.

1. INTRODUCTION

Learners' motivation is a central issue in education, as it is directly linked to engagement, success, and perseverance in learning. The multiplicity and diversity of research on this topic attest to its growing importance in the contemporary era.

Teaching and assessment activities influence learners' motivation and their commitment to persevering in their studies (Viau, 2009). The systematic adoption of the same pedagogical strategy can lead to student saturation. From this perspective, the renewal of pedagogical approaches is essential to break the monotony. Research has shown that diversifying active learning strategies supports learners' motivation (Pintrich & De Groot, 1990). In this context, it seems crucial to explore innovative learning and assessment approaches that can positively influence learners' engagement, perseverance, and motivation while also aligning with the anticipated expectations of AI integration in education.

In the spirit of renewing meaningful learning activities, this exploratory research was conceived, pursuing two objectives. First, it aims to analyze learners' motivation during the creation of mind maps based on a questionnaire that evaluates their situational motivation toward this pedagogical activity. Second, the study seeks to support the assessment approach for these mind maps by leveraging generative AI technologies, particularly the virtual assistant ChatGPT.

2. THEORETICAL FRAMEWORK

2.1 Assessment using mind maps

Mind maps are perceived as effective assessment tools, offering the possibility to evaluate a variety of both simple and complex skills, as well as cognitive tasks (De Broeck and Hausman, 2020). The creation of mind maps is a cognitive activity that demonstrates active understanding and meaningful learning. Numerous studies highlight their significance in this regard (Boukhari et al., 2024; Farrand, Hussain, and Hennessy, 2002; Shi et al., 2023; Weinstein and Mayer, 1983). Mind maps allow for the illustration of ideas (Balim, 2013; Shi et al., 2023) while emphasizing the learners' reflective process. This enables teachers to identify potential misconceptions or gaps in students' cognitive structures and take corrective action to improve learning. Furthermore, mind maps help visualize and simplify complex knowledge thanks to their visual layout, which aligns well with the way the human brain organizes and processes information, making them a powerful tool in various educational contexts (Buzan, 2024; Dambreville, 2014; Faouzi et al., 2019; Varsamidou, 2024; Yang, 2017). This assessment approach provides a richer evaluation framework, as it can measure transversal skills such as deep understanding, the ability to organize and structure knowledge, visual communication, critical thinking, and creativity. In contrast, other assessment methods, such as closed-ended or multiple-choice questions, are often exclusively focused on memorization skills.

2.2 The benefits of adopting AI in teaching

To adapt pedagogical practices to a fully connected generation and bridge the gap between the omnipresence of new technologies in learners' daily lives and their learning activities (Pratama, Sampelolo, and Lura, 2023; Walkington and Bernacki, 2020), the adoption of AI technologies in secondary education has become a central concern in educational research. The integration of artificial intelligence in education is seen as a powerful remedy for addressing technological challenges and meeting complex global demands (Liriwati, 2023). Furthermore, research on digital literacy recommends that learners develop a culture of AI technology usage from an early age (Long and Magerko, 2020; Su et al., 2023; Ng et al., 2021). As a result, AI-assisted teaching has become essential from preschool through the end of secondary education (Burgsteiner, Kandlhofer, and Steinbauer, 2016; Ng et al., 2021; Kandlhofer et al., 2016; Steinbauer et al., 2021). The integration of AI in education not only promotes adaptive learning (Pratama, Sampelolo, and Lura, 2023; Luckin and Holmes, 2016; Messaoudi, 2024; Rahman and Watanobe, 2023; Walkington and Bernacki, 2020; Yelubay et al., 2022), which facilitates an effective learning process, but it also ensures a higher level of motivation and engagement compared to traditional methods. Many studies highlight this aspect (Alasgarova and Rzayev, 2024; Bernate and Fonseca, 2023; Luckin and Holmes, 2016; Messaoudi, 2024; Moybeka et al., 2023; Panagiotidis, 2018; Pratama et al., 2023; Rizvi, 2023; Ruiz-Miranda, 2023; Yang, 2024; Zalte, 2023). Consequently, the adoption of AI technologies in educational activities positively contributes to improving learning outcomes (Hastie et al., 2016; Moybeka et al., 2023; Renz and Vladova, 2021; Rienties et al., 2020; Yang, 2024). In various contexts, artificial intelligence technologies, such as virtual assistants and intelligent tutoring systems, provide adaptive assessments and pedagogical solutions tailored to the individual needs of learners. For example, AI offers demonstrations and exercises that adjust to encountered difficulties, a topic explored in numerous studies (Rahman and Watanobe, 2023; Richter, 2019; Ruiz-Miranda, 2023). Personalized support enhances AI's motivational impact on educated individuals. Common definitions of personalized learning agree that it is based on the adaptation and customization of all pedagogical activities, including teaching approaches, educational sequences, learning experiences, assessment methods, and academic support, according to each learner's specific needs (Benhamdi et al., 2017; Christodoulou and Angeli, 2022; Johnson et al., 2016; Jung et al., 2019; Newman et al., 2013; Plass and Pawar, 2020; Walkington and Bernacki, 2020). In fact, personalized education, which adjusts to each learner's specificities—such as their needs, learning pace, and skills—represents a favorable approach that can strongly support motivation, satisfaction, and engagement (Liu et al., 2006; Gómez et al., 2014; Walkington and Bernacki, 2020). Referring to this point, it is evident that the goal of adaptive learning aligns with the principles of constructivist theory. This learning theory supports learner-centered pedagogical approaches, methods, and content while moving away from teacher-centered or outcome-focused approaches (Alamri et al., 2020; Barr and Tagg, 1995; Cuban, 1993; Watson et al., 2012). According to the constructivist perspective, the learner's role goes beyond active participation, as knowledge is constructed independently and individually (Barr and Tagg, 1995).

2.3 Complementary roles for educators and IA technologies

On one hand, in the educational context, the efficiency of AI adoption surpasses human intervention alone in terms of the permanent availability of AI tools, the ability to generate high-quality responses, and the capability to provide standardized assessments in a very short time (Celik, Dindar, Muukkonen, and Järvelä, 2022; Terzopoulos and Satratzemi, 2019). These factors strongly support the belief that teachers' tasks can be replaced by AI technology. Consequently, AI poses an unavoidable threat to administrative support functions in both educational and economic sectors (Chan and Tsi, 2023). On the other hand, human capabilities will always surpass AI in terms of emotional and social dimensions, reinforcing the crucial role of human educators in AI-assisted learning (Chiu et al., 2023; Frey and Osborne, 2017; Jarrahi, 2018). Many researchers argue that the synergy between AI technologies and educators creates a successful complementary relationship (Jarrahi, 2018; Popenici and Kerr, 2017). Siemens and Baker (2012) assert that this collaboration yields more promising results than an individual approach. Furthermore, a literature review (Roll and Wylie, 2016) has demonstrated that this collaboration fosters interactive learning environments. Therefore, in the context of optimizing learning, current research focuses more on streamlining pedagogical approaches based on the synergy between teachers and AI technologies. An example of a collaborative approach between AI and educators is the use of Intelligent Tutoring Systems (ITS), which provide real-time monitoring and tracking of each learner's educational progress, offering precise insights into their development. This allows teachers to better understand their students and intervene when necessary (Celik et al., 2022; Ma et al., 2014; VanLehn, 2006). Conversely, educators bring the essential human element that AI lacks by providing emotional support, fostering social interaction, and adding contextual depth to educational experiences. AI also has the potential to assist teachers by automating repetitive tasks, such as attendance management using facial recognition, thereby reducing time spent on administrative tasks (Haleem et al., 2022). As a result, the effective use of AI in education requires continuous teacher supervision. The design of this study aligns with the principle of teacher-AI collaboration, supporting the automated evaluation of mind maps using ChatGPT while maintaining the teacher's role in mediation and supervision. Educators can intervene, for instance, by providing emotional and physical support and correcting certain learning gaps. Successfully integrating AI into the teaching and learning process requires an exploration of the constraints that hinder AI implementation. It is therefore essential to address the challenges associated with AI adoption in education.

2.4 The challenges of adopting AI in education

Alongside the contributions of artificial intelligence (AI) technologies to improving the quality of teaching and learning, some field studies reveal that their use in schools—particularly in rural areas—faces several challenges. These include deficiencies in technical training and AI-related competencies for effective use (Chukwuere, 2024; Su and Zhong, 2022; Su et al., 2023), reliance on internet connectivity, and the continued necessity of educator intervention (Montiel-Ruiz and Ruiz, 2023). A literature review (Su et al., 2023) focusing on AI integration into teaching practices, particularly in preschool and secondary education, has identified another category of challenges, even in developed countries. These include the lack of well-designed educational resources (such as curricula and learning activities) and the absence of pedagogical guidelines for AI-assisted teaching. Similarly, in higher education, recent research (Labadze et al., 2023; Grassini, 2023; Michel-Villarreal et al., 2023; Siau and Wang, 2020; Chukwuere, 2024) underscores the growing need for explicit guidelines and reference frameworks to ensure the responsible use of AI technologies. Beyond the technical and pedagogical challenges, AI adoption in education also raises ethical concerns. These include the risk of algorithmic discrimination (Wogu, Misra, Olu-Owolabi, Assibong, and Udoh, 2018; Michel-Villarreal et al., 2023; Nah, 2023; Ntoutsi et al., 2020; Siau and Wang, 2020) and data security threats. Additionally, AI raises concerns regarding emotional privacy

(Hudlicka, 2016; Dignum, 2021), as these technologies may intrude upon users' right to personal space, emotions, and independent thought. To mitigate data reliability issues, the use of open-source AI is often recommended. Furthermore, other studies (Hastie et al., 2016; Popenici and Kerr, 2017; Richards and Dignum, 2019; Tuomi, 2018) argue that excessive reliance on AI-powered virtual assistants may lead to unintended consequences. While these assistants provide personalized, autonomous, and engaging learning experiences (Luckin and Holmes, 2016; Michel-Villarreal et al., 2023; Rahman and Watanobe, 2023), they may also foster dependency on AI technologies, thereby limiting learners' interactions with their surroundings. This, in turn, can negatively affect their socio-emotional and critical thinking skills (Iskender, 2023; Kasneci et al., 2023; Michel-Villarreal et al., 2023; Nah, 2023; Rahman and Watanobe, 2023; Wogu, Misra, Olu-Owolabi, Assibong, and Udoh, 2018). AI-generated responses tend to be automated and emotionally lacking (Felix, 2020; Pavlik, 2023), whereas emotional engagement strongly supports learners' motivation and involvement (Timms, 2016). Emotional aspects of learning, which cannot be automated by AI, remain essential (Schiff, 2021). Despite AI's ability to generate authentic content—including manuscripts, images, code, and videos—within seconds, as seen with generative AI models like ChatGPT (Chatterjee and Dethlefs, 2023; Kasneci et al., 2023; Lim, 2023; Morris, 2023; Nah, 2023), many studies highlight major issues such as inaccuracies, biases, and plagiarism (Chatterjee and Dethlefs, 2023; Ntoutsi et al., 2020; Stokel-Walker, 2022; Van Dis, 2023). For instance, ChatGPT-generated scripts are often flagged as plagiarism (Thorp, 2023) or AI-driven falsifications (Dibble, 2023; Lukpat, 2023). Other research warns that generative AI assistants may produce fabricated or biased data, misleading images, or false information (Ilieva et al., 2023; Laskar et al., 2023; Dwivedi et al., 2023; Lim, 2023; Lo, 2023).

One of the most significant challenges is AI hallucination, where the model generates inaccurate or fictitious content (Alkaissi and McFarlane, 2023; Kasneci et al., 2023; Nah, 2023; Susarla et al., 2023). A common example is the fabrication of nonexistent academic references (Nah, 2023; Thorp, 2023). Given these concerns, AI-generated content should undergo a rigorous verification and evaluation process before being accepted (Nah, 2023). For responsible AI use, recent research suggests strategies to ensure fairness and reduce bias, such as diversifying information sources (Gonzalez, 2023; Susarla et al., 2023).

2.5 Assessment using Chatgpt

In the context of improving pedagogical assessment methods, recent research has examined the significant potential of the ChatGPT chatbot across various disciplines. In medical education, ChatGPT has demonstrated its ability to provide adequate responses to open-ended questions in rheumatology (Lasnier Siron et al., 2023). In linguistics education, this tool has proven highly effective in evaluating text summaries and assessing the factual accuracy of text summaries (Luo et al., 2023; Gao et al., 2023), with performance comparable to that of human evaluators. Some teachers and students perceive AI generative technologies as potential tools for assessing student learning, taking on roles traditionally performed by educators. This generative assistant proves to be a valuable tool for assessment activities (Michel-Villarreal et al., 2023; Rahman and Watanobe, 2023).

2.6 Situational motivation

Situational intrinsic and extrinsic motivation refers to the motivation individuals experience when engaging in a given activity (Guay et al., 2000). It reflects the present state of motivation (Vallerand, 1997). Furthermore, several studies have confirmed that state motivation depends on psychological outcomes such as positive or negative impacts and vitality (Sheldon, Ryan, & Reiss, 1996). Consequently, measuring situational motivation at a specific moment provides a practical perspective on learners' state self-regulation mechanisms. Self-Determination Theory (Deci & Ryan, 1985) asserts that various types of motivation shape an individual's attitudes, namely intrinsic motivation, extrinsic motivation, and amotivation, which are distributed along a continuum ranging from high to low self-determination. Intrinsic motivation is based on the pleasure and satisfaction derived from completing a task (Deci, 1971). In contrast, extrinsic motivation encompasses a broad range of behaviors where the goals of the action extend beyond the activity itself. Self-Determination Theory has identified several types of extrinsic motivation, which can also be positioned along the self-determination continuum. The level of self-determination varies from lowest to highest, depending on external and identified regulations. When an individual's behavior is regulated by rewards or punishments, external regulation is at play, meaning the person feels compelled to behave in a certain way. Identified regulation, on the other hand, occurs when a behavior is perceived as a personal choice. However, the motivation remains external, as the task is not performed for its own sake but rather as a means to achieve a goal. To better understand human behavior, Deci and Ryan (1985) introduced the concept of amotivation, which refers to a lack of motivation that can be likened to learned helplessness (Abramson et al., 1978). When individuals are unmotivated, their actions are neither driven by a sense of duty nor by the expectation of a reward. To assess learners' momentary reactions during the execution of a particular activity, various situational motivation measures have been developed. Research typically relies on two categories of measures: behavioral measures and self-report measures. The different types of motivation outlined in Self-Determination Theory—such as intrinsic motivation, identified regulation, external regulation, and amotivation—deserve careful examination. Using this multidimensional approach provides a deeper understanding of motivational mechanisms.

This study employs a multidimensional tool, the Situational Motivation Scale (SIMS), to assess situational motivation. The items in this questionnaire are designed in accordance with the conceptual definition of motivation (Deci & Ryan, 1985; McClelland, 1985), which emphasizes the "why" behind behavior. As such, these items represent possible answers to the question: "Why are you currently engaged in this activity?" This definition focuses on the underlying factors that influence task engagement (Deci & Ryan, 1985; Harter, 1981; Vallerand, 1997).

3. PRACTICAL CONTEXT

3.1 The methodology

In the commendable effort to overcome, as much as possible, the challenges hindering the use of artificial intelligence in education—such as complexity, unequal access to these tools, and connectivity issues, as previously discussed—this study takes place in a pedagogical context where accessibility and ease of digital adoption are top priorities. There are multiple paid software programs dedicated to mind map creation. XMind, MindManager, and iMindMap are powerful tools in terms of advanced features and professional use.

The methodology of this research involves producing mind maps using a conventional tool: Microsoft Word, and evaluating them with recent artificial intelligence technologies, particularly ChatGPT. As mentioned earlier, the choice of this digital tool is based on several advantages, including its cost-effective alternative, wide availability, and flexibility. Word files are compatible with various formats (PDF or images), making it easy to share and/or convert them for other purposes. Mind maps created in Word can be easily converted into structured text or exported as images for analysis by AI tools such as Socratic or ChatGPT.

The pedagogical scenario followed these steps: Learners attended an introductory session on the mind map evaluation activity, as it was a new experience for the entire sample. The goal of this session was to introduce students to the exercise, provide instructions, and remind them of the evaluation criteria for the produced mind maps.

Students were invited to complete the formative assessment in the computer lab. The mind maps were sent via Gmail to the teacher for evaluation using ChatGPT, which performed semantic, cognitive, and structural analysis of these maps.

To analyze learners' motivation regarding the mind map evaluation activity (the second objective of the research), students were given instructions on completing a questionnaire measuring their situational motivation before and after the mind map creation task. They were assured that their responses would remain anonymous to ensure confidentiality.

3.2 Evaluation criteria for cards produced by ChatGPT

The evaluation of mind maps by AI assistants such as ChatGPT is based on various criteria: originality, the richness of concepts, and the structure of the map (coordination of ideas, logical organization, and readability of relationships). To ensure a methodical evaluative approach, certain assessment indicators can be customized by the teacher. For example, specific instructions regarding the visual aspects of the map, such as the minimum number of nodes and logical links, can be set. For content analysis, the scope of knowledge to be assessed must be clearly defined by the teacher, and all these basic instructions should be communicated to ChatGPT in advance.

In this study, the evaluation specifically focuses on the chemistry course "Chemical Reaction Equilibrium" from the second-year baccalaureate curriculum. The core knowledge and learning objectives of this course define the knowledge domain to be assessed in this formative evaluation. These objectives are clearly outlined in the document "Programs and Pedagogical Guidelines for Teaching Physics and Chemistry in High School" (2007) in Morocco. This document serves as a reference for planning, managing, and assessing learning in this subject at the secondary level. Based on these guidelines, ChatGPT automatically analyzes the created mind maps.

The evaluation using ChatGPT provides correction suggestions related to comprehension, hierarchy, reorganization, or idea development. It generates detailed, tailored feedback reports for each student, including practical improvements. For example, it can identify strengths and weaknesses, potential gaps or missing ideas, and difficulties encountered. By receiving this feedback, learners gain insight into their own cognitive processes, which can enhance their metacognitive skills. All these aspects contribute to the personalized evaluation capabilities of AI technologies.

3.3 Study sample

A quasi-experimental, analytical, and quantitative study was conducted with a randomly selected sample of learners. This population consists of 300 second-year scientific baccalaureate students (65.5% boys and 34.5% girls). The average age of the participants is 16.9 years, and they are from the Settat Casablanca Academy (Morocco) during the 2024-2025 academic year.

3.4 The measuring instrument

The questionnaire used to measure motivation is divided into two parts. The first part is related to sociodemographic data and students' experiences with digital learning and evaluation based on mind maps combined with AI technologies (13 items), including: age, gender, nationality, institution, study section (Arabic or French), grade repetition, residence area (rural or urban), prior experience with digital learning activities (courses, assessments, educational games, tests), frequency of digital tool usage for learning in class (every day, a few times a week, rarely, never), frequency of digital tool usage for learning at home (every day, a few times a week, rarely, never), the most used digital applications or platforms for studies (YouTube, WhatsApp, Moodle, Google Classroom, live social media sessions, ChatGPT), the most used devices/tools for accessing studies (laptop, desktop computer, smartphone, tablet), and prior experience with AI-assisted mind map-based digital learning activities. The second part of the questionnaire is a scale measuring situational motivation (SIMS-16). As mentioned earlier, the SIMS was designed by Guay et al., (2000), and its development is based on the self-determination theory (Deci & Ryan, 1985). It consists of 16 items. The 16 items are distributed across the following four subscales: intrinsic motivation, for example, "right now, I am doing this activity because I feel good doing it"; identified regulation, for example, "right now, I am doing the activity because I believe it is important"; external regulation, for example, "right now, I am doing this activity because I am supposed to do it"; and amotivation, for example, "right now, I am doing this activity, but I am wondering if I should continue it." All items from each dimension are assessed on a 7-point Likert scale, ranging from 1 (strongly disagree) to 7 (strongly agree). The subscales showed internal consistency values (Cronbach's α) such as intrinsic motivation ($\alpha = 0.95$), identified regulation ($\alpha = 0.80$), external regulation ($\alpha = 0.86$), and amotivation ($\alpha = 0.77$) (Guay et al., 2000). According to Nunnally's (1978) psychometric theory, self-assessment scales with internal consistencies ranging from 0.70 to 0.80 are considered acceptable for research studies. The SIMS subscales meet this condition.

4. RESULTS AND DISCUSSION

Statistical data are analyzed using SPSS. Significant results from the processing of sociodemographic data (first part of the questionnaire) include: The rate of digital tool usage for learning by the students, whether in class or at home, does not depend on the students' gender, age, or study section (Arabic or French). However, the rate of digital tool usage for learning depends on the area of residence (rural or urban). This result is consistent with several studies in different countries, such as South Africa, India, the Americas, and the United States. These studies affirm that the use of digital technologies in rural school environments faces more challenges than in urban environments, such as poor connectivity, lack of training and technical infrastructure, cultural barriers, and possibly electricity shortages (Das et al., 2021; Dube, 2020; Montiel-Ruiz and Ruiz, 2023; Valentine et al., 2021; Welser et al., 2019). This heterogeneity in the use of digital tools in learning reflects the weakness of digital skills among university students from rural areas compared to their peers from urban areas (Welser et al., 2019). Only 2.29% of learners reported having previously participated in digital learning activities in class (courses, assessments, educational games, tests), while most learners, 92%, selected the option "every day" for the frequency of using digital tools to learn at home. Additionally, 100% of the sample stated that they had never benefited from digital evaluation based on AI-assisted mind maps. This result shows that despite the lack of adoption of digital learning in the classroom, learners remain interested in using digital technology. Regarding the most used digital applications or platforms for studies, 74.6% of learners prefer WhatsApp, while 53% use YouTube. This result is highly expected, as the use of social media platforms has become a necessity for most learners (Ahmad et al., 2022; Appollis and Sutcliffe, 2022; Hassan et al., 2020; Patmanthara et al., 2019). For the descriptive analysis of the second part of the questionnaire, the comparison of average scores for the four dimensions of motivation before and after the digital mind map creation activity reveals a significant increase in students' situational motivation during this activity, particularly in the dimensions of intrinsic motivation and external regulation. For example, to measure intrinsic motivation self-determination, the item "right now, I am doing this activity because I find it interesting" shows an increase in the average score from 4.4524 to 6.3452, suggesting a significant improvement in students' perception and interest in learning. Another example for measuring external regulation self-determination, the item "right now, I am doing this activity because I feel like I have to do it" shows a decrease in the average score from 2.1 to 1.6. This decrease signals an improvement in the perception of learning in the present moment, as this item examines how much the learner perceives the current activity as a mandatory task. Table 1 summarizes the average scores for each dimension of motivation before and after the intervention

Table 1. average scores for each motivational dimension before and after the intervention.

Types of motivation	The average score	
	before activity	after activity
Intrinsic motivation	5,14	6,43
Regulation identified	4,39	5,78
Extern regulation	2,82	1,96
Amotivation	2,11	1,56

The statistical analyses of the four dimensions—intrinsic motivation, identified regulation, external regulation, and amotivation—show a significant increase in situational motivation during the mind mapping activity. These results can be interpreted by the fact that the first experience of using digital technology in the classroom is often unique, as adopting an unconventional pedagogical approach, whether for learning or assessment, is usually accompanied by much enthusiasm and curiosity from the learners. However, some believe that the first experience is frequently accompanied by concerns such as feelings of inability to use the technology effectively due to the complexity of the digital tools used and technical challenges. Yet, for the current study, the use of the classic Word tool did not raise such concerns. This made learners more enthusiastic and motivated about creating mind maps using Microsoft Word without worrying about the digital support itself.

These results are consistent with several related studies on the impact of artificial intelligence technologies on learner motivation (Richter, 2019; Ruiz-Miranda, 2023; Rahman and Watanobe, 2023). The personalized feedback and adaptive assessments provided by the virtual assistant ChatGPT ensure the motivational aspect of AI.

5. CONCLUSION

Formative assessment based on mind maps ensures authentic assessment, measuring both simple and complex competencies. However, evaluating these maps by the teacher is far from an easy task, especially with large numbers of learners. Initially, this study proposes a formative assessment approach based on mind maps combined with AI technologies, where the ChatGPT assistant ensures the automatic evaluation of the produced mind maps based on criteria that can be personalized by the teacher. Secondly, the study aims to assess the situational motivation of learners in relation to their experience in creating mind maps. The statistical analyses of the four dimensions—intrinsic motivation, identified regulation, external regulation, and amotivation—show a significant increase in situational motivation during the mind map creation activity, indicating that this intervention has a motivating effect. In conclusion, this evaluative approach encompasses a synergy between authentic assessment with mind maps and the pedagogical benefits of AI technologies.

REFERENCES

Abramson, L. Y., Seligman, M. E., & Teasdale, J. D. (1978). Learned helplessness in humans: Critique and reformulation. *Journal of Abnormal Psychology*, *87*(1), 49–74. DOI: 10.1037/0021-843X.87.1.49 PMID: 649856

Ahmad, T. S. A. S., Abedin, N. F. Z., Ahmad, I., Paramasivam, S., & Mustapha, W. Z. W. (2022). Awareness and Attitudes of Undergraduate Students towards Plagiarism: Are There Any Differences between Genders? *Asian Journal of University Education*, *18*(3), 597–605.

Alamri, H., Lowell, V., Watson, W., & Watson, S. L. (2020). Using personalized learning as an instructional approach to motivate learners in online higher education: Learner self-determination and intrinsic motivation. *Journal of Research on Technology in Education*, *52*(3), 322–352. DOI: 10.1080/15391523.2020.1728449

Alasgarova, R., & Rzayev, J. (2024). The role of Artificial Intelligence in shaping high school students' motivation. [IJTES]. *International Journal of Technology in Education and Science*, *8*(2), 311–324. DOI: 10.46328/ijtes.553

Alkaissi, H., & McFarlane, S. I. (2023). Artificial hallucinations in ChatGPT: Implications in scientific writing. *Cureus*, *15*(2), 1–4. DOI: 10.7759/cureus.35179 PMID: 36811129

Appollis, J., & Sutcliffe, C. M. (2022). The use of social media such as WhatsApp, YouTube and Instagram in enhancing rather than impeding the learning of College students: An investigative case study. *Journal of Education and Social Sciences*, *22*(1), 1–11.

Bagot, F. (2006). Élitaire pour tous: Entretiens sur les classes préparatoires aux grandes

Balim, A. G. (2013). The effect of mind-mapping applications on upper primary students' success and inquiry-learning skills in science and environment education. *International Research in Geographical and Environmental Education*, *22*(4), 337–352. DOI: 10.1080/10382046.2013.826543

Barr, R. B., & Tagg, J. (1995). From teaching to learning—A new paradigm for undergraduate education. Change: The magazine of higher learning, 27(6), 12-26.doi: . 10544672DOI: 10.1080/00091383.1995

Barr, R. B., & Tagg, J. (1995). From teaching to learning—A new paradigm for undergraduate education. Change: The magazine of higher learning, 27(6), 12-26.

Bearman, M., Nieminen, J. H., & Ajjawi, R. (2023). Designing assessment in a digital world: An organising framework. *Assessment & Evaluation in Higher Education, 48*(3), 291–304. DOI: 10.1080/02602938.2022.2069674

Ben Haman, O. (2021). The Moroccan education system, dilemma of language and think-tanks: The challenges of social development for the North African country. *Journal of North African Studies, 26*(4), 709–732. DOI: 10.1080/13629387.2019.1711061

Benhamdi, S., Babouri, A., & Chiky, R. (2017). Système de recommandation personnalisé pour environnement e-Learning. Éducation et Technologies de l'Information, 22, 1455-1477. DOI DOI: 10.1007/s10639-016-9504-y

Bernate, J. A. y Fonseca, I. P. (2023). Impacto de las Tecnologías de Información y Comunicación en la educación del siglo XXI: Revisión bibliométrica. Revistade ciencias sociales, 29(1), 227-242. https://doi.org/DOI: 10.31876/rcs.v29i1

Boukhari, S., Sadiq, M., Radid, M., Naciri, A., & Chemsi, G. (2024). *Mind Maps and Artificial Intelligence: Towards an Active Understanding of Redox in Secondary School Students. Lecture Notes in Networks and Systems* (Vol. 862). Springer., DOI: 10.1007/978-3-031-71429-0_1

Burgsteiner, H., Kandlhofer, M., & Steinbauer, G. (2016, March). Irobot: Teaching the basics of artificial intelligence in high schools. *Proceedings of the AAAI Conference on Artificial Intelligence, 30*(1) DOI: 10.1609/aaai.v30i1.9864

Buzan, T. (2024). *Mind map mastery: The complete guide to learning and using the most powerful thinking tool in the universe.* Jaico Publishing House.

Caro Dambreville, S. (2014). Mind maps: a paradigm shift in learning. Communication, technologies and development, (1).DOI: 10.4000/12746

Celik, I., Dindar, M., Muukkonen, H., & Järvelä, S. (2022). The Promises and Challenges of Artificial Intelligence for Teachers: A Systematic Review of Research. *TechTrends, 66*(4), 616–630. DOI: 10.1007/s11528-022-00715-y

Chan, C. K. Y., & Tsi, L. H. (2023). The AI revolution in education: Will AI replace or assist teachers in higher education? arXiv preprint arXiv:2305.01185. https://doi .org//arXiv.2305.01185DOI: 10.48550

Chatterjee, J., & Dethlefs, N. (2023). This new conversational AI model can be your friend, philosopher, and guide and even your worst enemy. Patterns, 4(1). DOI: 10.1016/j.patter.2022.100676

Chiu, TKF, Moorhouse, BL, Chai, CS, & Ismailov, M. (2023). Soutien des enseignants et motivation des élèves à apprendre avec un chatbot basé sur l'intelligence artificielle (IA). Environnements d'apprentissage interactifs, 32 (7), 3240–3256. DOI: 10.1080/10494820.2023.2172044

Christodoulou, A., & Angeli, C. (2022, June). Adaptive learning techniques for a personalized educational software in developing teachers' technological pedagogical content knowledge. In Frontiers in Education (Vol. 7, p. 789397). Frontiers Media SA. DOI: 10.3389/feduc.2022.789397

Chukwuere, J. E. (2024). *The Future of AI Chatbots in Higher Education*. Qeios., DOI: 10.32388/UE841K

Cuban, L. (1993). *How Teachers Taught: Constancy and Change in American Classrooms, 1890-1990*. Teachers College Press.

Darling-Hammond, L. (2006). Darling-, Linda. Constructing 21st-century teacher education. *Journal of Teacher Education*, *57*(3), 300–314. DOI: 10.1177/0022487105285962

Das, N. K., Sahoo, S., & Pati, L. (2021). Online learning: Challenges for education in rural and remote areas. suicide, 8(7). DOI: DOI: 10.17148/IARJSET.2021.8712

De Broeck, F., & Hausman, M. (2020). The potential of mind maps for assessment in times of pandemic. Assess. *International Journal of Research in Education and Training*, *1*, 85–96.

Deci, E. L. (1971). Effects of externally mediated rewards on intrinsic motivation. *Journal of Personality and Social Psychology*, *18*(1), 105–115. DOI: 10.1037/h0030644

Deci, E. L., & Ryan, R. M. (1985). *Intrinsic motivation and self-determination in human behavior*. Plenum. DOI: 10.1007/978-1-4899-2271-7

Dejours, R. (2017). Classes préparatoires. *Adolescence*, *35*(2), 361–370. DOI: 10.3917/ado.100.0361

Dibble, M. (2023). *Schools ban ChatGPT amid fears of artificial intelligence-assisted cheating*. VOA News.

Dignum, V. (2021). The role and challenges of education for responsible AI. *London Review of Education*, *19*(1), 1–11. DOI: 10.14324/LRE.19.1.01

Djouad, T., Settouti, L. S., Prié, Y., Reffay, C. & Mille, A. Un Système à Base de Traces pour la modélisation et l'élaboration d'indicateurs d'activités éducatives individuelles et collectives. Mise à l'épreuve sur Moodle.

Dube, B. (2020). Rural online learning in the context of COVID 19 in South Africa: Evoking an inclusive education approach. *Multidisciplinary Journal of Educational Research, 10*(2), 135–157. DOI: 10.17583/remie.2020.5607

Dwivedi, Y. K., Kshetri, N., Hughes, L., Slade, E. L., Jeyaraj, A., Kar, A. K., Baabdullah, A. M., Koohang, A., Raghavan, V., Ahuja, M., Albanna, H., Albashrawi, M. A., Al-Busaidi, A. S., Balakrishnan, J., Barlette, Y., Basu, S., Bose, I., Brooks, L., Buhalis, D., & Wright, R. (2023). Opinion paper: "So what if ChatGPT wrote it?" Multidisciplinary perspectives on opportunities, challenges and implications of generative conversational AI for research, practice and policy. *International Journal of Information Management, 71*, 1–63. DOI: 10.1016/j.ijinfomgt.2023.102642

Faouzi, L., Gourja, B., Belarbi, N., & Nachit, M. B. (2019). Mind Map Recognition in a Graphical Representation: An Evaluative Approach. Doi:DOI: 10.19044/esj.2019.v15n23p76

Farrand, P., Fearzana, H., & Hennessy, E. (2002). The efficacy of the mind map study technique. *Medical Education, 36*(5), 426–431. DOI: 10.1046/j.1365-2923.2002.01205.x PMID: 12028392

Felix, C. V. (2020). The Role of the Teacher and AI in Education. In Sengupta, E., Blessinger, P., & Makhanya, M. (Eds.), *International Perspectives on the Role of Technology in Humanizing Higher Education* (Vol. 33, pp. 33–48). Emerald Publishing Limited., DOI: 10.1108/S2055-364120200000033003

Fisher, R., Cavanagh, J., & Bowles, A. (2011). Assisting transition to university: Using assessment as a formative learning tool. *Assessment & Evaluation in Higher Education, 36*(2), 225–237. DOI: 10.1080/02602930903308241

Frey, C. B., & Osborne, M. A. (2017). The future of employment: How susceptible are jobs to computerisation? *Technological Forecasting and Social Change, 114*, 254–280. DOI: 10.1016/j.techfore.2016.08.019

Fui-Hoon Nah, F., Zheng, R., Cai, J., Siau, K., & Chen, L. (2023). IA générative et ChatGPT: Applications, défis et collaboration IA-humain. *Journal of Information Technology Case and Application Research, 25*(3), 277–304. DOI: 10.1080/15228053.2023.2233814

Gao, M., Ruan, J., Sun, R., Yin, X., Yang, S., & Wan, X. (2023). Human-like summarization evaluation with chatgpt. arXiv preprint arXiv:2304.02554. https://doi.org//arXiv.2304.02554DOI: 10.48550

Gikandi, J. W., Morrow, D., & Davis, N. E. (2011). Online formative assessment in higher education: A review of the literature. *Computers & Education, 57*(4), 2333–2351.

Gómez, S., Zervas, P., Sampson, D. G., & Fabregat, R. (2014). Context-aware adaptive and personalized mobile learning delivery supported by UoLmP. Journal of King Saud University-Computer and Information Sciences, 26(1), 47-61. DOI: 10.1016/j.rhum.2023.10.358

Gonzalez-Gonzalez, CS (2023). The impact of artificial intelligence on education: transforming the way we teach and learn. DOI: DOI: 10.25145/j.qurricul.2023.36.03

Grassini, S. (2023). Shaping the future of education: Exploring the potential and consequences of AI and ChatGPT in educational settings. *Education Sciences, 13*(7), 692. DOI: 10.3390/educsci13070692

Guay, F., Vallerand, R. J., & Blanchard, C. (2000). On the assessment of situational intrinsic and extrinsic motivation:The situational motivation scale. *Motivation and Emotion, 24*(3), 175–213. DOI: 10.1023/A:1005614228250

Haleem, A., Javaid, M., Qadri, M. A., & Suman, R. (2022). Understanding the role of digital technologies in education: A review. Sustainable operations and computers, 3, 275-285.

Harter, S. (1981). Une nouvelle échelle d'auto-évaluation de l'orientation intrinsèque et extrinsèque en classe: Composantes motivationnelles et informationnelles. *Developmental Psychology, 17*, 300–312. DOI: 10.1037/0012-1649.17.3.300

Hassan, M. M., Mirza, T., & Hussain, M. W. (2020). A critical review by teachers on the online teaching-learning during the COVID-19. *International Journal of Education and Management Engineering, 10*(5), 17–27. DOI: 10.5815/ijeme.2020.05.03

Hastie, H., Lim, M. Y., Janarthanam, S., Deshmukh, A., Aylett, R., Foster, M. E., & Hall, L. (2016). I remember you! interaction with memory for an empathic virtual robotic tutor.

Henderson, R. W., & Landesman, E. M. (1993, February). The Interactive Videodisc System in the Zone of Proximal Development: Academic Motivation and Learning Outcomes in Precalculus. [Internet]. *Journal of Educational Computing Research, 9*(1), 29–43. DOI: 10.2190/J53A-V7VT-22D0-VGEK

Hudlicka, E. (2016). Virtual affective agents and therapeutic games. In *Artificial intelligence in behavioral and mental health care* (p. 81–115). Academic Press., DOI: 10.1016/B978-0-12-420248-1.00004-0

Ilieva, G., Yankova, T., Klisarova-Belcheva, S., Dimitrov, A., Bratkov, M., & Angelov, D. (2023). Effects of generative chatbots in higher education. *Information (Basel)*, *14*(9), 492. DOI: 10.3390/info14090492

Iskender, A. (2023). Holy or unholy? Interview with open AI's ChatGPT. *European Journal of Tourism Research*, *34*(3414), 1–11. DOI: 10.54055/ejtr.v34i.3169

Jarrahi, M. H. (2018). Artificial intelligence and the future of work: Human-AI symbiosis in organizational decision making. *Business Horizons*, *61*(4), 577–586. DOI: 10.1016/j.bushor.2018.03.007

Jin, S. et Peng, L. (2022). Perception en classe dans l'enseignement supérieur: impact des facteurs spatiaux sur la satisfaction des étudiants dans les cours magistral par rapport aux salles de classe d'apprentissage actif. Frontières en psychologie, 13, 941285

Johnson, L., Adams Becker, S., Cummins, M., Estrada, V., Freeman, A., & Hall, C. (2016). NMC Horizon Report: 2016 Higher Education Edition. Austin, Texas: The New Media Consortium. https://www.learntechlib.org/p/171478/

Jung, E., Kim, D., Yoon, M., Park, S., & Oakley, B. (2019). The influence of instructional design on learner control, sense of achievement, and perceived effectiveness in a supersize MOOC course. *Computers & Education*, *128*, 377–388. DOI: 10.1016/j.compedu.2018.10.001

Kandlhofer, M., Steinbauer, G., Hirschmugl-Gaisch, S., & Huber, P. (2016, October). Artificial intelligence and computer science in education: From kindergarten to university. In 2016 IEEE frontiers in education conference (FIE) (p. 1-9). IEEE. DOI: DOI: 10.1109/FIE.2016.7757570

Kasneci, E., Seßler, K., Küchemann, S., Bannert, M., Dementieva, D., Fischer, F., Gasser, U., Groh, G., Günnemann, S., Hüllermeier, E., Krusche, S., Kutyniok, G., Michaeli, T., Nerdel, C., Pfeffer, J., Poquet, O., Sailer, M., Schmidt, A., Seidel, T., & Kasneci, G. (2023). ChatGPT for good? On opportunities and challenges of large language models for education. *Learning and Individual Differences*, *103*, 102274. DOI: 10.1016/j.lindif.2023.102274

Kong, S. C., Cheung, W. M. Y., & Zhang, G. (2022). Evaluating artificial intelligence literacy courses for fostering conceptual learning, literacy and empowerment in university students: Refocusing to conceptual building. *Computers in Human Behavior Reports*, *7*, 100223. DOI: 10.1016/j.chbr.2022.100223

Labadze, L., Grigolia, M., & Machaidze, L. (2023). Role of AI chatbots in education: Systematic literature review. *International Journal of Educational Technology in Higher Education*, *20*(1), 56. DOI: 10.1186/s41239-023-00426-1

Ladage, C., & Audran, J. (2011). Questions et test en ligne sur des plateformes EIAH: Des pratiques rétrocognitives réinterrogées par l'analyse des traces. Conférence EIAH 2011 Environnements informatiques pour l'apprentissage humain, 381-393. https://hal.archives-ouvertes.fr/hal00611391/document

Laskar, M. T. R., Bari, M. S., Rahman, M., Bhuiyan, M. A. H., Joty, S., & Huang, J. X. (2023). A systematic study and comprehensive evaluation of ChatGPT on benchmark datasets. arXiv preprint arXiv:2305.18486. /arXiv.2305.18486DOI: 10.18653/v1/2023.findings-acl.29

Lim, W. M., Gunasekara, A., Pallant, J. L., Pallant, J. I., & Pechenkina, E. (2023). Generative AI and the future of education: Ragnarök or reformation? A paradoxical perspective from management educators. *International Journal of Management Education*, *21*(2), 100790. DOI: 10.1016/j.ijme.2023.100790

Liriwati, F. Y. (2023). Transformasi Kurikulum. *Kecerdasan Buatan Untuk Membangun Pendidikan Yang Relevan di Masa Depan.*, *1*, 62–71.

Liu, R., Qiao, X., & Liu, Y. (2006). A paradigm shift of learner-centered teaching style: Reality or illusion? *Journal of Second Language Acquisition and Teaching*, *13*, 77–91.

Lo, C. K. (2023). What is the impact of ChatGPT on education? A rapid review of the literature. *Education Sciences*, *13*(4), 410. DOI: 10.3390/educsci13040410

Long, D., & Magerko, B. (2020, April). What is AI literacy? Competencies and design considerations. In *Proceedings of the 2020 CHI conference on human factors in computing systems* (p. 1-16). DOI: 10.1145/3313831.3376727

Luckin, R., & Holmes, W. (2016). Intelligence unleashed: An argument for AI in education

Lukpat, A. (2023). ChatGPT banned in New York City public schools over concerns about cheating, learning development. The Wall Street Journal.https://www.wsj.com/articles/chatgpt-banned-in-new-york-city-public-schools-over-concerns-about-cheating-learning-development-11673024059

Luo, Z., Xie, Q., & Ananiadou, S. (2023). Chatgpt as a factual inconsistency evaluator for text summarization. arXiv preprint arXiv:2303.15621. https://doi.org//arXiv.2303.15621DOI: 10.48550

Ma, W., Adesope, O. O., Nesbit, J. C., & Liu, Q. (2014). Intelligent tutoring systems and learning outcomes: A meta-analysis. *Journal of Educational Psychology, 106*(4), 901–918. DOI: 10.1037/a0037123

McClelland, D. C. (1985). How motives, skills, and values determine what people do. *The American Psychologist, 40*(7), 812–825. DOI: 10.1037/0003-066X.40.7.812

McGarr, O. (2009). A review of podcasting in higher education: Its influence on the traditional lecture. *Australasian Journal of Educational Technology, 25*(3), 25. DOI: 10.14742/ajet.1136

Messaoudi, A. (2024). The challenges of AI in education: from data protection to algorithmic biases. Mediations & mediatizations, (18), 148-160. DOI: 10.52358/mm.vi18.409

Michel-Villarreal, R., Vilalta-Perdomo, E., Salinas-Navarro, D. E., Thierry-Aguilera, R., & Gerardou, F. S. (2023). Challenges and opportunities of generative AI for higher education as explained by ChatGPT. *Education Sciences, 13*(9), 856. DOI: 10.3390/educsci13090856

Montiel-Ruiz, FJ and López Ruiz, M. (2023). L'intelligence artificielle comme ressource pédagogique dans une école groupée rurale. Revue interuniversitaire RiiTE de recherche en technologie éducative, (15), 28-40. DOI: 10.6018/riite.592031

Morris, M. R. (2023). Scientists' Perspectives on the Potential for Generative AI in their Fields. arXiv preprint arXiv:2304.01420.

Moybeka, A. M., Syariatin, N., Tatipang, D. P., Mushthoza, D. A., Dewi, N. P. J. L., & Tineh, S. (2023). Artificial Intelligence and English classroom: The implications of AI toward EFL students' motivation. Edumaspul. *Jurnal Pendidikan, 7*(2), 2444–2454.

Newman, A., Bryant, G., Stokes, P., & Squeo, T. (2013). Learning to adapt: Understanding the adaptive learning supplier landscape. Tyton Partners white paper

Ng, D. T. K., Leung, J. K. L., Chu, K. W. S., & Qiao, M. S. (2021). AI literacy: Definition, teaching, evaluation and ethical issues. *Proceedings of the Association for Information Science and Technology, 58*(1), 504–509. DOI: 10.1002/pra2.487

Nieminen, J. H., Bearman, M., & Ajjawi, R. (2023). Designing the digital in authentic assessment: Is it fit for purpose? *Assessment & Evaluation in Higher Education, 48*(4), 529–543.

Ntoutsi, E., Fafalios, P., Gadiraju, U., Iosifidis, V., Nejdl, W., Vidal, M. E., Ruggieri, S., Turini, F., Papadopoulos, S., Krasanakis, E., Kompatsiaris, I., Kinder-Kurlanda, K., Wagner, C., Karimi, F., Fernandez, M., Alani, H., Berendt, B., Kruegel, T., Heinze, C., & Staab, S. (2020). Bias in data-driven artificial intelligence systems—An introductory survey. *Wiley Interdisciplinary Reviews. Data Mining and Knowledge Discovery*, *10*(3), e1356. DOI: 10.1002/widm.1356

Nunnally, J. C. (1978). *Théorie psychométrique (2e édition).* Jossey-Bass.

Panagiotidis, P., Krystalli, P., & Arvanitis, P. (2018). Technology as a motivational factor in foreign language learning. *European Journal of Education*, *6*(1), 69–84. DOI: 10.2478/ejed-2023-0007

Patmanthara, S., Febiharsa, D., & Dwiyanto, F. A. (2019, October). Social media as a learning media: A comparative analysis of Youtube, WhatsApp, Facebook and Instagram utillization. In *2019 International Conference on Electrical, Electronics and Information Engineering (ICEEIE)* (Vol. 6, p. 183-186). IEEE. DOI: DOI: 10.1109/ICEEIE47180.2019.8981441

Pavlik, J. V. (2023). Collaborating With ChatGPT: Considering the Implications of Generative Artificial.Intelligence for Journalism and Media Education. Journalism & Mass Communication Educator, 107769582211495–. DOI: 10.1177/10776958221149577

Peraya, D. (2019a). Entre l'enseignement et la recherche, quelle place pour les Learning Analytics ? Distances et médiations des savoirs, 27, 1-4. DOI: 10.4000/dms.4080

Peraya, D. (2019b). Les Learning Analytics, entre fantasmes et réalités. Distances et médiations des savoirs, 28, 1-3. DOI: 10.4000/dms.4599

Pierrot, L. (2019). Les LA: Des réponses et des promesses. Distances et médiations des savoirs, 26, 1-7. DOI: 10.4000/dms.3764

Pintrich, P. R., & De Groot, E. V. (1990). Motivational and self regulated learning components of classroom academic performance. *Journal of Educational Psychology*, *82*(1), 33–40. DOI: 10.1037/0022-0663.82.1.33

Plass, J. L., & Pawar, S. (2020). Toward a taxonomy of adaptivity for learning. *Journal of Research on Technology in Education*, *52*(3), 275–300. DOI: 10.1080/15391523.2020.1719943

Poellhuber, B., & Roy, N. (2019). Quelques réflexions en lien avec l'analytique de l'apprentissage. Distances et médiations des savoirs, 26, 1-9. DOI: 10.4000/dms.3745

Popenici, S. A. D., & Kerr, S. (2017). Exploring the impact of artificial intelligence on teaching and learning in higher education. *Research and Practice in Technology Enhanced Learning*, *12*(1), 22–13. DOI: 10.1186/s41039-017-0062-8 PMID: 30595727

Pratama, M. P., Sampelolo, R., & Lura, H. (2023). Revolutionizing education: harnessing the power of artificial intelligence for personalized learning. Klasikal: Journal of education, language teaching and science, 5(2), 350-357. DOI: 10.52208/klasikal.v5i2.877

Rahman, M. M., & Watanobe, Y. (2023). ChatGPT for education and research: Opportunities, threats, and strategies. *Applied Sciences (Basel, Switzerland)*, *13*(9), 5783. DOI: 10.3390/app13095783

Renz, A., & Vladova, G. (2021). Reinvigorating the Discourse on Human- Centered Artificial Intelligence in Educational Technologies. 11(5).

Richards, D., & Dignum, V. (2019). Supporting and challenging learners through pedagogical agents: Addressing ethical issues through designing for values. *British Journal of Educational Technology*, *50*(6), 2885–2901. DOI: 10.1111/bjet.12863

Ricketts, C., & Wilks, S. (2002). *Improving student performance through computer-based assessment: Insights from recent research*. Assessment & Evaluation in Higher.

Rienties, B., Simonsen, H. K., Herodotou, C., & Levy, J. (2020). Defining the Boundaries Between Artificial Intelligence in Education, Computer- Supported Collaborative Learning, Educational Data Mining, and Learning Analytics: A Need for Coherence. 1–5. DOI: 10.3389/feduc.2020.00128

Roll, I., & Wylie, R. (2016). Evolution and Revolution in Artificial Intelligence in Education. *International Journal of Artificial Intelligence in Education*, *26*(2), 582–599. DOI: 10.1007/s40593-016-0110-3

Romero, M. (2019). Analyser les apprentissages à partir des traces: Des opportunités aux enjeux éthiques. Distances et médiations des savoirs, 26, 1-6. DOI: 10.4000/dms.3754

Ruiz Miranda, E. (2023). La révolution de l'intelligence artificielle dans l'éducation: une revue ChatGPT. Revue d'études et de recherches en psychologie et en éducation (REIPE), 10 (1), 156-160. DOI: 10.17979/reipe.2023.10.1.9594

Schiff, D. (2021). Out of the laboratory and into the classroom: The future of artificial intelligence in education. *AI & Society*, *36*(1), 331–348. DOI: 10.1007/s00146-020-01033-8 PMID: 32836908

Schmid, R., & Petko, D. (2019). Does the use of educational technology in personalized learning environments correlate with self-reported digital skills and beliefs of secondary-school students?. Computers & education, 136, 75-86.19.03.006 DOI: DOI: 10.1016/j.compedu.2019.03.006

Sheldon, KM, Ryan, R., & Reis, HT (1996). Qu'est-ce qui fait une bonne journée ? Compétence et autonomie dans la journée et chez la personne. Bulletin de psychologie sociale et de personnalité, 22 (12), 1270-1279. DOI: 10.1177/01461672962212007

Shi, Y., Yang, H., Dou, Y., & Zeng, Y. (2023). Effects of mind mapping-based instruction on student cognitive learning outcomes: A meta-analysis. *Asia Pacific Education Review*, *24*(3), 303–317. DOI: 10.1007/s12564-022-09746-9

Siau, K., & Wang, W. (2020). Artificial intelligence (AI) ethics: Ethics of AI and ethical AI. *Journal of Database Management*, *31*(2), 74–87. DOI: 10.4018/JDM.2020040105

Siemens, G., & Baker, R. (2012). Learning analytics and educational data mining: Towards communication and collaboration. *Proceedings of the 2nd International Conference on Learning Analytics and Knowledge*, 252-254. DOI: 10.1145/2330601.2330661

Siron, J. L., Bertrand, A., Kostine, M., Lichaud, O., Berard, E., Mehsen, N., & Germain, P. (2023). Evaluating artificial intelligence: 30 open-ended questions for ChatGPT. *Journal of Rheumatism*, *90*, A240.

Steinbauer, G., Kandlhofer, M., Chklovski, T., Heintz, F., & Koenig, S. (2021). A differentiated discussion about AI education K-12. *Kunstliche Intelligenz*, *35*(2), 131–137. DOI: 10.1007/s13218-021-00724-8 PMID: 34007103

Stokel-Walker, C. (2022). AI bot ChatGPT writes smart essays-should academics worry? *Nature*. Advance online publication. DOI: 10.1038/d41586-022-04397-7 PMID: 36494443

Su, J., Ng, DTK et Chu, SKW (2023). L'intelligence artificielle (IA) dans l'éducation de la petite enfance: défis et opportunités. Ordinateurs et éducation: intelligence artificielle, 4, 100124. DOI: 10.1016/j.caeai.2023.100124

Su, J., & Zhong, Y. (2022). Artificial intelligence (AI) in early childhood education: Curriculum design and future directions. *Computers and Education: Artificial Intelligence*, *3*, 100072. DOI: 10.1016/j.caeai.2022.100072

Susarla, A., Gopal, R., Thatcher, J. B., & Sarker, S. (2023). The Janus effect of generative AI: Charting the path for responsible conduct of scholarly activities in information systems. *Information Systems Research*, *34*(2), 1–10. DOI: 10.1287/isre.2023.ed.v34.n2

Terzopoulos, G., & Satratzemi, M. (2019). Voice Assistants and Artificial Intelligence in Education. *Proceedings of the 9th Balkan Conference on Informatics*, 1–6. DOI: 10.1145/3351556.3351588

Thomas, K. M., O'Bannon, B. W., & Bolton, N. (2013). Cell phones in the classroom: Teachers' perspectives of inclusion, benefits, and barriers. *Computers in the Schools*, *30*(4), 295–308.

Thorp, H. H. (2023). ChatGPT is fun, but not an author. Science. *Science*, *379*(6630), 313. DOI: 10.1126/science.adg7879 PMID: 36701446

Timms, M. J. (2016). Letting Artificial Intelligence in Education Out of the Box: Educational Cobots and Smart Classrooms. *International Journal of Artificial Intelligence in Education*, *26*(2), 701–712. DOI: 10.1007/s40593-016-0095-y

Tubaro, P. (2019). Les Learning Analytics vus par la sociologie. Distances et médiations des savoirs, 28, 1-8. DOI: 10.4000/dms.4608

Tuomi, I. (2018). The Impact of Artificial Intelligence on Learning, Teaching, and Education, JRC Science for Policy Report, European Joint Research Centre. https://publications.jrc.ec.europa.eu/repository/bitstream/JRC113226/jrc113226_jrcb4_the_impact_of_artificial_intelligence_on_learning_final_2.pdf

Valentine, A., Gemin, B., Vashaw, L., Watson, J., Harrington, C., & LeBlanc, E. (2021). Digital learning in rural K–12 settings: A survey of challenges and progress in the United States. Research Anthology on Developing Effective Online Learning Courses, 1987-2019. DOI: DOI: 10.4018/978-1-7998-8047-9.ch099

Vallerand, R. J. (1997). Toward a hierarchical model of intrinsic and extrinsic motivation. In Zanna, M. P. (Ed.), (pp. 271–360). Advances in experimental social psychology. Academic Press. DOI: 10.1016/S0065-2601(08)60019-2

Van Dis, E. A., Bollen, J., Zuidema, W., van Rooij, R., & Bockting, C. L. (2023). ChatGPT: Five priorities for research. *Nature*, *614*(7947), 224–226. DOI: 10.1038/d41586-023-00288-7 PMID: 36737653

VanLehn, K. (2006). The behavior of tutoring systems. *International Journal of Artificial Intelligence in Education*, *16*(3), 227–265.

Varsamidou, A. (2024). The pedagogical value of mind maps in the FLE classroom: How to integrate them into didactic scenarios to develop and assess language skills. *Journal of Languages and Translation*, *4*(2), 14–24. DOI: 10.70204/jlt.v4i2.375

Viau, R. (2009). *La motivation à apprendre en milieu scolaire*. Erpi.

Walkington, C., & Bernacki, M. L. (2020). Appraising research on personalized learning: Definitions, theoretical alignment, advancements, and future directions. *Journal of Research on Technology in Education*, *52*(3), 235–252. DOI: 10.1080/15391523.2020.1747757

Watson, W. R., Watson, S. L., & Reigeluth, C. M. (2012). A systemic integration of technology for new-paradigm education. *Educational Technology*, *52*, 25–29.

Welser, H. T., Khan, M. L., & Dickard, M. (2019). Digital remediation: Social support and online learning communities can help offset rural digital inequality. *Information Communication and Society*, *22*(5), 717–723. DOI: 10.1080/1369118X.2019.1566485

Wogu, I. A. P., Misra, S., Olu-Owolabi, E. F., Assibong, P. A., & Udoh, O. D. (2018). Artificial Intelligence, Artificial Teachers and the Fate of Learners in the 21st Century Education Sector: Implications for Theory and Practice. *International Journal of Pure and Applied Mathematics*, *119*(16), 2245–2259.

Yang, T. (2017, June). The mind map, a didactic tool to aid memorization for lexicon teaching/learning. In RJC2017-20èmes Rencontres des jeunes chercheurs en Sciences du Langage

Yang, T. (2024). Impact of Artificial Intelligence Software on English Learning Motivation and Achievement. In SHS Web of Conferences (Vol. 193, p. 02011). EDP Sciences. DOI: 10.1051/shsconf/202419302011

Zalte, S. M. (2023). Revolutionizing education: Leveraging ai-ml technologies to enhance teaching and learning outcomes. 12(12), 679–688. https://doi.org/DOI: 10.48047/ecb/2023.12.si12.058

Chapter 3
Student Engagement and Motivation in Video Microlearning Quizzes:
A Quantitative Study Based on Learning Traces and Measurement Scale

Ghizlane Chemsi
University Hassan II, Morocco

Aziz Naciri
https://orcid.org/0000-0001-7318-6633
University Hassan II, Morocco

Imane El Imadi
https://orcid.org/0000-0001-9076-5039
University Hassan II, Morocco

Mounir Sadiq
University Hassan II, Morocco

Assia Benabid
University Hassan II, Morocco

Mohammed Radid
https://orcid.org/0000-0002-8082-2009
University Hassan II, Morocco

ABSTRACT

Digital innovations are profoundly transforming teaching and learning methods. Research shows that integrating video microlearning quizzes as a pedagogical strategy promotes active student involvement and encourages them to adopt optimized learning approaches. The adoption of these technologies also generates a multitude of data that facilitates the evaluation of learners' behavioral engagement. This study aims to explore the impact of video microlearning quizzes on student engagement and motivation. Through a quantitative approach, the analysis of digital data from student activities provided insights into their degree of involvement and consequently their behavioral engagement. Additionally, a questionnaire based on

DOI: 10.4018/979-8-3373-0740-4.ch003

the Situational Motivation Scale (SIMS) was administered at the end of the semester to analyze student motivation. The results indicate that the majority of students actively engaged in completing the video microlearning quizzes.

INTRODUCTION

The rapid advent of information and communication technologies for education (ICT) has profoundly reoriented educational practices around the world. At the center of this transformation is the emergence of video microlearning, an innovative pedagogical approach that offers concise, interactive learning content via short videos (Brown et al., 2014). This method fits in perfectly with learners' current content consumption preferences, characterized by rapid information retrieval and fragmented attention (Guo et al., 2014). Video microlearning represents a direct response to the challenges posed by the digital age in education, providing a flexible, adaptive solution to individual learning needs. Moreover, this approach makes it possible to create more attractive and interactive learning experiences, paying particular attention to the interaction between learners and educational content (Baepler et al., 2014).

As video-based microlearning has evolved, assessment practices have also adapted to this new learning environment. Quizzes, in particular, have become one of the most popular formative assessment tools in microlearning environments. Strategically integrated with instructional videos, quizzes offer learners an additional opportunity to interact with the content, test their understanding and receive immediate feedback on their learning and adjust their learning accordingly (Clark & Mayer, 2023; Kizilcec et al., 2013). As a result, quizzes enrich the learning experience by providing opportunities for formative assessment and reinforcing learner engagement in the learning process.

Several studies have shown that video microlearning quizzes promote better knowledge retention and more effective learning by encouraging learners' active engagement (Guo et al., 2014). Furthermore, the strategic use of quizzes in video microlearning was associated with higher student engagement (Seo et al., 2021).

In the Moroccan context, the education system has begun its transition to digital transformation, supported by the strategic vision of the 2015-2030 reform. This reform aims to develop an open, diversified, high-performance and innovative teaching model, emphasizing the importance of integrating educational technologies into the learning process.

In this context, the present study aims to implement video microlearning quizzes and evaluate their impact on engagement and motivation with students enrolled in their first year at the Ben M'sik-Casablanca Faculty of Sciences. Our aim is to answer the following question: To what extent can the use of video microlearning quizzes stimulate student engagement and motivation in the teaching of the university work methodology module?

I. THEORETICAL FRAMEWORK

1. Microlearning video

Microlearning is an innovative and effective educational approach that meets the learning needs of the Alpha generation by providing concise learning content tailored to their individual needs(Fitria, 2022). Initially focused on short, targeted content, microlearning has expanded to encompass a variety of formats, such as educational videos, infographics, simulations and podcasts (Boring, 2020). This method is characterized by its modularity and accessibility, offering short, specific learning sessions adapted to consumption on various digital devices such as smartphones and tablets (Pappas et al., 2017). Microlearning responds to the contemporary preferences of learners, who are faced with time constraints and prefer shorter learning sessions. By providing stand-alone modules, it enables you to quickly fill specific knowledge gaps or revise key concepts, without the need for lengthy learning periods.

In a context where information is abundant and time is limited, the development of microlearning in various forms, notably video microlearning, represents an innovative response to these learning needs. This method is based on the creation and distribution of learning content in the form of short, interactive videos, designed to be easily accessible via various digital devices (Guo et al., 2014). It captures learners' attention with its concise, attractive presentation of information, facilitating comprehension and retention(Guo et al., 2014). Furthermore, the interactivity of videos, including embedded questions, simulations and practical exercises, promotes active participation and deeper learning. The flexibility of video microlearning enables learners to personalize their learning path according to their needs and interests, enhancing their engagement and intrinsic motivation(Baepler et al., 2014). By adapting to different skill levels, video microlearning offers a personalized learning experience, promoting better information retention and greater learner engagement.

2. Interactive formative quizzes.

Interactive quizzes play a crucial role in video microlearning, not only as engagement tools, but also as effective means of formative assessment. By integrating interactive quizzes into short educational videos, content creators can encourage learners to actively participate in their own learning process(Kizilcec et al., 2013). These quizzes can take a variety of forms, including multiple-choice questions, short-answer questions, matching questions, or even interactive exercises embedded directly in the video. Research shows that the use of interactive quizzes in video microlearning can improve learner engagement and comprehension of content (Abdul Jabbar & Felicia, 2015; Guo et al., 2014). Moreover, several studies have shown that quizzes embedded in videos can encourage learners to stay focused and follow the content attentively, thus increasing their retention of the information presented (Gegenfurtner & Ebner, 2019). In addition, interactive quizzes offer learners immediate feedback on their understanding, enabling them to quickly identify knowledge gaps and correct mistakes (Clark & Mayer, 2023; Nicol & Macfarlane-Dick, 2006)

As formative assessment tools, interactive quizzes in video microlearning enable learners to measure their own understanding and track their progress throughout the learning process (Kizilcec et al., 2013). By providing instant feedback, quizzes help learners identify areas in which they need improvement, facilitating self-directed learning and awareness of their own skills(Means et al., 2009). Learners' commitment and perseverance are key to their motivation and academic success. According to Viau (1994), engagement is a crucial indicator of academic motivation, as it represents the initiation of action and the active participation of learners in their learning process (Parent, 2014).

3. Behavioral engagement and digital traces of student work

Student behavioral engagement in the context of video microlearning is a crucial area of research for understanding learning dynamics in digital environments. Indeed, this engagement, defined by the visible actions of students during their learning process, is of particular importance in assessing the effectiveness of video microlearning(Fredricks et al., 2004). In video microlearning, this engagement materializes through various indicators, such as the frequency and duration of interactions with videos, participation in integrated interactive quizzes and exercises, as well as social interactions on e-learning platforms(Cai & Chen, 2018). Chen et al.'s (2018) studies demonstrated that students demonstrating high behavioral engagement in video microlearning were more likely to pass their assessments and demonstrate greater understanding of the concepts taught.

Meanwhile, the analysis of digital traces of students' work offers insight into their engagement and performance in the context of video microlearning (Kizilcec et al., 2017). These digital traces, such as the time spent on each video, the number of attempts at quizzes, the scores obtained, as well as social interactions, provide actionable data for assessing student engagement and progress in the learning process.

Integrating the findings of recent research such as Chemsi et al. (2019), which has also highlighted the importance of student behavioral engagement in digital learning environments, it becomes clear that understanding these aspects is crucial to designing effective learning experiences in video microlearning(Chemsi et al., 2019). By synthesizing this data, teachers and course designers can adjust their pedagogical approaches to maximize student engagement and foster better knowledge acquisition.

4. Self-determined motivation in video microlearning quizzes.

Motivation means that a person is energized or activated to accomplish a task or an activity, whereas an unmotivated person feels no drive to act (Deci & Ryan, 2000). The theoretical framework of this study is based on the self-determination theory (SDT) developed by(Deci & Ryan, 1985). SDT describes a continuum of three forms of motivation: amotivation, extrinsic motivation, and intrinsic motivation. These are differentiated based on the degree of self-determination. Amotivation during learning indicates a lack of intention and willingness to act in learning activities, representing the lowest degree of self-determination. Intrinsic motivation refers to the student's engagement for pleasure and personal vocation in the learning process. The student is self-motivated and self-determined. On the other hand, extrinsic motivation refers to the learner's involvement in the learning process for reasons external to the activities performed. Extrinsic motivation presents four modes of regulation. The first is external regulation, which means that the student's participation in activities is conditioned by external incentives such as rewards and the avoidance of punishment. The second is introjected regulation, which implies that individuals participate in educational activities to avoid the consequences of failure and guilt and to protect their self-esteem. The third is identified regulation, meaning that students engage in activities they find interesting and valuable and that align with their personal goals. The last style is integrated regulation, which occurs when students consider learning activities to be consistent with their core values and beliefs. Learners' self-determined motivation plays a central role in their engagement and success in learning environments, including in the context of video microlearning. According to Deci and Ryan's self-determination theory (1985), motivation can vary depending on the degree of satisfaction of basic psychological needs such as autonomy, competence, and social relatedness. In the context of video microlearning quizzes, learners' self-determined motivation can be fostered in various ways. First, autonomy is encouraged when learners have control over their learning process, notably by allowing them to choose when and how they interact with the quizzes. For example, by giving learners the option to decide when they want to take a quiz or to select the topics on which they want to be assessed, content designers promote a sense of control and autonomy in learners(Reeve & Jang, 2006). Furthermore, competence is stimulated when quizzes provide challenges that are appropriate to the learners' skill levels. The questions should be sufficiently challenging to maintain learners' interest while being achievable so that they feel competent in their ability to answer them(Ryan & Deci, 2022). The immediate feedback provided by the quizzes can also help reinforce the sense of competence by informing learners about their progress and helping them identify areas for improvement (Ryan & Deci, 2020).

Finally, social relatedness is encouraged through peer interactions facilitated by online quizzes. The ability for learners to compare their results with those of their peers, share their learning experiences, and collaborate on solutions to questions can enhance the feeling of belonging to a learning community(Ryan & Deci, 2020). Quizzes can also be designed to promote cooperation and healthy competition among learners, which can further stimulate their intrinsic motivation(Johnson & Johnson, 2009).

II. PRACTICAL FRAMEWORK

1. Type of study:

This formative study of educational design research (McKenney & Reeves, 2018) was conducted with 55 first-year students enrolled in the BCG program at the Faculty of Sciences Ben M'sik-Casablanca during the first semester.

2. Scenario used to conduct the experiment

In our study, we implemented a methodological scenario to assess students' engagement and motivation through the use of video microlearning quizzes. Here are the key steps of our approach:

a. **Design of Video Microlearning Quizzes**
    - We developed a series of short quizzes based on the key concepts of the university work methodology module.
    - Each quiz was designed to be interactive and engaging, featuring relevant questions and immediate feedback to reinforce learning.

b. **Integration of Quizzes into the Curriculum**
    - The quizzes were strategically integrated into the educational content of the module.
    - Students accessed the quizzes via the Moodle learning platform where the educational videos were hosted.

C. Communication and instructions to participants

Students were informed of the nature of the quizzes and their purpose in the learning process.

Clear instructions were provided on how to access the quizzes, complete them and benefit from immediate feedback.

3. Distribution of the SIMS questionnaire (Situational Motivation Scale).

Once the quizzes had been completed, we distributed the SIMS questionnaire to the participants. This questionnaire was designed to measure various aspects of student motivation during interaction with the video microlearning quizzes. The SIMS scale is a validated 16-item instrument developed by (Guay et al., 2000), and classified into the following subscales: intrinsic motivation, external regulation, identified regulation and amotivation. Each dimension comprises four items assessed on a 7-point Likert scale ranging from 1 (strongly disagree) to 7 (strongly agree).

4. Data analysis

The collected data were subjected to quantitative analysis to evaluate student engagement in the quizzes and their associated motivation. To assess learners' behavioral engagement during the video microlearning quizzes, we utilized log files provided by Moodle. These raw data were exported and processed using specialized software for analysis. The choice of indicators was based on Viau's (1994) model of motivation in a school context, favoring concrete and observable measures in the digital context, such as participation, timeliness in completing evaluation tests, the number of attempts (reflecting effort), and test completion tracking. Regarding the assessment of motivation, statistical analyses were conducted to identify the relationships between quiz usage, scores obtained, and motivation levels measured by the SIMS questionnaire.

5. Ethical considerations.

We obtained informed consent from participants, ensured data confidentiality and anonymity, and followed ethical research standards throughout the study.

III. RESULTS

2. ANALYSIS OF SIMS QUESTIONNAIRE RESULTS

2.1. Analysis of variability

The results of student motivation calculated through analysis of the questionnaire are summarized in Table 1 by type of motivation.

Table 1. Characteristics and motivation levels of the students taking part in the study.

Variable	N (Number of respondents)	Mean	Standard deviation
MI 1	55	3,73	2,857
MEI 2	55	3,58	2,424
MEE 3	55	2,76	2,054
AM 4	55	2,42	1,902
MI 5	55	2,73	2,068
MEI 6	55	3,55	2,898
MEE 7	55	3,15	2,505
AM 8	55	1,82	1,376
MI 9	55	1,76	1,515
MEI 10	55	2,04	2,081
MEE 11	55	1,85	1,704
AM 12	55	1,98	1,737
MI 13	55	2,71	2,401
MEI 14	55	2,40	1,862
MEE 15	55	2,31	2,142
AM 16	55	1,93	1,464

The analysis of the table data reveals that for:

Intrinsic Motivation (IM): The IM means indicate that levels of intrinsic engagement vary among learners. The standard deviations suggest diversity in the perception of intrinsic motivation, which aligns with the idea that learners are intrinsically motivated to varying degrees. This explains why video microlearning quizzes are perceived as motivating by most learners. For example, an average of 3.73 for IM 1 indicates a significant level of engagement, suggesting that students find these activities intrinsically interesting and beneficial.

Identified Regulation Motivation (IRM): The moderate means for IRM show that extrinsic factors moderately influence learners' engagement. The standard deviations indicate variability in the impact of these factors, implying that the effect of rewards and incentives may vary from one learner to another. An average of 3.58 for IRM 2, for example, may indicate that while external rewards play a role, they are not the only factor motivating learners.

External Regulation Motivation (ERM): The low means for ERM suggest that external rewards are not as motivating as intrinsic or identified factors. This could indicate that learners do not find external rewards sufficiently compelling to stimulate their engagement. The lower means for ERM variables might mean that external incentives, such as grades or rewards, are less effective in motivating learners. An average of 2.76 for ERM 3 shows that learners might not be as motivated by external factors compared to intrinsic or identified motivation.

Amotivation (AM): The low means for the AM dimension reveal a lack of personal motivation among some students. The low means for AM variables indicate a lack of personal motivation or disengagement from the video microlearning quizzes. For example, an average of 1.93 for AM 16 suggests that some learners may not see the relevance or usefulness of these activities in their learning.

1.1. Comparison of variables

Table 2 compares the means and standard deviations of the different motivational categories to identify which are most and least influenced by video microlearning quizzes.

Table 2. Comparaison entre les différentes catégories de motivation

Motivation category Mean score
MI (Intrinsic Motivation) 2,73
IEM (Identified Regulation Motivation) 2,89
MEE (Motivation by External Regulation) 2,52
AM (Amotivation) 2,04

Analysis of the mean scores for the different motivation categories reveals that students display moderate intrinsic motivation (IM, mean score 2.73), finding personal interest in learning activities without depending on external influences. They also show significant identified regulation motivation (IEM, mean score 2.89), recognizing the value of the activities in achieving their personal goals. In contrast, motivation by external regulation (MEE, mean score 2.52) seems to have less impact, suggesting that external rewards are less effective. Amotivation (AM), although present with the lowest mean score of 2.04, is not predominant. These results suggest that to enhance student engagement, it is essential to focus on improving intrinsic and identified motivation rather than external incentives. Understanding the causes of amotivation is crucial to developing targeted interventions that make learning more relevant and engaging for students.

3. ANALYSIS OF STUDENT ACTIVITY ON MOODLE: FROM PARTICIPATION, EFFORT AND PUNCTUALITY.

These are the actions that students have carried out in the assessment space, and which allow us to consider the student as active. In our case, we used periodicity of access, punctuality and effort provided by learners.

Figure 1. Assessing behavioral commitment: participation, effort and punctuality

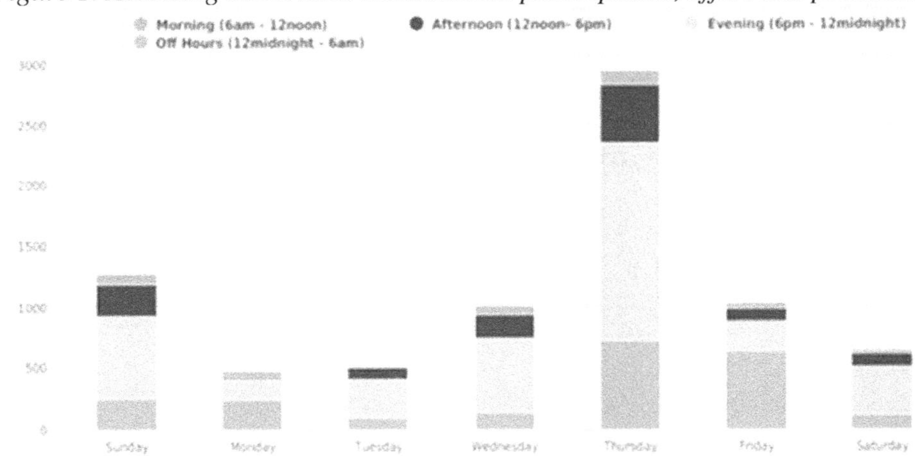

The graph above illustrates the process of student access to the system throughout the microlearning video quiz activity. In our case, the unit of measurement is the week, corresponding to the duration allocated for test completion. We observe that the majority of students take the assessment tests according to their availability (morning, noon, evening). The data shows that peak access occurs on Thursday, with 3000 attempts, corresponding to the deadline for completing the test. This indicates that students are motivated to complete tasks before set deadlines. Analysis of completion tracking statistics has allowed us to measure student engagement throughout the quiz period. These results reflect students' commitment and progress in completing evaluation tests. Analysis of the test traces left in the application will enable us to assess effort, persistence, and participation. (Thomas et al., 2017) demonstrate that it is not the score on self-assessment tests that significantly impacts learning quality, but rather the number of attempts, which serves as a positive predictor. Therefore, we observe that online formative assessment positively impacts learner engagement and perseverance.

VI. DISCUSSION

The results of this study highlight the potential effectiveness of video microlearning quizzes in enhancing learners' behavioral engagement and motivation. The observed averages for intrinsic motivation (IM) variables suggest that these digital educational tools are perceived as intrinsically motivating, which aligns with the principles of self-determination and autonomous learning (Deci & Ryan, 2000). This idea is reinforced by the work of (Chemsi et al., 2019), who emphasized the importance of self-determined motivation in the context of online educational activities. Previous studies have also highlighted the importance of active learner engagement in the learning process. For example, research on the use of serious games has shown that they can positively impact learner motivation, reinforcing the idea that interactivity and enjoyment in learning are key factors for maintaining learner interest and participation (Smith et al., 2015). In relation to this, Chemsi et al. (2019) explored behavioral engagement and found that engagement in online activities can significantly influence learners' motivation and behavioral engagement(Chemsi et al., 2019).

Furthermore, the results indicate that video microlearning quizzes may not be as effective in stimulating External Regulation Motivation (ERM), raising questions about the relevance of external rewards in digital learning strategies. This observation aligns with studies examining the impact of digital technologies on learner motivation, suggesting that learner-centered approaches are often more effective than performance-oriented ones(Johnson & Johnson, 2009). This means that digital tools are more effective in motivating students when they support a teaching approach that values learners' individual interests and needs rather than focusing solely on results and performance, which can lead to extrinsic motivation where learners are driven by external factors such as grades or rewards, potentially being less sustainable and engaging in the long term. Research by (Idrissi et al., 2022) on engagement in serious games supports this idea, showing that active engagement in playful tasks can enhance learning and retention. The low averages associated with Amotivation (AM) highlight the need for pedagogical strategies that make digital learning relevant and meaningful for each learner. This aligns with other research findings that emphasize the importance of cognitive and behavioral engagement for learners' performance in online learning environments(Williams, 2017). However, this study has certain limitations that should be considered. The sample size may limit the generalization of the results. Additionally, the study focuses on a specific form of educational technology, which may not reflect the entirety of available digital tools. For future research, it would be beneficial to explore the impact of other forms of educational technology on motivation and engagement, such as augmented and virtual realities, which offer immersive and interactive experiences likely to enhance learner engagement. Furthermore, expanding the sample to include learners from different educational and cultural contexts could provide a more comprehensive understanding of the impact of video microlearning quizzes on motivation and engagement (Nguyen et al., 2023).

CONCLUSION

This study highlighted the significant potential of video microlearning quizzes to enhance learners' behavioral engagement and motivation. The results demonstrated that when learners perceive these tools as intrinsically motivating, they are more likely to engage actively and autonomously in their learning process. This finding underscores the importance of designing digital learning activities that not only capture learners' interest but also meet their needs for autonomy and competence. The variability observed in learners' responses, particularly regarding extrinsic motivation and amotivation, indicates that video microlearning quizzes are not effective for all learners. This suggests the need for a more personalized approach to teaching, which could include diversifying pedagogical strategies and paying particular attention to individual preferences and motivations of learners. Finally, this study paves the way for future research to deepen our understanding of the impact of educational technologies on learner engagement and motivation. When well-designed and integrated into a comprehensive pedagogical strategy, video microlearning quizzes have the potential to become a valuable tool for enriching the educational experience of learners in the digital age.

REFERENCES

Abdul Jabbar, A. I., & Felicia, P. J. R. r. (2015). Gameplay engagement and learning in game-based learning. *Systematic Reviews*, *85*(4), 740–779.

Baepler, P., Walker, J., Driessen, M. J. C., & education. (2014). It's not about seat time: Blending, flipping, and efficiency in active learning classrooms. *78*, 227-236.

Boring, C. (2020). *Microlearning: An andragogical case study on knowledge retention, learner satisfaction, and behavior change*. Robert Morris University.

Brown, P. C., Roediger, H. L.III, & McDaniel, M. A. (2014). *Make it stick: The science of successful learning*. Harvard University Press.

Cai, W., & Chen, Q. (2018). An experimental research of augmented reality technology from the perspective of mobile learning. *2018 IEEE International Conference on Teaching, Assessment, and Learning for Engineering (TALE).*

Chemsi, G., Sadiq, M., Radid, M., & Talbi, M. (2019). Formative E-assessment and behavioral commitment of students. *Case of the Faculty of Science Ben M'sik.*, *14*(12), 4.

Clark, R. C., & Mayer, R. E. (2023). *E-learning and the science of instruction: Proven guidelines for consumers and designers of multimedia learning*. john Wiley & sons.

Deci, E. L., & Ryan, R. M. J. J. o. r. i. p. (1985). The general causality orientations scale: Self-determination in personality. *19*(2), 109-134.

Deci, E. L., & Ryan, R. M. J. P. i. (2000). The" what" and" why" of goal pursuits: Human needs and the self-determination of behavior. *11*(4), 227-268.

Fitria, T. N. (2022). Microlearning in teaching and learning process: A review. CENDEKIA: Jurnal Ilmu Sosial. *Bahasa Dan Pendidikan*, *2*(4), 114–135.

Fredricks, J. A., Blumenfeld, P. C., & Paris, A. H. J. R. o. e. r. (2004). School engagement: Potential of the concept, state of the evidence. *74*(1), 59-109.

Gegenfurtner, A., & Ebner, C. J. E. R. R. (2019). Webinars in higher education and professional training: A meta-analysis and systematic review of randomized controlled trials. *28*, 100293.

Guo, P. J., Kim, J., & Rubin, R. (2014). How video production affects student engagement: An empirical study of MOOC videos. Proceedings of the first ACM conference on Learning@ scale conference, Idrissi, W. E. M. E., Chemsi, G., Kababi, K. E., & Radid, M. (2022). The Impact of Serious Game on the Nursing Students' Learning, Behavioral Engagement, and Motivation. *17*(1), 18-35.

Johnson, D. W., & Johnson, R. T. J. E. r. (2009). An educational psychology success story: Social interdependence theory and cooperative learning. *38*(5), 365-379.

Kizilcec, R. F., Pérez-Sanagustín, M., & Maldonado, J. J. (2017). Self-regulated learning strategies predict learner behavior and goal attainment in Massive Open Online Courses. *Computers & Education*, *104*, 18–33.

Kizilcec, R. F., Piech, C., & Schneider, E. (2013). Deconstructing disengagement: analyzing learner subpopulations in massive open online courses. *Proceedings of the third international conference on learning analytics and knowledge.*

McKenney, S., & Reeves, T. (2018). *Conducting educational design research.* Routledge., DOI: 10.1145/2460296.2460330

Means, B., Toyama, Y., Murphy, R., Bakia, M., & Jones, K. (2009). Evaluation of evidence-based practices in online learning: A meta-analysis and review of online learning studies.

Nguyen, T. P. V., Lee, Y. F., Le, T. H., Nguyen, H. B. N. J. I. J. I., & Technology, E. (2023). Applying a Formative Assessment Model for a Blended Learning Environment to Promote Students'. *Engagement and Motivation.*, *13*(11), 1735–1740.

Nicol, D. J., & Macfarlane-Dick, D. J. S. i. h. e. (2006). Formative assessment and self-regulated learning: A model and seven principles of good feedback practice. *31*(2), 199-218.

Pappas, I. O., Giannakos, M. N., & Mikalef, P. J. J. o. C. i. H. E. (2017). Investigating students' use and adoption of with-video assignments: lessons learnt for video-based open educational resources. *29*, 160-177.

Parent, S. (2014). De la motivation à l'engagement: un processus multidimensionnel lié à la réussite de vos étudiants. Pédagogie collégiale vol. 27, no 3, printemps 2014.

Reeve, J., & Jang, H. (2006). What teachers say and do to support students' autonomy during a learning activity. *Journal of Educational Psychology*, *98*(1), 209.

Ryan, R. M., & Deci, E. L. (2022). Self-determination theory. In *Encyclopedia of quality of life and well-being research* (pp. 1–7). Springer. DOI: 10.1007/978-3-319-69909-7_2630-2

Ryan, R. M., & Deci, E. L. J. C. e. p. (2020). Intrinsic and extrinsic motivation from a self-determination theory perspective: Definitions, theory, practices, and future directions. *61*, 101860.

Seo, K., Dodson, S., Harandi, N. M., Roberson, N., Fels, S., Roll, I. J. C., & Education. (2021). Active learning with online video: The impact of learning context on engagement. *165*, 104132.

Smith, D., Cleak, H., & Vreugdenhil, A. J. A. s. w. (2015). "What are they really doing?" An exploration of student learning activities in field placement. *68*(4), 515-531.

Thomas, J. A., Wadsworth, D., Jin, Y., Clarke, J., Page, R., Thunders, M. J. H. E. R., & Development. (2017). Engagement with online self-tests as a predictor of student success. *36*(5), 1061-1071.

Williams, D. A. J. J. o. R. (2017). Exploring the issues of adult students with brain injuries in the online learning environment. *83*(3), 53-61.

Chapter 4
The Impact of Digital Platforms on Higher Education Through the Flipped Classroom and ICT

Asmaa Fathi
https://orcid.org/0009-0005-4909-5519
University Hassan II, Morocco

Assia Benabid
University Hassan II, Morocco

Imane El Imadi
https://orcid.org/0000-0001-9076-5039
University Hassan II, Morocco

ABSTRACT

This research investigates the impact of flipped classrooms and ICT on student learning in higher education. Data was collected through a questionnaire at the start of the first university semester. The study found that digital platforms enhance interactive, independent, and accessible learning by integrating the flipped classroom paradigm into ICT. These platforms can engage students, optimize knowledge acquisition, and meet contemporary pedagogical needs by providing flexibility and innovation. In conclusion, integrating digital platforms with flipped classrooms in higher education improves learning, cultivates student autonomy, and upholds teaching quality.

DOI: 10.4018/979-8-3373-0740-4.ch004

INTRODUCTION

Emergence of new technological tools such as chatbots and virtual reality has increased the versatility of the application of AI in school education (Bansal, H., & Khan, 2018). Chatbot systems like ChatGPT have added an interactive learning dimension for the students (Ranoliya, B. R., Raghuwanshi, N. & Singh, S., 2017). Virtual reality is an immersive medium of creating educational environments which promises a deeper immersion in the subject and hence, a more thorough understanding (Lo, 2023). AI now offers new possibilities at every stage of development and application for enhancing the efficiency and perfection of the educational process through new technologies and methods, with everything from classroom teaching to distance learning now possible (Price, 2019).

New technologies such as chatbots or VR have widened the horizons of application of applications of AI in school education (Bansal, H., Khan, 2018). Chatbot systems like ChatGPT provide an interactive dimension of learning and engaging support for students (Ranoliya, B. R., Raghuwanshi, N., & Singh, S., 2017). Virtual reality can create immersing educational environments, allowing a deeper immersion into the subject and a correspondingly better understanding (Lo, 2023). New possibilities at every stage of development and application have opened up avenues through which AI can improve the efficiency and perfection of the educational process with new technologies and methods (Price, 2019).

From what we've seen, knowledge-based learning systems make it possible to use AI and expert systems in the development of computer-based educational programmes which rely specifically on stored knowledge and expertise. They cater to individualised learning, curriculum adaptation, assessment of the learning process and feedback on progress to learners.

The quality of teaching at a university is increasingly becoming a topic of interest among lecturers, students, and administrative authorities. Such concerns have led many universities in the last decade to implement numerous reforms. Thus, there is a radical rethinking of pedagogies with the infusion of information and communication technologies (ICT) in education, making a big impact on teaching methods (David Castillo-Merino, Enric Serradell-López, Jordi Vilaseca-Requena, 2009).

In fact, information and communication technologies (ICTs) are called to present really genuine chances to considerably improve higher education quality and change the way knowledge is accessed to, as stated by the Organisation for Economic Co-operation and Development (De Clercq, 2023); quoted in (Ben Youssef and Hadhri, 2009), Mustafa Bensheikh, ex-Dean of the Faculty of Arts, Beni Meral University, in his book L'université marocaine à l'épreuve mentioned that from the start of this decade, 'universities have been facing a hidden crisis that no government has been able to resolve'.

These other researchers, for instance, (Zouaoui, 2006) who speaks of "the permanent cycle of perpetuating mediocrity from which the country is still struggling to get out": lacks regulatory power deans would resign themselves to those regulations which apply to their department for the sake of crisis avoidance and, at times, leave out basic operating principles, as stated by (Sidir and Benchenna, 2008). Several recent studies have gone into information and communication technologies (ICTs) in higher education universities in this recent official discussions in both Ministry of Education as well as the academic world. On one hand, this kind of research revealed that while 83 percent (Kaddouri, Bouamri, 2010) of students investigate the technologies in terms of leisure and personal communication, they rarely use them as tools for learning. On the contrary, teaching practices in universities overlook this reality and the changing use of ICTs in society. At the time of writing, an unexpected interruption in educational activities, due to the outbreak of the corona virus pandemic, has necessitated the re-examination of government policies on the management of the education system, with a resulting massive use of ICTs (Asmae Halimi, 2023). This has increased interest in things such as Distance Learning (DL) and the use of digital platforms like 'Teams' to have virtual classes with real-time interaction between teachers and students. While the introduction of ICT can improve, this only proves insufficient to enhance the quality of teaching. The idea of individuals learning by adaptive systems and intelligent tutors underlies this transformation but is not yet properly exploited within Moroccan academic institutions. These systems adapt the content and pace of learning to individual student needs for engaged and performing students. However, little research on these systems has been conducted in Morocco and warrants further investigation. Although ICT offers several benefits in terms of accessibility, flexibility, and diversification of teaching methods (Karsenti, 2002), several hurdles still exist against their integration. These include inadequate teacher training, nondiscriminated access to digital tools, and low resistance to change.

For some time now, artificial intelligence has been emerging as a real game-changer in the field of education. This is probably the major turning point of education systems- reinventing themselves entirely. AI is not solely about automating administrative functions or enhancing learning; it also provides remedies for the diversity of educational needs (Ouoba, 2024). Rephrase and rewrite in the above-defined way:

More recently, artificial intelligence (AI) is emerging as a catalyst for the transformation of education. This represents a significant turning point for the complete reinvention of education systems. AI will include not only the automation of many administrative tasks and improved learning processes; it can also provide solutions for diversified educational needs (Ouoba, 2024). Using advanced AI systems, education can now really personalize learning paths for all students according to their skills, speed and preferences. Such technologies do allow continuous assessments and real-time adjustments to educational content. Artificial Intelligence also improves educational data analytics, rewarding teachers and administrators with proven products for teaching excellence. AI chatbots offer personalized support anytime, while augmented reality and simulation further help make learning immersive and interactive. However, while adoption brings a great deal to the education scenario, it also raises ethical and practical issues, such as data confidentiality and equality of access, as well as faculty training on the best maximization of these technologies. Switch On Again for Students Studying Online: New Applications of Artificial Intelligence in Education Usage of Ap An extremely revolutionized method of learning has just been invented very recently through advanced AI systems, adapting learning paths for all students according to their own skills, pace, and preferences. Such technologies enable continuous assessment and real-time adaptation of educational content. Because of this, an AI could aid much improved analytics of educational data, much possible for teachers and administrators gleaning great ideas on improving holistic effectiveness in teaching. AI-based chatbots,' for instance, offer personal support anywhere at any time, while augmented and simulation experiences can be made even more immersive and interactive in this learning process. Nevertheless, the reality of AI application is opening many avenues, also casting ethical and practical questions in terms of data confidentiality, equity in access and teacher training to maximally exploit these new technologies.

Aims and assumptions of the study

The study was part of a sequence of studies that sought to elucidate the factors that play a role in academic achievement in higher education. This line of inquiry attempts to unravel the multiplicity of ways that students make use of artificial intelligence (AI) and information and communication technologies (ICT) in their learning.

This research gains relevance in this context. It aims to evaluate students' experiences of virtual learning environments and AI-supported tools, with emphasis on the impact of and the signs of adoption of these technologies. We want to find out to what extent AI uses promote students' engagement, academic performance, and satisfaction and, furthermore, to determine the factors that facilitate or hinder the adoption of these technological tools.

-Thus, as a means to prop up changes in higher education and enable students to adopt AI and ICTs as learning tools, it is imperative that the pedagogical styles of the faculty are adapted to fit environments whose best implementation is for learners. This means that teachers modify their pedagogical approaches to cater to different student learning profiles, using AI specifically to provide more personalised and engaging support.

(Anderson,1988) and (Chopin, 2006) have reinforced this proposition by demonstrating that the link that exists between the time spent and the performance of a student becomes much stronger when technological tools like AI are used to optimise their learning, thus further individualising it.

As stated by (Alves and al., 2010), it has been found that student satisfaction with learning tools is positively associated with satisfaction from higher education. It is AI and various learning platforms that bring along more flexibility and possibilities for interaction with teachers; this certainly counts as an important aspect in this whole interpretation.

In this research context, some questions arise:

- How do students use AI-based tools in their everyday learning?
- How does the integration of AI into teaching practices contribute to improving students' learning and performance in Moroccan universities?

Methodology

1)- Sample

The respondents targeted in this study were students from different disciplinary sections. The sample comprised a total of 195 participants, 60.5% of whom were enrolled in the scientific section and 39.5% in the literary section. Of these, 34.9% were at Bachelor's level, 27.7% at Master's level, 17.9% at Doctoral level, and 19.5% were university graduates. The sample was selected to reflect a diversity of academic backgrounds.

The results of the (table 1) show that most of the students are from the youth period and They are between 18 and 34 years old so this category is more active and productive research Young people make extensive use of information and communication technologies in their daily routine (Baron, Bruillard, 2008).

Table 1. Breakdown of students by age.

Age	18-24 years		25-34 years		35-44 years		45 years and over		Effective	
	N	%	N	%	N	%	N	%	N	%
Scientific section	52	44%	49	41,5%	10	8,5%	7	5,9%	118	60,5%
Literary section	30	38,9%	24	31,2%	16	20,8%	7	9%	77	39,5%
Effective	82	42%	73	37,4%	26	32,3%	14	7,2%	195	100%

2) The research process and data analysis

The study is premised on a survey of students to examine the use of digital platforms in relation to the flipped classroom and perceptions of this teaching methodology.

Initially, the survey was done in the time-slots scheduled with students at their convenience. The purpose of the survey was to assess how often they participated in online course learning, daily hours spent for digital classroom learning, the digital platforms most frequently used, and in particular, YouTube, Google Classroom, and Moodle.

Furthermore, it captured students' satisfaction with online study while assessing their overall experience, perception of benefits afforded by digital tools, and the effect of these tools on classroom engagement. It brought in the level of interaction these platforms encourage and the contribution they make toward improving educational interactions.

The study also looked into the effect that educational technology exerted on student academic performance by focusing on the hindrances in learning and methods adopted to counter the hindrances. A balanced interpretation of findings was sought by equally incorporating some of the constraints associated with the digital platforms like disparity in access to technological tools and problems in adjusting with the new methods of learning.

Finally, the students provided suggestions on how university learning could be improved, stressing the need for teaching to be suited to their needs. They stressed the need for digital platforms to be more harmoniously integrated into existing face-to-face teaching practices and for enhanced interactive and collaborative elements to be included in the classroom.

Table 3 shows the results of the Cronbach's alpha reliability test on the scale measuring the skills acquired during support courses in mathematics. The results indicate that the 17 items are highly correlated, given that the Cronbach's alpha correlation value of 0.730 is higher than the value of 0.700, often considered to indicate a strong correlation.

Table 2. Cronbach's Alpha reliability tests for the scale measuring soft skills.

Cronbach's Alpha	**Cronbach's Alpha based on standardised items.**	**Number of items**
.730	.722	17

The data was analysed using SPSS® (version 25, Chicago, IC, USA). To answer the research question, the results were examined using descriptive statistical analysis. The p-value is fixed ($p = 0.05$).

3) Measurement instrument.

This study adopted a quantitative approach to analyse the data and meet the research objectives. An anonymous electronic questionnaire was designed and structured into three main sections, allowing a complete and diversified collection of relevant data.

- First section: Frequency of attendance at online courses and management of time allocated per day.

The aim of this section was to explore students' habits in terms of participation in online courses. Participants indicated the frequency with which they attend courses (daily, several times a week, rarely, or never) and the amount of time they devote to online learning each day. These data provide an overview of digital learning practices and a better understanding of their influence on academic performance.

- Second section: Digital platforms and the online learning experience.

The aim of this section was to identify the platforms most used by university students for their learning activities (e.g. Moodle, Microsoft Teams, Google Classroom) and to assess their overall experience with online learning. It also included questions on students' level of satisfaction with distance university education, their perception of the effectiveness of digital tools for learning and their impact on academic success. Participants' answers were classified into several levels (very satisfied, moderately satisfied, not very satisfied, not satisfied).

- Third section: Barriers to learning and proposed solutions.

This section focused on the difficulties encountered by students when learning online. Multiple choice questions (MCQs) were used to identify the main obstacles (Internet connection, lack of interaction with teachers, lack of technical support, etc.) and the strategies used to overcome them. In addition, students were asked to put forward suggestions for improving the effectiveness of online courses, such as incorporating more interactive methods or developing teaching resources tailored to their needs.

Validation and research ethics: The questionnaire was validated by a committee of experts made up of two university lecturers, a doctor of education and two secondary school teachers. After revision, some questions were reworded to improve their clarity and scientific relevance. Participation was voluntary, and students were informed of their right to withdraw at any time without justification.

Data analysis and performance monitoring: The data collected was analysed using descriptive methods (averages and percentages), using Microsoft Office Excel 365 software. At the same time, an educational intervention was put in place, comprising personalised remediation and support sessions. These sessions, held for two hours a week for three months, were designed to meet the needs identified through the questionnaires. The students' progress was assessed each month using specific exams, enabling the impact of the solutions implemented on their academic success to be measured.

RESULTS

With regard to online courses (Table 3), undergraduates spent the most time on them, with 35% claiming to have a lot of time for them. On the other hand, a higher proportion of Master's (29%) and Doctorate (24%) students said they had less time for online courses. University graduates, meanwhile, tend to devote less time to online courses, with only 12% claiming to have a lot of time.

For face-to-face courses, undergraduates also say they spend a considerable amount of time on them, with 36% saying they have a lot of time. However, a significant proportion of PhD (35%) and Postgraduate (12%) students report having little time for face-to-face courses. This suggests a reduction in the timetable load as a function of the level of study and the maturation of students' academic autonomy.

In terms of the amount of teaching time allocated per day, Bachelor's students generally receive more teaching time, with 49% indicating that they have enough. By contrast, a significant proportion of Master's and Doctorate students say they have little time allocated each day, particularly for face-to-face courses. University graduates also seem to benefit from less daily teaching time. Students learn in an environment connected to the Internet (karsenti, 2002). The (Attali Commission, 2008) stressed the importance of including subjects such as group collaboration, English, computing and economics in the core of skills and knowledge that every French citizen should master, all without increasing the length of teaching hours. Similarly, we found that the amount of teaching time deployed per day is sufficient. There is a significant causal link between the duration of teaching on the one hand, and the results of teaching on the other (Chopin, 2006).

Table 3. Analysis of frequency and teaching time by learning mode and level of study

	Frequency of attendance at online courses						Frequency of attendance at face-to-face classes						Amount of teaching time allocated per day					
	A lot of time	%	Enough time	%	Little time	%	A lot of time	%	Enough time	%	Little time	%	A lot of time	%	Enough time	%	Little time	%
Bachelor's degree	12	35%	32	36%	24	33%	34	36%	23	31%	11	42%	21	49%	42	33%	5	22%
Master's degree	10	29%	23	26%	21	29%	32	34%	19	26%	3	12%	13	30%	34	26%	7	30%
Doctorate	8	24%	13	15%	14	19%	9	9%	17	23%	9	35%	5	12%	21	16%	9	39%
University graduates	4	12%	21	24%	13	18%	20	21%	15	20%	3	12%	4	9%	32	25%	2	9%
Number of students	34	100%	89	100%	72	100%	95	100%	74	100%	26	100%	43	100%	129	100%	23	100%

Table 4 shows the preferences for using e-learning platforms according to participants' level of education. Among the 439 respondents, YouTube stands out as the most popular platform, accounting for 33% of users, with particularly strong adoption among university graduates (42%) and undergraduates (32%). Google Classroom is in second place with 21% of users, largely adopted by Bachelor's (28%) and Master's (24%) students. Moodle, used by 9% of participants, is evenly distributed between the different levels of study. As far as specialised platforms are concerned, Coursera (12%) and LinkedIn Learning (10%) are mainly used by doctoral and Master's students. Free and accessible platforms, such as YouTube and Google Classroom, dominate at all levels, while specialised platforms are more attractive to students at higher levels. The data collected reveals that 57% of students consult YouTube. They subscribe to French-language channels and watch videos, documentaries and films (Benkrima, 2021), then google Classroom such that a third of the students surveyed observed that using Google Classroom proved effective in their learning for the subjects covered (Видавництво, 2021).

Table 4. Use of e-learning platforms by level of study.

	Bachelor's degree		**Master's degree**		**Doctorate**		**University graduates**		**Effective**	
	N	%	**N**	%	**N**	%	**N**	%	**N**	%
Coursera	9	7%	17	12%	23	23%	4	6%	53	12%
Udemy	6	5%	9	6%	6	6%	5	7%	26	6%
LinkedIn Learning	12	9%	14	10%	13	13%	3	4%	42	10%
Skillshare	3	2%	4	3%	1	1%	2	3%	10	2%
Codecademy	2	2%	2	1%	0	0%	0	0%	4	1%
OpenClassrooms	8	6%	9	6%	7	7%	5	7%	29	7%
YouTube	42	32%	43	30%	30	30%	28	42%	143	33%
Google Classroom	29	28%	34	24%	11	11%	12	18%	93	21%
Moodle	12	9%	11	8%	8	8%	8	12%	39	9%
Duolingo	14	11%	20	14%	23	23%	24	36%	81	18%
Effective	137	100%	143	100%	99	100%	67	100%	439	100%

The findings in Table 5 indicate that 35.9% of students rated their online learning experience as rather good. Similarly, the general satisfaction of the students regarding the university education is regarded as satisfactory—45.1%. In addition, 46.7% of students consider their ability to learn independently to be fairly good, while 47.7% grade their academic success to be fairly good. As (Alves and al., 2010) point out, these various dimensions are very important in the measurement of students' satisfaction with their learning and with their affective engagement.

Regarding academic performance, the results show a good number of students consider their academic performance the best on Even more, according to a concentration of 47.6%, which supports that the reform processes in pedagogy seem to have worked, especially those that incorporate ICT. In fact, lecturers are increasingly nudging students to use social media and other technological tools that could be adapted to the area or field of study in a bid to promote self-directed learning, thereby enhancing the learning process (Ennadi,2022).

According to (Pirot & Ketele, 2002), this interface of digital tools impacts positively on students concerning academic success and shows a good correlation between success levels rated in January and at the end of secondary education. The use of technology and diversified digital resources enables students to optimize their learning by providing greater access to educational content and enhancing their autonomy in the process of knowledge acquisition.

Table 5. Students' Perceptions of University Learning: Experiences, Abilities and Academic Results

		Bachelor's degree		Master's degree		Doctorate		University graduates		Effective	
		N	%	N	%	N	%	N	%	N	%
The online learning experience	Very good	6	5%	3	2,5%	3	2,5%	0	0%	12	5,9%
	Fairly good	19	15,8%	25	20,8%	12	10%	17	14,2%	73	35,9%
	Average	31	25,8%	17	14,2%	8	6,7%	12	10%	68	33,5%
	Fair Poor	4	3,3%	2	1,7%	2	1,7%	4	3,3%	12	5,9%
	Very poor	8	6,7%	7	5,8%	10	8,3%	5	4,2%	30	14,7%
	Total									195	100%
The face-to-face learning experience	Very good	34	28,3%	21	17,5%	16	13,3%	21	17,5%	92	50,3%
	Fairly good	22	18,3%	25	20,5%	14	11,7%	9	7,5%	70	38,3%
	Average	12	10%	6	5%	5	4,2%	8	6,7%	31	16,9%
	Fair Poor	0	0%	2	1,7%	0	0%	0	0%	2	1,1%
	Very poor	0	0%	0	0%	0	0%	0	0%	0	0%
	Total									195	100%
Ability to learn independently	Very good	21	17,5%	21	17,5%	15	12,5%	15	12,5%	72	36,9%
	Fairly good	32	26,7%	22	18,3%	21	17,5%	16	13,3%	91	46,7%
	Average	13	10,8%	10	8,3%	8	6,7%	7	5,8%	38	19,6%
	Fair Poor	2	1,7%	0	0%	0	0%	0	0%	2	1,1%
	Very poor	0	0%	1	0,8%	0	0%	0	0%	1	0,5%
	Total									195	100%

continued on following page

Table 5. Continued

		Bachelor's degree		Master's degree		Doctorate		University graduates		Effective	
		N	%	N	%	N	%	N	%	N	%
Satisfaction with university learning	Very good	15	12,5%	17	14,2%	8	6,7%	9	7,5%	49	25,1%
	Fairly good	33	27,5%	18	15%	18	15%	19	15,8%	88	45,1%
	Average	19	15,8%	17	14,2%	8	6,7%	10	8,3%	54	27,7%
	Fair Poor	1	0,8%	1	0,8%	1	0,8%	0	0%	3	1,5%
	Very poor	0	0%	1	0,8%	0	0%	0	0%	1	0,5%
	Total									195	100%
Level of academic success	Very good	9	7,5%	21	17,5%	13	10,8%	13	10,8%	56	28,7%
	Fairly good	40	33,3%	21	17,5%	18	15%	14	11,7%	93	47,7%
	Average	19	15,8%	11	9,2%	3	2,5%	11	9,2%	44	22,6%
	Fair Poor	0	0%	1	0,8%	1	0,8%	0	0%	2	1%
	Very poor	0	0%	0	0%	0	0%	0	0%	0	0%
	Total									195	100%

Broadly, these results (Table 6) indicate that nearly 31% of undergraduates see digital technologies as purely beneficial and about 33% perceive them to be somewhat beneficial-a clear positive disposition toward this type of technology at this level of learning. This trend continues among master's students, where 38% of respondents opine that digital technologies are entirely beneficial and 22% consider them to be fairly beneficial.

However, PhD students and university graduates are much more nuanced and show more moderate enthusiasm. Among PhD students, only 21% consider digital technologies to be entirely beneficial, while 22% consider them to be rather harmful. University graduates possess an even more reserved opinion, with only 11% seeing them as entirely beneficial and 25% seeing them as rather harmful.

That is why undergraduates and masters perceive digital technologies as effective learning tools, whereas doctoral students and graduates are more critical; the latter perhaps constitutes a part of the specific requirements for more advanced degrees. It should also be noted that the contextualization of digital technologies within higher education would bring this explanation for the differences in perception, such as that in the flipped classroom. The flipped classroom allows autonomous online preparation and face-to-face interaction using greater flexibility and highly personalized learning; this are the two main advantages cited by students as justifications for their use of the flipped classroom. However, this may not optimally fulfill such expectations as postgraduate students typically demand more extensive, specialized engagement of the content. Such differences in perception illustrate that the addition of digital technology cannot be simply usable in teaching as it will also need to factor in contexts (Endrizzi, 2012).

Table 6. Students' perceptions of the impact of digital technologies on learning

	Digital technologies are advantageous for education.											
	Quite beneficial		Somewhat beneficial		Neither beneficial nor harmful		Somewhat harmful		Quite harmful		Quite beneficial	
	N	%	N	%	N	%	N	%	N	%	N	%
Bachelor's degree	**22**	**31%**	**17**	**33%**	**8**	**50%**	**11**	**55%**	**10**	**28%**	**68**	**35%**
Master's degree	27	38%	11	22%	3	19%	4	20%	9	25%	54	28%
Doctorate	15	21%	11	22%	0	0%	1	5%	8	22%	35	18%
University graduates	8	11%	12	24%	5	31%	4	20%	9	25%	38	19%

The findings in (Table 7) suggest that 27.1% of university students tend to agree with the statement that the benefits of e-learning outweigh its disadvantages. This can be related to the flipped classroom approach, which blends the benefits of online learning, such as flexibility and independence, with those of in-person teaching, such as live student-teacher interaction. In an actual flipped classroom, students prepare content online, independently, before coming to class; thus, they master concise concepts before engaging in discussions and practicum activities. This validates the argument that well-designed online teaching can prove to be more holistic than that of traditional methods. Thus, we have a new textbook model that could also be perceived as offering an advantage over the traditional know-how of delivery-online as well as face-to-face (Walckiers & De Praetere, 2004).

In addition, 33.8% of students show strong conviction regarding the idea that learners learn better when they actively participate in the learning process. This lay down, active participation in the learning process comes one hundred percent in the spirit of the definition of the flipped classroom. In this model, teachers and students go about gaining knowledge through active participation and concretely linking with the real world, encouraging communication, collaboration, creativity and deep reflection with (Reverdy, 2013). Thus, the flipped classroom fosters these bounded spaces with active learning where student engagement is vital for its success since it emphasizes participation, group discussions and collaborative projects.

Teaching styles should respond to the learning styles of different students, according to 33.8% of students. This belief is directly linked to the flipped classroom model. Indeed, the teacher's role in a flipped classroom is not only to provide the resources online necessary for the course but to also adapt his/her actual teaching during the face-to-face sessions, depending on the requirements and pace of the students. In this case, the teachers become facilitators or guides on the student's journey for knowledge, aligning with an ideology of guiding students according to their needs in what is a differentiated pedagogy that is amenable to their various learning strategies (Bernabé, Dupont, 2001).

Finally, 69.2% of students strongly agree that learning by doing is more effective than theoretical learning. This is crucial when discussing flipped learning and its esteem for active, practically oriented learning. It involves allowing students to put theory into practice by working through pragmatic projects followed by discussions and practical work-a hallmark of implementation-focused learning encouraged by continuing education and professional development programs. Such practical, hands-on work is regarded as a gold standard for acquiring life skills through experience. (Morrocco and al., 2003).

Table 7. Perception des Étudiants sur les Méthodes d'Apprentissage et l'Adaptation des Enseignants

		Bachelor's degree		Master's degree		Doctorate		University graduates		
		N	%	N	%	N	%	N	%	N
The advantages of e-learning outweigh the disadvantages	Strongly agree	13	28,2%	12	26%	15	32,6%	6	13%	46
	Somewhat agree	18	33,9%	18	33,9%	8	15%	9	16,9%	53
	Neither agree nor disagree	16	34,7%	16	34,7%	7	15,21	8	17,3%	47
	Somewhat disagree	10	43,5%	4	17,4%	4	17,4%	5	21,7%	23
	Strongly disagree	11	42,3%	4	15,4%	1	3,8%	10	38,5%	26
Learners learn best by being active in the learning process	Strongly agree	18	27,3%	18	27,3%	18	27,3%	12	18,2%	66
	Somewhat agree	15	31,9%	17	36,2%	7	14,9%	8	17%	47
	Neither agree nor disagree	18	45%	11	27,5	6	15%	5	12,5%	40
	Somewhat disagree	7	41,2%	3	17,6%	2	11,8%	5	29,4%	17
	Strongly disagree	10	35,7%	8	28,6%	2	7,14%	8	28,6%	28
The teaching style of educators should be adjusted to the various modes of learning.	Strongly agree	18	27,2%	18	27,2%	18	27,2%	12	18,2%	66
	Somewhat agree	15	31,9%	17	36,2%	7	14,9%	8	17%	47
	Neither agree nor disagree	18	45	11	27,5%	6	15%	5	12,5%	40
	Somewhat disagree	7	41,2%	3	17,6%	2	11,8%	5	29,4%	17
	Strongly disagree	10	40%	5	20%	2	8%	8	32%	25
Teachers should adapt their teaching style to different learning styles	Strongly agree	40	29,6%	42	31,1%	24	17,7%	29	21,5%	135
	Somewhat agree	23	50%	8	17,4%	8	17,4%	7	8,7%	46
	Neither agree nor disagree	3	33,3%	2	22,2%	2	22,2%	2	22,2%	9
	Somewhat disagree	2	40%	2	40%	1	20%	0	0%	5
	Strongly disagree	0	0%	0	0%	0	0%	0	0%	0

Table 8. Study Obstacles and Proposed Solutions by Students

Study Obstacles	Proposed Solutions to Overcome Obstacles
Difficulty in finding books and journals	Conduct online research and seek help from colleagues to find books.
Poor guidance	Rely on bibliographic references and detailed documents.
A lot of confusion	Self-review to catch up on missed concepts.
Lack of information and simplification	Request clear explanations from teachers and engage in self-learning.
Difficulty in managing time and attending all classes	Plan a schedule and attend all classes.
Lack of practice	Engage in more practice through projects or hands-on exercises.
Lack of communication between students and teachers	Use electronic communication tools to facilitate interaction.
Work commitments preventing attendance at daily in-person classes	Participate in online training programs.
Traditional teaching methods used by some professors	Suggest adopting modern teaching methods such as flipped classrooms.
Language barriers	Use language learning applications to improve skills.
Difficulty in attending in-person training sessions for PhD students	Replace in-person training with online courses.
Lack of university courses in online PDF format	Conduct online research to find course materials.
Lack of information on free online resources and absence of an online library for students	Seek help from colleagues or use external resources to access books and materials.
Difficulty in selecting appropriate references for research papers	Consult citation guides and seek advice from colleagues or professors.
Mandatory self-learning	Utilize online tools and resources to improve self-learning efficiency.
Overwhelming number of books to read simultaneously	Prioritize reading based on urgency and relevance.
Poor use of technology	Take training courses to better understand digital tools.
High costs of online courses	Look for alternatives such as free MOOCs or apply for scholarships and discounts.
Poor internet connection	Improve the connection or use tools that allow downloading content for offline access.
Overcrowded academic programs and lack of fundamental resources	Establish associations or learning centers to help address this issue.
Differences in shyness and learning styles among students	Reorganize groups, assign specific tasks, and encourage active participation.
Lack of structured online courses	Propose well-structured and clearly designed online courses.

Table 9. Desired Improvements by Students and Their Link to the Flipped Classroom Method

Desired Improvements	Link to the Flipped Classroom Method
Practice and training	The flipped classroom allows more time for in-class practice after independent online preparation.
Digital resources	The use of digital tools and MOOCs facilitates students' independent preparation before in-person sessions.
Teaching methods	The flipped classroom is based on innovative teaching methods tailored to different learning styles.
Teacher-student interaction	The flipped classroom promotes interaction between students and teachers during in-person sessions through prior preparation.
Internships and professional preparation	The flipped classroom can incorporate practical projects and internships, enabling students to better prepare for these activities in advance.
Educational resources and tools	The flipped classroom relies on digital educational resources and online tools to support independent learning.
Facilities and supervision	The flipped classroom may require enhanced supervision to support students in their independent learning before in-person classes.
Hybrid learning	The flipped classroom is inherently a hybrid learning method, combining online self-learning with in-person sessions.
Library and book access	The flipped classroom requires access to online resources, such as digital books, for students to prepare in advance.
Training and personal development	In the flipped classroom model, recorded sessions and accessible online training allow for independent learning, contributing to students' personal development.

DISCUSSION

Whether or not they are of benefit to their learning is therefore an issue which would appear to support ICT integration. From this evidence, it is clearly witnessed that ICT integration helps. Using technology in science subjects evidently would assist most students and perhaps improve the quality of their learning, as cited in (Guennoun and Benjelloun, 2016).

Information and communication technology basically works as a tool for accessing information. (Margarian and al., 2008) mentioned that one of the major obstacles for university students concerning the advantages of ICT is easy access to diverse information that is decentralized, is available by anyone, from anywhere, at anytime, and is often given free of charge (Rogers, 2001).

Here, ICT also permits the efficient employment of images in students' long-term storage of the information provided. This really does help in the communication progress; students can also find information without having to go to the library. It creates access to different vantage approaches toward the same subject matter, allowing users to support varied tools or processes. The integration of ICT into courses and academic practices works to nearly everyone's benefit and is likely to enhance the learning experience, according to (Guennoun and Benjelloun, 2016). E-learning capital investment can potentially save universities money and consolidate digital technologies' economic benefits, as articulately argued by David Castillo-Merino, Enric Serradell-López, and Jordi Vilaseca-Requena (2009).

The students have greatly benefited from an expanded and enriched educational system with techno-pedagogy to be able to address the holistic development of learners through a global experience. The educational materials could be made accessible through ICT, and students could collaborate and submit assignments for evaluation. Online learning platforms therefore argued to be an invaluable, forward-thinking approach with numerous advantages (Admin, 2021).

Most university students affirm that many advantages come with the incorporation of technologies for learning into higher education, which help in learning and enhance the development of content. In support of this, (Karsenti and Larose, 2001 ; Oulmaati and al., 2017) went on to further mention that ICT integration into education carries several benefits, including the possibility of increased motivation for learners, better communication, wider access to information and knowledge, enhancement of educational processes with greater personalisation, and greater autonomy for learners.

To some students, ICT is very handy in the process of learning. On one hand, they believe that the explanations provided by the teachers are not always clear and good. On the other hand, they also consider some professors as people who do not mind teaching and rather appreciate the students to teach themselves. For some students, this kind of work is just an excuse to gap in the classroom on a daily basis, thus missing out on hands-on experience or even access to vital resources.

While some students like the mixed hybrid system of in-person courses and online courses, others state that they prefer traditional classes. This accentuates the importance of traditional education while requesting the improvement of e-learning in Morocco.

Based on student feedback, some changes they wish to see implemented in their university education include the free availability of the books on the web. Some concerns raised by students are the upgrading of present teaching methods, use of digital platforms, educational software and making more MOOCs available for a variety of subjects. Beyond these changes, students also emphasized the recording of lectures, increased practical training, teaching online research courses, and conducting live classes with a university professor. (Krajcik and al., 1998) and (Reverdy, 2013) underline the need to develop varied media for student support in coping with complexity.

E-learning helps in acquiring knowledge among university students. However, its effectiveness is also configured by several factors to enhance access to e-learning platforms reasonable communication with the teachers, (Ennadi, 2022). 147 It is thus proposed that an investment in e-learning by universities would enhance quality education. Such investment would sustain the continuity of e-learning and redress historical challenges.

CONCLUSION

The digitalization brought in by higher education in the running of the flipped classroom is a path-breaking measure in education. It has given-way for easy access to the learning resources, facilitating independent learning through strengthened teacher-student interactions using such platforms as YouTube, Google Classroom and Moodle. This research proves that such platforms increase student engagement to learn more flexibly and interactively. These notwithstanding, challenges remain in the adoption of flipped classrooms and ICT in teaching universities. The limitations include a small sample, student diversity, and methodological constraints and point to a need for other approaches that would enrich the evaluation of these tools' impact. Moreover, the effectiveness of these technologies will likely be influenced also by the infrastructure, potential support for teachers, and accessibility to digital resources for all students.

Thus, research needs to be continued into different contexts and thus rigorous evaluations. Teaching practices would have to transform along an optimal spectrum of ICT use with constant training for teachers and a very appropriate student fitment. In sum, this is promising but would require adjustments and institutional commitment in order to be effectively and equitably recognized in higher education.

REFERENCES

Видавництво, П. А. І. С. (2021, avril). Expérience d'utilisation de Google Classroom dans le processus d'étude des étudiants francophones à l'Académie de médecine de Dnipropetrovsk. *The DSMU Repository*. https://repo.dma.dp.ua/7211/

Alves, S., Gosse, B., & Sprimont, P. (2010). Dimensions et conséquences de la satisfaction au travail des apprentis. *Revue internationale de psychosociologie, 16*(40), 161–180. https://doi.org/DOI: 10.3917/rips.040.0161

Anderson, L. W. (1988). Opportunity to learn. In Dunkin, M. J. (Ed.), *The International encyclopedia of teaching and teacher education* (pp. 368–372). Pergamon Press.

Attali, J. (2008). *Rapport de la Commission pour la libération de la croissance française* (245 p.). https://www.liberationdelacroissance.fr/files/rapports/rapportCLCF.pdf

Bansal, H., & Khan, R. (2018). A review paper on human computer interaction. *International Journal of Advanced Research in Computer Science and Software Engineering, 8*(4), 53. DOI: 10.23956/ijarcsse.v8i4.630

Baron, G. (2008). Technologies de l'information et de la communication et indigènes numériques: quelle situation? https://hal.science/hal-00696420

Ben Youssef, A., & Hadhri, W. (2009). Les dynamiques d'usage des TIC par les enseignants universitaires. *Reseaux (London), 155*(3), 23–54.

Benkrima, F. (2021). *Le développement de la compétence orale chez les étudiants pendant le confinement: Cas des étudiants de 3e année licence français à l'Université Kasdi Merbah Ouargla — Promotion 2019-2020.* http://dspace.univ-ouargla.dz/jspui/handle/123456789/28593

Bernabé, E., & Dupont, P. (2001). *Le leadership pédagogique: Une approche managériale du style d'enseignement.*

Castillo-Merino, D., Serradell-López, E., & Vilaseca-Requena, J. (2009). Usage des technologies de l'information et de la communication dans l'enseignement supérieur. *Reseaux (London), 155*(3), 55–80. DOI: 10.3917/res.155.0055

Chopin, M. (2006). Temps d'enseignement et temps didactique: Approche didactique de la question du temps dans l'enseignement des mathématiques au cycle 3 de l'école élémentaire. *Carrefours de l'éducation, 21*(1), 53–71. https://doi.org/DOI: 10.3917/cdle.021.0053

De Clercq, M. (2023). Les défis de l'enseignement supérieur: entre accessibilité, équité et réussite. *Diversité. Revue d'actualité et de réflexion sur l'action éducative*, (202), volume 1.

Endrizzi, L. (2012). *Les technologies numériques dans l'enseignement supérieur, entre défis et opportunités*. https://ens-lyon.hal.science/ensl-01651604

Ennadi, M. (2022, 1 septembre). L'apprentissage en ligne et l'expérience des étudiants universitaires à l'utilisation des TIC. *Revue de Management et Cultures*. https://revues.imist.ma/index.php/REMAC/article/view/34249/17561

Guennoun, B., & Benjelloun, N. (2016). Regards des étudiants sur l'intégration des TIC dans l'enseignement supérieur scientifique. *Revue internationale des technologies en pédagogie universitaire, 13*(1), 61. https://doi.org/DOI: 10.18162/ritpu-2016-v13n1-05

Halimi, A. (2023). L'enseignement à distance dans l'université marocaine après la Covid-19: Cas de l'université Hassan II. Disponible sur https://revues.imist.ma/index.php/IAJESP/index

Kaddouri, M., & Bouamri, A. (2010). Usage de plateformes d'enseignement à distance dans l'enseignement supérieur marocain: Avantages pédagogiques et difficultés d'appropriation. *Questions Vives*, *5*(14), 107–118. DOI: 10.4000/questionsvives.642

Karsenti, T. (2001). Pédagogies et nouvelles technologies: Former des enseignants pour le nouveau millénaire. Dans *Actes du IXe sommet de la Francophonie, Colloque Éthique et nouvelles Technologies, l'appropriation des savoirs en question* (Beyrouth, 24–28 septembre).

Karsenti, T. (2002). L'alphabétisation et les technologies de l'information à l'aube du nouveau millénaire: Nouvelle conception, nouvelles perspectives. *Canadian Journal for the Study of Adult Education*, *15*(2), 37–60. DOI: 10.56105/cjsae.v15i2.1916

Krajcik, J. S., Blumenfeld, P. C., Marx, R. W., Bass, K. M., Fredricks, J., & Soloway, E. (1998). Inquiry in project-based science classrooms: Initial attempts by middle school students. *Journal of the Learning Sciences*, *7*(3–4), 313–350. DOI: 10.1080/10508406.1998.9672057

Lo, C. K. (2023). What is the impact of ChatGPT on education? A rapid review of the literature. *Education Sciences*, *13*(4), 4. Advance online publication. DOI: 10.3390/educsci13040410

Margaryan, A., Nicol, D., Littlejohn, A., & Trinder, K. (2008). Students' use of technologies to support formal and informal learning. In Luca, J., & Weippl, E. (Éds.), *Proceedings of World Conference on Educational Multimedia, Hypermedia and Telecommunications (ED-MEDIA) 2008* (pp. 4257–4266). Chesapeake, VA: Association for the Advancement of Computing in Education (AACE).

Morroco, C. C., Walker, A., & Lewis, L. R. (2003). Access to a schoolwide thinking curriculum: Leadership challenges and solutions. *Journal of Special Education Leadership*, *1*(1), 5–14.

Oulmaati, K., Ezzahri, S., & Samadi, K. (2017). Usage des TIC et apprentissages des étudiants inscrits en études islamiques à l'Université Abdelmalek Essaadi. *Revue internationale des technologies en pédagogie universitaire, 14*(1), 40. https://doi.org/DOI: 10.18162/ritpu-2017-v14n1-03

Ouoba, N. E. (2024). L'intégration des outils d'intelligence artificielle dans l'enseignement supérieur: perceptions, usages et défis. *Les Cahiers de l'ACAREF, 4.*

Pirot, L., & De Ketele, J. (2002). L'engagement académique de l'étudiant comme facteur de réussite à l'université: Étude exploratoire menée dans deux facultés contrastées. *Revue des Sciences de l'Education, 26*(2), 367–394. DOI: 10.7202/000127ar

Price, A. M., Perkins, K. K., Holmes, N. G., & Wieman, C. E. (2019). How and why do high school teachers use PhET interactive simulations? In *2017 Physics Education Research Conference Proceedings*. https://doi.org/DOI: 10.1119/perc.2018.pr.Price

Ranoliya, B. R., Raghuwanshi, N., & Singh, S. (2017). Chatbot for university related FAQs. In *2017 International Conference on Advances in Computing, Communications and Informatics (ICACCI)* (pp. 1525–1530). Udupi. DOI: 10.1109/ICACCI.2017.8126057

Reverdy, C. (2013). *Des projets pour mieux apprendre?* https://hal.science/hal-01657236

Rogers, P. L. (2001). Traditions to transformations: The forced evolution of higher education. *AACE Journal*, *9*(1), 47–60.

Sidir, M., & Benchenna, A. (2008). Du recours aux TICE en temps de crise? Le cas des universités marocaines. *Distances Et Savoirs*, *6*(2), 211–236. DOI: 10.3166/ds.6.211-236

Walckiers, M., & De Praetere, T. (2004). L'apprentissage collaboratif en ligne, huit avantages qui en font un must. *Distances Et Savoirs*, *2*(1), 53–75. DOI: 10.3166/ds.2.53-75

Zouaoui, M. (2006). L'enseignement supérieur depuis l'indépendance: la dégradation de la qualité était-elle inéluctable? In *Cinquante ans de développement humain au Maroc et perspectives 2025* (pp. 159–195).

Chapter 5
The Impact of E-Assessment on Students' Cognitive Engagement:
An Empirical Study

laaziz Youssef
https://orcid.org/0000-0002-0306-1314
University Hassan II, Morocco

Ghizlane Chemsi
University Hassan II, Morocco

Marouane Moukhliss
University Hassan II, Morocco

Mohamed Latifi
Center of Training Education' Inspectors, Rabat, Morocco

Mohamed Radid
https://orcid.org/0000-0002-8082-2009
University Hassan II, Morocco

ABSTRACT

This article presents the results of a study aimed at implementing a dynamic E-assessment prototype in a group of university students in order to examine its influence on their cognitive engagement. This research is based on the Design-Based Research approach (Brown, 1992). We opted for a mixed methodology to examine students' cognitive engagement and the influence of E-assessment on it, in a mathematics didactics course at the École Supérieure d'Éducation et de Formation of

DOI: 10.4018/979-8-3373-0740-4.ch005

the Université Chouaib Doukali El jadida, for the benefit of second-year students specializing in primary education, using the Cognitive Engagement Questionnaire (Leduc, Kozanitis and Lepage, 2018) as well as two group interviews. The results show that this E-assessment modality was beneficial for students' cognitive engagement. It enabled them to deploy and implement in-depth study strategies and to self-regulate their preparation for the final exam.

INTRODUCTION

1. Background to the study

In recent years, Moroccan open-access universities have consistently experienced a significant explosion in student numbers. In a presentation to the Government Council for the start of the 2023/2024 academic year, the Minister of Higher Education, Scientific Research and Innovation, Abdellatif Miraoui, pointed out that the number of students had risen by 6.7% compared with 2022/2023 (Ministry of Higher Education, Scientific Research, and Innovation, 2025). This significant increase in student enrolment has led to a reduction in the quality of teaching and training. Indeed, several studies show that this massification can lead to a deterioration in learning conditions, affecting both student engagement and academic results.

On the other hand, according to the world university ranking drawn up by the British magazine Times Higher Education (THE), which evaluates more than 1,900 universities in 108 countries and regions, Moroccan universities, although they have made significant progress in research indicators, are still below the world average. Cela soulève des inquiétudes quant à la compétitivité du système éducatif marocain sur la scène internationale. En parallèle, l'enseignement en contexte de grand groupe a un impact défavorable sur l'engagement cognitif des étudiants, ce qui se traduit par un abaissement de leurs performances scolaires et de leur taux de réussite (Youssef, Chemsi, & Radid, 2023).

Faced with this situation of increasing enrolment on Moroccan campuses and the rapid emergence of information and communication technologies (ICT), Morocco has recognized the crucial role they can play in improving the quality of academic and vocational education and training. This has led to the initiation of programs aimed at the widespread use and integration of ICTs in higher education (Mastafi & Bouhlou, 2016). In this context of improving the quality of higher education, Morocco has embarked on a new reform in line with the guidelines of the National Education and Training Charter and the promulgation of Law 01-00 governing the organization of higher education, thus reinforcing the legitimacy of the reforms adopted.

However, despite efforts to improve and promote assessment in higher education, a number of weaknesses persist. For example, the cumbersome organization of evaluation, due to the phenomenon of massification, is particularly problematic in open-access establishments. What's more, the absence of formative assessment, whose function would be to support student progress while allowing programs to be adjusted, is a major obstacle to academic success. This diversity of assessment practices, in terms of systems, procedures and criteria, also raises questions about the effectiveness of current methods (Kaaouachi, 2004).

To establish relevant and rigorous evaluation procedures, it is imperative to create an evaluation culture among all educational players. This requires not only training in evaluation, but also a redefinition of evaluation principles and operational mechanisms, adapted to the specificities of the local context (Kaaouachi, 2010).

2. Problematic

In this context, our general research question is as follows: how can a dynamic e-assessment be a vehicle for stimulating students' cognitive engagement in a large-group context at university?

This question raises crucial issues for the future of higher education in Morocco. It questions not only current assessment practices, but also the integration of ICT as a potential lever for countering the negative effects of massification. By exploring this issue, our study aims to contribute to the debate on improving the quality of higher education, while meeting the challenges posed by an ever-growing student population and ever-increasing pedagogical requirements.

3. Research objectives and relevance

This research project proposes to implement a dynamic e-assessment device via the Quizizz application in a large-group context, with the aim of examining the extent to which it influences students' cognitive engagement. This study also aims to explore the advantages and/or disadvantages of e-assessment in terms of cognitive engagement compared to traditional methods, e-assessment via Quizizz could help improve the pedagogical situation based on empirical and theoretical knowledge drawn from the literature.

Studies concerning the integration of digital learning environments to optimize the pedagogical structure of large university groups are few and far between (Timmis, Broadfoot, Sutherland, & Oldfield, 2016), which is why this study is of particular importance in terms of pedagogical spin-offs on this subject. Similarly, the scientific knowledge gained and practical experience gained from this project could also be used as a basis for future experiments in implementing e-assessment in university courses.

4. Research hypotheses

H0: We believe that dynamic e-assessment could be an effective solution and a foundation for engaging students cognitively in a large group context at university.

H1: We believe that e-assessment could not contribute to increasing students' cognitive engagement in a large-group context at university.

I. CONCEPTUAL FRAMEWORK

Following our research question, which aims to measure the influence of e-assessment on students' cognitive engagement, our conceptual framework will be based mainly on the following concepts:

- Cognitive engagement in a large-group context;
- Cognitive engagement in the context of this study;
- Innovative assessment and cognitive engagement
- Dynamic e-assessment;
- Quizziz.

Cognitive engagement in large-group contexts

The importance of students' cognitive engagement at university, particularly in large groups, is an important topic in the field of education and pedagogy. More recently, a review of several articles (Cuseo, 2007) highlights two key factors that are responsible for the low cognitive engagement experienced in this context. The first concerns the teaching and assessment strategies used by teachers (Lepage, 2018). Indeed, to meet the constraints of the large group, the lecture technique is adopted by the majority of teachers, as is the multiple-choice exam (Biggs & Tang, 2011).

As is well known, lecturing allows a great deal of information to be conveyed to a large group in a short space of time, while ensuring the transmission of well-structured and clear information, however, it is not recommended to use it as a dominant strategy especially as it can lead to challenges in maintaining the attention of all students and assessing their understanding (Daele & Berthiaume, 2010). This teaching practice is now widespread and predominant among large groups of students, leading to cognitive passivity, a lack of interaction with the teacher and peers, and a lack of feedback on learning, resulting in a lower success rate (Youssef,

Chemsi, & Radid, 2023). What's more, the large-group context not only leads to surface learning, but also to an answer-choice test, i.e., to the memorization and retrieval of knowledge (Timmis et al., 2016). Indeed, the response-choice test may therefore be more appropriate for assessing skills at the lower and middle levels of Bloom's taxonomic scale, while assessing skills at the higher levels proves more difficult (Ernoult & Talamoni, 2006).

The second factor held responsible for low cognitive engagement in large-group contexts is the lack of feedback perceived by the student regarding his or her learning (Kerr, 2011). Many researchers and pedagogues define feedback as information that the teacher provides to the student about how to accomplish learning activities. This feedback can take place in a formal or informal context, and at different points in the learning process (Lambert, Rossier, Daele, & Lenzo, 2009). Exam marking certainly highlights the errors made, but it offers little opportunity for the student to engage cognitively with his or her learning and be able to self-regulate to achieve the course objectives (Lepage, 2018). Well-done feedback supports learning, improves subsequent performance, develops learner autonomy and also enables the teacher to regulate and adjust his or her teaching (Boucher, 2015). Notwithstanding the fact that the majority of players in the world of education consider feedback to be important for learning, at university level, however, this practice remains underdeveloped due to the lack of pedagogical and didactic resources on the part of teachers, which keeps it at a preliminary stage (Glazer, 2014).

Cognitive engagement in this study

Although cognitive engagement presents a daily challenge and topic of concern to teachers and educational institutions, it remains largely unexplored, particularly in the context of higher education, and we are only at the beginning of understanding its crucial role in the full development potential of human learning (Coates, 2008). It is defined by the level of intellectual engagement as the student's use of cognitive and metacognitive strategies during learning (Greene, 2015). Cognitive engagement therefore manifests itself in the choice to engage and interest in the course, the intensity of that engagement and perseverance in completing the task (Leduc, Kozanitis, & Lepage, 2018). Cognitive engagement is a guiding and important vector for learning, which refers to the student's responsibility and efforts to succeed. Cognitive engagement is associated with the student's desire to understand. Conversely, low cognitive engagement is correlated with superficial learning stemming from a desire to perform (Dinsmore & Alexander, 2012).

A number of researchers are studying and understanding cognitive engagement, including Miller et al. (1996), who define cognitive engagement as a concept for measuring:

- Cognitive strategies used to learn;
- Reflection on the best way to learn;
- The mental effort expended to organize strategies and thoughts for learning.

Given that the questionnaire adopted in our study is the one developed by Miller and colleagues (1996), cognitive engagement refers to the three aspects that make it up, namely, 1) learning strategies used (surface or deep), 2) self-regulatory skills and 3) time/effort expended by the student (Leduc, Kozanitis, & Lepage, 2018).

Surface learning and deep learning

Cognitive engagement takes two distinct forms: surface and deep (Greene, 2015). It is considered superficial when the student's learning is based on memorization (Leduc, Kozanitis, & Lepage, 2018). As a result, a student who is cognitively engaged on the surface is not interested in understanding notions and concepts in order to assimilate and master them; indeed, he or she limits himself or herself to restituting memorized knowledge by rote, aiming for performance goals such as getting a good grade or progressing to a higher academic level (Miller, Greene, Montalvo, Ravindran, & Nichols, 1996).

When the student exploits his or her prior knowledge in a creative way, or when he or she explains how he or she arrives at his or her conclusions, cognitive engagement is said to be in depth (Baeten, Kyndt, Struyven, & Dochy, 2010). Thus, learning is qualified as deep if it is characterized by the use of complex cognitive functions. It occurs as soon as the learner chooses to incorporate new information into pre-existing knowledge structures.

Self-regulation

Self-regulation is defined as a process aimed at achieving a goal and involving sub-processes related to goal setting, planning, monitoring learning and self-reflection and response (Greene, 2015). For 25 years, educational psychologist Zimmerman conducted research into student behavior, highlighting a positive correlation between students' good academic results and their practices and attitudes. These results suggest that high achievers are distinguished by their ability to set specific learning goals, use effective study strategies, carefully monitor the progress of their learning, and systematically adjust their efforts according to the results achieved and desired (Zimmerman & Martinez-Pons, 1988).

Contemporary studies characterize self-regulation by three skills: metacognition, motivation and active participation in the learning process (Fréchette, 2008). These skills can be strongly influenced by the forms of feedback they receive (Zimmerman & Labuhn, 2012). Moreover, feedback processes in teaching methods play an important role in the development of self-regulation skills (Boud & Molloy, 2013). The constant feedback provided to the student has a significant impact on their cognitive engagement, therefore, providing continuous feedback encourages the student to invest sustained and diligent effort in their studies, thus promoting success (Zimmerman & Labuhn, 2012).

Briefly, cognitive engagement is manifested through deep or surface learning strategies, the student's self-regulatory processes and efforts to achieve study goals (Leduc, Kozanitis, & Lepage, 2018). Cognitive engagement and motivation are strongly linked, with the former frequently perceived as a behavioral manifestation of the latter (Pintrich, 2004). According to Greene, understanding the mechanisms of cognitive engagement is a mediating factor in explaining the links between motivation and success, although success is not always directly associated with deep cognitive engagement (Greene, 2015). Nevertheless, various researchers have observed significant results concerning the negative correlation between superficial engagement and academic success (Greene & Azevedo, 2010). In reality, successful students possess a set of strategies, whether superficial or in-depth, which they use in accordance with the demands and requests of the teacher, taking into account the teaching-learning contexts. In reality, different context-specific variables impact cognitive engagement, such as environmental demands, reference values, relationships with the environment, peers and teachers (Bailey, 2005).

Innovative assessment and cognitive engagement

In education, a great deal of research has focused on pedagogical innovation since the 1990s (Lison, 2011), but in higher education, it is less present, even though it has been perceptible in many sectors (Lison, Bédard, Beaucher, & Trudelle, 2014). Today, however, in the digital age and following the introduction of the new law 01-00, higher education in Morocco is also embracing pedagogical innovation, as reflected in the introduction of digital platforms covering the disciplines taught at university.

Since assessment is an integral part of teaching and learning, it can be an essential source of innovation (Hamdan, 2022). Before the university began experimenting with so-called innovative online assessment, traditional assessment (written exam, essay, multiple-choice test) was commonly used (Martell, 2007), yet teaching assessment at Moroccan universities was initiated by some teachers anxious to receive feedback in order to improve the quality of their teaching (Hamdan, 2022).

The need for innovation in the field of assessment has become inescapable through the introduction of techno-pedagogical solutions for all educational systems, and so-called e-assessment practices, on the one hand, due to the transformations induced by the advent of the Covid-19 pandemic, on the other, to insert feedback devices via digital learning environments would be a way of implementing proven and effective feedback methods with the aim of turning students into "feedback seekers", leading them to develop their attitudes and self-evaluate their learning themselves (Boud & Molloy, 2013). What's more, recent experiments in large groups that have incorporated formative e-assessment (and therefore feedback) into learning have shown promising results (Jiao, 2015). Thus, inserting feedback into the large-group context could represent a promising and interesting opportunity to integrate pedagogical principles that support cognitive engagement (Lepage, 2018).

Dynamic e-assessment

E-assessment is a flexible, highly innovative tool that can be adapted to meet the needs of a wide range of educational contexts worldwide. It offers many advantages, such as flexibility and speed. As such, it is designed to encourage metacognition and self-regulation on the part of the student, important characteristics for cognitive engagement (Leung, 2007).

Dynamic e-assessment is an interactive approach to assessment, not only focusing on the task to be performed, but also on the interaction between student and teacher, generating information about what helps the student to progress (Blais, 2023).

Dynamic assessment can thus be an effective tool for analyzing an individual's cognitive processes and exploring the circumstances that contribute to efficient learning (Greenberg, 2000). It also encourages students to self-regulate by assessing their own progress in relation to the knowledge targeted by the course, while benefiting from the support of a form of tutoring to guide them. Finally, it directly fills the feedback gap experienced in larges groups (Lepage, 2018).

Quizizz

Quizizz is an online assessment tool that allows all students to practice together on their computer, smartphone or I Pad (Ju & Adam, 2018). As well as enabling teachers to create customized quizzes to assess students' knowledge in a fun and interactive way, it offers an interactive experience that can make learning more stimulating and engaging for students.

Several studies have highlighted the advantages of Quizizz, such as interactivity, competitiveness and ease of access (Zhao, 2019). In addition, Quizizz can be used as a formative assessment tool, enabling teachers to see how students are progressing and to adjust their teaching according to the results obtained. It is a self-assessment tool for students (Rahayu & Purnawarman, 2019). It is used to improve interaction between teacher and students, and to stimulate student motivation, commitment and learning (Chaiyo & Nokham, 2017).

Research methodology

In this study, we opted for Desing-Based-Research (DBR), an action research approach that is part of the methodological current of collaborative educational research (Sanchez & Monod-Ansaldi, 2015), characterized by an iterative process involving the design of educational interventions, their implementation, and the collaborative analysis of results (Fauré, 2017).

Desing-Based-Research (DBR) conforms to the pragmatic paradigm. This philosophical current emphasizes activity (or, more precisely, interactivity) and considers interaction to be the founding principle of this pragmatic approach (Verlot & Suijs, 2000). It considers that knowledge is constructed through concrete experience, and that learning is rooted in reality and takes place in specific contexts. Furthermore, the pragmatic approach of Desing-Based-Research (DBR) emphasizes that the construction of knowledge during action encourages students to reflect on their cognitive choices (Tardif, 2015).

The choice of methodological approach for this research was based on numerous considerations, not least because this approach aims to feed both practice and theory by taking into account the context and its reality both ecologically and in terms of its actors (Burguete, 2021). Field-based: research is conducted in the "real world where participants interact socially" (Wang & Hannafin, 2005), and is interactive, iterative and contextual (Mandran et al., 2021). Moreover, pedagogical practices in universities are influenced by globalization and the massification of higher education. Consequently, the integration of information and communication technologies (ICT) is crucial to improving the quality of teaching. However, little empirical research has addressed pedagogical choices in larges groups (Doan, 2021), so class size and teacher delivery are almost inextricably linked. Indeed, teaching in large groups generally favors the traditional method, both dis and in small groups, the emphasis is mainly on discussion (McKeachie, 1978).

DBR (Design-Based Research) stems from a desire to promote collaboration between educational researchers and practitioners. This approach aims to address a number of concerns, such as the e-assessment experiments currently underway in universities, which use technology for its own sake without any underlying pedagogical principles (Age, 2018). It appears that e-assessments carried out under such conditions cannot be useful and could even be harmful and detrimental (Farrell & Rushby, 2016).

In our study, we use this approach to understand the influence of e-assessment via quizzes on the cognitive engagement of university students in a large-group context.

Features of the approach

Figure 1. represents the steps involved in the process of developing a DBR research project. These features are: 1) assessment and analysis of the context related to the identified problem, 2) design of an intervention to solve the problem, 3) testing and improvement of the proposed intervention and 4) evaluation and analysis aimed at formulating theoretical and practical principles from the results of the intervention.

Figure 1. Refinement of Problems, Solutions,Methods, and Desing Principles (Reeves, 2000)

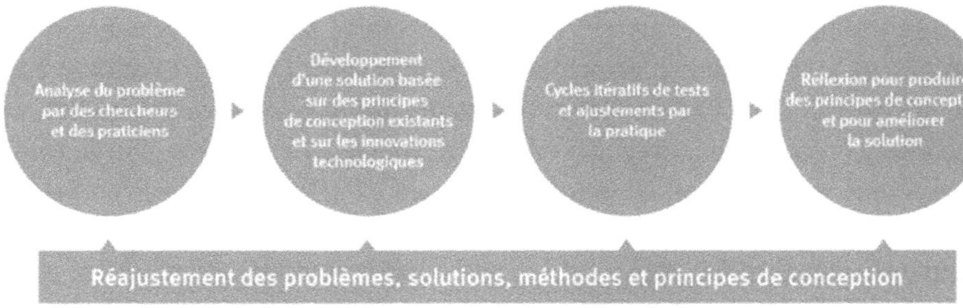

Context assessment

In the DBR approach, the context in which the intervention is carried out is of primary importance (Collins, Joseph, & Bielaczyc, 2016). The assessment of the context is based on writings concerning the problem situation as well as on information collected from individuals directly involved in this situation, such as teachers and students. The researcher engages actively and directly in the context of his research and remains at the heart of the action, collaborating closely with the stakeholders concerned (Anderson & Shattuck, 2012). For this ongoing project, we first carried out a literature review on learning in a large group context, cognitive engagement and e-assessment methods. We then contacted the professor collaborating on the research to discuss the topic and understand his perspective. Finally, we examined in detail the course curriculum, the teaching approaches and the assessment methods, as well as the course objectives in order to understand all aspects of it.

The iterative process

DBR is a research approach that involves an iterative process to create and implement a prototype to solve a problem experienced in the context of learning. The number of iterations in DBR is variable, between 2 (Ozverir, Osam, & Herrington, 2017), or 3 (Kim, Suh, & Song, 2015) and up to 5 iterations (Vanderhoven, Schellens, Vanderlinde, & Valcke, 2016). Indeed, before considering a prototype as complete, various tests and adjustments are carried out (Bannan, 2009).

The iterative process can take various forms (Amiel & Reeves, 2008), however its objective always remains to explore, adjust and continuously improve prototypes and solutions, while ensuring the quality of the research conducted (Mandran, Prior, & Vermeulen, 2020). This project includes two iterations that are deployed in several phases.

Sample and context

The project takes place in a fourth-session mathematics teaching course at the Higher School of Education and Training of Chouaib Doukali El Jadida University for second-year students specializing in primary education. The course is offered to two groups and has a total of 139 students. Of this number, group number 1 of 71 students, including ten boys, is subjected to a formal formative e-assessment via the Quizizz application, in the form of a quiz, for 18 hours of lessons divided into 12 sessions of 1h30min each. The other group, number 2, is made up of 68 students, including eight boys, and is subjected to an informal formative assessment for 12 lessons as well.

This course is taught by the same professor in two different time slots. The teaching strategy adopted by the professor is the lecture.

The tests are constructed based on the manual designed by the professor and which is communicated to the students at the beginning of the first course. These courses are considered as material for the final exams. After each course, a quarter of an hour is allocated for a formative e-assessment in the form of a quiz.

Data collection tools

Data collection was done using two tools:

- The Cognitive Engagement Questionnaire (Leduc, Kozanitis and Lepage, 2018);
- Two group interviews of ten students each.

We opted for a mixed research in order to acquire an in-depth and broad understanding of the contribution of e-assessment on the cognitive engagement of students in a large group context, which allowed us to collect a lot of factual information.

Data collection was done using two tools:

1) The cognitive engagement questionnaire (Leduc, Kozanitis and Lepage, 2018);
2) Two group interviews of 10 students each.

Our questionnaire is intended for students of the El Jadida Higher School of Education and Training, it allowed us to interview a larger number of individuals, which allows us to collect data from several sources. However, among the 139 questionnaires distributed, only 128 students responded to our survey.

Our questionnaire aims to measure students' cognitive engagement with e-assessment via the Quizizz application, in order to verify its influence on their cognitive engagement as students. The choice fell on the cognitive engagement scale questionnaire by Miller et al. (1996), whose French translation has recently been validated (Leduc, Kozanitis and Lepage, 2018).

This questionnaire allows us to measure the following four dimensions of cognitive engagement:

1- Learning strategies used (surface or deep);
2- Self-regulation skills;
3- Perseverance in study and efforts deployed;
4- Situational cognitive engagement.

29 items, constructed on a 6-level Likert scale ranging from "totally disagree" to "strongly agree", are associated with these dimensions.

The analysis of the internal consistency of the items of our questionnaire reveals a strong association between them for the four dimensions of cognitive engagement. According to the significant values of Cronbach's alpha presented in Table 1, it is very clear that the items of this questionnaire constitute a coherent whole.

Table 1. Reliability statistics

Variables	Cronbach's Alpha	Cronbach's Alpha Based on Standardized Items	Number of Items
In-depth cognitive strategies	0.762	0.771	6
Surface cognitive strategies	0.719	0.732	9
Self-regulation	0.634	0.640	5

continued on following page

Table 1. Continued

Variables	Cronbach's Alpha	Cronbach's Alpha Based on Standardized Items	Number of Items
Perseverance	0.813	0.819	5
Situational engagement	0.917	0.921	4

In addition, the choice of the interview in our research is explained by the fact that this research device is frequently used in action research, and allows us to collect specific data (Baribeau, 2009). Similarly, group interviews require less time, encourage expression on "sensitive" subjects and allow social representations to emerge (Baribeau & Germain, 2010). This technique allows to artificially create a framework of social interactions where participants can express common or divergent points of view on a specific subject (Morgan, 1996).

The group interview was chosen in our research in order to explore students' perceptions of the learning context experienced and their experience of formal and informal formative assessment.

Two group interviews with six students each were conducted. The choice of the number of participants was based on the recommendations of the researchers, who estimate that the ideal number of group interviews is between six and twelve participants (Davila & Domínguez, 2010).

The group interviews lasted two hours: one hour for each group.

Result

To test our research hypothesis, we adopted the Mann-Whitney U test, because the conditions for using parametric tests are not verified due to the non-normality of the study variables.

Tables 2, 3, 4, 5 and 6 present the cognitive engagement test according to its five dimensions, carried out on students from the two groups: the control group and the experimental group.

The influence of E-assessment on cognitive engagement on the side of:

- Deep cognitive strategies
- Surface cognitive strategies;
- Self-regulation;
- Perseverance;
- Situational engagement

was tested using the Mann-Whitney U test.

Table 2. In-depth cognitive strategies

Items	Group	N	Mean Rank	Sum of Ranks	Mann-Whitney U	P
Before a quiz or exam, I plan how I'll study the material	2	68	36,49	2481,00	135,00	0.00
	1	71	102,10	7249,00		
	Total	139				
When I finish an assignment, I check for errors.	2	68	37,49	2549,50	203,50	0.00
	1	71	101,13	7180,50		
	Total	139				
I organize my study time well for this course	2	68	42,04	2858,50	512,50	0.00
	1	71	96,78	6871,50		
	Total	139				
I make memory cards to prepare for assessments	2	68	35,14	2389,50	43,50	0.00
	1	71	103,39	7340,50		
	Total	139				
When I'm having trouble with an assignment, I tend to try and guess the answer instead of looking in books to try and understand it.	2	68	64,82	4408,00	2062,00	0,12
	1	71	74,96	5322,00		
	Total	139				
When I study, I compare and distinguish between different concepts.	2	68	77,47	5268,00	1906,00	0,02
	1	71	62,85	4462,00		
	Total	139				

According to the results mentioned in Table 2, E-assessment has a significant impact on the deep learning strategy dimension of cognitive engagement with respect to the following items: "Before a quiz or exam, I plan how I will study the material" [Mann-Whitney U = 135.00; P = 0.000 < 0.05], "When I finish an assignment, I check for mistakes" [Mann-Whitney U = 203.50; P = 0.000 < 0.05], "I organize my study time well for this course" [Mann-Whitney U = 512.50; P = 0.000 < 0.05], "I make flashcards to prepare for assessments" [Mann-Whitney U = 43.50; P = 0.000 < 0.05], "When I study, I compare and distinguish between different concepts" [Mann-Whitney U = 1906.00; P = 0.02 < 0.05].

For the item "When I have difficulty with an assignment, I tend to try to guess the answer instead of looking in books to try to understand" [Mann-Whitney U = 2062.00; P = 0.12 > 0.05], the result is not significant and would be considered random.

Table 3. Cognitive strategies on the surface

Items	Group	N	Mean Rank	Sum of Ranks	Mann-Whitney U	P
I find that the best way to pass the assessments is to anticipate the questions and try to remember the answers.	2	68	88,43	6013,50	1160,500	0.00
	1	71	52,35	3716,50		
	Total	139				
If I have trouble doing an assignment in the book, I copy the answer at the end of the book if it's there.	2	68	104,49	7105,50	68,500	0.00
	1	71	36,96	2624,50		
	Total	139				
Highlighting with a marker is a good way to prepare for assessments	2	68	47,40	3223,50	877,500	0.00
	1	71	91,64	6506,50		
	Total	139				
I try to memorize the answers to the questions in the revision documents so that I can the test	2	68	105,14	7149,50	24,500	0.00
	1	71	36,35	2580,50		
	Total	139				
When I learn new concepts, I try to think of applications practices.	2	68	43,95	2988,50	642,500	0.00
	1	71	94,95	6741,50		
	Total	139				
When I have trouble doing my homework, I try to find someone to do it for me.	2	68	104,04	7074,50	99,500	0.00
	1	71	37,40	2655,50		
	Total	139				
When I'm studying, I try to combine the various elements of the material in a way that makes sense to me new	2	68	66,46	4519,50	2173,500	0,297
	1	71	73,39	5210,50		
	Total	139				
To learn is to store information with a view to reproducing it.	2	68	94,10	6399,00	775,000	0.00
	1	71	46,92	3331,00		
	Total	139				
I mentally organize different information from the course in an order that makes sense meaning for me	2	68	49,03	3334,00	988,000	0.00
	1	71	90,08	6396,00		
	Total	139				

According to the results reported in Table 3, E-assessment has a significant impact on the surface cognitive strategies dimension of cognitive engagement with respect to the following items: "I find that the best way to succeed on assessments is to anticipate the questions and try to remember the answers" [Mann-Whitney U = 1160.500; $P = 0.000 < 0.05$], "If I have difficulty doing an assignment in the book, I copy the answer from the back of the book if it is there" [Mann-Whitney U = 68.500; $P = 0.000 < 0.05$], "Highlighting with a marker is a good way to prepare for assessments" [Mann-Whitney U = 877.500; $P = 0.000 < 0.05$], "I try to memorize the answers to the questions on the review materials for the exam"

[Mann-Whitney U = 24.500; P = 0.000 < 0.05], "When I learn new concepts, I try to think of practical applications." [Mann-Whitney U = 642.500; P = 0.000 < 0.05], "When I have difficulty doing my homework, I try to get someone to do it for me" [Mann-Whitney U = 99.500; P = 0.000 < 0.05], "Learning is storing information with a view to reproducing it" [Mann-Whitney U = 775.000; P = 0.000 < 0.05], "I mentally organize different pieces of information from the course in an order that makes sense to me" [Mann-Whitney U = 988.000; P = 0.000 < 0.05]. For the item "When I study, I try to combine the various elements of the material in a new way" [Mann-Whitney U = 2173.500; P = 0.297 > 0.05], the result is not significant and would be considered random.

Table 4. Self-regulation skills

Items	Group	N	Mean Rank	Sum of Ranks	Mann-Whitney U	P
When I read something in the book that I don't understand, I move on thing and I hope the teacher explains it in class.	2	68	101,62	6910,00	264,000	0.00
	1	71	39,72	2820,00		
	Total	139				
During assessments, I get by memorizing key elements rather than try to understand them	2	68	34,88	2372,00	26,000	0.00
	1	71	103,63	7358,00		
	Total	139				
I have evaluated the usefulness of the ideas presented in this course	2	68	35,17	2391,50	45,500	0.00
	1	71	103,36	7338,50		
	Total	139				
I try to think of a strategy before I start my homework or studying.	2	68	36,04	2451,00	105,000	0.00
	1	71	102,52	7279,00		
	Total	139				
I try to think of a strategy before starting homework or studying	2	68	35,70	2427,50	81,500	0.00
	1	71	102,85	7302,50		
	Total	139				

According to the results mentioned in the table, the E-assessment has a significant impact on the perseverance dimension of cognitive engagement with regard to the following items:

- When I read something I don't understand in the book, I move on and hope the teacher explains it in class [U = 264.000; P = 0.00]: Group 2 has a significantly higher mean rank than Group 1, indicating that members of Group 2 are more likely to move on when they encounter difficulties in their learning, relying on the teacher to clarify in class. The difference is statistically significant (p = 0.00), suggesting a marked tendency of Group 2 toward this learning strategy.

- When taking assessments, I cope by memorizing key elements rather than trying to understand them [U = 26.000; P = 0.00]: The difference in mean ranks is significant, indicating that Group 1 adopts learning strategies based on understanding rather than simple memorization when taking assessments, compared to Group 2.
- I rated the usefulness of the ideas presented in this course [U = 45.500; P = 0.00]: The result of this test indicates that Group 1 uses a more thoughtful approach to assessing course content.
- I believe that a good way to study for an exam is to review examples seen in the book or seen in class [U = 105.00; P = 0.00]: Group 1 has a higher mean rank than Group 2, indicating that members of Group 1 believe more in reviewing examples as an effective method of studying for exams. The difference is statistically significant (p = 0.00), reflecting a preference of Group 1 for this method of study.
- I try to think of a strategy before starting my homework or studying [U = 81.500; P = 0.00]: There is a statistically significant difference (p = 0.00) between two groups in their tendency to think of a strategy before starting their homework or studying, indicating that group 1 uses a well-thought-out and adequate strategy before starting studies.

In summary, for all the items analyzed, the differences between the groups are significant. Group 1 is distinguished by a greater use of active and deep learning strategies, while group 2 adopts less engaging methods, such as memorization and giving up in the face of difficulties.

Table 5. Perseverance

Items	Group	N	Mean Rank	Sum of Ranks	Mann-Whitney U	P
If I'm having trouble with an assignment, I persevere until I get it right.	2	68	34,80	2366,50	20,500	**0.00**
	1	71	103,71	7363,50		
	Total	139				
I learn new material by mentally linking new ideas with similar ones I already know.	2	68	35,02	2381,50	35,500	**0.00**
	1	71	103,50	7348,50		
	Total	139				
I make sure I understand what I'm studying	2	68	35,18	2392,50	46,500	**0.00**
	1	71	103,35	7337,50		
	Total	139				

continued on following page

Table 5. Continued

Items	Group	N	Mean Rank	Sum of Ranks	Mann-Whitney U	P
I read the course texts mainly to get the information I need for the exam.	2	68	104,44	7102,00	72,000	0.00
	1	71	37,01	2628,00		
	Total	139				
I learn certain elements by heart, repeating them several times.	2	68	36,19	2461,00	115,000	0.00
	1	71	102,38	7269,00		
	Total	139				

According to the results mentioned in Table 2.15, the E-assessment has a significant impact on the perseverance dimension of cognitive engagement with regard to the following items:

- If I have difficulty with an assignment, I persevere until I succeed in understanding [U = 20.500; P = 0.00]: Group 1 presents a significantly higher mean rank than Group 2, which indicates that members of Group 1 are more persevering than members of Group 2 and adopt a more resilient attitude in the face of academic difficulties.
- I learn new material by mentally connecting new ideas with similar ideas that I already know [U = 35.500; P = 0.00]: The difference is significant (p = 0.00), showing that Group 1 uses more integrative and connective learning strategies. However, Group 2 is less likely to connect new ideas to pre-existing knowledge to learn.
- I make sure I understand what I am studying [U = 46.500; P = 0.00]: Group 1 focuses more on deep understanding of the material studied. The difference is statistically significant (p = 0.00), suggesting a stronger engagement in understanding concepts by this group.
- It is mainly to have the necessary information for the exam that I read the course texts [U = 72.000; P = 0.00]: Group 2 has a significantly higher mean rank than Group 1, indicating that Group 2 mainly reads the course texts to obtain specific information for the exams. The difference is statistically significant (p = 0.00), showing a tendency for Group 2 to focus more on short-term preparation rather than on overall understanding.
- I learn some items by heart by repeating them several times [U = 115.000; P = 0.00]: Group 1 has a higher mean rank than Group 2, suggesting that members of Group 1 are more willing to use repetition to memorize items. The difference is significant (p = 0.00), so Group 1 has a more repetition- and memorization-oriented approach.

To conclude, the results show that group 1 adopts more in-depth and active learning strategies, such as persistence in the face of difficulties, deep understanding, and connecting new ideas with existing knowledge. In contrast, group 2 seems more focused on exam preparation strategies, such as repetition to memorize course elements.

Table 6. Situational commitment

Items	Group	N	Mean Rank	Sum of Ranks	Mann-Whitney U	P
I am committed to the tasks of this course	2	68	40,61	2761,50	415,500	0.00
	1	71	98,15	6968,50		
	Total	139				
I invest a lot of intellectual effort in this course	2	68	35,71	2428,00	82,000	0.00
	1	71	102,85	7302,00		
	Total	139				
I would like to be able to continue the work undertaken in this course for another year moment	2	68	36,19	2461,00	115,000	0.00
	1	71	102,38	7269,00		
	Total	139				
I'm so involved in this course that I've forgotten everything around me.	2	68	35,43	2409,50	63,500	0.00
	1	71	103,11	7320,50		
	Total	139				

According to the results mentioned in the table, the E-assessment has a significant impact on the situational engagement dimension of cognitive engagement with regard to the following items:

- I am engaged in the tasks to be completed in this course [U = 415.000; P = 0.00]: Group 1 has a significantly higher mean rank than group 2, which reveals that they are much more engaged in the tasks to be completed in the course than the students in group 2. The difference is highly significant ($p < 0.001$).
- I invest a lot of intellectual effort in this course [U = 82.000; P = 0.00]: Group 1 again has a significantly higher mean rank than group 2, which shows that students in group 1 deploy much more intellectual effort in the course compared to group 2. The difference is highly significant ($p < 0.001$).
- I would like to be able to continue the work undertaken in this course for a while longer [U = 115.000; P = 0.00]: The difference is highly significant ($p < 0.001$), meaning that students in group 1 are more interested in continuing the work in this course than those in group 2.

- I am so involved in this course that I forget everything around me [U = 63.500; P = 0.00]: While there is a difference between the two groups, students in Group 1 are more likely to feel deeply involved in the course to the point of forgetting their surroundings, compared to students in Group 2.

For all four items measured, group 1 has significantly higher mean ranks than group 2. This indicates that group 1 is overall more engaged, invested and involved in the course, both in terms of tasks to be accomplished and intellectual efforts, perseverance or immersion in learning. All results show a statistically highly significant difference ($p < 0.001$), demonstrating a marked distinction between the two groups.

Table 7. Comparative table of responses from two groups

Thèmes	Groupe témoin Groupe 2	Groupe d'expérience Groupe 1
Type d'apprentissage	Sept étudiants se concentrent sur la mémorisation sans chercher à comprendre en profondeur. Une étudiante privilégie la prise de notes pour réussir l'examen sans comprendre le contenu. Deux étudiants révisent intensivement avant l'examen sans comprendre le cours en profondeur	Cinq étudiants établissent des liens entre les nouvelles informations et les connaissances antérieures. Trois étudiants prennent le temps d'analyser le cours en profondeur pour comprendre ses nuances et ses implications Deux étudiants discutent du cours avec leurs pairs ou leur professeur pour renforcer leur compréhension
Autorégulation	Un étudiant déclare une perte de concentration fréquentes pour des raisons personnelles. Sept étudiants soulignent que la monotonie du cours entraîne des distractions. Deux étudiants hésitent à poser des questions au professeur par timidité devant leurs camarades	Six étudiants soulignent qu'ils demandent d'explications supplémentaires au professeur en cas de difficultés. Deux étudiants affirment relier le cours avec leurs intérêts personnels. Un étudiant planifie et élabore un emploi du temps et le suivre rigoureusement. Un étudiant souligne qu'il fixe d'objectifs et utilise des stratégies d'auto-motivation
Rétroaction	Six étudiants estiment que la rétroaction fournie par les professeurs lors des évaluations formatives est trop succincte pour les aider à progresser au contraire s'elle était plus détaillée et plus fréquente elle serait bénéfique. Trois étudiants déclarent que la rétroaction actuelle ne répond pas à leurs besoins individuels. Un étudiant aurait préféré plus d'occasions de discuter individuellement avec le professeur	Neuf étudiants confirment que la rétroaction immédiate pendant la E-évaluation s'est avérée pertinente, en les aidant à renforcer leurs compétences académiques. Un étudiant affirme que la rétroaction l'a aidé à cibler ses efforts d'étude.

continued on following page

Table 7. Continued

Thèmes	Groupe témoin Groupe 2	Groupe d'expérience Groupe 1
Affects	Huit étudiants ne ressentent pas de changement significatif dans leur engagement cognitif avec l'évaluation formative informelle. Deux étudiants n'ont pas d'opinion claire sur cet impact	Les dix étudiants confirment que la E-évaluation formative les a aidés à comprendre les concepts en profondeur et à identifier leurs lacunes. Ils considèrent ces quiz comme un outil utile leur permettant à ajuster leur méthode d'étude, en réduisant le stress habituellement associé aux évaluations.
Appréciation générale	Les dix étudiants s'accordent sur le fait que l'évaluation formative informelle est jugée importante, mais insuffisante pour une réelle aide à l'apprentissage.	La E-évaluation formative est appréciée par les dix étudiants interviewés et soulignent que les quiz hebdomadaires rendent leur apprentissage plus efficace

The results of this table, after comparing the responses of the two groups (control group and experimental group) according to the different themes studied: type of learning, self-regulation, feedback, affective aspects and general appreciation show that for:

- Type of learning: Students in the experimental group appear to adopt a more in-depth and reflective approach to learning compared to the control group, which could be related to the assessment method used in the Experimental Group.
- Self-regulation: The experimental group demonstrated a better self-regulation capacity compared to the control group, which could reflect a positive impact of the assessment methods adopted.
- Feedback: The experimental group receives more relevant and constructive feedback, which could contribute to a relevant promotion of a better understanding of courses and higher academic performance compared to the control group.
- Affect: Formative e-assessment appears to have a greater positive impact on cognitive engagement and emotions associated with assessment in the experience group.
- General assessment: The assessment method used in the experimental group is widely appreciated and considered more effective and efficient compared to the non-formal formative assessment of the control group.

The exploitation of this interview suggests that the experimental group demonstrates a better understanding of the content, a reinforced self-regulation, a more constructive feedback, as well as a more favorable cognitive engagement compared to the control group after having benefited from the E-assessment which indicates that this method of assessment is more effective to support learning and improve the performance of the students.

Discussion

This study aims to examine the impact of formative e-assessment on students' cognitive engagement in large group settings at university. The results, as presented in Tables 2 to 6, show that most of the items studied have a p-value less than 0.001, with the exception of two items. These statistically significant results confirm the hypothesis that e-assessment has a significant effect on students' cognitive engagement.

Previous research has demonstrated that integrating information and communication technologies (ICT) into teaching improves student engagement and academic achievement (Saunders & Klemming, 2003). These findings are consistent with our results: students in the experimental group, who used e-assessment, obtained overall better grades than those in the control group, who followed informal assessments. This performance differential was rigorously measured, and analysis of the results reveals that e-assessment contributes to greater cognitive involvement of students.

As a pedagogical practice, assessment (including e-assessment) constitutes an essential lever in improving learning processes (Talbot, 2009). In particular, the interactivity specific to e-assessment reinforces learners' self-regulation processes (Bedin & Broussal, 2011), a dimension that our results confirm. Students subjected to e-assessment tend to adopt deep learning strategies, valuing the construction of knowledge and the development of sustainable skills (Jouquan & Parent, 2013). Conversely, students in the control group, who were subjected to informal assessment, often adopted a more superficial approach, focusing more on getting good grades than on acquiring knowledge.

Regarding perseverance, the questionnaire shows that students in the experimental group, who benefited from e-assessment, show greater persistence in the face of learning challenges, unlike students in the control group. Those in the experimental group actively pursue their cognitive and affective efforts, even in the presence of obstacles, demonstrating a continued commitment to the learning process (Pintrinch & Schunk, 2002).

For situational engagement, students assessed via Quizizz report that this assessment modality motivates them to be more involved in class. On the other hand, those who took informal assessments seem less engaged, being mainly concerned with succeeding with minimal effort.

Finally, the interviews reveal that feedback is perceived as crucial in both groups. However, students in the experimental group believe that feedback provided via e-assessment is more effective because of its immediacy, which allows them to quickly adjust their study efforts. Conversely, students in the control group find that feedback from informal assessments, although potentially relevant, is too succinct and takes longer to deliver, reducing its usefulness in their progress.

In summary, the combined analysis of the questionnaire and interviews highlights that e-assessment has a significant impact on students' cognitive engagement in all dimensions explored by this study, compared to informal assessment.

CONCLUSION

This article presents the results of a mixed research, which aimed to examine the influence of formative e-assessment on the cognitive engagement of university students, in a large group context. Through a rigorous methodology combining quantitative and qualitative analyses, we explored this question by formulating a hypothesis according to which e-assessment would promote deeper cognitive engagement among students.

After having presented the problem and defined our theoretical framework, the analysis of the results confirms that formative e-assessment constitutes an effective pedagogical lever to refocus teaching on learning, particularly in environments with a high student density. Our results demonstrate that e-assessment encourages students to adopt in-depth learning strategies and to self-regulate their study behavior, particularly when preparing for exams.

The use of Quizizz, a central tool in this research, has allowed to create an interactive and engaging learning environment. However, it is important to emphasize that Quizizz does not represent a universal or exclusive solution. It is one tool among a multitude of other available platforms, such as Kahoot, Blackboard Learn, ProProfs Quiz Maker, Socrative or Edmodo, which can also contribute to the implementation of dynamic e-assessment devices. These technologies, when used thoughtfully, allow to diversify assessment methods and to engage students more actively in their learning.

In conclusion, this study makes a significant contribution to understanding the impact of formative e-assessment in higher education, particularly in large group contexts. It shows that e-assessment is not only an assessment tool, but also a pedagogical practice that encourages students to actively engage in their learning, develop self-regulation skills, and adopt deep cognitive strategies. These results reinforce the idea that the integration of educational technologies can positively transform pedagogical practices and improve students' cognitive engagement.

Limitations of the study and suggestions for future research

The integration of ICT in the teaching-learning-assessment process in higher education has become crucial, as it plays a fundamental role in motivating students and stimulating their cognitive engagement, especially through formative assessment, whether through applications or university platforms. This approach allows the teacher to have a clear vision of the individual progress of each student while providing them with immediate feedback, thus promoting more effective self-regulation.

However, this study has some limitations that are important to mention. First, a significant number of teachers have difficulty integrating digital tools into their teaching practices, particularly in the context of formative assessment. This situation mainly stems from a lack of adequate training in educational technologies, which limits the effectiveness of the approach. Furthermore, although e-assessment relies on the use of digital tools, it poses challenges for some students, particularly regarding access to smartphones and stable internet connection, which are essential conditions to fully participate in these assessments. These factors can therefore create disparities in access to e-assessment and limit its positive impact on cognitive engagement, particularly in environments where access to technologies remains unequal.

REFERENCES

Age, I. L. (2018). L'influence D'une E-Évaluation Dynamique Sur L'engagement Cognitif D'étudiants En Contexte De Grand Groupe À L'université.

Amiel, T., & Reeves, T. C. (2008). Design-based research and educational technology: Rethinking technology and the research agenda. *Journal of Educational Technology & Society*, *11*(4), 29–40.

Anderson, T., & Shattuck, J. (2012). Design-based research: A decade of progress in education research? *Educational Researcher*, *41*(1), 16–25. DOI: 10.3102/0013189X11428813

Baeten, M., Kyndt, E., Struyven, K., & Dochy, F. (2010). Using student-centred learning environments to stimulate deep approaches to learning: Factors encouraging or discouraging their effectiveness. *Educational Research Review*, *5*(3), 243–260. DOI: 10.1016/j.edurev.2010.06.001

Bailey, T. R. (2005). Paths to persistence: An analysis of research on program effectiveness at community colleges.

Bannan, B. (2009). The integrative learning design framework: An illustrated example from the domain of instructional technology. An introduction to educational design research, 53-73.

Baribeau, C. (2009). Analyse des données des entretiens de groupe. *Recherches Qualitatives*, *28*(1), 133–148. DOI: 10.7202/1085324ar

Baribeau, C., & Germain, M. (2010). L'entretien de groupe: Considérations théoriques et méthodologiques. *Recherches Qualitatives*, *29*(1), 28–49. DOI: 10.7202/1085131ar

Bedin, V., & Broussal, D. (2011). L'évaluation interactive des apprentissages dans l'enseignement supérieur: intérêt pédagogique et limites. Les dossiers des sciences de l'éducation, (26), 133-144.

Biggs, J., & Tang, C. (2011). Teaching for Quality Learning at University: What the Student Does. Open University Press (4e éd.). New-York: USA.

Blais, S. (2023). L'évaluation dynamique en mathématiques: des avantages et des limites de l'utilisation de cette approche auprès d'un élève du 2e cycle du primaire en difficulté d'apprentissage.

Boucher, C. (2015). La rétroaction: élément phare pour l'apprentissage de nos étudiants. Le tableau, 4(3).

Boud, D., & Molloy, E. (2013). Rethinking models of feedback for learning: The challenge of design. *Assessment & Evaluation in Higher Education*, *38*(6), 698–712. DOI: 10.1080/02602938.2012.691462

Brown, A. L. (1992). Design experiments: Theoretical and methodological challenges in creating complex interventions in classroom settings. *Journal of the Learning Sciences*, *2*(2), 141–178. DOI: 10.1207/s15327809jls0202_2

Burguete, E. (2021). Proposition d'une méthodologie de conception et d'évaluation d'un SPOC en microlearning. Adjectif: analyses et recherches sur les TICE, 2021(1).

Chaiyo, Y., & Nokham, R. (2017, March). The effect of Kahoot, Quizizz and Google Forms on the student's perception in the classrooms response system. In 2017 International conference on digital arts, media and technology (ICDAMT) (pp. 178-182). IEEE.

Coates, H. B. (2008). Attracting, engaging and retaining: New conversations about learning.

Collins, A., Joseph, D., & Bielaczyc, K. (2016). Design research: Theoretical and methodological issues. In *Design-based Research* (pp. 15–42). Psychology Press.

Cuseo, J. (2007). *The Empirical Case Against Large Class Size: Adverse Effects on the Teaching*. Learning, and Retention of First-Year Students.

[] Daele, A., & Berthiaume, D. (2010). Choisir ses stratégies d'enseignement.

Davila, A., & Domínguez, M. (2010). Formats des groupes et types de discussion dans la recherche sociale qualitative. *Recherches Qualitatives*, *29*(1), 50–68. DOI: 10.7202/1085132ar

Dinsmore, D. L., & Alexander, P. A. (2012). A critical discussion of deep and surface processing: What it means, how it is measured, the role of context, and model specification. *Educational Psychology Review*, *24*(4), 499–567. DOI: 10.1007/s10648-012-9198-7

Doan, B. K. V. (2021). Quels motifs amènent des professeurs d'université à mettre en place des pratiques pédagogiques non magistrales dans le contexte de l'enseignement à de grands groupes?.

Ernoult, M., & Talamoni, C. (2006). Le QCM: un outil pour la formation et l'évaluation. Bulletin vert de l'APMEP, (462).

Farrell, T., & Rushby, N. (2016). Assessment and learning technologies: An overview. *British Journal of Educational Technology*, *47*(1), 106–120. DOI: 10.1111/bjet.12348

Fauré, L. (2017). Co-enseignement et développement professionnel des enseignants en agroéquipements de l'enseignement agricole (Doctoral dissertation, Université Toulouse le Mirail-Toulouse II).

Figari, G. (1994). *Évaluer: quel référentiel?* De Boeck.

Fréchette, S. (2008). Autorégulation de l'apprentissage de l'exercice du rôle de soutien à la motivation de l'élève au secondaire dans le cadre de la formation des enseignants (Doctoral dissertation, Université du Québec à Montréal).

Glazer, N. (2014). Formative plus Summative Assessment in Large Undergraduate Courses: Why Both? *International Journal on Teaching and Learning in Higher Education*, *26*(2), 276–286.

Greenberg, K. H. (2000). Inside professional practice: A collaborative, systems orientation to linking dynamic assessment and intervention. Dynamic assessment: Prevailing models and applications, 489-519.

Greene, B. A. (2015). Measuring cognitive engagement with self-report scales: Reflections from over 20 years of research. *Educational Psychologist*, *50*(1), 14–30. DOI: 10.1080/00461520.2014.989230

Greene, J. A., & Azevedo, R. (2010). The measurement of learners' self-regulated cognitive and metacognitive processes while using computer-based learning environments. *Educational Psychologist*, *45*(4), 203–209. DOI: 10.1080/00461520.2010.515935

Hamdan, Y. (2022). L'innovation dans l'enseignement supérieur marocain au temps de la digitalisation: Bilan, défis et perspectives. *Revue Marocaine de Didactique et Pédagogie*, *2*(1).

Jiao, H. (2015). Enhancing students' engagement in learning through a formative e-assessment tool that motivates students to take action on feedback. *Australasian Journal of Engineering Education*, *20*(1), 9–18. DOI: 10.7158/D13-002.2015.20.1

Jouquan, J., & Parent, F. (2013). *Les enjeux épistémologiques et méthodologiques de l'évaluation des pratiques professionnelles en santé. Parent F, Jouquan J. Penser la formation des professionnels de la santé. Une perspective intégrative*. De Boeck.

Ju, S. Y., & Adam, Z. (2018). Implementing Quizizz as game based learning in the Arabic classroom. *European Journal of Social Science Education and Research*, *5*(1), 194–198. DOI: 10.26417/ejser.v12i1.p208-212

Kaaouachi, A. (2004). Evaluation des acquis des étudiants dans l'université marocaine. *Prospecfive Pédagogique*, *27*, 37–41.

Kaaouachi, A. (2010). L'évaluation dans le système d'enseignement supérieur au Maroc: Bilan des réalisations, limites et principaux défis. Towards an Arab Higher Education Space: International Challenges and Societal Responsibilities, 409-422.

Kerr, A. (2011). L'enseignement et l'apprentissage dans les classes nombreuses des universités ontariennes: Teaching and learning in large classes at Ontario universities: an exploratory study.

Kiesler, C. A. (1971). The psychology of commitment: Experiments linking behavior to belief.

Kim, P., Suh, E., & Song, D. (2015). Development of a design-based learning curriculum through design-based research for a technology-enabled science classroom. *Educational Technology Research and Development*, *63*(4), 575–602. DOI: 10.1007/s11423-015-9376-7

Kozanitis, A. (2021). Évaluation des apprentissages en formation à distance: les situations authentiques à la rescousse. Revue internationale des technologies en pédagogie universitaire, 18(1), 276-290.

Leduc, D., Kozanitis, A., & Lepage, I. (2018). L'engagement cognitif en contexte postsecondaire: Traduction, adaptation et validation d'une échelle de mesure. *McGill Journal of Education*, *53*(3). Advance online publication. DOI: 10.7202/1058412ar

Lepage, I. (2018). L'influence d'une e-évaluation dynamique sur l'engagement cognitif d'étudiants en contexte de grand groupe à l'université.

Leung, C. (2007). Dynamic assessment: Assessment for and as teaching? *Language Assessment Quarterly*, *4*(3), 257–278. DOI: 10.1080/15434300701481127

Lison, C. (2011). *Programmes innovants en formation des enseignants du secondaire: perceptions, conceptions et pratiques*. Université de Sherbrooke.

Lison, C., Bédard, D., Beaucher, C., & Trudelle, D. (2014). De l'innovation à un modèle de dynamique innovationnelle en enseignement supérieur. Revue internationale de pédagogie de l'enseignement supérieur, 30(30 (1)).

Mandran, N., Planche, M., Marzin-Janvier, P., Vermeulen, M., Karoui, A., Ham, C. D., & Hoffmann, C. (2021). Comment construire un processus d'évaluation en EIAH fondé sur le Design-Based Research? *Sciences et Technologies de l'Information et de la Communication pour l'Éducation et la Formation*, *28*(1), 139–168.

Mandran, N., Prior, E., & Vermeulen, M. (2020). Comment outiller la méthode Design-Based-Research?.

Martell, K. (2007). Assessing student learning: Are business schools making the grade? *Journal of Education for Business, 82*(4), 189–195. DOI: 10.3200/JOEB.82.4.189-195

Mastafi, M., & Bouhlou, H. (2016). Intégration des TIC dans l'enseignement supérieur marocain: réflexions et perspectives. Penser les TIC dans les universités du Maghreb.

McKeachie, W. J. (1978). *Teaching tips: A guidebook for the beginning college teacher*. DC Heath.

Miller, R. B., Greene, B. A., Montalvo, G. P., Ravindran, B., & Nichols, J. D. (1996). Engagement in academic work: The role of learning goals, future consequences, pleasing others, and perceived ability. *Contemporary Educational Psychology, 21*(4), 388–422. DOI: 10.1006/ceps.1996.0028 PMID: 8979871

Ministry of Higher Education, Scientific Research, and Innovation. (2025). *Official website of the Ministry of Higher Education, Scientific Research, and Innovation*. https://www.enssup.gov.ma/fr

Morgan, D. L. (1996). *Focus groups as qualitative research* (Vol. 16). Sage publications.

Ozverir, I., Osam, U. V., & Herrington, J. (2017). Investigating the effects of authentic activities on foreign language learning: A design-based research approach. *Journal of Educational Technology & Society, 20*(4), 261–274.

Pintrich, P. R. (2004). A conceptual framework for assessing motivation and self-regulated learning in college students. *Educational Psychology Review, 16*(4), 385–407. DOI: 10.1007/s10648-004-0006-x

Pintrinch, P. R., & Schunk, D. H. (2002). *Motivation in education : theory, research, and applications*. Merrill Prentice Hall.

Rahayu, I. S. D., & Purnawarman, P. (2019, June). The use of Quizizz in improving students' grammar understanding through self-assessment. In *Eleventh Conference on Applied Linguistics (CONAPLIN 2018)* (pp. 102-106). Atlantis Press.

Reeves, T. C. (2000). Enhancing the worth of instructional technology research through "design experiments" and other development research strategies. International perspectives on instructional technology research for the 21st century, 27(1), 1-15.

Sanchez, É., & Monod-Ansaldi, R. (2015). Recherche collaborative orientée par la conception: Un paradigme méthodologique pour prendre en compte la complexité des situations d'enseignement-apprentissage. Éducation et didactique, 2, 73-94.

Saunders, G., & Klemming, F. (2003). Integrating technology into a traditional learning environment: Reasons for and risks of success. *Active Learning in Higher Education*, *4*(1), 74–86. DOI: 10.1177/1469787403004001006

Talbot, L. (2009). *L'évaluation formative: comment évaluer pour remédier aux difficultés d'apprentissage*. Armand Colin.

Tardif, J. (2015). La construction des connaissances. 2, Les pratiques pédagogiques. v. 11, no 3, mars 1998, p. 4-9 Pédagogie collégiale.

Timmis, S., Broadfoot, P., Sutherland, R., & Oldfield, A. (2016). Rethinking assessment in a digital age: Opportunities, challenges and risks. *British Educational Research Journal*, *42*(3), 454–476. DOI: 10.1002/berj.3215

Timmis, S., Broadfoot, P., Sutherland, R. et Oldfield, A. (2016). Repenser l'évaluation à l'ère numérique: opportunités, défis et risques. Journal britannique de recherche pédagogique, 42 (3), 454-476.

Vanderhoven, E., Schellens, T., Vanderlinde, R., & Valcke, M. (2016). Developing educational materials about risks on social network sites: A design based research approach. *Educational Technology Research and Development*, *64*(3), 459–480. DOI: 10.1007/s11423-015-9415-4

Verlot, M., & Suijs, S. (2000). L'apprentissage pragmatique de l'interculturel. *Diversité*, *120*(1), 111–125.

Wang, F., & Hannafin, M. J. (2005). Design-based research and technology-enhanced learning environments. *Educational Technology Research and Development*, *53*(4), 5–23. DOI: 10.1007/BF02504682

Youssef, L., Chemsi, G., & Radid, M. (2023). The Effect of Group Size on Students' Cognitive and Behavioral Engagement. *International Journal of Emerging Technologies in Learning*, *18*(15).

Zhao, F. (2019). Using Quizizz to integrate fun multiplayer activity in the accounting classroom. *International Journal of Higher Education*, *8*(1), 37–43. DOI: 10.5430/ijhe.v8n1p37

Zimmerman, B. J., & Labuhn, A. S. (2012). Self-regulation of learning: Process approaches to personal development.

Zimmerman, B. J., & Martinez-Pons, M. (1988). Construct validation of a strategy model of student self-regulated learning. *Journal of Educational Psychology*, *80*(3), 284–290. DOI: 10.1037/0022-0663.80.3.284

Chapter 6
Recommendation System in the Educational Context:
Experience in Morocco

Hasna Mahmoud
https://orcid.org/0009-0006-5457-3594
Faculty of Sciences, Ibn Zohr University, Agadir, Morocco

Omar Zioudi
Faculty of Sciences, Ibn Zohr University, Agadir, Morocco

Es-Said Boulmane
Faculty of Sciences, Ibn Zohr University, Agadir, Morocco

Mohamed Badouch
https://orcid.org/0000-0003-0495-3784
Faculty of Sciences, Ibn Zohr University, Agadir, Morocco

Mehdi Boutaounte
https://orcid.org/0009-0001-0459-7532
National School of Commerce and Management, Ibn Zohr University, Dakhla, Morocco

ABSTRACT

The advent of artificial intelligence (AI) has transformed many aspects of daily life, particularly in the field of education. .This article presents a study on student guidance and recommender systems, focusing on the needs of students and exploring the potential integration of recommender systems to support their academic and

DOI: 10.4018/979-8-3373-0740-4.ch006

career decisions. The research is based on a survey conducted with 253 students in Morocco, collecting both qualitative and quantitative data about their career paths, challenges, decisions, and the use of academic or career guidance services. The findings reveal that 72,8% of students lack sufficient information about career opportunities . Additionally, 76.7% of students express strong interest in recommender systems, particularly in receiving personalized recommendations for their academic and professional choices. These results provide valuable insights for career counselors and can inform the development of more effective, tailored recommender systems for career guidance in universities.

1. INTRODUCTION

The rapid advancement of technology over the past few decades has significantly transformed various sectors, including education.Technology has not only enhanced the way knowledge is delivered and accessed but has also opened new avenues for personalized learning(Elmourabit et al., 2024), remote education, and efficient administrative management .Personalization is an essential element that differentiates online education from classical face-to-face (Baidada et al., 2021) teaching, which offers common content to a group of learners, without taking into account their specificities.

The issue we pinpointed in our research revolves around addressing the academic and professional guidance requirements of students. Utilizing a questionnaire, our objective was to pinpoint the hurdles encountered by students and explore the potential benefits of employing an AI-based recommendation system to assist them in their decision-making journey. By prioritizing the specific needs of students, our goal is to create a personalized and efficient guidance tool that considers their unique interests, abilities, and aspirations.

This study makes a key contribution to the understanding and application of recommender systems in academic and career guidance. Based on a survey of 253 participants, it analyzes user perceptions and needs. The article explores key approaches to recommender systems, including collaborative filtering, content-based filtering, and hybrid methods, and suggests ways to effectively integrate them into career guidance platforms. By providing personalized recommendations, these systems aim to improve the support provided to students and young professionals, guiding them toward informed choices that are tailored to their aspirations.

This article is organized as follows: Section 2 presents the state-of-the-art concerning various types of recommendation systems, followed by Section 3, which explains the concept of academic and career guidance. Section 4 outlines the methodology employed to address student needs, emphasizing the importance of recommendation systems and exploring other research questions. Next, in Section 5, the study's findings are discussed, and finally, in Section 6, we conclude the article by summarizing the key points discussed.

2. LITERATURE REVIEW

2.1. Recommendation filtering techniques

Recommender systems (RS) are software tools (Urdaneta-Ponte et al., 2021) that assist users in the decision-making process by applying information filtering, data mining, and prediction algorithms. The development of RS has a history, they emerged in the early 1990s(Aucancela et al., 2023)and used algorithms that identified other users with similar tastes and combined their ratings into a personalized weighted average.Fig 1 shows the general concept for the recommender system while matching the user profile with other users profile rate for the common items between them and recommend the difference between them.

Figure 1. General model of the recommendation process(Mohamed et al., 2019)

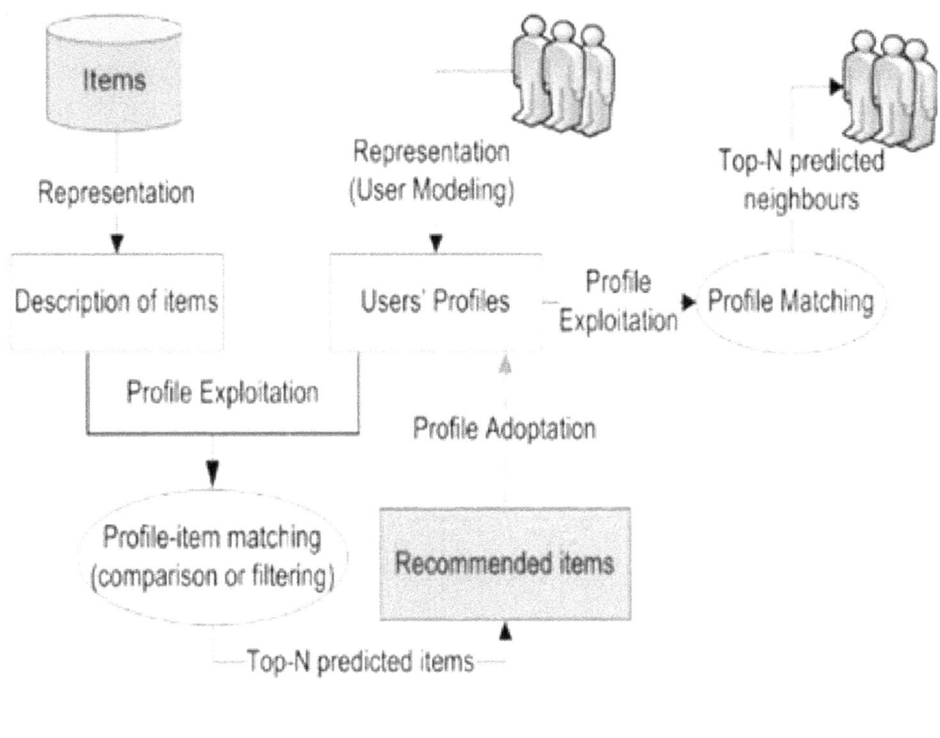

Recommender systems have different types of filtering such as (Collaborative,content-based, and hybrid)(Badouch & Boutaounte, 2023) to make an effective recommendation engine as shown below:

Content-Based Filtering: Content-Based Filtering: This approach is a widely used approach for personalized recommendations in which items are recommended to users based on their preferences for certain features or content(Badouch & Boutaounte, 2023). The system builds a profile of the user's interests based on the attributes of items they have previously(Zhang et al., 2021)liked or interacted with. This method focuses on the attributes of the items themselves, such as genres, descriptions, or tags, to make recommendations.

Collaborative Filtering: Unlike content-based filtering, collaborative filtering makes recommendations based on the preferences and behaviors of other users(Cai et al., 2022). This method relies on identifying patterns and similarities among users to predict how a user might rate or enjoy an item that they have not yet encountered. It operates under the principle that users who agreed in the past will likely have similar preferences in the future.For instance, this method is used by LinkedIn(Wu et al., s. d.)for recommending peoples, jobs,companies,groups,and other entities recommendations.Collaborative Filtering (CF) models are classified into two categories: memory-based techniques and model-based techniques(S. Li & Li, 2020). Memory-based techniques are further divided into user-based methods and item-based methods [badouch]. The first type of methods generates recommendations by considering user preferences within their neighborhood (recommending new items based on ratings given by similar users), while the second type uses the neighborhood of items in calculating similarities between items (recommending items similar to those the user has rated in the past). These two types of methods are also called the "k Nearest Neighborhood method (KNN)"(Choi et al., 2023) because they rely on their neighbors in the calculation of similarity measures between two users or two items. In the literature, we can find several measures for these similarities, such as Pearson correlation, cosine similarity, Jaccard coefficient, and Manhattan distance. Unlike memory-based methods that use the neighborhood of users or items, model-based methods utilize other approaches such as matrix factorization, fuzzy systems, Bayesian classifiers, and neural networks, among others.

Figure 2. Collaborative filtering technique(Aucancela et al., 2023)

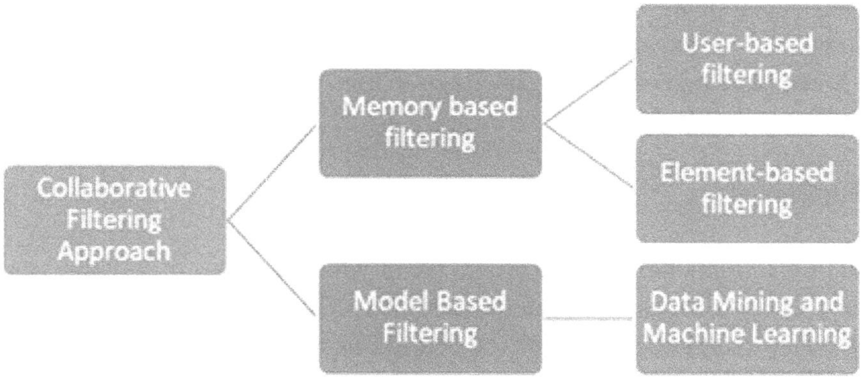

Hybrid recommender systems combine the two previous methods.This approach is to enhance the efficiency of the recommender model and get over the issues(Dhahri & Khribi, 2021)of other types of recommender such as collaborative and content-based filtering.

2.2. Challenges in Recommendation Systems

The recommendation system faces many challenges that need to be investigated and solved and in this section we will introduce some of them.

Cold-start problem:The cold start problem in recommendation systems refers to the problem of recommending to new users or recommending new items with few or no interactions(Mashayekhi et al., 2023).This real issue can undermine the quality of CF significantly. It can occur in three different scenarios: a) when a new user enters b) a new item is introduced c) a new community group is formed(Patel et al., 2023) .

Data sparsity problem:The Sparsity Problem is a significant challenge in recommender systems. it's happening when a user has large matrix contain buy items or watch movies or listing for music. Sparsity evolved when the user didn't rate these items. While recommender systems depend on users rating matrix users to recommend to the others(Mohamed et al., 2019).

Scalability:Scalability is a major challenge in recommender systems due to the rapid growth of information. Large datasets make it difficult to efficiently find relevant neighbors for users, especially with millions of users and items. To address this, techniques like clustering segment users into smaller groups to speed up predictions, while Singular Value Decomposition (SVD(Fayyaz et al., 2020) reduces dimensionality, mapping similar users and items to shared features. These methods enhance performance by reducing computational demands and improving scalability.

Privacy: privacy is one of the important challenges in recommender systems. Recommender systems to recommend items matching their interests, we must know some information about the user data. Users need to know which information needed to recommend more preferably items to him, and how it applied(Mohamed et al., 2019).

2.3. Guidance

Guidance is support(Westman et al., 2021) which consists of helping young people in their educational and professional career. This support includes decision-making related to the choice of a course of study, a discipline, educational resources, or a career.

Figure 3. Types of Orientation

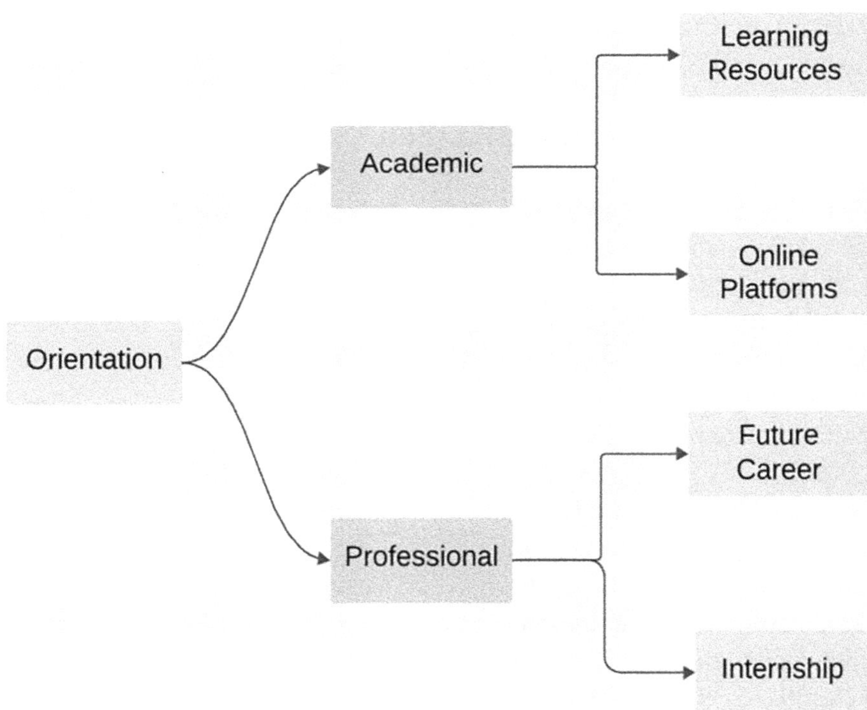

2.3.1. Academic Guidance

Recommending online platforms and learning resources improves the academic advising(Iatrellis et al., 2024)process, providing students with the tools and knowledge necessary for a successful educational journey. As technology continues to advance, these platforms help create a personalized and adaptive academic (Moharm, 2019) support system.

1. Recommendation of online platforms

The e-learning platform (Reddy et al., 2022) is a digital environment designed to facilitate the delivery of educational content(Elmourabit et al., 2024) and activities over the internet . It serves as a virtual space where educators can create, organize, and deliver instructional resources, while learners can access and engage with these resources from anywhere(Xu et al., 2021). These platforms vary widely in features, functionalities, and purposes, catering to diverse educational needs.Popular examples of e-learning platforms include social media platforms (Facebook and WhatsApp) (Zayet et al., 2023), video conferencing tools (Zoom, WebEx, and MS Teams(Zayet et al., 2023), and learning management systems, namely Moodle, Blackboard, and Google Classroom.and many others. These platforms have become instrumental in modern education, providing flexibility, accessibility(Rathod et al., 2024), and interactivity for learners and educators alike.

2. Recommendation of Learning Resources
   - **The recommendation of recently viewed resources**(Tadlaoui et al., 2015)enhances collaborative learning in a system. It provides users with a list of resources recently accessed by others with similar interests. This benefits collaborative learning(G. M. et al., 2024) by enabling users to synchronize their learning experiences with friends.
   - **Recommendation of useful resources**(Tadlaoui et al., 2015): entails evaluating users' preferences, interests, and previous engagements to propose pertinent learning materials. These materials may span textbooks, articles, videos, online courses(J. Li & Ye, 2020), or other educational content customized to suit the user's requirements. Based on the learning domains relevant to the user, a curated list of resources can be suggested to facilitate their educational journey(Hurst, 2024).
   - **Recommendation of popular resources"** refers to suggesting learning materials that have received high ratings and endorsements from the user's friends or peers. This feature allows users to discover educational

content (Kamal et al., 2024) that comes highly recommended by individuals they trust and share their interests.

Table 1. Description of Metadata Retained for Educational Resources

General	**Language**	**Arabic,French,English**
Technical	Format	Video, Document (pdf, slides, ...), Web article,module interactif
Educational	Resource type	Course, Tests or exercises, Forum
Educational Context	Education Level	primary, college, secondary, higher education
Category	Metadata	Values

2.3.2. Professional Guidance

Career guidance(Kiselev et al., 2020)plays an essential role in helping students make informed career decisions(*Crişan et al. - 2015 - A Need Assessment on Students' Career Guidance.pdf*, s. d.) and define their future career, with the integration of AI providing personalized recommendations based on individual data to improve this support(Gedrimiene et al., 2024).

There are leading online platforms such as Glassdoor (Dillahunt et al., 2021), Indeed.com(Oliveira, s. d.)and LinkedIn, each pursuing specific objectives in the areas of job search, career development and employer branding. These platforms all integrate AI-based recommendation systems to optimize the user experience.

Overview of Career Platforms

Here are some popular online platforms for employment:

1. LinkedIn: Primarily a professional networking platform, LinkedIn also features job search functionalities and allows users to apply directly through the platform.
2. Indeed(Dave et al., 2018): A global platform that aggregates job listings from various sources, enabling users to search for jobs based on different criteria.
3. Glassdoor: In addition to job listings, Glassdoor provides company reviews, salary information, and details about interviews, offering a comprehensive view of employers(Dillahunt et al., 2021).
4. CareerBuilder(Ruijt & Bhulai, 2021): Provides job search services, career exploration, and workforce-related advice.

3. METHODOLOGY

This study is based on data collection using an online questionnaire created with Google Forms. The questionnaire is composed of 14 questions aimed at collecting relevant information to achieve the objectives of the study. Participants are encouraged to answer the questions honestly and as accurately as possible.

Participants

The demographic and occupational breakdown of our survey participants offers a comprehensive overview of the diverse perspectives collected. With a total of 253 respondents, the gender distribution leans slightly towards females, comprising 143 participants, while males account for 110, ensuring a balanced representation of views across genders.

In terms of age, the survey predominantly attracted younger adults, with the largest group, 137 participants, falling between 18 and 25 years. This is closely followed by those aged between 25 and 35 years, numbering 78 participants, indicating a strong representation from individuals in their early academic and career stages. The participation of younger teenagers (15 to 17 years, 7 participants) and those over 35 years (31 participants) adds further diversity, encompassing a wide age range that enhances the survey's depth and relevance.

In terms of current situations, pupils/students form the majority, with 165 indicating their primary engagement with education. This is complemented by 60 employees, reflecting those actively engaged in the workforce. The survey also captures the perspectives of the self-employed (8 participants), unemployed (16 participants), and even a retired individual, painting a holistic picture of varied life and career phases among the respondents.

4. RESULTS AND DISCUSSION

Main Challenges as a Student

Figure 4. Main Challenges as a Student

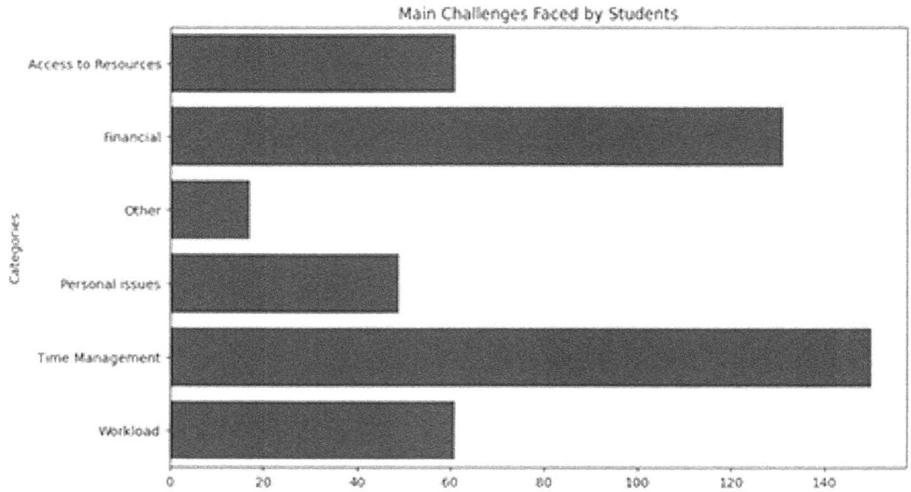

The survey results show the main challenges students face. Financial problems are a big issue, with 131 students saying it's their main challenge. This shows the need for better financial support, scholarships, and flexible job opportunities for students.

The most-mentioned problem is time management. The survey yielded 150 responses saying it is hard to combine tasks implied by academic life with adequate personal time. The implication here is that students need to be equipped with the skills and strategies on how to effectively deal with their schedules as well as reduce the pressure and stress through prioritization of tasks.

Time management stands out as the most cited challenge, with 150 students expressing difficulties in balancing academic responsibilities with personal time. This underscores the importance of providing students with tools and strategies to effectively manage their schedules, prioritize tasks, and reduce stress.

Approximately 61 students highlighted workload and access to resources as key challenges. The workload issue points to the need for curriculum adjustments that promote a balanced approach to course assignments and expectations. Additionally, improving access to resources such as libraries, learning materials, and technological tools is crucial in ensuring all students can engage fully with their studies and succeed academically.Personal issues, mentioned by 49 respondents, reveal the impact of non-academic factors on student well-being and success.

The category labeled "Other" (17 respondents) indicates a variety of less common challenges, suggesting that student experiences are diverse and multifaceted.

Changes in Academic or Professional Paths

Figure 5. Changes in Academic or Professional Paths

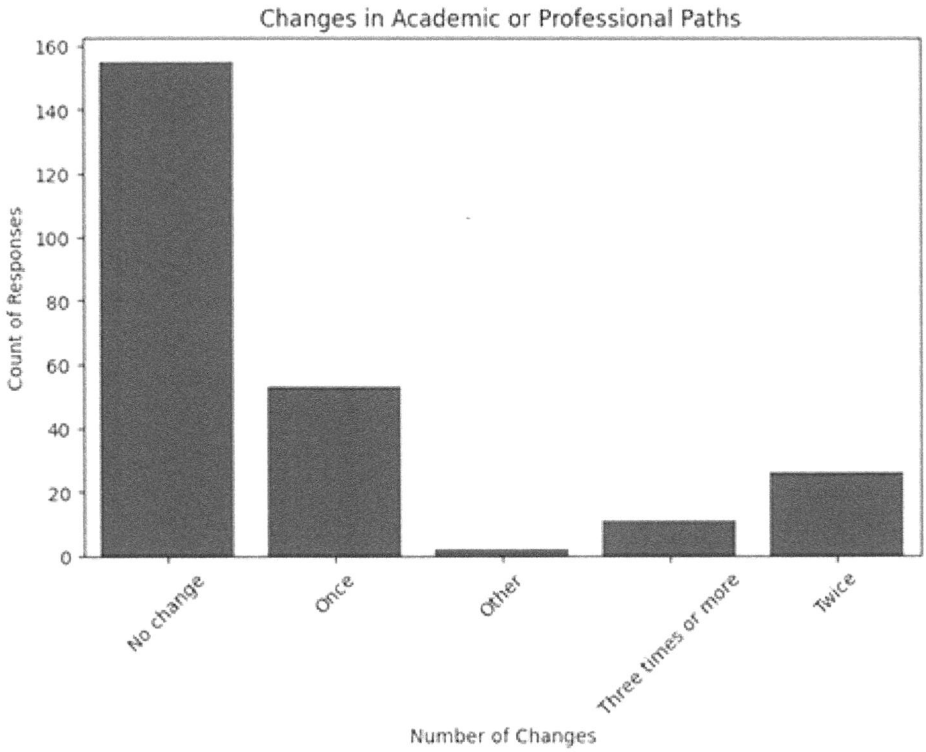

The bar graph represents the responses to the question on the frequency of changes in individuals' academic or professional careers. To discuss the results, the following points can be considered:

No change: This is the most frequent response, indicating that the majority of respondents have not changed their academic or professional path. This could suggest a tendency to follow a linear path or satisfaction with the initial path chosen.

Once: A significant number of people have changed their path once, which could indicate a common reorientation after an initial experience or the discovery of a new passion or opportunity.

Twice and Three times or more: A smaller number of respondents reported switching two or more times. These multiple changes could reflect broader career exploration, a changing work environment, or personal changes that require professional adaptation.

Use of school or career guidance services

Figure 6. Use of Guidance Services

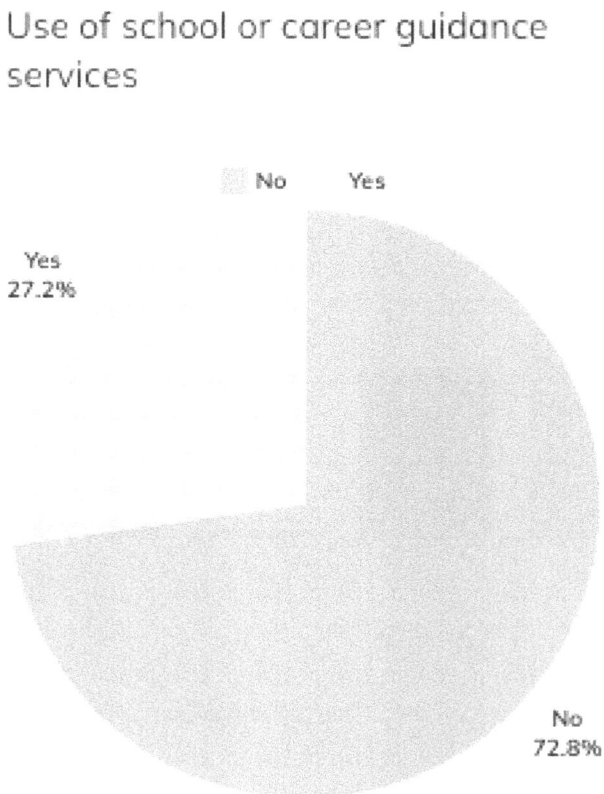

The pie chart shows that only 27.2% of respondents use career or school counseling services, while 72.8% do not. This low adoption could be explained by a lack of accessibility, awareness or interest in these services. These data highlight an opportunity for improvement, particularly through innovative solutions like artificial intelligence-based recommendation systems. These could better meet the individual needs of users and increase their use of guidance.

Recommender Systems

Figure 7. Knowledge of recommendation systems

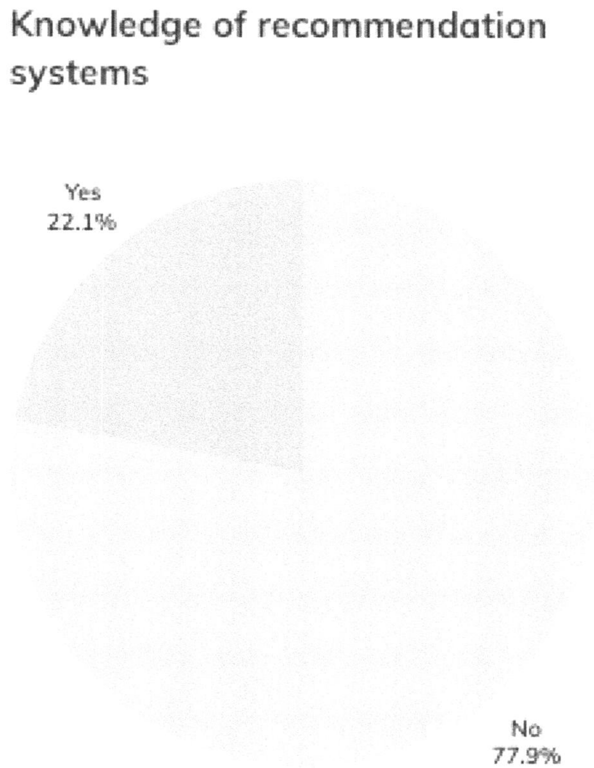

Figure 8. Follow suggested videos on streaming platforms

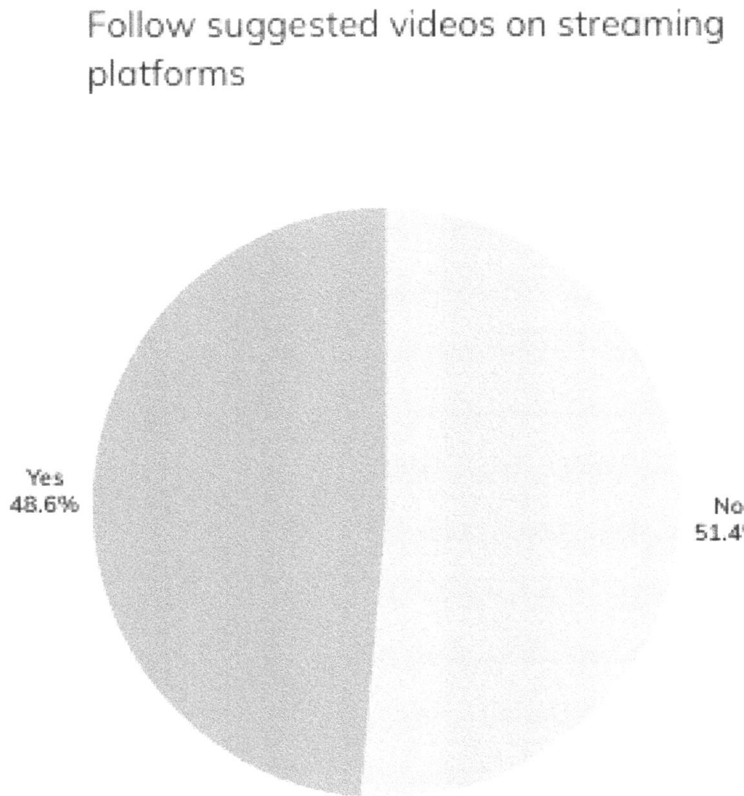

Based on the information provided in the graphs, the following observations can be made: About 22.1% of people are aware of recommender systems, which are algorithms used to suggest content on platforms like YouTube. Almost half of people, or 48.6%, follow suggested videos on streaming platforms. This could suggest that even though not everyone is aware of the mechanisms behind recommender systems, a good portion of them interact with the results of these systems by following suggested videos.

Figure 9. Interest in using recommendation systems for academic / career choices

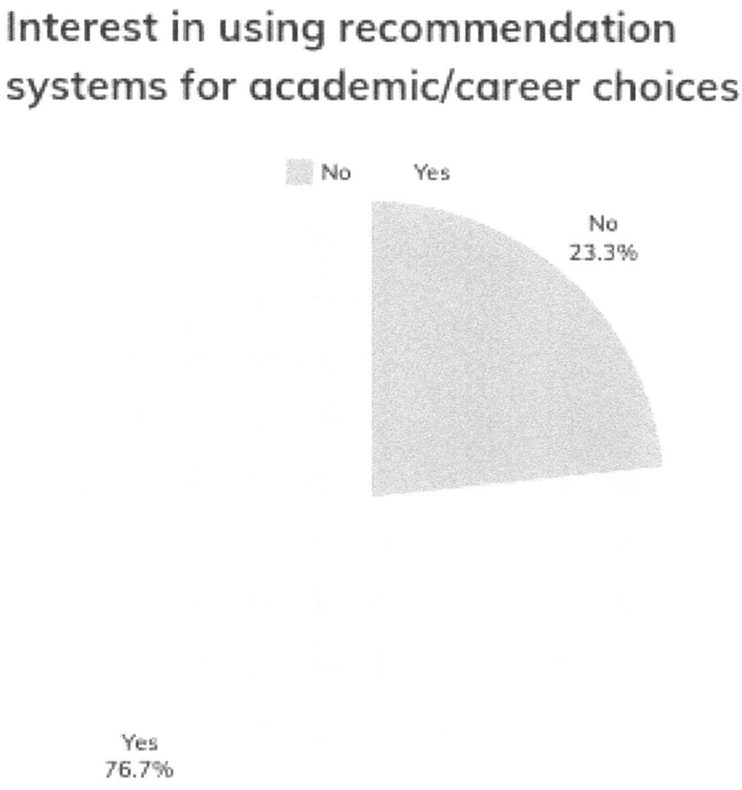

There is a strong interest (76.7%) in using recommendation systems for academic or career choices. This could suggest that people trust recommendation technologies to help them with important choices, even if they don't do not fully understand how these systems work.

Figure 10. Types of recommendations

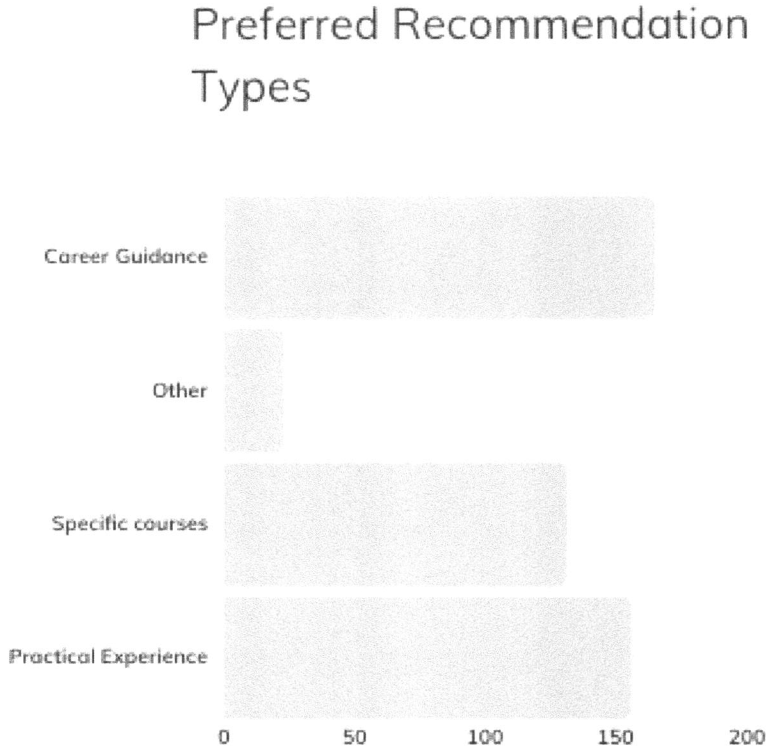

The graph represents respondents' preferences for the types of recommendations or information they would like to receive from a recommender system for academic or career guidance. The categories, listed in descending order of interest, appear to be:

Career Guidance: This is the most popular category, indicating high interest in career planning-related recommendations.

Practical Experience: This category likely includes internships, apprenticeships, or other forms of work experience.

Specific courses: Respondents also show significant interest in information about educational opportunities.

Other: This indicates that some respondents are interested in international opportunities, whether educational or professional.

Figure 11. Personalized Recommendations

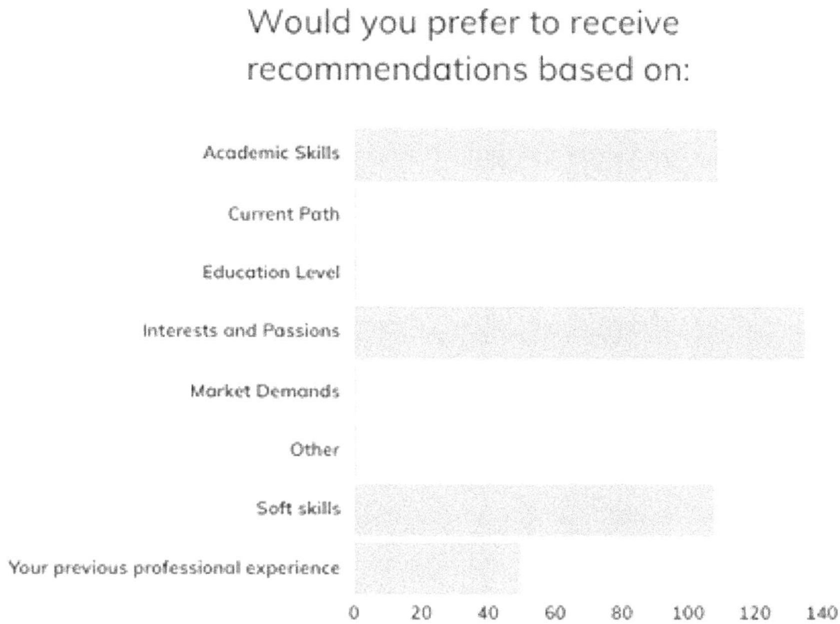

The individuals surveyed appeared to prioritize their personal characteristics and past experiences when making their educational and career decisions, rather than considering market requirements or available paths in the market. This may make sense, especially if the individual seeks to choose a path that aligns with their personal skills and interests, thus increasing their chances of success in their chosen field. However, it may also be beneficial for individuals to consider future market requirements and needs when making educational and career decisions, to ensure that they are equipped with the skills and knowledge necessary to succeed in the future work environment.

5. CONCLUSION AND FUTURE WORK

This study highlights the importance of recommendation systems in academic and professional orientation. It emphasizes the integration of these systems into student counseling programs to address the multiple challenges students face throughout their academic journey.By leveraging the capabilities of these systems, students can receive personalized advice that matches their unique interests, skills, and career aspirations.

In future work,We are planning to use a hybrid model based recommendation system in future to enhance the accuracy of the recommendation. We are also planning to use recommender systems to suggest career options to students.

REFERENCES

Aucancela, M., Briones, A. G., & Chamoso, P. (2023). *Educational Recommender Systems : A Systematic Literature Review*. 933-951. DOI: 10.22492/issn.2435-9467.2023.74

Badouch, M., & Boutaounte, M. (2023). Personalized Travel Recommendation Systems : A Study of Machine Learning Approaches in Tourism. *Journal of Artificial Intelligence. Machine Learning and Neural Network*, *33*(33), 35–45. DOI: 10.55529/jaimlnn.33.35.45

Baidada, M., Mansouri, K., & Poirier, F. (2021). Hybrid Filtering Recommendation System in an Educational Context : Experiment in Higher Education in Morocco. *International Journal of Web-Based Learning and Teaching Technologies*, *17*(1), 1–17. DOI: 10.4018/IJWLTT.294573

Cai, Y., Ke, W., Cui, E., & Yu, F. (2022). A deep recommendation model of cross-grained sentiments of user reviews and ratings. *Information Processing & Management*, *59*(2), 102842. DOI: 10.1016/j.ipm.2021.102842

Choi, S.-M., Lee, D., Jang, K., Park, C., & Lee, S. (2023). Improving Data Sparsity in Recommender Systems Using Matrix Regeneration with Item Features. *Mathematics*, *11*(2), 292. DOI: 10.3390/math11020292

Crişan, C., Pavelea, A., & Ghimbuluţ, O. (2015). A need assessment on students' career guidance. *Procedia: Social and Behavioral Sciences*, *180*, 1022–1029.

Dave, V. S., Zhang, B., Al Hasan, M., AlJadda, K., & Korayem, M. (2018). A Combined Representation Learning Approach for Better Job and Skill Recommendation. *Proceedings of the 27th ACM International Conference on Information and Knowledge Management*, 1997-2005. DOI: 10.1145/3269206.3272023

de Ruijt, C., & Bhulai, S. (2021). *Job Recommender Systems : A Review* (No. arXiv:2111.13576). arXiv. https://doi.org//arXiv.2111.13576DOI: 10.48550

Dhahri, M., & Khribi, M. K. (2021). *A REVIEW OF EDUCATIONAL RECOMMENDER SYSTEMS FOR TEACHERS*.

Dhananjaya, G. M., Goudar, R. H., Kulkarni, A. A., Rathod, V. N., & Hukkeri, G. S. (2024). A Digital Recommendation System for Personalized Learning to Enhance Online Education : A Review. *IEEE Access : Practical Innovations, Open Solutions*, *12*, 34019–34041. DOI: 10.1109/ACCESS.2024.3369901

Dillahunt, T. R., Israni, A., Lu, A. J., Cai, M., & Hsiao, J. C.-Y. (2021). Examining the Use of Online Platforms for Employment : A Survey of U.S. Job Seekers. *Proceedings of the 2021 CHI Conference on Human Factors in Computing Systems*, 1-23. DOI: 10.1145/3411764.3445350

Elmourabit, Z., Asmaâ Retbi, & Nour-Eddine El Faddouli. (2024). The Impact of Generative Artificial Intelligence on Education : A Comparative Study. *European Conference on E-Learning, 23*(1), 470-476. DOI: 10.34190/ecel.23.1.2975

Fayyaz, Z., Ebrahimian, M., Nawara, D., Ibrahim, A., & Kashef, R. (2020). Recommendation Systems : Algorithms, Challenges, Metrics, and Business Opportunities. *Applied Sciences (Basel, Switzerland)*, *10*(21), 7748. DOI: 10.3390/app10217748

Gedrimiene, E., Celik, I., Kaasila, A., Mäkitalo, K., & Muukkonen, H. (2024). Artificial Intelligence (AI)-enhanced learning analytics (LA) for supporting Career decisions : Advantages and challenges from user perspective. *Education and Information Technologies*, *29*(1), 297–322. DOI: 10.1007/s10639-023-12277-4

Hurst, R. A. (2024). Analysis of the Impact of Personalized Learning Paths in Mobile Learning Platforms on the Development of Self-Directed Learning Strategies Among Brazilian College Students. *Research and Advances in Education*, *3*(3), 9–14. DOI: 10.56397/RAE.2024.03.02

Iatrellis, O., Samaras, N., Kokkinos, K., & Panagiotakopoulos, T. (2024). Leveraging Generative AI for Sustainable Academic Advising : Enhancing Educational Practices through AI-Driven Recommendations. *Sustainability (Basel)*, *16*(17), 7829. DOI: 10.3390/su16177829

Kamal, N., Sarker, F., Rahman, A., Hossain, S., & Mamun, K. A. (2024). Recommender System in Academic Choices of Higher Education : A Systematic Review. *IEEE Access : Practical Innovations, Open Solutions*, *12*, 35475–35501. DOI: 10.1109/ACCESS.2024.3368058

Kiselev, P., Kiselev, B., Matsuta, V., Feshchenko, A., Bogdanovskaya, I., & Kosheleva, A. (2020). Career guidance based on machine learning : Social networks in professional identity construction. *Procedia Computer Science*, *169*, 158–163. DOI: 10.1016/j.procs.2020.02.128

Li, J., & Ye, Z. (2020). Course Recommendations in Online Education Based on Collaborative Filtering Recommendation Algorithm. *Complexity*, *2020*, 1–10. DOI: 10.1155/2020/8882813

Li, S., & Li, X. (2020). Collaborative Filtering Recommendation Algorithm Based on User Characteristics and User Interests. *Journal of Physics: Conference Series, 1616*(1), 012032. DOI: 10.1088/1742-6596/1616/1/012032

Mashayekhi, Y., Li, N., Kang, B., Lijffijt, J., & Bie, T. D. (2023). *A challenge-based survey of e-recruitment recommendation systems* (No. arXiv:2209.05112). arXiv. https://doi.org//arXiv.2209.05112DOI: 10.48550

Mohamed, M. H., Khafagy, M. H., & Ibrahim, M. H. (2019). Recommender Systems Challenges and Solutions Survey. *2019 International Conference on Innovative Trends in Computer Engineering (ITCE)*, 149-155. DOI: 10.1109/ITCE.2019.8646645

Moharm, K. (2019). A Framework for Adaptive Personalized E-learning Recommender Systems. *International Journal of Intelligent Information Systems*, *8*(1), 12. DOI: 10.11648/j.ijiis.20190801.13

Oliveira, M. (s. d.). *Intelligence artificielle appliquée au processus de recrutement—Les perceptions des recruteurs.*

Patel, D., Patel, F., & Chauhan, U. (2023). Recommendation Systems : Types, Applications, and Challenges. *International Journal of Computing and Digital Systems, 13*(1), 851–868. DOI: 10.12785/ijcds/130168

Rathod, V. N., Goudar, R. H., Kulkarni, A., M, D. G., & Hukkeri, G. S. (2024). A Survey on E-Learning Recommendation Systems for Autistic People. *IEEE Access : Practical Innovations, Open Solutions*, *12*, 11723–11732. DOI: 10.1109/ACCESS.2024.3355589

Reddy, K. S. V., Reddy, M. A., Kaur, V., & Kaur, G. (2022). Career Guidance System Using Ensemble Learning. SSRN *Electronic Journal*. DOI: 10.2139/ssrn.4157249

Tadlaoui, M., Sehaba, K., & George, S. (2015). Recommendation of Learning Resources based on Social Relations: *Proceedings of the 7th International Conference on Computer Supported Education*, 425-432. DOI: 10.5220/0005452304250432

Urdaneta-Ponte, M. C., Mendez-Zorrilla, A., & Oleagordia-Ruiz, I. (2021). Recommendation Systems for Education : Systematic Review. *Electronics (Basel)*, *10*(14), 1611. DOI: 10.3390/electronics10141611

Westman, S., Kauttonen, J., Klemetti, A., Korhonen, N., Manninen, M., Mononen, A., Niittymäki, S., & Paananen, H. (2021). Artificial Intelligence for Career Guidance – Current Requirements and Prospects for the Future. *IAFOR Journal of Education*, *9*(4), 43–62. DOI: 10.22492/ije.9.4.03

Wu, L., Shah, S., Choi, S., Tiwari, M., & Posse, C. (2014). The browsemaps: Collaborative filtering at LinkedIn. RSWeb@ RecSys, 1271.

Xu, G., Jia, G., Shi, L., & Zhang, Z. (2021). Personalized Course Recommendation System Fusing with Knowledge Graph and Collaborative Filtering. *Computational Intelligence and Neuroscience*, *2021*(1), 9590502. DOI: 10.1155/2021/9590502 PMID: 34616447

Zayet, T. M. A., Ismail, M. A., Almadi, S. H. S., Zawia, J. M. H., & Mohamad Nor, A. (2023). What is needed to build a personalized recommender system for K-12 students' E-Learning? Recommendations for future systems and a conceptual framework. *Education and Information Technologies*, *28*(6), 7487–7508. DOI: 10.1007/s10639-022-11489-4 PMID: 36532791

Zhang, Q., Lu, J., & Jin, Y. (2021). Artificial intelligence in recommender systems. *Complex & Intelligent Systems*, *7*(1), 439–457. DOI: 10.1007/s40747-020-00212-w

Chapter 7

Personalized Learning Through Simulation: Assessing the Structured Communication Tool's Effect on Nurse-Physician Communication – A Pilot Study

Abdelkader Amechghal
https://orcid.org/0009-0004-7103-7457
Faculty of Medicine and Pharmacy, Ibn Zohr University, Morocco

Aziz Naciri
https://orcid.org/0000-0001-7318-6633
University Hassan II, Morocco

Fouzia Zaroual
Higher Institute of Nursing Professions and Health Techniques, Morocco

Nouhaila Lagrini
Higher Institute of Nursing Professions and Health Techniques, Morocco

Doha Rmili
Higher Institute of Nursing Professions and Health Techniques, Morocco

Kamal Takhdat
Higher Institute of Nursing Professions and Health Techniques, Morocco

Hicham Nassik
Faculty of Medicine and Pharmacy, Agadir, Morocco

ABSTRACT

A lack of standardized communication was identified among Intesive Care Unite (ICU) providers in a public hospital in southern Morocco. This quasi-experimental pre-post test study aimed to evaluate the effectiveness of personalized simulation-based learning using the SAED tool (French adaptation of SBAR) to enhance structured communication between nurses and physicians in intensive care. Eleven

DOI: 10.4018/979-8-3373-0740-4.ch007

nurses participated in the study, which employed three data collection instruments: a sociodemographic questionnaire, a SAED knowledge assessment, and an evaluation of communication as perceived by the recipient. Data analysis through SPSS revealed significant improvements in participants' theoretical knowledge of the SAED tool and their performance in structured communication during telephone calls with physicians. The study demonstrates the effectiveness of this approach in enhancing ICU nurses' communication skills, suggesting potential benefits for patient safety and quality of care, although further research with larger samples is recommended to validate these findings.

INTRODUCTION

According to the Joint Commission (2012), about 80% of serious medical errors are related to poor communication between healthcare providers. Communication is undeniably fundamental to all human interactions and professional fields. It shapes our exchanges with others and our understanding of the world around us. Beyond facilitating social interactions, it plays a pivotal role in professional practices. In healthcare, institutions must ensure clear and effective communication with both internal and external stakeholders. The interaction between healthcare establishments and patients constitutes a unique interface, with a major impact on the organization's communications strategy (Vujadinovic, 2020).

In nursing, effective communication between staff is very important, either to improve the quality of care or to guarantee patient safety during their stay in the hospital. Communication in nursing care aims to coordinate the appropriate care of the patient collaboratively. This involves sharing accurate and relevant information between different healthcare professionals, which promotes continuity of care (Le Levier et al., 2018).

Indeed, 70-80% of medical errors have been attributed to communication failures among healthcare professionals. Ineffective communication can lead to adverse events and suboptimal care management (Leonard et al., 2004; Dimova et al., 2018). In addition, interprofessional tensions arising from human factors and professional disparities can compromise effective information exchange and workplace quality. These communication challenges are particularly pronounced between novice and experienced professionals (A. Cohen et al., 2021).

Consequently, some National Patient Safety Improvement Programs (NPSIPs), such as the Agency for Healthcare Research and Quality (AHRQ), have recommended the development and use of standardized tools to facilitate communication among healthcare professionals for effective interprofessional care (AHRQ, 2015). Among existing tools, the SBAR (Situation, Background, Assessment, Recommendation) tool is specially designed to enable team communication in emergencies. The French National Authority for Health adapted the SBAR tool to create SAED (*Situation, Antécédents, Évaluation, Demande*) for French-speaking healthcare settings (Le Levier et al., 2018). This scale contributes to enhancing communication, collaboration, and safety culture (A. Cohen et al., 2021).

Clinical communication is a fundamental factor in ensuring both continuity and quality of care in intensive care settings. This importance was only emphasized when an error was clearly attributed to a transmission failure (Cecile & Richard, 2018). Furthermore, Communication and transfer of clinical information are essential for quality care in the ICU. However, its significance was only fully recognized following the publication of studies analyzing the root causes of medical errors (Peters & Peters, 2007).

The use of structured communication tools such as SAED tool can reduce communication errors between nurses and physicians by 11 to 31%. This tool facilitates the concise structuring of shared information, promotes both intra- and interdisciplinary communication, and is adaptable to all medical specialties. Its application reduces stress among healthcare professionals, lowers hospital costs, and enhances work efficiency and on-the-ground stakeholder satisfaction (Michiels, 2018).

Simulation-based learning in healthcare improves the communication skills of learners (students and practitioners) by providing a safe and controlled environment (Foronda et al., 2013; Thomas et al., 2009) in complex clinical settings where effective communication is critical. This pedagogical method is under the principles of personalized learning, which tailors educational experiences to the needs, preferences, and performance of individuals (Bloom, 1968). In healthcare training, the use of personalized learning through simulation can optimize skills acquisition and prepare trainees for real-life scenarios. This method enhances effective learning with fewer hands-on trials, ensuring readiness for patient encounters (Elsaadany et al., 2023). This association between the advantages of SBL and personalized learning can enhance patient safety and quality of care, particularly in complex clinical environments where effective communication is crucial (Gaba, 2004; McGaghie et al., 2011).

In this context, this study aims to evaluate the effectiveness of personalized learning through simulation training using the SAED tool to improve structured communication between intensive care nurses and physicians during patient care management. More specifically, the aim is to examine the extent to which the use of this tool contributes to optimizing the transmission of clinical information and strengthening interprofessional collaboration. Thus, the research question guiding this study is: what is the effect of personalized simulation-based learning, using the SAED tool, on the theoretical knowledge of ICU nurses regarding the use of this structured communication tool and their communication performance during telephone calls with ICU physicians?

METHODS

Study design

A quasi-experimental, pre-and post-test design, without a control group, was used in this pilot study.

Study Setting and Period

The study was conducted between March 1, 2024, and June 30, 2024, in the intensive care unit of a public hospital in southern Morocco. This unit is designed to provide medical and post-surgical resuscitation care.

Population

The study population was all nurse practitioners at the intensive care unit, with a total of 11 participants.

Inclusion and Exclusion Criteria.

All intensive care unit nurse practitioners were included. No exclusion criteria were specified.

Data collection

Sociodemographic data were collected using a structured questionnaire, including sociodemographic characteristics such as age (in years), gender, total years of professional experience, specific experience in the intensive care unit, nursing specialty (e.g., general nurse, nurse anesthetist), and prior experience with simulation-based training (Yes/No). Additionally, participants were asked to report their previous experience (Never, Occasionally, Regularly) with the SAED communication tool. Furthermore, we administered two standardized questionnaires: (1) the knowledge assessment questionnaire for healthcare professionals regarding SAED communication tool usage, and (2) the caller evaluation questionnaire assessing communication between healthcare professionals (caller-to-called interaction). Both questionnaires are publicly available and can be accessed through the French Health Authority website (HAS, 2014)

Variables of Study

The dependent variables were the acquisition of theoretical knowledge regarding the use of the SAED communication tool and communication performance during a telephone call between a nurse and an intensivist. The independent variable was simulation training for nurse-physician communication using the SAED tool.

Data analysis

Data analysis was performed using the Statistical Package for Social Sciences (SPSS) version 26.0. Participants' socio-demographic characteristics were described using frequencies and percentages for categorical variables (n(%)) and median with interquartile range median [IQR: 25–27]. for continuous variables. McNemar's test was used to assess the difference in knowledge of the SAED structural communication tool and nurse-physician telephone communication performance between the pre-test and post-test. A frequency table was constructed to analyze the distribution of responses to multiple-choice items, allowing for a comparison of results between the pre-test and post-test. Statistical significance was tested at a p-value <.05.

RESULTS

Socio-demographic characteristics of participants

The sociodemographic characteristics of the participants are summarized in Table 01 below. The sample consisted of eleven participants with a median age of 26 years (IQR: 25–27). The majority were female (72.7%, n=8. According to the nursing practice field, 45.5% (n=5) were nurse anesthetists, and 54.5% (n=6) were multi-skilled nurses. In terms of total professional experience, 63.6% (n=7) had less than 5 years of experience, while 36.4% (n=4) had between 5 and 10 years. All participants (100%, n=11) had less than 5 years of professional experience in the intensive care unit.

Table 1. Socio-demographic characteristics of participants (n=11)

n=11	
Age*	**26(25;27)**
Gender**	
• Male	3(27.3)
• Femel	8(72.7)
Field of nursing practice**	
• nurse anesthetist,	5(45.5)
• multi-skilled nurse	6(54.5)
Total Professional experience (year)**	
• < 5	7(63.6)
• **5-10**	4(36.4)
Professional experience in the intensive care unit (year)**	
• < 5	11(100)

*: mediane (interquartile range: Q1-Q3) ; **: effectif(percentage)

Effect of Simulation Training on ICU Nurses' Knowledge of the SAED Communication Tool

Table 2 below shows the pre-test and post-test frequencies recorded for each item on the SAED knowledge assessment questionnaire. A comparison was also carried out between the pre-test and post-test results. Before the intervention, the average SAED acronym demonstrated a limited level of SAED knowledge for structural communication in ICU, with only 18.2% (n=2) of participants correctly identifying "*Situation*", 36.4% (n=4) for "*Antécedents*" (Background), 45.5% (n=5) for "*Evaluation*" (Assessment) and 45.5% (n=5) for "*Décision*" (Decision). After the simulation training, a significant improvement was observed for all participants correctly identifying "Situation" (p=0.016), Antecedents (p=0.016), and "Assessment" (p= 0.031). Participants showed a significant improvement in identifying the elements to be included in each component in terms of the practical application of the tool. For the "Situation" component, the most notable improvements concerned the correct identification of background (from 18.2% to 100%, p=0.004) and the assessment of the situation (from 27.3% to 100%, P= 0.008). For the "History" component, significant progress was observed in understanding current treatments (from 9.1% to 100%, p=0.002) and known allergies (from 18.2% to 100%, p=0.004). Perception of the tool's usefulness also improved, notably in structuring communication among the ICU nurses (from 54.5% to 100%, p=0.031) and transmitting concise, clear information (from 27.3% to 100%, p= 0.008).

Table 2. Descriptive statistics and non-parametric analysis of the SAED knowledge assessment questionnaire (n=11)

Question	Pre-Test	Post-Test	*P* value*
Subscale 1 ***: Que signifie SAED*** ***S***			
Situation	7(18.2)	11(100)	0.016
Service	2(18.2)	00(00)	0.063
Security	2(18.2)	00(00)	0.063
A			
Anesthesia	1(9.1)	00(00)	
Background	4(36.4)	11(100)	0.016
Anticipate	2(18.2)	00(00)	0.063
Aid	4(36.4)	00(00)	0.125
E			
Evolution	4(36.4)	00(00)	0.0625
Evaluation	5(45.5)	11(100)	0.031
Education	2(18.2)	00(00)	0.500
D			
Decision	5(45.5)	00(00)	0.063
Demand	4(36.4)	11(100)	0.016
Detect	2(18.2)	00(00)	0.500
Subscale 2: ***For the S part of SAED, what do I specify?***			
My identity	6(54.5)	11(100)	0.031
My service	4(36.4)	11(100)	0.016
Patient identity	6(54.5)	11(100)	0.031
Patient's current location	4(36.4)	11(100)	0.016
History	2(18.2)	11(100)	0.004
My request	11(100)	11(100)	1.000
Current situation motivating my call	7(63.6)	11(100)	0.125
Current vital signs motivating my call	5(45.5)	00(00)	0.063
My assessment of the situation	3(27.3)	11(100)	0.0008
Current clinical signs motivating my call	5(45.5)	11(100)	0.031
I write these data on the notepad to prepare my call	3(27.3)	11(100)	0.008
Subscale 3: For part A of SAED, what do I specify?			
Situation analysis	4(36.4)	11(100)	0.016
All the patient's history since birth	5(45.5)	11(100)	0.031

continued on following page

Table 2. Continued

Question	Pre-Test	Post-Test	*P* value*
Only medical history related to his care	5(45.5)	11(100)	0.031
Known allergies	2(18.2)	11(100)	0.004
The patient's normal condition (confused, in pain, etc.)	3(27.3)	11(100)	0.008
Ongoing treatments	1(9.1)	11(100)	0.002
My request	11(100)	11(100)	1.000
My assessment of the situation	1(9.1)	11(100)	0.002
Interventions and invasive procedures related to the current management	1(9.1)	11(100)	0.002
The admission date and the diagnosis made upon admission	1(9.1)	11(100)	0.002
When the situation started to change, prompting my call	3(27.3)	11(100)	0.008
Subscale 4 : For part E of Saed, what do I specify?			
My request	1(9.1)	11(100)	0.002
My interpretation of the patient's condition progression	10(90.9)	11(100)	1.000
The main reason for my concern	2(18.2)	11(100)	0.004
Subscale 5 : For part D of Saed, what do I specify?			
My request	9(81.8)	11(100)	0.500
My diagnosis	3(27.3)	11(100)	0.008
My assessment of the situation	3(27.3)	11(100)	0.008
Patient history	11(100)	11(100)	1.000
Subscale 6: ***En conclusion, à quoi sert la grille SAED ?***			
Trace a call that has been made so that it can be filed in the patient's file	2(18.2)	11(100)	0.004
Prepare a call to be made to facilitate communication with the caller	8(72.7)	11(100)	0.250
Structure communication between healthcare professionals	6(54.5)	11(100)	0.031
Save time	5(45.5)	11(100)	0.031
Communicate clear, concise information	3(27.3)	11(100)	0.008
Prevent misunderstandings and tensions between healthcare professionals	3(27.3)	11(100)	0.008
Reinforce self-confidence and legitimacy during a call	3(27.3)	11(100)	0.008
If we note in the patient's file that we called another healthcare professional, can we specify that we used the SAED tool?			
Yes	5(45.5)	11(100)	0.031

Evaluation of the caller's (nurse) communication by the recipient (intensivist) during the use of the SAED tool

The table below on the evaluation of ICU nurses' communication performance by the intensivist physician shows the results of a pre-and post-training evaluation using the SAED (Situation, Antecedents, Evaluation, Demand) tool. Data analysis reveals an overall improvement in structured communication skills. Immediately after the telephone call, the doctors evaluated the nurses using "*the communication evaluation questionnaire to be completed by a professional (called)" for each call.* The results showed significant improvement in several areas. For situation description (Subscale 1), quality improved from a predominantly "average" level (54.5% for Clarity of Wording(CW) and Relevance of Purpose (RP)) to "excellent" (54.5% for CW and 18.2% for RP) and "very good" (100% for CW and 9.1% for RP), with a statistically significant improvement (p=0.031 for CW). For history-taking (Subscale 2), a notable progression was observed, from a scattered assessment (27.3% "acceptable" for CW) to "excellent" (36.4% for CW and RP) with a significant improvement (p=0.031 for R). Situation assessment (Subscale 3) also improved, moving from a majority of "good" (45.5% for C) to "excellent" (27.3% for C), with significant p-values (p=0.016 for C and p=0.031 for R). Request quality (Subscale 4) progressed from "average" and "good" (27.3% each for C) to "excellent" (36.4% for C and 27.3% for R), showing significant improvement (p=0.008 for C and p=0.031 for R). Finally, call time (Subscale 5) improved considerably, from "acceptable" to "average" (54.5% and 45.5%) to "excellent" (72.7%), with a very significant improvement (p=0.001).

Table 3. Descriptive and non-parametric analysis of the use of the SAED tool in communication between the caller (nurse) and the recipient (intensivist physician) (n=11)

Question	Pre-Test*		Post- Test*		P-value**	
	CW	RP	CW	RP	CW	RP
Subscale 1: The situation described by the calling professional						
Acceptable	1(9.1)	2(18.2)	00(00)	00(00)	0.031	0.5
Fair	6(54.5)	6(54.5)	00(00)	00(00)		
Good	2(18.2)	2(18.2)	00(100)	1(9.1)		
Very good	1(9.1)	00(00)	00(100)	1(9.1)		
Excellent	00(00)	00(00)	6(54.5)	7(18.2)		
Not specified	00(00)	1(9.1)	5(45.5)	2(18.2)		

continued on following page

Table 3. Continued

Question	Pre-Test*		Post- Test*		P-value**	
	CW	RP	CW	RP	CW	RP
Subscale 1: The situation described by the calling professional						
Subscale 2: Background to the situation, as described by the calling professional						
Fair	00(00)	3(27.3)	00(00)	00(00)	0.063	0.031
Acceptable	3(27.3)	00(00)	00(00)	00(00)		
Average	3(27.3)	1(9.1)	00(00)	00(00)		
well	2(18.2)	5(45.5)	00(00)	00(00)		
Very good	2(18.2)	1(9.1)	00(00)	1(9.1)		
Excellent	1(9.1)	1(9.1)	4(36.4)	4(36.4)		
No opinion	00(00)	00(00)	7(63.6)	6(54.5)		
Subscale 3: Calling professional's assessment of the situation						
Fair	2(18.2)	00(00)	00(00)	00(00)	0.016	0.031
Acceptable	00(00)	2(18.2)	00(00)	00(00)		
Average	1(9.1)	2(18.2)	00(00)	00(00)		
well	5(45.5)	4(36.4)	00(00)	00(00)		
Very good	1(9.1)	1(9.1)	1(9.1)	00(00)		
Excellent	2(18.2)	00(00)	3(27.3)	00(00)		
No opinino	00(00)	00(00)	7(63.3)	00(00)		
Subscale 4: The request made by the calling professional						
Acceptable	1(9.1)	3(27.3)	00(00)	00(00)	0.008	0.031
Fair	3(27.3)	00(00)	00(00)	00(00)		
Good	3(27.3)	5(45.5)	00(00)	00(00)		
Very good	00(00)	1(9.1)	3(27.3)	1(9.1)		
Excellent	00(00)	1(9.1)	4(36.4)	3(27.3)		
No opinion	00(00)	1(9.1)	4(36.4)	7(63.6)		
Subscale 5: Call time adapted to context						
Acceptable	6(54.5)		00(00)		0.001	
Average	5(45.5)		00(00)			
Excellent	00(00)		8(72.7)			
No opinion	00(00)		3(27.3)			

CW: Clarity of wording ; RP: Relevance of Purpose ; *: n(%); **<0.05 ; N=11

DISCUSSION

This study was conducted to evaluate the effectiveness of a personalized simulation-based approach in improving individual nurse practitioner outcomes, including knowledge acquisition on the use of the SAED tool for structured communication and nurses' telephone communication performance after simulation training on the use of the SAED tool for structured communication between nurses and physicians in ICU.

The simulation-based personalized learning approach significantly improved knowledge acquisition on the use of the SAED tool. This suggests that simulation facilitates the effective assimilation of key concepts. These results are consistent with those of the systematic review by Cook et al. (2011) who showed that simulation improves technical knowledge and skills, such as communication skills. Simulation provides a safe environment for rehearsing and assimilating complex information. These results imply that this method could be integrated into continuing education programs to enhance healthcare professionals' knowledge of structured communication.

The ICU nurses demonstrated a significant improvement in telephone communication performance following the training. This suggests that simulation enhances the ability to communicate clearly and systematically. It was demonstrated that structured tools like SBAR tool or SAED tool, in the French context, improve communication by providing a clear framework for exchanges (Haig et al., 2006). Similarly, Thomas et al. (2009) found that using structured tools reduces communication errors by 30% in intensive care units. The SAED tool provides a structured format for organizing information, thereby reducing communication errors and enhancing exchange efficiency. Riesenberg et al. (2010) also highlighted that standardized communication tools improve the transmission of critical information among healthcare professionals, which is crucial for patient safety. Furthermore, simulation-based training enhances communication skills, particularly in high-stress settings such as intensive care (E. R. Cohen et al., 2010). These findings suggest that using a SAED tool could improve communication and enhance patient safety in clinical settings.

This training significantly improved communication performance between ICU nurses and intensive physicians. The findings suggest that simulation enhances the ability to communicate clearly and systematically. These findings are supported by Zwarenstein et al. (2009), who showed that targeted interventions improve interprofessional collaboration. Simulation enables realistic scenarios to be practiced, reinforcing mutual understanding. This could contribute to a more collaborative working culture and effectiveness patient outcomes.

This study has several limitations that should be considered. As a pilot study, it was conducted with a limited sample of 11 participants, which restricts the generalization of results. The small sample size, single-cohort and a single-site prevents extrapolation of findings to other settings or populations. Additionally, the absence of a control group limits the ability to establish robust comparisons.

Future studies should include a larger and more diverse sample, along with a control group to assess the actual impact of simulation training. It would also be relevant to explore the long-term effect of this approach on communication skills and patient safety. Moreover, the use of objective measurement tools, such as audio recordings or peer evaluations, could strengthen the validity of the results. Despite these limitations, this study provides promising perspectives for integrating personalized learning simulation using structured communication tools like SAED in nursing education.

CONCLUSION

This study aimed to evaluate the effectiveness of a personalized simulation-based learning approach for nurse practitioners. The results showed a significant improvement in participants' knowledge of how to use the SAED tool and their performance in structured interprofessional communication. They suggest that simulation and the SAED tool could enhance interprofessional collaboration, quality of care and patient safety. However, the study has limitations, including a limited sample of 11 participants. Future research is needed to validate these results on a larger, more diverse sample. The inclusion of a control group and evaluation of long-term impact are also recommended. Finally, this study contributes to our understanding of the benefits of personalized learning and simulation in nursing.

REFERENCES

Agency for Healthcare Research and Quality. *Team Strategies & Tools to Enhance Performance & Patient Safety.* (2014). https://www.ahrq.gov/teamstepps-program/index.html

Bloom, B. S. (1968). Learning for Mastery. Instruction and Curriculum. Regional Education Laboratory for the Carolinas and Virginia, Topical Papers and Reprints, Number 1. *Evaluation Comment, 1*(2). https://eric.ed.gov/?id=eD053419

Cecile, C. D. Q., & Richard, T. (2018). Étude De La Communication Interprofessionnelle Entre Medecins Et Infirmiers Exercant En Maisons De Sante Pluri-Professionnelles (Doctoral dissertation). file:///C:/Users/az/Downloads/THm_2018_CARNEIRO_DE_QUEIROZ_Cecile_et_TY_Richard%20(1).pdf

Cohen, A., Doucède, G., Clouqueur, E., Debarge, V., Béhal, H., Rubod, C., & Hanssens, S. (2021). Utilisation de l'outil SAED : Évaluation de l'intérêt d'une formation courte sur la qualité de la communication entre soignants à court et à long terme. *Gynécologie, Obstétrique, Fertilité & Sénologie*, *49*(11), 823–829. Advance online publication. DOI: 10.1016/j.gofs.2021.04.010 PMID: 33933673

Cohen, E. R., Feinglass, J., Barsuk, J. H., Barnard, C., O'Donnell, A., McGaghie, W. C., & Wayne, D. B. (2010). Cost Savings From Reduced Catheter-Related Bloodstream Infection After Simulation-Based Education for Residents in a Medical Intensive Care Unit. *Simulation in Healthcare*, *5*(2), 98–102. DOI: 10.1097/SIH.0b013e3181bc8304 PMID: 20389233

Cook, D. A., Hatala, R., Brydges, R., Zendejas, B., Szostek, J. H., Wang, A. T., Erwin, P. J., & Hamstra, S. J. (n.d.). *Technology-Enhanced Simulation for Health Professions Education*. 11.

Dimova, R., Stoyanova, R., & Doykov, I. (2018). Mixed-methods study of reported clinical cases of undesirable events, medical errors, and near misses in health care. *Journal of Evaluation in Clinical Practice*, *24*(4), 752–757. DOI: 10.1111/jep.12970 PMID: 29947085

Elsaadany, I. K., Gonzalez-Vargas, J. M., Moore, J. Z., & Miller, S. R. (2023). Progressive Medical Simulation: An Analysis of the Integration of Progressive and Personalized Learning in Central Line Simulators. *Proceedings of the Human Factors and Ergonomics Society Annual Meeting*, *67*(1), 1868–1874. DOI: 10.1177/21695067231192713 PMID: 38450121

Foronda, C., Liu, S., & Bauman, E. B. (2013). Evaluation of Simulation in Undergraduate Nurse Education: An Integrative Review. *Clinical Simulation in Nursing*, *9*(10), e409–e416. DOI: 10.1016/j.ecns.2012.11.003

Gaba, D. M. (2004). The future vision of simulation in health care. *BMJ Quality & Safety*, *13*(suppl 1), i2–i10. DOI: 10.1136/qshc.2004.009878 PMID: 15465951

Haig, K. M., Sutton, S., & Whittington, J. (2006). SBAR: A Shared Mental Model for Improving Communication Between Clinicians. *Joint Commission Journal on Quality and Patient Safety*, *32*(3), 167–175. DOI: 10.1016/S1553-7250(06)32022-3 PMID: 16617948

Haute Autorité de Santé (HAS). *SAED: Un guide pour faciliter la communication entre professionnels de santé*. (2014, October). Haute Autorité de Santé. https://www.has-sante.fr/jcms/c_1776178/fr/saed-un-guide-pour-faciliter-la-communication-entre-professionnels-de-sante

Le Levier, C., Cluzel, F., Hadjeb, L., & Lemée, F. (2018). Transposition de la méthodologie SAED en formation aide-soignante. *L'Aide-Soignante*, *32*(202), 26–28. DOI: 10.1016/j.aidsoi.2018.10.009

Leonard, M., Graham, S., & Bonacum, D. (2004). The human factor: The critical importance of effective teamwork and communication in providing safe care. *BMJ Quality & Safety*, *13*(suppl 1), i85–i90. DOI: 10.1136/qshc.2004.010033 PMID: 15465961

McGaghie, W. C., Issenberg, S. B., Cohen, E. R., Barsuk, J. H., & Wayne, D. B. (2011). Does Simulation-Based Medical Education With Deliberate Practice Yield Better Results Than Traditional Clinical Education? A Meta-Analytic Comparative Review of the Evidence. *Academic Medicine*, *86*(6), 706–711. DOI: 10.1097/ACM.0b013e318217e119 PMID: 21512370

Michiels, I. (2018). Etude de l'impact potentiel d'une formation par e-learning au Situation-Background-Assessment Recommendation (SBAR) auprès d'étudiants infirmiers (Master's thesis). https://luck.synhera.be/bitstream/handle/123456789/300/18%20mai-MICHIELS%20Isabelle-M2%20PASI-Me%20moire-1.pdf?sequence=1

Peters, G. A., & Peters, B. J. (2007). *Medical Error and Patient Safety: Human Factors in Medicine*. CRC Press., DOI: 10.1201/9781420064797

Riesenberg, L. A., Leisch, J., & Cunningham, J. M. (2010). Nursing Handoffs: A Systematic Review of the Literature. *The American Journal of Nursing*, *110*(4), 24–34. DOI: 10.1097/01.NAJ.0000370154.79857.09 PMID: 20335686

Thomas, C. M., Bertram, E., & Johnson, D. (2009). The SBAR Communication Technique: Teaching Nursing Students Professional Communication Skills. *Nurse Educator*, *34*(4), 176–180. DOI: 10.1097/NNE.0b013e3181aaba54 PMID: 19574858

Vujadinovic, N. (2020). Communication and Public Relations in Healthcare. In *Health Information Management: Empowering Public Health* (pp. 42–51). IOS Press. https://doi.org/DOI: 10.3233/SHTI200664

Zwarenstein, M., Goldman, J., & Reeves, S. (2009). Interprofessional collaboration: Effects of practice-based interventions on professional practice and healthcare outcomes. *The Cochrane Library*. Advance online publication. DOI: 10.1002/14651858.CD000072.pub2 PMID: 19588316

Chapter 8
Personalized Adaptive Learning Among Midwifery and Nursing Students: A Scoping Review

Aziz Naciri
https://orcid.org/0000-0001-7318-6633
Higher Institute of Nursing Professions and Health Techniques of Laàyoune, Morocco

Lahoucine Benyahya
https://orcid.org/0000-0001-8366-6446
Faculty of Sciences Ben M'Sik, University Hassan II, Morocco

Mohamed Radid
https://orcid.org/0000-0002-8082-2009
Faculty of Sciences Ben M'Sik, University Hassan II, Morocco

Ghizlane Chemsi
Faculty of Sciences Ben M'Sik, University Hassan II, Morocco

ABSTRACT

Purpose: Personalized adaptive learning uses technology to adjust teaching strategies in real time, adapting to the characteristics, performance and evolution of each learner. This scoping review aims to explore and synthesize existing knowledge on the application of personalized, individualized, intelligent or responsive learning systems in the training of nursing and midwifery students. Methods: This review

DOI: 10.4018/979-8-3373-0740-4.ch008

followed exploratory review methodology in accordance with PRISMA guidelines. Searches were conducted in the main international databases: Scopus, PubMed, ScienceDirect. Results: The included studies reported that Adaptive Learning improves students' academic performance and promotes engagement, with an increase in learner involvement. Likewise, it enables learning to be personalized by adjusting content to individual student needs. Conclusion: This study explored the use of personalized adaptive learning among midwifery and nursing students. Further research is needed to address technological challenges and enhance its implementation in education.

INTRODUCTION

As digital technologies continue to reshape educational practices, adaptive learning technologies stand out as a promising innovation to cater to the diverse needs of learners (Sacré et al., 2020). These systems, based on artificial intelligence and data analysis, enable the personalization of educational pathways according to each individual's skills, preferences, and learning pace (Martin et al., 2020). With their ability to dynamically adjust educational content, these tools aim to optimize the knowledge acquisition process while supporting learners' motivation and engagement (Belfer et al., 2022). Nevertheless, their adoption sparks discussions on both pedagogical and technical fronts. Although these technologies provide clear benefits, including personalized learning experiences, accurate progress monitoring, and instant feedback, they also come with notable drawbacks. These include high implementation costs, greater reliance on technology, diminished human interactions, and ethical issues surrounding the handling of learners' personal data (Jares et al., 2019; Zotou et al., 2020).

In nursing education, adapting teaching practices to the needs of students is crucial to ensure high-quality training. Adaptive learning technologies, based on artificial intelligence and data analysis, allow for the personalization of content, pace, and learning methods, thereby enhancing the clinical and theoretical skills of future nurses (Andersen et al., 2021; De Gagne & health, 2023). The scope of application of adaptive learning technologies in nursing education is vast. They can be used in online learning platforms to deliver theoretical courses, in virtual simulators to practice technical skills, or in assessment modules to track learners' progress. These technologies are applicable both in initial and continuing education, offering essential flexibility for professionals in career transition or skill enhancement.

Objective

The purpose of this scoping review is to explore and analyze the various approaches to personalized adaptive learning implemented in the training of midwifery and nursing students. It focuses on examining the teaching strategies and technologies used, while evaluating their effects on the teaching and learning process.

METHODS

1. Study design

This scoping review was described according to the Preferred Reporting Items for Systematic Reviews and Meta-Analyses (Page et al., 2021). These guidelines aim to ensure transparency, rigor, and standardization in conducting systematic reviews. They include a series of points to follow, such as source identification, inclusion/ exclusion criteria, and result presentation.

2. Eligibility criteria

The inclusion and exclusion criteria were defined using the Population, Intervention, Comparison, Outcome, and Study Design (PICOS) (table 1).

Table 1. Inclusion and exclusion criteria.

Variable	Description
Population	Nursing and midwifery students.
Intervention	This scoping review will include studies investigating adaptive and personalized learning, focusing on impact on educational outcomes.
comparison	The comparison between groups of students employing traditional methods and those using adaptive or personalized learning highlights critical differences in teaching approaches and their impact on student outcomes.
Outcome	To be eligible for inclusion, studies must evaluate the impact of adaptive and personalized learning on student outcomes in academic settings.
Study Design	This scoping review included quantitative and mixed-method studies, such as randomized controlled trials, case-control studies, cross-sectional studies, and mixed-method studies, to ensure a rigorous and diverse analysis of the available data. Conversely, qualitative studies, letters to the editor, editorials, conference abstracts, book chapters, and literature reviews were excluded due to their descriptive or non-empirical nature, in order to maintain a high level of reliability and comparability of the results.

3. Information sources

The literature search was conducted in the following databases: PubMed, ScienceDirect, and Scopus. Only studies published in English from the inception of the databases to Novembre 2024 were included. The final search check was completed on Novembre 20, 2024.

4. Search strategy

Two researchers (A.N and G.C.) collaboratively identified the terms, keywords, and combinations for inclusion in each database, as illustrated in Table 2.

Table 2. Search strategy and terms according to the databases

Data base	Combination
Scopus	(Title-Abs ("Personalized learning" or "Individualized learning" or "Intelligent learning systems" or "Responsive learning")) and (Title-abs ("Midwife" or "Nursing student" or "Nursing education"))
Pubmed	(((("Personalized learning"[Title/abstract]) or ("Individualized learning"[Title/abstract])) or ("Intelligent learning systems"[Title/abstract])) or ("Responsive learning"[Title/abstract])) and ((("Midwife"[Title/abstract]) or ("Nursing student"[Title/abstract])) or ("Nursing education"[Title/abstract]))
Science direct	Title, abstract, keywords: ("Personalized learning" or "Individualized learning" or "Intelligent learning systems" or "Responsive learning") and ("Midwife" or "Nursing student" or "Nursing education")

5. Selection and data collection process

Two authors, A.N and L.B, conducted independent reviews following the defined inclusion and exclusion criteria. They examined titles, abstracts, full-text articles, and keywords. Duplicate entries were electronically identified and removed using EndNote X9. The selection and screening process was then managed using Rayyan QCRI (Ouzzani et al., 2016). Articles deemed potentially eligible were downloaded for detailed and thorough analysis. Any disagreements regarding study selection were resolved through consultation with a third researcher, M.R.

6. Data items

The following data was extracted from the included studies: the author and year of publication, which situates each study within its temporal context; the country of origin, providing a geographical perspective on the research conducted; the study design, indicating the methodology adopted; the sample size, essential for assessing the statistical robustness of the findings; the nature of the intervention, which specifies the type of action or program studied; the educational content, detailing the pedagogical or informational elements included in the intervention; the frequency and duration, which provide insights into the intensity and timeframe of the intervention; the measurement instruments, used to evaluate the outcomes and ensure their reliability; and finally, the key findings, which summarize the most significant results of each study. This information enables a thorough analysis and a nuanced understanding of the educational interventions documented in the literature.

RESULTS

1. Study selection

The database search identified a total of 53 articles: 20 in Scopus, 14 in Science-Direct, and 19 in PubMed. These articles were imported into the EndNote software to remove duplicates, resulting in the elimination of 23 studies. Of the remaining 30 studies, 17 were excluded based on inclusion and exclusion criteria by analyzing the titles and abstracts of the articles using the systematic review application Rayyan. The 13 potentially eligible articles were downloaded for in-depth analysis. Finally, 4 studies were included in the present review. The study selection process for this review is illustrated in (Fig. 1) through a PRISMA diagram.

Figure 1. PRISMA flowchart of selected studies.

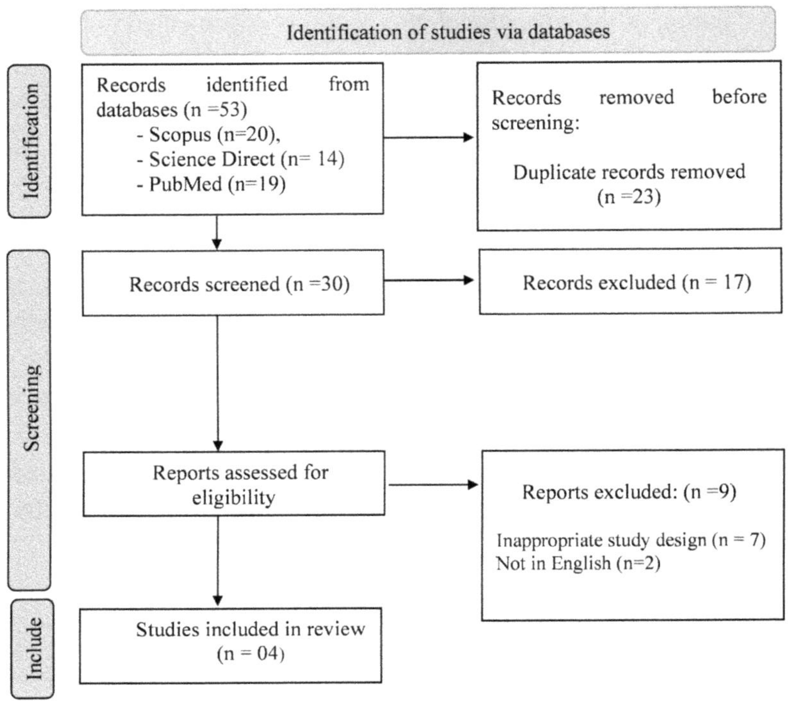

2. Study characteristics

The four studies included in this review focus on nursing education tailored to students pedagogical needs, with particular emphasis on diverse educational contexts, involving a total of 292 participants. Firstly, Govindan et al. (Govindan et al., 2023) conducted a study involving 54 students enrolled in an anatomy and physiology course, comparing a blended learning approach (e-books and interactive activities) with traditional teaching. Similarly, Hinkle et al. (Hinkle, 2023) studied 116 students in a pathophysiology and pharmacology course, exploring the impact of personalized learning through the Canvas Mastery Paths platform. In addition, Kim et al (Kim et al., 2017) examined two flipped classroom models applied to 62 students as part of practical nursing training. Meanwhile, In Jordan, Azizeh et al. (Sowan & Jenkins, 2013) conducted a study with 60 students, divided between hybrid and distance learning in a nursing communication course enhanced with online modules. It is important to highlight that all participants are nursing students enrolled in courses related to their professional practice, including anatomy, physiology, communication, pharmacology, or practical skills. Furthermore, sample sizes range from 54 participants (Govindan et al., 2023) to 116 (Hinkle, 2023). Notably, the educational contexts reflect contrasting environments: two studies are from developed countries (Hinkle, 2023; Kim et al., 2017) and two from developing countries (Govindan et al., 2023; Sowan & Jenkins, 2013). This distinction underscores that geographical and socio-economic diversity potentially influences pedagogical approaches and access to resources.

Moreover, the methodologies adopted in these studies also illustrate a variety of approaches. Govindan et al. used a quasi-experimental method to compare a control group (traditional teaching) with an experimental group (blended learning) (Govindan et al., 2023). In contrast, Hinkle et al. conducted a pilot study over two semesters to evaluate the effect of personalized learning on academic performance (Hinkle, 2023). Additionally, Kim et al. (Kim et al., 2017) conducted a randomized controlled trial to compare two flipped classroom models, whereas, Sowan et al. (Sowan & Jenkins, 2013) employed a mixed descriptive approach combining satisfaction questionnaires, academic performance analysis, and tracking of access to online content.

The learning designs adopted reflect innovative and diverse pedagogical strategies. For instance, Govindan et al. (Govindan et al., 2023) developed a blended learning approach integrating e-books, videos, dissections, and interactive notes to promote student autonomy. Similarly, Hinkle et al. (Hinkle, 2023) implemented personalized learning based on weekly quizzes via Canvas. In a different context, Kim et al. tested flipped classroom models incorporating pre-class videos, reflective journals, and in-class activities focused on practical skills (Kim et al., 2017). Finally, Sowan et al. (Sowan & Jenkins, 2013) designed a hybrid or distance learning course using platforms such as Blackboard and Tegrity, while also enriching the learning experience with interactive modules, online discussions, and collaborative assignments

Table 3. Overview of Studies Included in the Review

Author/ Country/ Year	Study Design	Sample Size	Nature of Intervention	Educational Content	Frequency and Duration	Measurement Instruments	Key Findings
(Govindan et al., 2023) Malaysia	Quasi-experimental approach with a non-equivalent control group	Control group: 24 students Intervention group: 30 students	Blended learning using e-books Compared to traditional teaching	Anatomy and Physiology course	30 minutes of online lectures 90 minutes of participatory activities	Self-Directed Learning Readiness (SDLR) Scale	SDLR scores significantly higher in the intervention group (P=0.019) Improvements in self-management and self-control subscales
(Hinkle, 2023) Usa	Pilot study using a personalized learning	Fall 2021: 57 students Spring 2022: 59 students	Redesign of a nursing course using Canvas© Mastery Paths	Pathophysiology and pharmacology course	Weekly quizzes during the Spring 2022 semester	Course grades, exam grades, and Canvas© New Analytics data	Significant improvement in course grades with personalized learning (P=0.018) Positive correlation between quiz and course outcomes
(Kim et al., 2017) South Korea	Randomized controlled trial	Initial: 69 participants; Final: 62 participants (after dropout)	Two flipped learning models for clinical placements: 1. Flipped-Mastery Classroom Model (FMCM) 2. Flipped-Mastery Practicum Model (FMPM)	Pre-class videos, reflective journals, in-class activities and follow-up discussions focusing on basic nursing skills	Pre-class activities: 3 days Internship period: 2 weeks	1. Academic motivation questionnaire (ARCS model) 2. Satisfaction questionnaire 3. Visual Analog Confidence Scale	Both groups showed an increase in confidence in basic skills. Satisfaction was higher for the FMCM model.
(Sowan & Jenkins, 2013) Jordan	Descriptive study with mixed methodology	60 students in total: 25 in distance learning and 35 in hybrid classes	Nursing communication course designed using Blackboard and Tegrity	Online modules: learning objectives, interactive videos (max. 20 min.), glossary, manuals, forum questions, individual and group assignments	16 weeks (a full semester, autumn), with face-to-face meetings once a month for distance learners	Satisfaction questionnaire (27 items, Likert scale), academic performance	High satisfaction with distance learning courses (average score: 4.14/5). Performance of distance students (80 ± 8.2) higher than that of hybrid students (72.2 ± 9.5).

3. Main findings

The four studies included in this scoping review explore innovative pedagogical approaches aimed at improving student learning in nursing education. Although they differ in their pedagogical methods, they all converge on the idea that adaptive and personalized learning plays a crucial role in enhancing student learning. Each approach emphasizes the importance of adapting teaching to the individual needs of learners, whether through blended, flipped, or online methods.

1) Self-directed learning and motivation

The results of the studies conducted by Govindan et al. and Kim et al. (Govindan et al., 2023; Kim et al., 2017) demonstrate how adaptive learning promotes autonomy and motivation. The blended learning approach described by Govindan et al. (Govindan et al., 2023) enables students to take greater responsibility for their own learning, thereby fostering self-management and self-regulation critical skills in the nursing field. Similarly, Kim et al.(Kim et al., 2017) how that flipped classroom models focused on practical skills not only enhance student motivation but also build confidence in their abilities, which are key elements for professional development.

2) Personalized learning

Hinkle et al. (Hinkle, 2023) highlight the benefits of truly personalized learning through platforms like Canvas. By adapting educational content to the individual needs of students and providing personalized tracking of their progress, the study demonstrated significant improvements in academic performance. This approach aligns seamlessly with the concept of adaptive learning, in which each student benefits from instruction and support specifically tailored to their needs, thereby maximizing their potential.

3) Blended and distance learning formats

Sowan et al. (Sowan & Jenkins, 2013), on the other hand, provide valuable reflections on hybrid and distance learning modalities. While technology and resources have significantly evolved since this study, it nonetheless raises pertinent questions about the effectiveness of fully distance-based learning. In the context of an adaptive learning framework, these formats have the potential to offer more flexible and personalized solutions. However, issues related to resource access and infrastructure management continue to represent significant challenges that require careful consideration.

4) Impact on adaptive and personalized learning

These results underscore a key phenomenon: adaptive and personalized learning significantly enhance student engagement, motivation, and performance. By placing students at the center of their learning process and employing varied approaches tailored to their individual needs, they are more likely to develop self-directed learning skills and effectively manage their academic journey. For example, the learning formats proposed by Govindan et al. (Govindan et al., 2023), Kim et al. (Kim et al., 2017), Hinkle et al. (Hinkle, 2023), and and Sowan et al. (Sowan & Jenkins, 2013) foster a more active pedagogy, where the student becomes the principal agent of their own development an essential aspect in the training of future healthcare professionals.

These studies converge on the conclusion that pedagogical innovation whether based on digital tools, flipped models, or personalized approaches significantly enhances student engagement and learning outcomes. Nevertheless, they also reveal key divergences: while Govindan et al. (Govindan et al., 2023) and Kim et al. (Kim et al., 2017) primarily focus on fostering self-direction and motivation, Hinkle et al. (Hinkle, 2023) and Sowan et al. (Sowan & Jenkins, 2013) emphasize academic performance and student satisfaction. Moreover, the effectiveness of these interventions appears to depend heavily on the quality of available infrastructure and resources, which remains a significant challenge in contexts where these tools are either inaccessible or insufficiently mastered.

Overall, these four studies underscore the pressing need to reform nursing education to better align with the expectations and needs of modern students. Technological tools and innovative pedagogical approaches demonstrate significant potential to enhance motivation, autonomy, and academic results. However, further research involving larger sample sizes, diverse educational contexts, and long-term analysis is essential to fully evaluate the effectiveness and sustainability of these interventions.

DISCUSSION

The results of the included studies clearly demonstrate the effectiveness of various innovative pedagogical approaches in nursing education, highlighting significant improvements in academic performance, self-directed learning, self-confidence, and student satisfaction. Govindan et al. (Govindan et al., 2023) emphasize the positive impact of blended learning on student autonomy, with significantly higher scores in self-management and self-control. These findings are consistent with previous research (Bernard et al., 2018; Nortvig et al., 2018), suggesting that the integration of interactive and digital resources, such as e-books, not only facilitates knowledge acquisition but also promotes the development of essential skills for self-directed learning—a crucial competency in nursing education. Furthermore, these results support the notion that pedagogical approaches incorporating digital tools can better prepare students for the demands of professional practice, where autonomy and self-management are indispensable.

The study conducted by Hinkle et al. (Hinkle, 2023) validates the effectiveness of personalized learning using the Canvas platform, demonstrating a significant improvement in course grades and a positive correlation between weekly quizzes and overall academic performance. Similarly, these findings align with the results of prior studies (Bernacki et al., 2021; Rubio-Arraez, 2022; Sahni & Education, 2019), highlighting the importance of adaptability in teaching by addressing the specific needs of students. This underscores the role of digital platforms in facilitating differentiated learning pathways, while also boosting motivation and engagement. In another context, Kim et al. (Kim et al., 2017) explored two flipped classroom models, reporting an increase in students' confidence in their practical skills, with higher satisfaction for the FMCM model. These results are consistent with other studies (Bergmann, 2012; Naciri et al., 2022; Zheng et al., 2020), illustrating that the combination of pre-class activities (e.g., videos and reflective journals) and interactive in-class practices can optimize active learning and prepare students for clinical settings. The preference for the FMCM model may be attributed to its more structured framework, which enhances the overall learning experience. This finding underscores the effectiveness of well-structured online courses, equipped with interactive tools and accessible resources, even in resource-limited environments. Moreover, these results highlight the importance of access to learning technologies in improving outcomes, particularly in developing countries such as Jordan.

In summary, these findings emphasize that innovative teaching methods integrating technologies can simultaneously improve academic performance and foster the personal development of nursing students. However, their effectiveness appears to be influenced by factors such as cultural context, the quality of educational infrastructures, and the design of pedagogical interventions.

CONCLUSION

This scoping review highlights that innovative teaching methods, such as adaptive and personalized learning, play a crucial role in enhancing student engagement, motivation, and performance in nursing education. The findings from the included studies suggest that these methods foster student autonomy and professional development, while offering flexible solutions tailored to individual needs. However, their effectiveness is largely contingent upon the quality of available infrastructure and resources, underscoring the need for a broader and more thoughtful adoption of these technologies. Therefore, it is essential to continue investing in educational technologies, ensuring that both teachers and students have the necessary resources to fully leverage these innovations. Future research involving larger sample sizes and long-term interventions will provide a more comprehensive assessment of the effectiveness of these methods in nursing education, taking into account the rapid advancement of educational technologies and the evolving needs of students.

CONFLICTS OF INTEREST

No potential conflict of interest relevant to this article was reported.

FUNDING

None.

REFERENCES

Andersen, B. L., Jørnø, R. L., & Nortvig, A.-M. J. C. E. T. (2021). Blending adaptive learning technology into nursing education: A scoping review. *14*(1), ep333.

Belfer, R., Kochmar, E., & Serban, I. V. (2022). Raising student completion rates with adaptive curriculum and contextual bandits. International Conference on Artificial Intelligence in Education, Bergmann, J. (2012). Flip your classroom: Reach every student in every class every day. DOI: 10.1007/978-3-031-11644-5_74

Bernacki, M. L., Greene, M. J., & Lobczowski, N. G. J. E. P. R. (2021). A systematic review of research on personalized learning: Personalized by whom, to what, how, and for what purpose (s)?, *33*(4), 1675-1715.

Bernard, R. M., Borokhovski, E., & Tamim, R. M. (2018). The state of research on distance, online, and blended learning: Meta-analyses and qualitative systematic reviews. In *Handbook of distance education* (pp. 92–104). Routledge. DOI: 10.4324/9781315296135-8

De Gagne, J. C. J. I. j. o. e. r., & health, p. (2023). The state of artificial intelligence in nursing education: Past, present, and future directions. In (Vol. 20, pp. 4884): MDPI.

Govindan, S. N., Singh, H. K., Ling, L. W., Sekar, M. J. J. o. E., & Promotion, H. (2023). Effect of blended self-directed learning on nursing students: Quasi-experimental approach. *12*(1), 229.

Hinkle, J. F. J. S. O. N. (2023). Personalization and Learning Outcome in a Nursing Pathophysiology and Pharmacology Course: Canvas© Mastery Adoption Pilot Study. *9*, 23779608231186030.

Jares, T. E., Wilcox, W., Cahalan, R., & Dickey, G. J. T. A. e. j. (2019). An examination of the effectiveness of online adaptive learning technologies. *29*(1).

Kim, H. S., Kim, M. Y., Cho, M. K., & Jang, S. J. J. I. J. o. N. P. (2017). Effectiveness of applying flipped learning to clinical nursing practicums for nursing students in Korea: A randomized controlled trial. *23*(5), e12574.

Martin, F., Chen, Y., Moore, R. L., Westine, C. D. J. E. T. R., & Development. (2020). Systematic review of adaptive learning research designs, context, strategies, and technologies from 2009 to 2018. *68*(4), 1903-1929.

Naciri, A., Hajji, M. E., Radid, M., Kharbach, A., & Chemsi, G. J. E. J. o. G. M. (2022). Exploring Student Motivation and Performance in the Flipped Classroom: A Case Study of Nursing Students. *19*(3).

Nortvig, A.-M., Petersen, A. K., & Balle, S. H. J. E. J. o. E.-l. (2018). A literature review of the factors influencing e-learning and blended learning in relation to learning outcome, student satisfaction and engagement. *16*(1), pp46-55-pp46-55.

Ouzzani, M., Hammady, H., Fedorowicz, Z., & Elmagarmid, A. (2016). Rayyan—A web and mobile app for systematic reviews. *Systematic Reviews*, *5*(1), 1–10. DOI: 10.1186/s13643-016-0384-4 PMID: 27919275

Page, M. J., McKenzie, J. E., Bossuyt, P. M., Boutron, I., Hoffmann, T. C., Mulrow, C. D., Shamseer, L., Tetzlaff, J. M., Akl, E. A., Brennan, S. E., Chou, R., Glanville, J., Grimshaw, J. M., Hróbjartsson, A., Lalu, M. M., Li, T., Loder, E. W., Mayo-Wilson, E., McDonald, S., & Moher, D. (2021). The PRISMA 2020 statement: An updated guideline for reporting systematic reviews. *BMJ (Clinical Research Ed.)*, *372*(71), n71. Advance online publication. DOI: 10.1136/bmj.n71 PMID: 33782057

Rubio-Arraez, S. (2022). Improving academic performance through the combination of canvas and blackboard learn platforms in master's degree students. In *EDULEARN22 Proceedings* (pp. 8856-8862). IATED.

Sacré, M., Toczek, M. C., Policard, F., Serres, G., Paulet, C., Petit, S., ... & Lafontaine, D. (2020). L'efficacité d'un dispositif d'enseignement hybride en fonction des caractéristiques des étudiants. Revue internationale des technologies en pédagogie universitaire, 17(2), 9-29.

Sahni, J. J. J. o. E.-l., & Education, H. (2019). Does blended learning enhance student engagement? Evidence from higher education. *2019*(2019), 1-14.

Sowan, A. K., & Jenkins, L. S. J. I. j. o. m. i. (2013). Designing, delivering and evaluating a distance learning nursing course responsive to students needs. *82*(6), 553-564.

Zheng, L., Bhagat, K. K., Zhen, Y., Zhang, X. J. J. o. E. T., & Society. (2020). The effectiveness of the flipped classroom on students' learning achievement and learning motivation. *23*(1), 1-15.

Zotou, M., Tambouris, E., Tarabanis, K. J. E. T. R., & Development. (2020). Data-driven problem based learning: Enhancing problem based learning with learning analytics. *68*(6), 3393-3424.

Chapter 9
Enhancing Engagement and Equity in Personalized Learning Through Adaptive Systems

Mohsen Mahmoudi-Dehaki
https://orcid.org/0000-0002-4962-6827
Islamic Azad University, Najafabad, Iran

Nasim Nasr-Esfahani
https://orcid.org/0000-0002-2388-6524
Islamic Azad University, Isfahan, Iran

ABSTRACT

The chapter discusses personalized learning and adaptive systems, emphasizing their role in enhancing student engagement and equity. It highlights how these approaches tailor educational experiences to meet individual needs through real-time data analysis. Key features include continuous assessment, immediate feedback, and customized learning pathways that allow students to progress at their own pace, fostering motivation and ownership of their learning. Adaptive systems also address educational disparities by providing targeted support for underperforming students, ensuring equitable access to resources. By personalizing the learning experience, these technologies enable students to choose pathways that align with their interests and learning styles, promoting a sense of autonomy. Ultimately, the chapter argues that integrating adaptive systems into personalized learning frameworks is essential for creating an equitable educational environment where all students can thrive.

DOI: 10.4018/979-8-3373-0740-4.ch009

INTRODUCTION

The evolution of personalized learning and adaptive systems is a complex narrative that intertwines educational philosophy, societal needs, and technological advancements. The philosophical underpinnings of personalized learning can be traced back to the Enlightenment, particularly through the works of Jean-Jacques Rousseau. In his seminal work, Emile, or On Education, Rousseau advocated for education that respects the natural development of children, emphasizing individualized learning experiences tailored to each child's unique needs and interests. This perspective laid the groundwork for later educational reforms that sought to prioritize the learner's experience over rigid curricula. During the Victorian era, educational reformers began implementing more structured approaches to personalization. The monitorial system, popularized by Joseph Lancaster, allowed advanced students to assist in teaching their peers, effectively creating a tiered learning environment. This model aimed to address the educational needs of large groups while still providing some level of individualized instruction

The early 20th century marked a significant shift towards progressive education, largely influenced by John Dewey. In his 1916 book Democracy and Education, Dewey argued for an educational framework centered on student engagement and active learning. He believed that education should foster critical thinking and social interaction within small learning communities, which are directly aligned with personalized learning principles. Simultaneously, Maria Montessori developed her educational philosophy, emphasizing self-directed activity and hands-on learning. Her methods encouraged children to explore their interests at their own pace within a prepared environment. Montessori's approach reinforced the idea that education should be tailored to individual learners, further enriching the discourse on personalized education.

The 1960s and 1970s saw the emergence of competency-based education models. Fred Keller's Personalized System of Instruction (PSI) allowed students to progress through content at their own pace, with assessments determining readiness for advancement. This mastery-oriented approach was revolutionary in its recognition of individual learning trajectories. Benjamin Bloom's research during this period further validated personalized approaches. His studies indicated that when students were given opportunities for mastery learning—where they could revisit material until they achieved proficiency—they significantly outperformed peers in traditional settings. Bloom's findings reinforced the importance of adapting instruction to meet individual student needs.

The advent of digital technology has transformed personalized learning into a more scalable and accessible model. Online platforms and adaptive learning technologies now allow for real-time data collection on student performance, enabling educators to tailor instruction dynamically based on individual progress. This shift marks a departure from earlier models by leveraging technology to facilitate personalized experiences on a larger scale. In 2005, Dan Buckley articulated two distinct forms of personalized learning: "personalization for the learner," where educators design tailored experiences, and "personalization by the learner," where students actively shape their own educational journeys. This duality reflects contemporary practices that empower students while still providing necessary guidance from educators.

Integrating adaptive systems to enhance engagement and equity in personalized learning has become increasingly vital in the evolving educational landscape. Personalized learning is an instructional approach that tailors education to meet individual students' diverse needs, interests, and abilities (Rickabaugh, 2016). By leveraging adaptive systems, which utilize advanced algorithms and data analytics, educators can create dynamic learning environments that respond to student performance and foster a deeper level of engagement. Adaptive learning is defined by its ability to adjust instructional content, pace, and assessment based on real-time learner progress and preferences analysis (Saba & Shearer, 2017). This innovative approach utilizes sophisticated algorithms to gather and interpret data on student interactions with learning materials, enabling the system to provide customized educational experiences that resonate with each learner's unique profile. For instance, adaptive learning platforms can modify the difficulty of tasks or suggest additional resources based on a student's demonstrated understanding of concepts, ensuring that instruction remains relevant and appropriately challenging.

The effectiveness of adaptive learning in enhancing student engagement is particularly noteworthy. By presenting content that aligns with individual interests and strengths, adaptive systems can significantly increase motivation and enjoyment in the learning process. Research (e.g., Cheng et al., 2010) indicates that students who engage with personalized content are more likely to remain focused and invested in their education. Furthermore, adaptive learning environments allow learners to progress at their own pace, which helps mitigate feelings of boredom or frustration often associated with traditional, one-size-fits-all educational models. This individualized pace caters to faster learners and supports those who require additional time to grasp complex concepts.

A critical component of adaptive learning is its emphasis on continuous assessment and immediate feedback (Benosman, 2016). Unlike traditional assessments that may occur infrequently, adaptive systems offer ongoing evaluations through various formats—such as interactive simulations or real-world problem-solving exercises. This real-time feedback loop enables students to identify areas needing improvement promptly, fostering a sense of self-efficacy and encouraging continuous growth. By addressing misconceptions as they arise and reinforcing understanding through tailored feedback, learners develop metacognitive skills that enhance their overall educational experience.

Equity in education is another significant benefit of implementing adaptive systems within personalized learning frameworks. These technologies ensure that all students have access to resources tailored to their specific needs, thereby addressing disparities that have historically plagued educational outcomes. Adaptive systems can identify gaps in knowledge and provide targeted interventions for underperforming students, ensuring they receive the necessary support to succeed. This commitment to equitable access helps close achievement gaps and fosters an inclusive environment where every learner can thrive.

Moreover, adaptive systems promote equity and enhance student engagement and motivation (Levy, 2015). By personalizing the learning experience, these technologies allow students to progress at their own pace, choosing pathways that resonate with their interests and learning styles. This autonomy fosters a sense of ownership over their education, encouraging students to take an active role in their learning journey. As they encounter challenges tailored to their skill level and receive immediate feedback, students are more likely to remain motivated and invested in their studies. Ultimately, this increased engagement contributes to a more dynamic and responsive educational environment where learners feel empowered to explore their potential fully.

As we explore the integration of engagement, equity, and personalized learning through adaptive systems, it becomes evident that this multifaceted approach enhances educational experiences and aligns with broader social justice goals within education. By effectively harnessing technology to meet diverse learner needs, we can create a more equitable educational landscape that empowers all students to reach their full potential. The future of education lies in our ability to adapt content and pedagogical strategies to embrace every learner's unique journey.

1. UNDERSTANDING ADAPTIVE SYSTEMS

Adaptive learning technologies refer to educational systems that utilize data-driven algorithms to customize learning experiences for individual students (Kuhlthau & Maniotes, 2010). By analyzing a learner's interactions, preferences, and performance metrics in real-time, these systems can modify the educational content, pacing, and instructional strategies to optimize learning outcomes. The goal is to create a more engaging and effective learning environment that meets the diverse needs of students.

1.1. Types of Adaptive Learning Systems

Adaptive learning encompasses several types of systems designed to enhance educational experiences. Intelligent tutoring systems (ITS) emulate the personalized support offered by human tutors, providing tailored guidance, hints, and feedback as learners engage with problem-solving tasks (Wenger, 2014). These systems are particularly beneficial in subjects like mathematics or science, where they can adaptively present problems based on a student's previous answers.

Exploratory learning environments empower students to navigate their learning paths based on personal interests and goals (De Freitas, 2013). While promoting autonomy and self-directed exploration, these systems also incorporate adaptive feedback mechanisms that help guide learners toward relevant resources and activities.

Game-based learning platforms integrate gamification elements to engage students through interactive gameplay while adapting challenges according to individual performance levels (Prensky, 2007). By leveraging game mechanics such as rewards and levels, these systems motivate learners to progress at their own pace while receiving adaptive support.

Basic tutoring systems utilize decision trees or rule-based approaches to provide structured feedback based on predetermined criteria. Although these systems may not offer the same level of adaptability as more advanced technologies, they can still effectively guide learners through specific content areas. Many modern learning management systems (LMS) also incorporate adaptive features, allowing personalized course delivery. These LMS analyze learner data to suggest resources or modify course materials based on student performance and engagement levels (Foreman, 2017).

1.2. Mechanisms of Adaptation

Adaptive learning technologies employ a variety of mechanisms to adjust educational content based on student interactions and performance data (McLeod & Graber, 2018). Ongoing assessment is a key feature; unlike traditional assessments that occur at fixed points, adaptive learning systems continuously evaluate student performance throughout the learning process. This real-time assessment enables immediate adjustments to the learning path, ensuring that students are consistently challenged without becoming overwhelmed.

Instantaneous feedback is another crucial element in adaptive learning environments. Providing immediate responses helps reinforce concepts and correct misunderstandings. Adaptive systems deliver real-time feedback on student actions, guiding learners toward mastery of the material while clarifying mistakes (Pollock, 2012). Customized learning pathways are created for each learner, allowing them to follow a distinct trajectory through the curriculum tailored to their strengths, weaknesses, and preferences (Williamson, 2017). For instance, if a student struggles with a specific topic, the system can offer additional practice exercises or alternative explanations to enhance understanding.

Data-driven insights play an essential role in adaptive systems as they leverage advanced data analytics and machine learning techniques to interpret vast amounts of information regarding student behavior and performance trends (Caballe & Clariso, 2016). This analysis helps identify learners' common challenges and informs decisions about what content should be presented next.

Cognitive modeling is also incorporated into some sophisticated adaptive learning technologies. These models simulate expert tutoring behaviors by understanding how learners process information and develop skills (Busemeyer & Diederich, 2010). This understanding allows for tailored instructional strategies, pacing, and task complexity to maximize each student's learning experience. Learning analytics further enhance adaptive learning environments by collecting and analyzing data on student engagement, progress, and outcomes (Srinivasa & Kurni, 2021). This information helps educators understand individual learner needs and informs curriculum design and instructional practices.

2. THE IMPORTANCE OF ENGAGEMENT IN LEARNING

Learner engagement is fundamental to educational success, significantly influencing motivation and academic performance. This section delves deeper into the theoretical frameworks that inform our understanding of learner engagement, mainly focusing on Self-Determination Theory (SDT), and examines the empirical evidence that connects engagement to enhanced learning outcomes.

2.1. Theoretical Framework

SDT (Deci & Ryan, 2000) is fundamental to comprehending learner engagement. The theory asserts that motivation is driven by satisfying three core psychological needs: autonomy, competence, and relatedness.

- **Autonomy** signifies the desire for individuals to have control over their actions and choices. In educational settings, students are more likely to engage deeply with the content when they can make decisions regarding their learning activities. Research indicates that environments supporting autonomy enhance intrinsic motivation, which is essential for ongoing engagement.

- **Competence** refers to feeling adequate and skilled in one's endeavors. Students who believe they are competent are more inclined to tackle challenging tasks and persevere through obstacles. Studies demonstrate that when educators provide constructive feedback and opportunities for skill enhancement, students' feelings of competence increase, leading to greater engagement.
- **Relatedness** involves the need for social connections and a sense of belonging within a learning community. When students feel connected to their peers and instructors, they are more likely to participate in learning activities actively. Research has shown that cultivating a supportive classroom atmosphere can significantly enhance students' emotional engagement and satisfaction with their educational experiences.

Engagement itself is a multifaceted construct that includes behavioral (participation in tasks), emotional (affective responses), and cognitive (mental effort) components. The interaction among these dimensions can be effectively understood through SDT, which emphasizes that fulfilling students' psychological needs promotes higher levels of engagement across all areas.

2.2. Effects on Learning Outcomes

Student engagement is consistently associated with improved academic outcomes in higher education. Research shows that engaged students achieve high grades, have better retention rates, and experience greater satisfaction with their learning. Engagement has positively affected first-year college grades and persistence, with consequential benefits for historically underserved students (Kuh et al., 2008). In online learning environments, student engagement is crucial for reducing dropout rates and improving retention (Lu, 2020). Timely and substantive instructor feedback facilitates engagement, learning, and student satisfaction (Lu, 2020). While student engagement lacks a universally accepted definition, both attitudinal and behavioral measures have been used to assess its impact on academic performance and commitment. Also, learning analytics are increasingly used to track and support student engagement in digital learning environments.

Furthermore, during the shift to online education prompted by the COVID-19 pandemic, research highlighted that digital support strategies catering to students' psychological needs were essential in maintaining high levels of engagement (Chiu, 2022). Students who felt their autonomy and competence were supported were more likely to participate actively in online learning activities, resulting in better academic outcomes.

These findings emphasize the importance of developing educational environments that prioritize student engagement. Educators can enhance motivation by implementing strategies that promote autonomy—such as providing choices in assignments—and fostering a sense of community among learners. Such approaches improve student satisfaction and contribute to better academic performance. Recognizing the significance of learner engagement through frameworks like SDT offers valuable insights for improving educational practices. By addressing students' psychological needs and promoting high levels of engagement, educators can significantly enhance learning outcomes across diverse educational contexts.

3. EQUITY IN PERSONALIZED LEARNING

Equity in education is a fundamental concern that has gained increasing attention, particularly with the rise of personalized learning models in K-12 education. Personalized learning aims to tailor educational experiences to meet each student's needs, skills, and interests. However, for this approach to be efficient, it must be underpinned by principles of equity. This section explores the barriers to access that hinder equitable educational experiences and discusses comprehensive strategies for inclusion to ensure all learners benefit from personalized learning.

3.1. Barriers to Access

The digital divide (Ragnedda & Muschert, 2013) is one of the most significant barriers to equitable access to personalized learning. Many students, particularly those from low-income families or rural areas, lack reliable access to technology and high-speed internet. According to the Pew Research Center, approximately 15% of U.S. households with school-aged children do not have a reliable internet connection. This lack of access limits students' ability to engage with online learning platforms, participate in virtual classrooms, and utilize adaptive technologies crucial for personalized learning experiences. Schools must recognize this divide and advocate for policies that expand broadband access and provide necessary devices to underserved populations.

Also, socioeconomic status significantly impacts students' educational experiences (Mirowsky, 2017). Students from lower-income families often face multiple barriers that can hinder their academic success, including inadequate housing, food insecurity, and limited access to healthcare. These challenges can lead to increased stress and absenteeism, making it difficult for students to focus on their studies or fully engage with personalized learning tools. Furthermore, schools in low-income areas may have fewer resources and less experienced teachers, exacerbating existing inequities in educational quality.

Additionally, language proficiency is another critical factor influencing equitable access to personalized learning (Neugebauer et al., 2023). English Language Learners (ELLs) may struggle with personalized learning systems that do not accommodate their language needs or provide sufficient support for language acquisition. If educational materials are not available in students' native languages or if instructional strategies do not consider their linguistic backgrounds, these learners may miss out on valuable personalized experiences designed to enhance their understanding and engagement.

Furthermore, students with disabilities often encounter significant barriers within personalized learning frameworks that do not adequately address their unique needs (Halder & Argyropoulos, 2019). Many adaptive learning technologies are not designed with accessibility in mind, which can prevent these students from fully benefiting from personalized instruction. For instance, a student with visual impairments may struggle with platforms lacking screen reader compatibility or alternative image text options. In regard to promoting equity, educational technology must be inclusive and provide necessary accommodations for all learners.

Moreover, the legacy of systemic inequities—such as redlining, school segregation, and discriminatory policies—continues to affect educational access and quality today (Pease, 2021). Students from historically marginalized communities often attend underfunded schools with fewer resources and opportunities for advanced coursework or enrichment programs. These historical factors contribute to ongoing disparities in academic achievement and limit the effectiveness of personalized learning initiatives if they do not address these underlying issues.

Finally, a lack of cultural responsiveness in educational content can also create barriers to equitable access in personalized learning environments (Grant & Sleeter, 2012). Learners may feel disconnected or disengaged from the material when curricula do not reflect all students' diverse backgrounds and experiences. This disconnect can hinder their motivation and participation in personalized learning experiences.

3.2. Strategies for Inclusion

Implementing Multi-Tiered Systems of Support (MTSS) can create a more equitable framework for personalized learning by providing varying levels of support based on individual student needs (Brown-Chidsey & Bickford, 2015). MTSS involves tiered interventions that range from universal support for all students to targeted interventions for those who require additional assistance. By identifying students at risk early on and providing appropriate interventions, educators can ensure that all learners receive the support they need to succeed.

Utilizing design thinking with an equity focus encourages educators to create personalized learning experiences that are inclusive and accessible for all students. This approach involves critically assessing and redesigning existing systems based on student feedback and diverse perspectives. By actively involving stakeholders—students, parents, and educators—in the design process, schools can develop solutions that address specific equity concerns and promote engagement among all learners.

Comprehensive professional development is essential for equipping teachers with the skills necessary to implement personalized learning strategies while being mindful of equity issues. Training should focus on culturally responsive teaching practices, differentiation strategies, and the use of technology in ways that enhance accessibility for all students. Educators should also be encouraged to reflect on their biases and understand the diverse needs of their students through ongoing training and collaboration.

Engaging families and communities in the educational process fosters a more inclusive environment where diverse voices are heard and valued. Schools should actively seek input from parents and community members when designing personalized learning initiatives or selecting educational technologies. Establishing partnerships with local organizations can also help provide additional resources and support for students who may face barriers outside of school.

Collecting and analyzing data on student performance is crucial for identifying gaps in achievement and tailoring approaches accordingly. Schools should utilize data analytics tools to monitor student progress closely, disaggregating data by demographics such as race, socioeconomic status, and disability status to identify trends and disparities. Educators can proactively adjust their strategies by understanding which groups are underperforming or facing challenges within personalized learning frameworks.

Creating flexible classroom settings that allow for various learning modes can effectively accommodate different student needs. This might include blended learning models that combine online instruction with face-to-face interaction or project-based learning opportunities that encourage collaboration among peers with diverse skill sets. Flexibility also extends to assessment methods; offering multiple ways for students to demonstrate their understanding can help ensure that all learners have an opportunity to succeed.

Developing a curriculum that reflects students' diverse backgrounds is essential for promoting engagement in personalized learning environments. Culturally relevant pedagogy emphasizes the importance of connecting academic content with students' cultural contexts, encouraging them to see themselves reflected in what they learn. This approach enhances motivation and fosters a sense of belonging among students from various backgrounds.

Finally, advocating for local, state, and national policy changes is vital for addressing systemic inequities in education. Policymakers should prioritize funding initiatives to close the digital divide, support underserved schools, and ensure equitable access to high-quality educational resources across all communities.

While personalized learning offers significant potential for enhancing educational equity by tailoring instruction to individual needs, addressing the barriers preventing access and effectively implementing comprehensive inclusion strategies is essential. By focusing on systemic changes—rooted in equity principles—and fostering inclusive practices within classrooms, educators can create a more just educational landscape where every student can thrive academically and personally.

4. ENHANCING ENGAGEMENT THROUGH ADAPTIVE SYSTEMS

Adaptive learning systems are revolutionizing education by tailoring learning experiences to meet individual student needs. This approach enhances engagement and fosters a more personalized and effective learning environment. Below, we explore practical strategies for educators to enhance student engagement through adaptive systems, focusing on designing engaging content and utilizing feedback mechanisms.

4.1. Designing Engaging Content

Providing students with options in their learning pathways can significantly boost engagement. By allowing students to choose from various activities—such as visual aids, podcasts, or hands-on projects—educators can cater to different learning styles. This differentiation fosters intrinsic motivation and ensures all students feel challenged and involved in their learning journey. Also, educational technology can enhance engagement by offering adaptive tools that personalize learning experiences. Platforms that adjust content based on individual progress allow for real-time adjustments, ensuring students receive the necessary support or challenges tailored to their abilities. For example, online quizzes with instant feedback can help identify areas needing improvement, while gamified elements can make learning more enjoyable

Besides, Gamification strategies can increase motivation by introducing game-like elements into the learning process. This could include earning rewards for completing tasks or competing in friendly challenges with peers. Such features make learning fun and encourage students to engage more deeply with the material, leading to improved retention and mastery of concepts. Active learning techniques such as group discussions, role-playing, and project-based assignments can significantly enhance student involvement. These methods require students to actively participate in their education rather than passively receiving information, which can lead to a deeper understanding of the subject matter. Finally, linking content to real-world applications helps students see the relevance of their learning. When students understand how their studies apply outside the classroom, they are more likely to engage with the material and take ownership of their learning.

4.2. Utilizing Feedback Mechanisms

Real-time feedback is critical for enhancing student involvement and self-regulation within adaptive systems. Adaptive systems continuously assess student performance and adjust the difficulty of tasks accordingly. For example, if a student struggles with a concept, the system can provide more straightforward questions or additional resources tailored to that specific topic, ensuring that students remain engaged without feeling overwhelmed. Also, educators receive valuable data analytics from adaptive systems highlighting individual student performance trends. This information allows teachers to identify which students require additional support or intervention, enabling targeted assistance that enhances overall engagement.

By providing tools for self-assessment, such as reflection journals or progress trackers, students can actively monitor their learning journey. This self-regulation encourages accountability and motivates students to engage more deeply with their studies. Besides, advanced adaptive systems utilize predictive analytics to foresee potential learning challenges based on historical data and current performance trends. By anticipating these challenges, educators can proactively adjust instructional strategies or provide additional resources before issues arise.

Moreover, encouraging a culture where feedback is viewed positively can enhance student motivation. When constructive feedback focuses on growth rather than just evaluation, students are more likely to engage with the material and strive for improvement.

Enhancing engagement through adaptive systems involves a comprehensive approach that combines innovative content design with effective feedback mechanisms. By implementing these strategies, educators can create dynamic learning environments where students feel empowered, motivated, and actively involved in their educational journeys. Adaptive systems personalize learning and foster a culture of continuous improvement for students and educators alike.

5. TEACHER PROFESSIONAL DEVELOPMENT

Teacher professional development (TPD) is vital to educational reform, particularly as adaptive learning technologies become increasingly prevalent in classrooms. We can enhance teaching practices and improve student outcomes by equipping educators with the skills to implement these systems effectively. This section delves deeper into the significance of TPD, focusing on training programs and strategies for building supportive communities among educators.

5.1. Training Programs

Professional development initiatives focused on adaptive learning technologies aim to provide educators with the tools and knowledge they need to leverage these systems effectively. The education landscape is evolving, and teachers must be prepared to meet the diverse needs of their students through personalized learning experiences. Key components of effective training programs include:

- **Needs Assessment:** Before implementing training, it's essential to conduct a needs assessment to identify the specific skills and knowledge gaps among educators. This ensures that the professional development offered is relevant and targeted.
- **Integration of Technology:** Training programs should focus on the theoretical aspects of adaptive systems and include practical, hands-on experiences. Educators should have opportunities to experiment with various adaptive learning tools, understand their functionalities, and explore how they can be integrated into their existing curricula.
- **Differentiated Learning Opportunities:** Just as adaptive systems cater to individual student needs, professional development should also accommodate teachers' diverse learning styles and paces. Various formats—such as online courses, in-person workshops, and blended learning options—can help meet these diverse needs.
- **Evaluation and Feedback:** Continuous evaluation of professional development programs is crucial for ensuring their effectiveness. Gathering feedback from participants can inform future training sessions and help refine content delivery methods.

Here are some examples of effective training programs:

- **Online Learning Platforms:** Many organizations offer online courses designed for teachers to learn about adaptive technologies. These platforms often include interactive modules, video tutorials, and forums for discussion.
- **Workshops Led by Experts:** Bringing in experts in adaptive learning can provide teachers with insights into best practices and emerging trends. These workshops can also facilitate networking opportunities among educators.
- **Collaborative Projects:** Engaging teachers in collaborative projects where they can design adaptive learning experiences together fosters teamwork and encourages innovative thinking.

5.2. Building a Supportive Community

Creating a supportive community among educators is essential for sharing best practices related to adaptive teaching methods. Here are several strategies that can enhance collaboration:

- **Establishing Professional Learning Communities (PLCs):** PLCs are groups of educators who meet regularly to discuss their practices, share resources, and support each other in implementing adaptive strategies. These communities encourage continuous improvement through shared accountability.
- **Utilizing Technology for Collaboration:** Online platforms such as Google Classroom or Microsoft Teams can facilitate communication among educators, allowing them to share resources, lesson plans, and feedback asynchronously.
- **Organizing Peer Observations:** Encouraging teachers to observe one another's classrooms can provide valuable insights into different teaching styles and the implementation of adaptive technologies. This practice fosters a culture of openness and mutual support.
- **Creating Resource Sharing Platforms:** Developing a centralized repository where educators can upload and access lesson plans, assessment tools, and technology guides promotes resource sharing and reduces duplication of effort.

School leaders play a critical role in fostering a collaborative culture among educators. They can:

- **Model Collaborative Practices:** Leaders should demonstrate collaboration by engaging in professional development alongside their staff, participating in PLCs, or co-facilitating workshops.

- **Encourage Risk-Taking:** Creating an environment where teachers feel safe to experiment with new technologies without fear of failure encourages innovation and growth.
- **Provide Time for Collaboration:** Allocating time within the school schedule for teachers to collaborate is essential. This could involve scheduled planning periods or dedicated professional development days focused on collaboration.

Recognizing and celebrating the achievements of educators who successfully implement adaptive learning strategies reinforces positive behavior and motivates others to engage in similar practices. This could take the form of:

- **Showcasing Success Stories:** Highlighting case studies or testimonials from teachers who have effectively used adaptive systems can inspire peers.
- **Awards and Recognition Programs:** Establishing awards for innovative teaching practices encourages educators to strive for excellence in their use of technology.

6. THE ROLE OF STAKEHOLDERS IN IMPLEMENTATION

The successful implementation of adaptive systems in educational settings is a collaborative effort that involves various stakeholders, each contributing unique perspectives and resources. This section delves deeper into the roles of educators, administrative support, and community involvement, highlighting the interconnectedness of these roles and their impact on fostering equitable practices and effective technology integration.

6.1. Educators' Responsibilities

Educators are at the forefront of implementing adaptive systems, and their responsibilities extend beyond merely using technology in the classroom. They must engage in culturally responsive teaching by integrating culturally relevant materials and practices into their lessons. Understanding students' backgrounds allows educators to create more meaningful learning experiences that resonate with diverse learners. Additionally, differentiated instruction strategies enable educators to tailor their teaching methods to accommodate various learning styles and abilities. This approach ensures that all students, including those with special needs or English language learners, receive appropriate support. PLCs can also be beneficial for teachers. By participating in PLCs, educators can collaborate with colleagues to share best practices, discuss challenges, and explore innovative uses of adaptive technologies. This collective approach fosters a culture of continuous improvement. Moreover, educators should leverage data generated by adaptive systems to inform their instructional strategies. Teachers can identify learning gaps and adjust their teaching methods by analyzing student performance data.

6.2. Administrative Support

The role of school administrators is critical in creating an environment conducive to successfully implementing adaptive systems. Administrators must articulate a clear vision for integrating technology into education. This includes setting strategic goals that align with the school's mission and values while ensuring that all stakeholders understand the importance of adaptive systems. Effective technology integration requires robust infrastructure, including reliable internet access and up-to-date hardware. Administrators should prioritize investments in technology infrastructure to support seamless implementation. Establishing mechanisms for monitoring the effectiveness of adaptive systems is also essential. Regular evaluations can help identify areas for improvement and ensure that the technology meets educational goals. Additionally, administrators should encourage risk-taking and experimentation among educators by creating a supportive atmosphere where teachers feel comfortable trying new approaches.

6.3. Community Involvement

Community involvement is essential for creating an equitable educational environment that supports all students. Schools can develop outreach programs to educate families about the importance of technology in education. Workshops or informational sessions can empower parents to engage with their children's learning processes actively. Collaborating with local organizations can provide additional resources for schools. For example, partnerships with tech companies may lead to donations of devices or software licenses, enhancing access for underserved students. Community stakeholders can work together to advocate for policies promoting equitable technology access. This may involve lobbying for funding or resources from local governments or educational bodies to support disadvantaged schools. Establishing channels for community feedback regarding technology use and accessibility is also crucial. Engaging families in discussions about their needs and concerns can lead to more effective solutions tailored to the community's context.

6.4. The Interconnectedness of Roles

The roles of educators, administrators, and community members are deeply interconnected. Collaborative professional development opportunities that involve community experts or organizations specializing in adaptive technologies can enhance educators' training experiences. Establishing shared goals among stakeholders fosters a unified approach to implementing adaptive systems. When educators, administrators, and community members work together toward common objectives, they create a cohesive strategy that enhances student learning outcomes. Continuous engagement from all stakeholders is vital for sustaining momentum in implementing adaptive systems. Regular check-ins, community meetings, and collaborative events can keep everyone informed and invested in the process.

7. ETHICAL CONSIDERATIONS IN ADAPTIVE LEARNING TECHNOLOGIES

Adaptive learning technologies offer personalized educational experiences by leveraging data to tailor content and instructional methods to individual student needs. While these innovations can enhance learning outcomes, they also raise significant ethical considerations that must be carefully addressed. This extended discussion delves deeper into three critical ethical issues: data privacy concerns, algorithmic fairness, and informed consent while exploring additional dimensions such as accountability, transparency, and the role of stakeholders.

7.1. Data Privacy Concerns

The collection of vast amounts of data is intrinsic to the functionality of adaptive learning systems. This data includes personal information, academic performance, behavioral patterns, and emotional responses. The risks associated with data breaches are significant. The more data collected, the greater the risk of unauthorized access or exploitation. Educational institutions have a responsibility to protect sensitive student information from cyber threats. High-profile data breaches in various sectors highlight the vulnerability of personal information, making it imperative for schools to adopt rigorous cybersecurity measures. Additionally, questions arise regarding how long student data should be stored and who has access to it. Institutions must develop clear policies that dictate data retention periods and ensure that data is anonymized or securely deleted when it is no longer needed.

Compliance with regulations such as the Family Educational Rights and Privacy Act (FERPA) in the U.S. or the General Data Protection Regulation (GDPR) in Europe is essential. These laws provide frameworks for protecting student privacy and outline rights regarding personal data. Engaging students, parents, and educators in discussions about data privacy can help institutions understand community concerns and expectations. Regular workshops or informational sessions can increase awareness and foster a culture of privacy consciousness.

7.2. Algorithmic Fairness

Algorithmic fairness addresses the potential biases in the algorithms that drive adaptive learning technologies. These biases can lead to unequal educational opportunities and outcomes. Biased algorithms may lead to certain groups of students receiving less effective learning paths. For example, if an algorithm favors content based on prior success metrics that predominantly reflect one demographic, it may inadvertently disadvantage students from different backgrounds or learning styles. The implications of algorithmic bias extend beyond immediate educational outcomes; they can affect students' long-term academic trajectories and career opportunities. Ensuring fairness in adaptive learning systems is crucial for promoting social equity.

To address these biases, developers should prioritize using diverse datasets representing a wide range of demographics, experiences, and learning styles during algorithm training. This approach helps create more inclusive algorithms that cater to all learners. Continuous evaluation of algorithms through audits can help identify biases early. Institutions should implement testing protocols assessing algorithms' performance across different demographic groups to ensure equitable treatment.

7.3. Informed Consent

Informed consent is fundamental in ethical research and practice, mainly when dealing with minors in educational settings. Institutions should ensure that consent forms are written in plain language that is easily understandable by both students and parents. This includes providing information about what data will be collected, how it will be used, and the potential risks involved. Schools should consider adopting an opt-in model for data collection where explicit consent is required before any data is collected. This empowers parents and students to make informed choices about their participation. Establishing a continuous dialogue with stakeholders about data practices fosters trust and transparency. Regular updates about student data use can help alleviate concerns and reinforce a commitment to ethical practices. Providing training sessions for students and parents about digital literacy, privacy rights, and the implications of data sharing can empower them to make informed decisions regarding their participation in adaptive learning programs.

As adaptive learning technologies evolve, establishing accountability structures becomes essential. Educational institutions should develop ethical frameworks that guide the implementation of adaptive technologies. These frameworks should outline responsibilities regarding data collection, algorithm development, and stakeholder engagement. Forming oversight committees comprised of educators, technologists, ethicists, and community representatives can help ensure adherence to ethical standards. These committees can review practices regularly and provide recommendations for improvement. Engaging various stakeholders—students, parents, educators, and technology providers—is crucial in addressing ethical considerations effectively.

Schools should work closely with technology providers to ensure that ethical considerations are integrated into product design. This collaboration can lead to more responsible technology development that prioritizes student welfare. Involving the community in discussions about adaptive learning technologies can help identify local concerns and values related to education. Community forums or surveys can serve as platforms for gathering input from diverse perspectives.

8. FUTURE DIRECTIONS IN ADAPTIVE LEARNING RESEARCH

The field of adaptive learning is rapidly evolving, driven by technological advancements and the need for personalized education. This section outlines two significant areas for further research: Innovations in Technology and Longitudinal Studies on Impact. By delving deeper into these topics, we can better understand the potential of adaptive learning systems and their implications for the future of education.

8.1. Innovations in Technology

AI-driven systems can create dynamic learning pathways that adapt to a student's progress in real-time. By continuously assessing performance and engagement, these systems can recommend resources or activities that align with individual learning styles. This personalized approach not only helps students master concepts but also fosters a sense of ownership over their learning journey. Educators can use predictive analytics to identify at-risk students early in their academic careers. AI can flag students who may need additional support by analyzing data patterns, such as assignment completion rates and assessment scores. This proactive intervention can lead to timely assistance and improved educational outcomes.

Gamification introduces elements of competition into the learning environment, which can be particularly motivating for students. Leaderboards, badges, and achievement levels encourage learners to strive for excellence while fostering community among peers. This competitive spirit can enhance motivation and drive engagement. With advancements in virtual reality (VR) and augmented reality (AR), gamification can take on new dimensions. Immersive experiences allow students to explore complex subjects interactively, making learning more engaging and memorable. For instance, VR simulations can provide hands-on experiences in science or history, deepening understanding through experiential learning.

Deep learning models can revolutionize assessment methods by creating adaptive tests that adjust difficulty based on student responses. This approach ensures that assessments accurately reflect a student's knowledge level, providing more meaningful insights into their understanding of the material. Natural language processing (NLP) technologies enable adaptive systems to analyze student interactions in real-time, offering personalized feedback on written assignments or discussions. By understanding context and sentiment, these systems can provide tailored suggestions that help students improve their communication skills.

8.2. Longitudinal Studies on Impact

While the immediate benefits of adaptive systems are becoming evident, there is a pressing need for longitudinal studies to assess their long-term effects on engagement and equity in education. Longitudinal studies should investigate how different adaptive strategies maintain student interest over extended periods. Factors such as content variety, challenge levels, and feedback mechanisms play crucial roles in sustaining engagement. Understanding these dynamics will help educators design more effective adaptive learning environments. Research could also explore how early exposure to adaptive learning influences attitudes toward lifelong learning. Students who engage with personalized educational tools may develop a greater propensity for self-directed learning and curiosity beyond formal education settings.

Longitudinal studies should assess how access to technology affects adaptive learning systems implementation across diverse socioeconomic groups. Understanding disparities in access will inform efforts to bridge the digital divide and ensure equitable opportunities for all students. Evaluating whether adaptive systems are culturally responsive is vital for promoting equity. Research should focus on how well these systems accommodate diverse cultural backgrounds and learning preferences, ensuring all students feel represented and valued within the educational framework.

To fully understand the effectiveness of adaptive systems, researchers should develop comprehensive evaluation metrics that go beyond traditional academic performance indicators. Metrics could include social-emotional development, critical thinking skills, and collaborative abilities, contributing to holistic educational outcomes. Establishing feedback loops between educators, students, and technology developers is essential for refining adaptive systems. Longitudinal studies can facilitate ongoing dialogue about what works well and what needs improvement, leading to more effective educational practices.

9. ADAPTIVE LEARNING IN THE MENA REGION

Adaptive learning, characterized by its ability to customize educational experiences based on individual learner needs, is becoming increasingly prominent in the Middle East and North Africa (MENA) region. This transformation is primarily fueled by technological advancements, particularly in artificial intelligence (AI), which enable more personalized and effective learning environments.

Artificial intelligence and machine learning are revolutionizing how students learn. These technologies analyze vast amounts of data to identify individual learning patterns, preferences, and areas needing improvement. By doing so, adaptive learning platforms can offer tailored content that adjusts in real-time based on a student's performance, ensuring that learners are neither bored with material that is too easy nor overwhelmed by content that is too challenging.

With the high penetration of smartphones across the MENA region, mobile learning applications are becoming a vital tool for adaptive education. These platforms allow students to access learning materials anytime and anywhere, making education more flexible and accessible. This is particularly beneficial in remote or underserved areas where traditional educational resources may be lacking.

The adaptive learning market in the MENA region is experiencing rapid growth. As of 2023, it was valued at approximately USD 0.2 billion and is expected to reach around USD 0.72 billion by 2024. This surge can be attributed to several factors, including increased demand for personalized education. Parents and educators are recognizing the limitations of one-size-fits-all approaches, leading to a growing expectation for educational solutions that cater to diverse learning needs. Additionally, many governments in the region are prioritizing educational reform and digital transformation as part of their broader economic strategies. Investments in technology-enhanced education are seen as essential for preparing a skilled workforce for the future.

Adaptive learning is not limited to traditional education settings; it is also making significant strides in corporate training programs. Organizations are increasingly adopting AI-driven platforms to enhance employee training and development. These systems assess employees' skills and knowledge gaps, enabling companies to create personalized training programs that align with their business objectives. For instance, large corporations in countries like the United Arab Emirates (UAE) and Saudi Arabia are leveraging adaptive learning technologies to ensure their workforce remains competitive in a rapidly changing job market. Companies can enhance productivity and employee satisfaction by providing employees with tailored training experiences.

Research conducted in various MENA countries has demonstrated the effectiveness of adaptive learning systems. For example, studies in Saudi Arabia indicate that students using AI-based adaptive learning tools show marked improvements in academic performance compared to those receiving traditional instruction. These findings underscore the potential of personalized education to address diverse student needs effectively. Additionally, longitudinal studies conducted across Jordan, Egypt, and Saudi Arabia have highlighted the positive effects of adaptive learning technologies on early literacy skills among young children. These systems help foster foundational skills critical for future academic success by providing customized reading interventions.

Despite the promising developments in adaptive learning within the MENA region, several challenges persist. Many educational institutions still lack the necessary technological infrastructure to support advanced adaptive learning systems. Issues such as unreliable internet access and outdated hardware can impede implementation efforts. Furthermore, the disparity in digital literacy levels among educators and students poses a significant barrier to effective technology integration. Training programs aimed at enhancing digital skills are essential to ensure all stakeholders can fully leverage adaptive learning tools.

Looking ahead, there are significant opportunities for growth and innovation in adaptive learning within the MENA region. Educational institutions can collaborate with technology companies to develop tailored solutions that address local needs while leveraging global best practices. Investing in professional development for educators will be crucial for successful implementation; teachers equipped with the skills to utilize adaptive technologies can better support their students' diverse learning journeys. Continued government support through policies that promote digital education initiatives will also be vital for scaling adaptive learning solutions across the region.

10. SUMMARY

The roots of personalized learning can be traced back to Enlightenment thinkers like Jean-Jacques Rousseau, who emphasized individualized education tailored to children's natural development. This philosophy influenced later educational reforms that prioritized learner experiences over rigid curricula. Joseph Lancaster's monitorial system introduced structured personalization, allowing advanced students to assist peers, thus addressing large group educational needs while maintaining some individual instruction. In the early 20th century, John Dewey advocated for student engagement and active learning in his work "Democracy and Education," while Maria Montessori promoted self-directed learning, both reinforcing the need for personalized education.

The 1960s and 1970s saw the rise of competency-based education, exemplified by Fred Keller's PSI, which allowed students to progress at their own pace. Research by Benjamin Bloom supported these methods, showing significant benefits for mastery learning. The advent of digital technology has made personalized learning more scalable through online platforms and adaptive technologies that utilize real-time data to tailor educational experiences based on individual student performance.

Adaptive learning technologies employ data-driven algorithms to customize learning experiences. Key features include ongoing assessments, immediate feedback, customized learning pathways, and the use of cognitive modeling to enhance instructional strategies. Various adaptive systems exist, including intelligent tutoring systems, exploratory learning environments, game-based platforms, and modern learning management systems that incorporate adaptive features. Engagement is crucial for academic success and is influenced by factors such as autonomy, competence, and relatedness, as outlined in SDT. Engaged students tend to achieve better academic outcomes. Adaptive systems promote equity by providing tailored resources that address individual student needs, helping to close achievement gaps and foster inclusive learning environments. In conclusion, the integration of personalized learning and adaptive systems represents a significant shift in educational practices aimed at meeting diverse learner needs. This approach enhances student engagement and aligns with broader social justice goals in education.

REFERENCES

Benosman, M. (2016). *Learning-based adaptive control: An extremum seeking approach–theory and applications*. Butterworth-Heinemann.

Brown-Chidsey, R., & Bickford, R. (2015). *Practical handbook of multi-tiered systems of support: Building academic and behavioral success in schools*. Guilford Publications.

Busemeyer, J. R., & Diederich, A. (2010). Cognitive modeling. *Sage (Atlanta, Ga.)*.

Caballe, S., & Clariso, R. (2016). Formative assessment, learning data analytics and gamification. In *ICT education*. Morgan Kaufmann.

Cheng, I., Safont, L. V., & Basu, A. (2010). *Multimedia in education: Adaptive learning and testing*. World Scientific. DOI: 10.1142/7111

Chiu, T. K. (2022). Applying the self-determination theory (SDT) to explain student engagement in online learning during the COVID-19 pandemic. *Journal of Research on Technology in Education*, *54*(1), 14–30. DOI: 10.1080/15391523.2021.1891998

De Freitas, S. (2013). *Education in computer generated environments*. Routledge. DOI: 10.4324/9780203094709

Deci, E. L., & Ryan, R. M. (2000). The" what" and" why" of goal pursuits: Human needs and the self-determination of behavior. *Psychological Inquiry*, *11*(4), 227–268. DOI: 10.1207/S15327965PLI1104_01

Foreman, S. D. (2017). *The LMS guidebook: Learning management systems demystified*. Association for Talent Development.

Grant, C. A., & Sleeter, C. E. (2012). *Doing multicultural education for achievement and equity*. Routledge. DOI: 10.4324/9780203831397

Halder, S., & Argyropoulos, V. (2019). *Inclusion, equity and access for individuals with disabilities*. Springer. DOI: 10.1007/978-981-13-5962-0

Kuh, G. D., Cruce, T. M., Shoup, R., Kinzie, J., & Gonyea, R. M. (2008). Unmasking the effects of student engagement on first-year college grades and persistence. *The Journal of Higher Education*, *79*(5), 540–563. DOI: 10.1080/00221546.2008.11772116

Kuhlthau, C. C., & Maniotes, L. K. (2010). *Guided inquiry: Learning in the 21st century. Libraries Unlimited. Levy, J. C. (2015). Adaptive learning and the human condition*. Routledge.

Lu, H. (2020). Online learning: The meanings of student engagement. *Education Journal*, *9*(3), 73–79. DOI: 10.11648/j.edu.20200903.13

McLeod, S., & Graber, J. (2018). *Harnessing technology for deeper learning: Solutions for creating the learning spaces students deserve*. Solution Tree Press.

Mirowsky, J. (2017). *Education, social status, and health*. Routledge. DOI: 10.4324/9781351328081

Neugebauer, S. R., Galloway, E. P., & Dobbs, C. L. (2023). *Reimagining language instruction: New approaches to promoting equity*. Teachers College Press.

Pease, B. (2021). *Undoing privilege: Unearned advantage and systemic injustice in an unequal world*. Bloomsbury Publishing.

Pollock, J. E. (2012). *Feedback: The hinge that joins teaching and learning*. Corwin Press.

Prensky, M. (2003). *Digital game-based learning. Computers in entertainment*. Paragon House.

Ragnedda, M., & Muschert, G. W. (2013). *The digital divide*. Routledge. DOI: 10.4324/9780203069769

Rickabaugh, J. (2016). *Tapping the power of personalized learning: A roadmap for school leaders*. ASCD.

Saba, F., & Shearer, R. L. (2017). *Transactional distance and adaptive learning: Planning for the future of higher education*. Routledge. DOI: 10.4324/9780203731819

Srinivasa, K. G., & Kurni, M. (2021). *A beginner's guide to learning analytics*. Springer.

Vytasek, J. M., Patzak, A., & Winne, P. H. (2020). Analytics for student engagement. *Machine learning paradigms: Advances in Learning Analytics*, 23-48.

Wenger, E. (2014). *Artificial intelligence and tutoring systems: Computational and cognitive approaches to the communication of knowledge*. Morgan Kaufmann.

Williamson, B. (2017). Big data in education: The digital future of learning, policy and practice. *Sage (Atlanta, Ga.)*. Advance online publication. DOI: 10.4135/9781529714920

ADDITIONAL READING

Gligorea, I., Cioca, M., Oancea, R., Gorski, A. T., Gorski, H., & Tudorache, P. (2023). Adaptive learning using artificial intelligence in e-learning: A literature review. *Education Sciences*, *13*(12), 1216. DOI: 10.3390/educsci13121216

Gransden, C., Hindmarsh, M., Lê, N. C., & Nguyen, T. H. (2024). Adaptive learning through technology: A technical review and implementation. *Higher Education. Skills and Work-Based Learning*, *14*(2), 409–417. DOI: 10.1108/HESWBL-05-2023-0121

Raj, N. S., & Renumol, V. G. (2024). An improved adaptive learning path recommendation model driven by real-time learning analytics. *Journal of Computers in Education*, *11*(1), 121–148. DOI: 10.1007/s40692-022-00250-y

Sajja, R., Sermet, Y., Cikmaz, M., Cwiertny, D., & Demir, I. (2024). Artificial intelligence-enabled intelligent assistant for personalized and adaptive learning in higher education. *Information (Basel)*, *15*(10), 596–608. DOI: 10.3390/info15100596

Wang, S., Christensen, C., Cui, W., Tong, R., Yarnall, L., Shear, L., & Feng, M. (2023). When adaptive learning is effective learning: Comparison of an adaptive learning system to teacher-led instruction. *Interactive Learning Environments*, *31*(2), 793–803. DOI: 10.1080/10494820.2020.1808794

KEY TERMS AND DEFINITIONS

Adaptive System: An adaptive system is a framework that adjusts its operations based on feedback from its environment or users. In educational contexts, adaptive systems utilize algorithms and artificial intelligence to modify learning experiences according to individual learner needs, strengths, and weaknesses. This personalization enhances engagement and improves educational outcomes by allowing learners to progress at their own pace and receive tailored support.

Augmented Reality (AR): AR refers to technology that superimposes digital information—such as images, sounds, or other data—onto the real world. This interactive experience enhances users' perception of their environment, often through devices like smartphones or AR glasses. AR is widely used in various fields, including education, where it can create immersive learning experiences by blending digital content with physical surroundings.

Family Educational Rights and Privacy Act (FERPA): The FERPA is a U.S. federal law that protects the privacy of student education records. It grants parents and eligible students the right to access these records and request necessary corrections. FERPA ensures that educational institutions cannot disclose personally identifiable information without consent, thereby safeguarding student data in various educational settings.

General Data Protection Regulation (GDPR): The GDPR is a comprehensive data protection law enacted in the European Union that governs how personal data is collected, processed, and stored. It aims to enhance individuals' control over personal information and establish strict guidelines for organizations handling such data. GDPR emphasizes transparency, user consent, and the right to data access, significantly impacting how companies manage user privacy in digital environments.

Intelligent Tutoring System: ITS is a computer-based educational tool that provides personalized instruction and feedback to learners. Utilizing artificial intelligence, ITS can adapt to individual learning styles and needs, offering tailored exercises and assessments. An ITS aims to simulate one-on-one tutoring by analyzing student performance and adjusting instructional strategies accordingly.

Learning Management System (LMS): LMS is software designed to facilitate the administration, documentation, tracking, reporting, and delivery of educational courses or training programs. LMS platforms provide a centralized location for course materials, assessments, and communication between instructors and students. They are widely used in both academic institutions and corporate training environments.

Multi-Tiered Systems of Support (MTSS): MTSS is an educational framework aimed at providing varying levels of support to students based on their individual needs. It integrates academic and behavioral interventions across multiple tiers: universal support for all students, targeted interventions for those at risk, and intensive support for students with significant challenges. MTSS promotes early identification of student needs and data-driven decision-making.

Natural Language Processing (NLP): NLP is a branch of artificial intelligence that focuses on the interaction between computers and human language. It involves enabling machines to understand, interpret, and respond to human language in a meaningful way. NLP applications include language translation, sentiment analysis, chatbots, and voice recognition systems.

Personalized System of Instruction: PSI is an educational approach that emphasizes individualized learning through self-paced study and mastery of content before progressing. PSI typically involves a combination of written materials, instructional videos, and assessments that allow learners to control their learning trajectory based on their understanding of the subject matter.

Professional Learning Community (PLC): PLC is a collaborative approach among educators focused on improving teaching practices and student outcomes through collective inquiry and shared learning experiences. PLCs encourage ongoing professional development by fostering a culture of collaboration where teachers can share strategies, analyze student data, and reflect on their practices.

Self-Determination Theory (SDT): SDT is a psychological framework emphasizing intrinsic motivation's importance in driving human behavior. It posits that individuals are most motivated when they feel autonomous, competent, and connected to others. SDT suggests that fostering these conditions can enhance student engagement and learning outcomes in educational settings.

Teacher Professional Development (TPD): TPD refers to ongoing training and education for teachers aimed at enhancing their skills, knowledge, and effectiveness in the classroom. TPD can take various forms—workshops, seminars, coaching—and focuses on improving instructional practices to meet students' needs better.

Virtual Reality (VR): VR is an immersive technology that creates a simulated environment with which users can interact using specialized equipment such as VR headsets. In education, VR offers experiential learning opportunities by allowing students to explore virtual worlds or scenarios that enhance understanding through active participation rather than passive observation.

Chapter 10

Design and Evaluation of an Adaptive VLE for a Flipped Classroom Emergency Care course

Rachid Gouifrane
https://orcid.org/0000-0003-0810-6275
ISPITS Casablanca, Morocco

Halima Lajane
ISPITS Casablanca, Morocco

Mounir Arai
ISPITS Casablanca, Morocco

Rabia Qaisar
ISPITS Casablanca, Morocco

Abderrahmane Lamiri
ISPITS Casablanca, Morocco

Wissam El Machtani El Idrissi
https://orcid.org/0000-0002-2851-5925
ISPITS Casablanca, Morocco

Amina Lhbibani
ISPITS Casablanca, Morocco

Maria Mazouri
ISPITS Casablanca, Morocco

Omar Abidi
ISPITS Casablanca, Morocco

Ghizlane Chemsi
Hassan II University of Casablanca, Morocco

Mohamed Radid
https://orcid.org/0000-0002-8082-2009
Hassan II University of Casablanca, Morocco

ABSTRACT

Nursing students face several difficulties in understanding the material of an emergency care course. This study describes the design and evaluation of a virtual learning environment (VLE) integrated into a flipped classroom approach to address these

DOI: 10.4018/979-8-3373-0740-4.ch010

issues. Using the ADDIE model, the VLE incorporated adaptive learning mechanisms to personalize content based on student progress and performance. The pilot implementation involved 56 second-year nursing students in Casablanca, Morocco, who accessed online resources and participated in class activities. Results showed moderate resource usage, with peaks before assessments, and highlighted multiple-choice questions as the most utilized and appreciated resource. Students expressed overall satisfaction with the course design, resource variety, and user-friendliness. However, limited use of interactive tools like forums was observed, and no significant correlation was found between content usage frequency and exam scores. The study suggests that flipped classrooms and VLEs can effectively support nursing education.

INTRODUCTION

The emergency care course is a major module in the training program for future nurses. It is composed of several foundational chapters that constitute the core of the nursing profession. The main objective of this course is to equip the student with the necessary resources to behave competently in front of critical clinical situations. Classically, each chapter of the course is taught in an academic setting. Subsequently, clinical simulation sessions are offered to students before they enter the clinical settings.

Many students find it challenging to understand the concepts covered in this course. The extensive volume of material to be covered within a limited timeframe hinders students' ability to integrate and apply the knowledge effectively. In addition, the invasive nature of the majority of chapters and the lack of learning opportunities in the clinical settings increase the frequency of difficulties. This situation often leads students to adopt "surface learning strategies", as the knowledge learned does not remain in memory for long, and is quickly forgotten following exams (Charlin et al., 2003).

So-called traditional teaching methods are often suggested as one of the factors promoting these difficulties. (Chamberland et al, 1995; Billings & Halstead, 2012; Schwerdt & Wupperman, 2010). These methods encourage passive learning and provide little opportunity for feedback (Billings & Halstead, 2012). They are effective for delivering large volumes of information; however, they often fail to ensure high-quality learning experiences and do not adequately support personalized learning (Collins & Halverson, 2018).

As a result, several recommendations have advocated for the integration of virtual learning environments (VLEs) into nursing education programs, not only as a complement to traditional methods but also as a core component of the flipped classroom approach (French National Authority for Health [HAS], 2015; Liu et al.,

2016). Using the strategies provided by these VLEs could support students to learn the emergency course more effectively.

Currently, many well-developed VLEs are used in higher education to facilitate learning. “Canvas” is an example of a VLE used in thousands of universities especially in the United States. According to Keefe and Wharrad (2012) the use of VLEs promotes the integration of knowledge and increases student motivation and satisfaction. The various techno-pedagogical tools offered by these VLEs promote sustainable learning according to the pace and needs of various learner styles.

Beyond the simple online distribution of content, VLEs can perform several functions. In particular, they provide visibility into student progress even outside of regular teaching hours through resource usage statistics. These systems address individual strengths and weaknesses, fostering improved academic performance and deeper understanding (Graf et al, 2011). They also support personalized learning experiences by integrating adaptive feedback mechanisms tailored to individual needs (Yang & Wu, 2009). Consequently, these features enhance educators' ability to deliver targeted and effective individual support (Green et al., 2006).

Over the past decade, numerous empirical studies, conducted in different contexts, show that the use of VLEs in nursing education as part of flipped classroom approach represents a potential superior or, at least, equivalent to a traditional course. In this sense, several comparative studies have shown significant improvement in flipped classroom groups in terms of satisfaction (Ahmed Mersal et al, 2014; Bloomfield and Jones, 2013; Hsu, 2012; Li et al, 2019; Pangandaman, 2018; Shorey et al, 2018; Shorey et al, 2017; Smyth et al, 2012) and knowledge acquisition (Ahmed Mersal et al, 2014, Chen and Chuang, 2012; Gerdprasert et al, 2011; Tan et al, 2017; Kim et al, 2019; Zhu et al, 2019) compared to the control groups. Several authors also add that the use of VLEs was more effective in improving nursing students' critical thinking and clinical reasoning skills (Dehghanzadeh and Jafaraghaie, 2018; Jang and Hong, 2016; Park and Park, 2017; Sadhuwong et al, 2016). However, other experimental studies did not find significant differences between comparison groups in terms of motivation and theoretical knowledge acquisition (Horiuchi et al, 2009; Bloomfield et al, 2010; Li et al 2014). Similarly, Sung et al (2008) did not find significant differences between the two groups in terms of acquisition of medication administration ability.

In brief, these studies have evaluated the effects of introducing VLEs to support the learning of several courses including medication administration (Sung et al, 2008), hand washing (Bloomfield et al, 2010), pain management (Keefe and Wharrad, 2012), and postpartum care (Gerdprasert et al, 2011). Nevertheless, there is a dearth of literature examining the use of VLEs to support emergency care. Thus, the present study describes an experience of designing and using a VLE “Canvas” to support nursing students undertaking a flipped classroom emergency care course, with a focus on adaptive mechanisms employed to address the specific needs of individual students. The study also aims to describe student perceptions on flipped classroom and the e-learning resources used.

LITERATURE REVIEW

Flipped classroom

The flipped classroom is an innovative pedagogical model that redefines the traditional dynamics of classroom and out-of-class learning activities. It is a subset of blended learning that shifts the delivery of instructional content outside the classroom, often through multimedia resources such as pre-recorded video lectures. These asynchronous materials enable students to learn at their own pace, thereby optimizing classroom time for synchronous, interactive, and student-centered learning activities (Critz & Knight, 2013; Missildine et al., 2013; Patanwala et al, 2017; Wells-Beede, 2020).

In this approach, content traditionally delivered through in-class lectures is assigned as pre-class work. Students engage with video lectures or other online exercises before attending in-person sessions. Classroom time is then dedicated to applying acquired knowledge through collaborative and interactive activities facilitated by the instructor. This restructured approach transforms the classroom into an active learning environment, where students challenge and refine their understanding of the material through group-based exercises and discussions (Guilbault & Viau-Guay, 2017).

The flipped classroom model is often characterized by three core components: (1) mandatory pre-class preparation involving content acquisition, (2) active learning strategies during in-person sessions focused on discussing and analyzing pre-learned content, and (3) structured participation from all students during classroom interactions (Charnet, 2019). While the idea of pre-class preparation is not new, technological advancements have significantly enhanced students' ability to engage with preparatory materials through virtual learning environments (Park & Park, 2017).

Over the past decade, the flipped classroom has gained prominence in nursing education, where its efficacy has been widely documented. Research indicates that this model promotes deeper learning in the classroom and fosters higher levels of student engagement (Critz & Knight, 2013; Missildine et al., 2013; Smith & McDonald, 2013; Gilboy et al., 2015). One of its main advantages lies in freeing up classroom time for more effective discussions and problem-solving activities. By doing so, it encourages students to engage with higher-order cognitive skills, such as application, analysis, and synthesis, as outlined in Bloom's taxonomy (Gilboy et al., 2015).

In healthcare education, the advantages of the flipped classroom are particularly pronounced. Online video lectures can effectively deliver foundational knowledge while offering flexibility in pacing for learners. Consequently, in-class activities such as simulations and clinical case studies become the primary focus, enhancing knowledge retention, critical thinking, and problem-solving skills (McLaughlin et al., 2014; Rose et al., 2016; Ward et al., 2018). Furthermore, evidence suggests that the flipped classroom enhances active learning (Betihavas et al., 2016; Lewis et al., 2018; Park & Park, 2017), promotes collaborative engagement (Critz & Knight, 2013), and facilitates self-directed learning (Lewis et al., 2018). By leveraging this approach, students develop greater autonomy and engagement, ultimately taking more responsibility for their educational outcomes (Betihavas et al., 2016).

However, despite its many advantages, the pedagogical success of the flipped classroom is heavily contingent on students' adequate preparation before in-class sessions (Patanwala et al, 2017). Effective implementation also requires optimal use of classroom time, emphasizing interactive and collaborative activities (Guilbault & Viau-Guay, 2017). Additionally, the success of this approach depends significantly on the competency of instructors, particularly in selecting appropriate digital tools and integrating active learning strategies effectively (Wells-Beede, 2020).

Virtual learning environments (VLEs)

The initial development of VLEs can be traced back to the 1990s. Early e-learning systems featured asynchronous communication tools, including email and basic discussion forums, and supported the uploading and distribution of pre-recorded lectures, multimedia, and textual content. By the early 2000s, the emergence of innovative training modalities such as blended learning significantly transformed VLEs. These platforms began integrating advanced features like synchronous communication, discussion forums, videoconferencing, blogs, wikis, and podcasts (Atun et al., 2015).

Blended learning programs, like fully online courses, rely heavily on VLEs for their design and delivery. Various terms are often used interchangeably to describe VLEs, including Virtual Learning Environments (VLEs), Learning Management Systems (LMS), Learning Content Management Systems (LCMS), and educational or learning platforms. While differences exist among these systems, they share core functionalities: enabling the creation, management, and distribution of online courses (Ghirardini, 2012). Moreover, they combine content delivery with a suite of techno-pedagogical tools designed to foster communication, interactivity, and support for teaching and learning processes.

Currently, numerous VLEs are available, offering varying levels of complexity. Technically, these platforms are software systems hosted on servers and accessible as web-based applications. Access is typically secured via licensing agreements for proprietary systems (e.g., Blackboard, Angel, Canvas, eCollege) or through open-source solutions like Moodle. Users are granted distinct permissions based on their roles—administrators, educators, or learners. These platforms ensure secure connections, restricting access to course content to enrolled students and assigned instructors. While technical support is often available, instructors generally retain full control over their course pages and content (Bristol & Zerwekh, 2011).

From a pedagogical perspective, VLEs typically feature three main functional spaces:

1. A course space, that organizes course content and supplementary materials in diverse formats.
2. A communication and collaboration space, enabling interaction through forums, chats, emails, and similar tools.
3. A management space, dedicated to tracking learner progress and training activities (Assaad, 2016).

Advancements in VLEs now allow for the extension of their basic functionalities through plug-ins and add-ons, enhancing the versatility and adaptability of these systems (Ghirardini, 2012).

Beyond acting as repositories for online content, VLEs offer several benefits. They enable educators to design, organize, and manage all aspects of their courses, providing tools to upload diverse resources such as lesson plans, learning objectives, teaching strategies, and interactive activities. Additionally, most platforms include tracking systems that allow educators to collect both individual and collective data on student progress. These systems facilitate the monitoring of key metrics, including:

- Scores from assessed activities such as online quizzes.
- Statistical reports on content engagement.
- Participation rates in forums and collaborative activities.
- Responses to interactive tasks (e.g., online tests, forums) (Bristol & Zerwekh, 2011).

The analysis of these tracking data, often referred to as "learning analytics," is an emerging area of research. Metrics such as login times, test scores, and forum participation provide insights into student progress and enable timely interventions in case of anomalies. These analytics can also provide valuable insights into students' cognitive processes, particularly in contexts requiring the development of clinical reasoning skills (HAS, 2015).

For students, VLEs facilitate access to course materials, enabling them to engage with educational resources and communicate with peers and instructors outside of traditional learning hours. These environments support cognitive engagement by providing opportunities for concrete experiential learning. Furthermore, VLEs promote collaborative and interactive learning at a distance, which complements in-class communication (Legros et al., 2002). Students can ask questions online, complete exercises, take part in online assessments, and review their grades (Bristol & Zerwekh, 2011).

Despite their advantages, VLEs have been criticized for perpetuating a traditional teacher-centered model of education, primarily focused on knowledge transmission. Marcel Lebrun notably described them as "Teaching Management Systems" rather than "Learning Management Systems," emphasizing their orientation toward supporting instructors in creating and managing courses rather than fostering student-driven learning processes (Assaad, 2016). It is evident that VLEs, as tools, cannot independently ensure effective learning outcomes. Their effectiveness largely depends on how they are utilized and the degree of student engagement they foster.

Techno-pedagogical tools in VLEs

VLEs typically offer educators a wide range of digital tools, including collaboration and communication tools, content creation and dissemination tools, assessment tools, and administrative tools. These tools are primarily asynchronous (e.g., quizzes, recorded lectures, discussion forums). However, synchronous methods, such as live chat sessions and online video conferencing, are also available to facilitate real-time interaction (HAS, 2015). Selecting techno-pedagogical tools should be guided by their pedagogical value within the training framework and their alignment with learning objectives (Pelaccia, 2016).

Content creation and dissemination tools

Content creation and dissemination tools enable educators to share digital learning materials in various formats, including text, images, videos, tutorials, and glossaries. For instance, the "learning pathway" tool allows educators to design a course or sequence of content as web pages, files, multimedia resources (videos, audio, images), and activities (tests, discussions, assignments). This tool structures learning content into coherent stages, enabling educators to monitor learners' progress at each step. Additionally, prerequisites can be defined to ensure that learners complete one stage before advancing to the next. For pathways exceeding three stages, it is recommended to include clear descriptions of the primary activities expected of learners.

The “document” or “resource” tool facilitates the creation and dissemination of files in various formats, such as MS Word, PowerPoint, Excel, PDF, MP3, and AVI. These resources are easily accessible, modifiable (e.g., edit, relocate, or delete), and can be integrated into learning pathways. Similarly, the “assignments” tool allows learners to upload individual or group work assignments for submission to instructors. Educators can set detailed instructions and submission deadlines, making it easier to manage submissions and provide feedback, including grades and comments (HAS, 2015).

Educational videos

Instructional videos, including short video capsules and videoconferences, are dominant resources in online and hybrid learning environments. The literature highlights that various types of videos are utilized based on specific learning objectives. Video capsules and videoconferences are particularly effective for delivering theoretical knowledge in hybrid learning contexts. These resources enable students to review materials asynchronously before face-to-face sessions.

Research advocates for creating short video capsules of 10 to 20 minutes rather than lengthy videoconferences, enhancing engagement and knowledge retention (Smith & McDonald, 2013). Additionally, simulation videos have been widely employed to develop clinical skills, offering realistic demonstrations of best practices in clinical settings (Hansen, 2011; Holland et al., 2013). These resources help bridge the gap between theoretical knowledge and practical application, boosting learners' confidence in clinical settings (Stone et al., 2019).

Key advantages of instructional videos include unlimited accessibility and on-demand repetition, particularly through mobile devices. Videos can be paused, replayed, or revisited multiple times, catering to diverse learning styles and optimizing classroom time. Moreover, pre-recorded videos can be reused across academic years, reducing teachers' workload and spreading production costs over time. However, the primary limitation of videos is the lack of interaction between students and instructors or among peers (Viel et al., 2014).

To address this limitation, interactive elements can be added to videos, transforming them from passive to active learning tools. Features such as embedded tasks, reflective questions, hyperlinks, or prompts encourage deeper engagement and critical thinking (Fontaine, 2016). While these interactive features enhance learning, they remain optional for students who prefer to proceed without additional materials (Brahimi et al., 2008).

The creation of educational videos has also become more accessible and cost-effective. Various free and paid software solutions enable educators to produce video capsules. Educators can appear on screen using a webcam, narrate presentations, or record their screens and voice. Some VLEs support live videoconferencing, which can be recorded and uploaded to the platform for asynchronous viewing (Peraya, 2017).

Collaboration and communication tools

Interaction is a cornerstone of effective online and hybrid learning. Singh (2003) emphasizes that communication and collaboration in blended learning environments enhance knowledge construction and sharing. Various technological tools, both asynchronous (e.g., discussion forums, wikis) and synchronous (e.g., videoconferencing, email, chat), support online interaction. Among these, discussion forums are the most commonly used tools.

Discussion forums

Discussion forums are integral to VLEs, providing a virtual space for asynchronous interaction. They enable students to engage with peers and instructors beyond traditional learning hours, fostering collaboration and knowledge exchange (Holenko & Hoi-Bozic, 2008). Rooted in the socioconstructivist framework (Vygotskiĭ, 1978), forums promote peer interaction as a significant support mechanism for learning.

In these forums, students engage in diverse cognitive activities, such as posing questions, generating ideas, offering critiques, and analyzing peers' contributions. Forums encourage constructive disagreement and help learners identify and rectify misconceptions (Holenko & Hoi-Bozic, 2008). Additionally, Forums enable students to comment on course content or collaborate on specific tasks and projects, thereby fostering critical reflection and shared learning (Nandi et al., 2011).

Despite the abundant research on discussion forums in distance learning, their effectiveness in hybrid learning and nursing education remains underexplored. Studies indicate that collaborative learning opportunities in online discussions enhance student engagement and support knowledge construction activities (Sternberger, 2002; Nor et al., 2010). Asynchronous forums, in particular, provide students with the flexibility to engage thoughtfully at their own pace and preserve discussion records for future reference (Christopher et al., 2004).

Discussion forums in VLEs offer the advantage of preserving records of exchanges. These archives are valuable for students, especially when frequently asked questions arise, and for educators, who can identify areas of ambiguity or learning difficulties (Abel et al., 2010). The literature also highlights the potential of discussion forums to foster critical thinking among learners. By participating in these forums, students enhance their decision-making and problem-solving skills (Sternberger, 2002; Afify, 2019). Activities or questions that prompt students to apply course knowledge to clinical scenarios or to compare and critique specific issues have been demonstrated to enhance higher-order thinking skills (Craig, 2015).

Given these benefits, discussion forums have become a common feature of online and blended learning environments, enabling asynchronous communication between students and educators regardless of time and location (Nandi et al., 2011). However, challenges such as time constraints or student shyness sometimes hinder participation in face-to-face discussions, underscoring the value of blended learning's in-person component. Forums are particularly beneficial for students who may not actively participate in physical classroom discussions (Al-Huneidi & Schreurs, 2012).

Despite their strengths, forums also present limitations. Rovai (2007) notes issues such as an overwhelming volume of messages, the dominance of discussions by a few students, the risk of miscommunication, and reduced motivation to participate. Research confirms that forum participation is not uniformly distributed (Abel et al., 2010; Nandi et al., 2011; Nandi et al., 2012). Nandi et al. (2012) categorized students into three groups based on their participation levels: (a) passive readers who do not contribute, (b) posters who share their opinions with limited interaction, and (c) active participants who engage consistently in discussions.

The success of online discussions depends on various factors, including the design of the forum, the topics addressed, group size, and students' intrinsic motivation to engage in asynchronous discussions (Afify, 2019). Several strategies have been proposed to optimize forum interaction. Researchers recommend dividing forums into thematic sections, facilitating focused navigation and discussion (Holenko & Hoi-Bozic, 2008; Abel et al., 2010). Creating small discussion groups has also been shown to foster higher levels of knowledge and critical thinking compared to larger groups (Schellens & Valcke, 2006; Kim, 2013; Afify, 2019). Rovai (2007) emphasizes the importance of instructor "social presence," with regular feedback to prevent student isolation.

Online Assessment tools

Online assessment tools are increasingly integrated into distance learning programs, typically encompassing self-assessment quizzes or tests scheduled for specific dates and times (Bristol & Zerwekh, 2011).

Multiple Choice Questions (MCQs)

Many VLEs and software applications allow educators to design online MCQs that are automatically graded. Similar to traditional written MCQs, they can serve formative or summative purposes. These assessments enable instructors to monitor student progress and evaluate course effectiveness, while students can track their learning and enhance their skills accordingly (Honey & Marshall, 2003). However, a significant limitation of online MCQs is the difficulty in supervising students during summative assessments, which is why they are frequently utilized for self-assessment purposes. Self-assessment quizzes allow students to identify knowledge gaps and address them without fear of poor grades.

These tools provide unlimited accessibility and instant feedback, making them a valuable resource for exam preparation (Thérèse & Warnier, 2016). From the instructor's perspective, response data and usage statistics help identify misconceptions and adapt course content. VLEs provide detailed analytics, including individual scores, question difficulty levels, and patterns of overall student performance, allowing instructors to efficiently identify areas for improvement (Honey & Marshall, 2003).

The cognitive levels measured by MCQs remain a topic of debate. According to Thérèse and Warnier (2016), MCQs—whether online or paper-based—primarily assess the first four levels of Bloom's taxonomy: knowledge, comprehension, application, and analysis. While higher-order cognitive skills are less frequently evaluated, case-based or context-rich MCQs can address analytical and clinical reasoning skills. These questions often begin with a brief clinical vignette, followed by options that require hypothesis formulation and application of prior knowledge (Charlin et al., 2003; Perrier, 2014). They help students recall care-related problems and prepare for safe and effective clinical decision-making (Bristol & Zerwekh, 2011).

VLEs typically include quiz tools allowing instructors to create interactive exercises with diverse question types, such as:

- Multiple-choice questions with single or multiple answers.
- True/false questions.
- Matching tasks between two lists.
- Fill-in-the-blank questions…

Quiz tools often allow instructors to provide tailored feedback, linking students to relevant course materials or web resources. Questions can be categorized by topic or difficulty level, and random question generation ensures varied test formats, especially for multiple attempts. Educators can also set attempt limits and incorporate multimedia elements into questions (Thérèse & Warnier, 2016).

Adaptive Mechanisms in VLEs

A significant development in VLEs is the integration of adaptive mechanisms that customize educational content and experiences based on individual learner needs, preferences, and behaviors. Adaptive mechanisms utilize advanced algorithms and real-time analytics to create personalized learning pathways, catering to diverse learner needs and characteristics (Scott et al, 2017). The integration of Artificial Intelligence (AI) has significantly enhanced these adaptive mechanisms by enabling systems to process vast amounts of learner data, recognize complex patterns, and predict future learning needs. AI-driven mechanisms, such as machine learning algorithms and natural language processing, facilitate dynamic adjustments in content delivery, feedback, and assessment, thereby fostering more effective and engaging learning experiences (Xu, 2024).

Adaptive mechanisms within VLEs refer to system functionalities that modify the presentation of content, learning paths, or feedback based on the analysis of learner interactions and characteristics. They aim to create personalized learning experiences that optimize engagement and comprehension. For example, adaptive learning environments can analyze learner data to adjust content complexity, pacing, and sequencing, thereby improving knowledge retention and motivation (El-Sabagh, 2021). These mechanisms rely on robust data collection and processing technologies to deliver real-time adaptations that align with individual learning needs (Katsaris & Vidakis, 2021).

Adaptive mechanisms in VLEs can be categorized into content adaptation, pacing adaptation, assessment adaptation, and navigation adaptation. Content adaptation involves modifying instructional materials to suit learners' prior knowledge and preferences, enhancing their engagement and comprehension. Pacing adaptation dynamically adjusts the speed of content delivery based on learners' performance, promoting optimal learning experiences. Assessment adaptation tailors evaluation methods to individual learning needs, providing customized feedback that supports mastery (Bober et al, 2007; Talaghzi et al, 2020). Navigation adaptation reorganizes learning sequences to align with learners' progress and goals, facilitating efficient knowledge acquisition (Scott et al, 2017).

Recent research highlights diverse applications of adaptive mechanisms in VLEs. Adaptive 3D virtual environments, for instance, dynamically adjust scenarios and challenges based on learners' interactions, fostering immersive and engaging experiences (Scott et al., 2017). Cluster-based adaptive learning systems utilize algorithms to group learners with similar characteristics, enabling the delivery of customized learning pathways (Fadieieva, 2023). Furthermore, adaptive e-learning systems integrate learning style preferences into content delivery and assessment processes, enhancing personalization and effectiveness (Graf et al, 2011).

Despite their potential, implementing adaptive mechanisms in VLEs presents several challenges. The technical complexity of designing and maintaining adaptive systems requires advanced algorithms, substantial computational resources, and specialized expertise (Smith & Ragan, 2016). Furthermore, the collection and analysis of learner data raise concerns about privacy and compliance with regulatory frameworks, necessitating robust data protection measures (Bober et al, 2007). Scalability is a significant concern, as adaptive systems must perform effectively across diverse learner populations with varying needs and contexts (Talaghzi et al, 2020).

REFERENCE FRAMEWORK

Any course that integrates e learning must be based on a pedagogical engineering approach. Currently, there are two main models for the implementation of distance learning: the ADDIE model (acronym for Analysis, Design, Development, Implementation, Evaluation), and the SAM model (Successive Approximation Model) (HAS, 2015).

The ADDIE model is the classic and popular model in e-learning engineering. It consists of five steps. Given its characteristics, it was chosen to accompany the design process of this course (Figure 1) (Ghirardini, 2012).

Figure 1. ADDIE model applied to e-learning (source: Ghirardini B. FAO 2012)

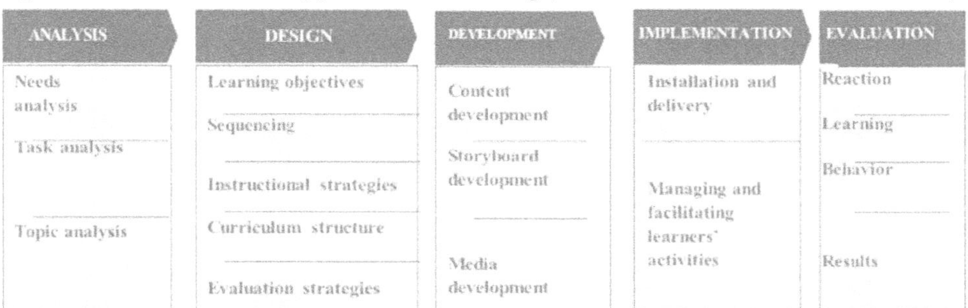

METHOD

Course design

The emergency care course is a 30-hour course addressed to second year nursing students at a Faculty in Casablanca, Morocco. During the 2023/2024 academic year, this course was delivered using a flipped classroom approach, through which the student is invited to consult the content online and actively participate in the recommended classroom activities.

The course design was based on the ADDIE model (Ghirardini, 2012):

1. Analysis:

Data related to the study context, the level of the students and their learning difficulties as well as the pedagogical objectives of the course were analyzed. Besides, technical predisposition and computer skills are a primary condition before starting a flipped classroom course (Petit dit Dariel, 2011). In this course, all students were used to handling IT (information technology) tools with unlimited access to computers and smartphones. After receiving specific training, the students were introduced to using the different educational resources implemented on Canvas. Each student has a personal account accessible using a Login and Password. In case of access problems or technical difficulties, students can contact the IT department of the institution directly. At the end of this phase, the learning objectives have been developed and decisions regarding the delivery of the course have been made.

2. Design:

At the end of this phase, the general structure of the course and its content were defined. The instructional objectives were translated into learning objectives. The pedagogical sequences, learning activities and evaluation methods were determined.

The course was designed in seven chapters (Table 1). The overall time commitment for face-to-face sessions was set at 24 hours. In addition, for the preparation of the content, decisions were made regarding the various learning situations to be proposed.

3. Development:

The development of learning resources is the most important step in the design process of a flipped classroom course. This phase consists of producing the necessary resources and supporting materials for the course. Based on the University of

Ottawa's Quality Hybrid Course grid (SAEA, 2016), the course content was carefully prepared in terms of the quality of the learning materials, the organization of online and face to face activities, the teaching strategies, and the assessment approach.

These included micro conferences, written care procedures, simulation videos, interactive videos, illustrations, online tests through formative multiple choice questions (MCQs) and discussion forums. These online resources have been developed to establish an engaging learning environment where the learner is able to learn anywhere, anytime, and independently. At the same time, statements of the tutorials scheduled during these sessions were developed (Table 1).

Table 1. Course design

Chapters	**E-learning**	**Face to face learning**
First Aid and Emergency Care	Micro conferences Care procedures Illustrations Simulation videos Interactives videos MCQs self-assessment Discussion forums	Discussions Tutorials Explanatory interviews Practical activities
Life-Threatening Emergencies		
Trauma and Prehospital Emergency Care		
Common Medical Emergencies		
Pediatric and Obstetric Emergencies		
Specialized Skills in Emergency Care		
Disasters and Exceptional Situations		

The online resources have been developed to establish an engaging learning environment where the learner is able to learn anywhere, anytime, and independently. Similarly, learning activities were designed to encourage learners to interact and collaborate with their peers and to facilitate formative assessment. The main purpose of this structure was to:

- Facilitate the learning of basic theoretical knowledge.
- Promote the acquisition of procedural knowledge before integrating the practical sessions and internships.
- Promote the development of clinical reasoning skills for the most frequent clinical situations.

The choice of online resources has been carefully considered to select pedagogical strategies that are appropriate to the types of knowledge to be acquired and to the various learning styles of the students:

✓ **Educational micro conferences**

In order to facilitate the learning of declarative knowledge, audio lectures were recorded for each chapter of the course. The student could thus benefit, at a distance and at his own pace, from the same qualities of a face-to-face conference. The use of this method allows communicating a large amount of information while providing the student with the ability to manipulate the video as needed, allowing more time to organize the knowledge in their long-term memory.

Seven micro conferences (Table 5), averaging 15 minutes per lecture, were recorded. These videos were recorded based on PowerPoint (2013) presentations using the "record slideshow" tool. Thus, audio explanations were added to accompany each video.

✓ **Simulation videos**

Traditionally, procedural knowledge is learned during practical sessions and internships. The use of online simulation videos could facilitate the early acquisition of this type of knowledge. In addition, the virtual consultation of clinical situations can help students avoid risks and professional misconducts in front of real patients.

In this sense, 05 video sequences were put on the VLE (Table 4). Before consulting the video simulation, the student is led to consult the written procedure. This chronology could promote visual and mental repetition before integrating the practical sessions.

In addition, interactive elements, such as quizzes, were created on several videos using the free online software "Visia". When viewing the video, quiz questions appear in specific sequences of the procedure. The student will be asked to identify the correct answers and possible errors before continuing the viewing. Hyperlinks may lead the student to other sources for more information on the topic. At the end, the student is given a score and feedback.

✓ **MCQs self-assessment**

In order to allow students to identify their strengths and weaknesses, online MCQs related to the learning objectives of the course have been used as a method of self-assessment. Apart from the advantages offered by these online tests (unlimited accessibility, immediate feedback...), they allow the student to perceive his progress without any risk of receiving a bad grade.

For the seven course chapters, seven self-assessment tests (127 questions) were rephrased according to the rules synthesized by Thérèse and Warnier (2016). Each test had an average of eighteen MCQs depending on the consistency of the chapter. Simple MCQs to assess memorization, comprehension, and dose calculation skills; and clinical case-based MCQs to assess analysis and decision-making skills. This last type of MCQs starts with short vignettes describing some possible clinical situations related to the chapters studied. This diversification of MCQ types aimed to assess various taxonomic levels (Table 2).

Table 2. Types and Purposes of Online MCQs

Educational objectives	**Learning outcomes**	**Chapters**							**Total**
		Ch1	**Ch2**	**Ch3**	**Ch4**	**Ch5**	**Ch6**	**Ch7**	
Knowledge and comprehension	**Memorize facts, interpret and reproduce them**	**8 true false questions+ 13 simple MCQs**		**40 simple MCQs**					**61 questions**
Application	Calculate a dosage						12 simple MCQs		12 questions
Analysis	Make a decision	54 clinical case-based MCQs							54 questions

Access to the MCQs was only allowed after consulting the teaching materials according to instructions and timetables previously set by the teacher. The number of attempts allowed was unlimited. Each test consisted of a core question and several distractors. The shuffle setting was used to shuffle both the order of the questions and the distractors, which makes it difficult to learn the answers by heart.

Once the answer is validated by the student, the latter immediately receives a grade and constructive feedback previously introduced by the teacher. The student may be referred to specific instructional sequences for further clarification.

In addition to the quizzes and standard sections for each chapter, a range of other resources were also available to support learning. These included the course outline, a PDF basic document, external links and discussion forums.

✓ **Discussion forums:**

In order to answer all pedagogical questions early on and to avoid isolating learners, thematic discussion forums have been created on the VLE. This e-learning resource allows students to meet virtually in order to benefit from exchanges and interactions between teachers and students and between pairs. This approach is in line with the socio-constructivist theory (Vygotskiĭ, 1978) where the promotion of interaction between students is considered a real support for learning. Exchanges between learners or with the tutor take place via modes of communication that do not require simultaneous connection (asynchronous mode).

These forums were facilitated by the tutor and students, divided into groups, to discuss the weekly curriculum after viewing the content. Students were encouraged to post their responses and comment on the responses of others on questions and topics previously introduced in the discussion forum. Some of these topics included discussion of scientific publications related to the course chapters. Students were also encouraged to post their own questions online and to respond to the questions of others.

4. Implementation:

All of the above online resources have been implemented on the Canvas platform. Each chapter of the course has been placed in a separate section. The design of the course on the VLE was carefully considered to facilitate the mastery of the learning objectives. In addition, the course chapters were taught sequentially and the resources appeared on a thoughtful schedule that began with the micro conferences and ended with the MCQs self-assessment. This process was intended to allow more focus on similar knowledge without overloading the student with a range of new information.

The proposed flipped classroom model consisted of a variety of online and face-to-face learning activities. After an introductory session on the use of the VLE: Canvas, access to the online learning resources was available via a login and password one week prior to the face-to-face sessions. Access to the online resources was available 24 hours a day throughout the academic year.

The learning process began with a face-to-face session to provide an overview of the course outline, the learning objectives as well as the learning strategies and methods that would be used. The timeline for consulting the online resources was scheduled by the instructor. For each chapter of the course, the students were asked to consult, through their computers or smartphones, specific sequences following a logical order before integrating the face-to-face sessions. The order of consultation began with the micro conferences and ended with the self-assessment by MCQ. The classroom sessions were an opportunity both to clarify ambiguities and to apply the knowledge gained through the clinical case studies. In the final session, students attend a practical activity before entering the clinical simulation sessions (figure 2).

Adaptive learning mechanisms

Various adaptive learning mechanisms have been implemented within the VLE to tailor educational content according to learners' progress and performance. Conditional release rules have been implemented to ensure that educational content is made accessible only after the learning prerequisites have been fulfilled. Moreover, online MCQs dynamically adjust in difficulty: they become more challenging if the learner performs well or simpler if the learner encounters difficulties. Additionally, automated personalized feedback systems, based on learners' responses, have been integrated to help them identify their strengths and areas for improvement. In cases of difficulty, learners are directed to automated recommendations for supplementary resources to deepen their understanding or clarify misunderstood concepts. Finally, learning Analytics provides detailed visualizations of engagement and performance data (time spent, resources accessed, scores achieved). These insights enable educators to identify individual learner needs and make informed decisions to adapt content and pedagogical strategies accordingly.

5. Evaluation

The assessment method used in this model is a combination of online and traditional assessment. The teacher assesses student interactions, participation, responses and assignments in the online activities. Analysis of this data allows the teacher to provide individualized feedback based on the needs of each learner.

In the classroom, the teacher assesses students based on their care plans and their performance on written assessments. In addition, explanatory interviews were used as a formative assessment method to promote reflective practice. Through this instrument, the learner was led, by means of questioning, to mentally present the care procedure and to verbalize his actions. This method is likely to reveal a lot of information about the origin of the errors and difficulties encountered. Figure 2 and Table 3 show the process of our flipped classroom model and the main roles assigned to the teacher and student.

Figure 2. Flipped classroom process

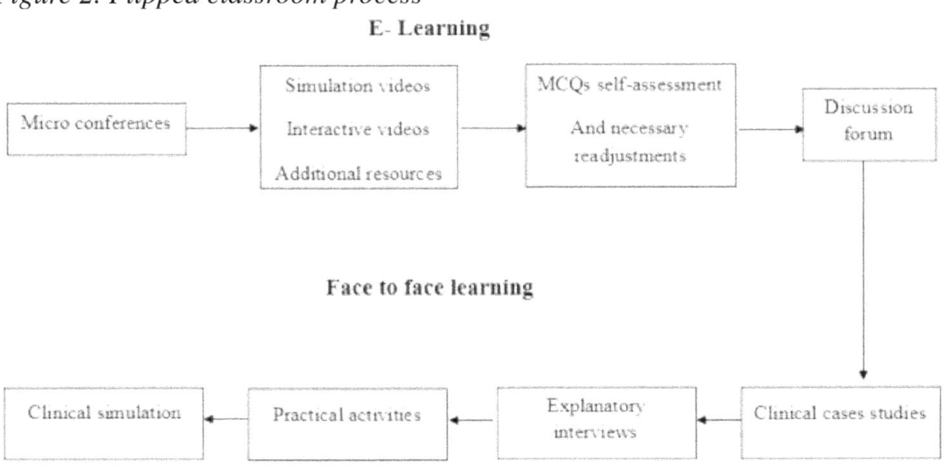

Table 3. Position of the teacher and the student in the flipped classroom model

Teacher's role	Student's role	Evaluation methods
e-Learning		
Communicate instructions for using online educational resources. Analyze the degree of consultation of the resources (number of pages and duration). Analyze the responses of students (MCQs and interactive video). Analyze the content and quality of online interactions. Provide feedback and guidance based on the analysis. Identify deficiencies in terms of knowledge acquisition. Provide individualized feedback via discussion forums.	Consult the micro conferences (following the instructions, several times, a delay before the face-to-face session). Consult the written care procedure. View the video simulation. View and perform the exercises contained in the interactive videos. Correct according to the feedbacks. Pass the MCQ test. Make corrections based on automatic feedback Consult, via the hyperlinks, the necessary additional information. Interact via the discussion forums in case of ambiguity or questioning.	Quiz/MCQs Interactives videos Learning analytics

Data collection and analysis

In this quantitative descriptive study, Data were collected through content usage results and a satisfaction questionnaire. Descriptive statistics regarding the use of online resources by all registered students (n = 56) were analyzed. We monitored learners' activities on the VLE. For each learner, we recorded his or her contributions, learning trajectories, number of online pages visited, time spent in each page, results of online assessments, and number of posts in the discussion forums. With the exception of the online MCQs, the level of use of the VLE was measured in terms of the number and duration of access to the online pages. It should be noted that this does not necessarily mean that the student has used the content of the page. To ensure the reliability of the results, students were not allowed to download and/or print the materials on the VLE until after the experimental phase was completed.

Data collection was conducted over a 92-day period from October 01, 2023 to December 31, 2023, which is the entire period between the start of the course and the end-of-semester exam. Data were imported into Excel and SPSS version 20 from the VLE. Pearson's correlation coefficient was used to test the relationship between final exam scores and, respectively, the number and duration of online page views.

The satisfaction questionnaire was an adapted version of the "flipped classroom Satisfaction Scale" developed by Hsu (2011). All students were asked to respond to 22 statements on a scale of one (strongly disagree, not at all useful) to five (strongly agree, very useful). The questionnaire included questions regarding students' perceptions of flipped classroom and its effects, as well as the VLE and the online resources used. Descriptive statistics were used to describe the data obtained. At the end of the questionnaire, students were asked to write suggestions and comments under the headings "What aspects of the course did you find most useful? " and "What aspects of the course could be improved? ". The internal consistency of the measurement instrument in this study was .953 (Cronbach's alpha)

Ethical considerations

This study was carried out after the approval of the management of the Higher Institute of Nursing Professions and Health Techniques of Casablanca. The consent of the students who participated in this experiment was obtained. They were reassured that their answers would remain confidential. The data were processed anonymously.

RESULTS

1. Use of online resources

1.1. Access and use of the online pages

Figure 3. Number of accesses per day between October 01 and December 30, 2023

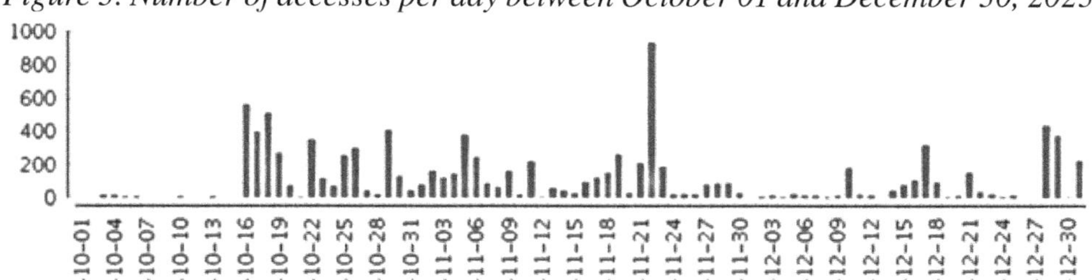

Figure 3 illustrates the general pattern of access to online content from the beginning of the course instruction to the day before the first semester exam. With the exception of a short period of relatively intense access at the beginning of the course, two inflations of usage can be observed one in late November 2023 and the other in late December 2023.

Figure 4. Frequency of access to online resources between October 18 and December 31, 2023

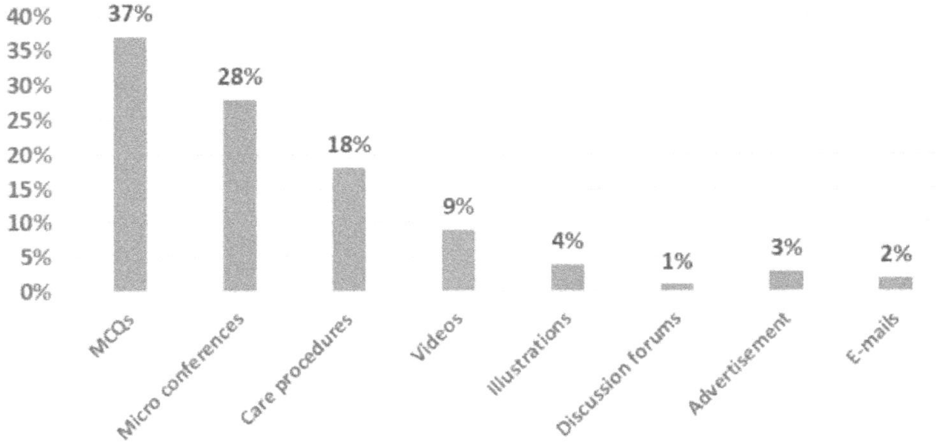

Self-assessment by MCQs and micro conferences were the most frequently used elements. However, the degree of online interaction, through discussion forums and e-mail, was low.

1.2. Use of online MCQs

Table 4. The use of online MCQs between October 18 and December 31, 2023

Indicators	Values
Number of validated attempts	343
Average number of attempts per student	16
Success rate for first attempts	36%
Success rate for last attempts	75%
Total duration of attempts	35,11 hours
Average time per student	1,67 hour (19,55% of total time online)

Online MCQs represent the most used e-learning resource by students. An average of 16 attempts per student were made throughout the trial period. Furthermore, the success rate of attempts increased significantly towards the end of the last attempts (Table 4).

1.3. Use of educational videos

Table 5. Use of educational videos

Video	Duration (min: sec)	Average viewing time (hour: min)
Micro conferences		
First Aid and Emergency Care	15:09	2:76
Life-Threatening Emergencies	15:02	2:65
Trauma and Prehospital Emergency Care	15:06	2:90
Common Medical Emergencies	13:45	1:41
Pediatric and Obstetric Emergencies	12:36	2:05
Specialized Skills in Emergency Care	14:51	3:80
Disasters and Exceptional Situations	20:09	3:73
Total	**105:58**	**19:30**
Simulation videos		
Cardiopulmonary Resuscitation (CPR)	05:11	0:41
Recovery Position	02:09	0:22
Airway Clearance for Obstruction	06:48	0:53
Emergency Extraction from the Accident Scene	05:06	0:35
Management of an Unconscious Victim	04:34	0:29
Total	**23:48**	**3:00**

The total viewing time of the micro conferences was 19 hours and 30 minutes (1170 minutes). Students viewed each lecture an average of 11 times. Similarly, the total viewing time of the simulation videos was 3 hours (180 minutes). Students viewed each video an average of approximately 7.6 times throughout the experimental period.

1.4. Use of discussion forums

The discussion forums were not widely used. An average of 19 posts were exchanged each week by students. Analysis of the data reveals that a significant number of students (23) do not access or post to the discussion forum.

1.5. Individual use of online resources

All students successfully met the predefined criteria for unlocking new content, albeit at varying rates. The various resources made available online were accessed 21392 times during the period 10/18/23 to 12/30/23, an average of 382 accesses per student. The frequency with which students accessed these resources varied from student to student and ranged from one time to 775 times. The average amount of time spent viewing online content was 8.11 hours per student. This time varied by student from 15 minutes to 57.88 hours.

2. The student's satisfaction with flipped classroom approach and the VLE

2.1. Perceptions of flipped classroom approach and the VLE

Table 6. Perceptions of flipped classroom approach and the VLE

Item	Mean ± SD	Perception (n)				
		Strongly agree	Agree	Neutral	disagree	Strongly disagree
I like the practice of flipped classroom (a combination of online learning with classroom learning)	4.47±0.74	37	21	0	1	0
I found this course better organized than other traditional courses	4.28±0.95	27	24	3	0	3
Compared to traditional-style classroom learning, I found myself working harder in this course	4.19±0.87	27	16	11	3	0
I found myself learning more through flipped classroom	4.19±0.87	24	21	8	3	0
Access to Canvas and online resources was easy	4.57±0.50	32	24	0	0	0
I spend more time on online learning than classroom learning	4.57±0.50	29	21	5	0	0
I was able to employ various learning strategies (online MCQs, videos, etc.) in this course	4.47±0.60	29	24	0	3	0
Compared to classroom learning, I found it easier to participate in online discussions in flipped classroom	3.14±1.35	4	5	5	4	3
The quantity of my interactions with the teacher increased in this course	4.14±0.85	8	9	3	1	0
The quality of my interactions with classmates improved in this course	3.57±1.16	13	21	19	3	0
I think blended learning has helped me learn emergency course better	4.47±0.74	27	19	11	0	0
Flipped classroom helped me to develop skills in theory and clinical practice	4.52±0.51	29	21	5	0	0

continued on following page

Table 6. Continued

Item	Mean ± SD	Perception (n)				
		Strongly agree	Agree	Neutral	disagree	Strongly disagree
Flipped classroom allows me to improve my clinical reasoning skills.	4.52±0.51	21	24	8	3	0
I think flipped classroom allows me a better preparation to take care of patients on clinical settings	4.38±0.65	21	21	13	0	0
I think flipped classroom has a positive effect on the quality of nursing for patients	4.33±0.73	27	24	3	3	0
I would like to have the opportunity to participate in this type of course	4.71±0.46	40	16	0	0	0

The survey results indicate a positive perception of flipped classroom and the VLE among students. The only item that had a mean score below 3.5 was "Compared to classroom learning, I found it easier to participate in online discussions in flipped classroom." Most students (M = 4.42; SD = 0.72) considered themselves good at using various learning strategies (educational videos, online MCQs etc.). Overall, students rated the quality of the flipped classroom approach, online resources and their effects on learning highly. The majority of items had average scores between 4.00 and 4.71 (the highest score was 5).

2.2. The usefulness of online resources

Table 7. The usefulness of online resources as perceived by students

Online resources	Mean ± SD	Perceptions (n)				
		Very useful	useful	Neutral	Not very useful	Not at all useful
Canvas	4.47±0.74	12	8	0	1	0
Micro conferences	4.52±0.81	14	5	1	1	0
Online MCQs	4.76±0.53	17	3	1	0	0
Interactives videos	4.57±0.87	16	2	2	1	0
Simulation videos	4.19±1.12	11	6	2	1	1
Discussion forums	2.90±1.26	3	4	4	8	2

The vast majority of students (M = 4.47; SD = 0.74) rated the VLE as useful or very useful. Only one student indicated that he did not like using Canvas. Students rated all of the online resources favorably except for the discussion forums which scored less than 3 (M = 2.90; SD = 1.26).

2.3. Correlation of frequency and duration of resource use with final exam scores

Table 8. Correlation between frequency of online page views and final exam score

Correlations			
		Exam score	**Page views**
Exam score	Pearson's correlation	1	,157
	Sig. (2-tailed)		,496
	N	21	21
Page views	Pearson's correlation	,157	1
	Sig. (2-tailed)	,496	
	N	21	21

Table 9. Correlation between the duration of consultation of online resources and final exam score

Correlations			
		Exam score	**Duration (h)**
Exam score	Pearson's correlation	1	,097
	Sig. (2-tailed)		,675
	N	21	21
Duration (h)	Pearson's correlation	,097	1
	Sig. (2-tailed)	,675	
	N	21	21

Data analysis shows that there is no statistically significant correlation between the number of pages consulted and final exam scores ($r = 0.157$, $p = 0.496$). The data also shows that there is no statistically significant correlation between page viewing time and final exam scores.

Discussion

The participants in this study demonstrated positive perceptions of the VLE used and the flipped classroom experience. In total, 19 items (out of 22) showed high average scores above 4 (the highest was 5). Participants were particularly satisfied with the quality of the flipped classroom approach, the digital resources, and the learning outcomes (knowledge, skills, and clinical reasoning abilities). This result appears consistent with findings from studies that have evaluated the effects of flipped classroom on student perceptions and satisfaction (Pangandaman, 2018); Shorey et al, 2018; Shorey et al, 2017; Bloomfield and Jones, 2013; Ahmed Mersal et al, 2014; Hsu, 2012; Smyth et al, 2012; Sung et al, 2008; Li et al, 2019).

The majority of participants rated the course and the VLE as "very useful" or "useful". Students were able to use a variety of online and face-to-face learning resources and strategies (micro conferences, online MCQs, interactive videos, discussion forums...) in this course. Using a mix of constructivist elements could facilitate critical thinking, group discussions, and individualized learning among learners (Hsu, 2011).

Technically, the use of Canvas by students and lecturers does not require a high level of information technology expertise. In this course, students report experiencing few problems accessing content and easily solving the small difficulties that did arise. Nevertheless, it must be recognized that the use of a VLE requires at least one training session at the beginning of the course.

Learning analytics on the VLE provided deeper insights into students' activities, enabling the optimization of learning processes. Notably, the pedagogical resources available on the platform were accessed by all registered students. During the experimentation period, two peaks of use were noticed. The first and second peaks of use, observed respectively in late November and late December 2023, could be attributed to the preparation period for the summative evaluation and exam.

The literature review shows that the use of VLEs in flipped classroom is a factor that can create increased motivation to learn compared to traditional methods (Gagnon et al, 2013; Gerdprasert et al, 2011; Jang and Hong, 2016). Although students were strongly encouraged to use the VLE, the frequency of use of the available resources varied from student to student in terms of both pages viewed and duration of viewing. The majority of students seemed to appreciate these resources and used them frequently, while a minority used them to a moderate or low degree. These results are consistent with those observed by Green et al. (2006) in an experiment to design a VLE to support the learning of anatomy and physiology course.

Regarding the online MCQs, all students completed all the tests. The average number of attempts reached 16 per student with a 75% success rate towards the end of the last attempts, which is still positive and logical. Furthermore, similar to Honey and Marshal's (2003) study, the survey revealed that students found the online MCQs to be very useful and useful for their learning. Students reported a high level of satisfaction with the adaptive progression in MCQ difficulty levels, as well as the personalized feedback and supplementary resources provided to support their learning. Learners specifically mentioned that the hyperlinks in the feedback encouraged them to read their course more thoroughly.

Besides, participants rated the instructional videos positively and had adequate viewing time for the micro conferences and simulation videos. Each student viewed the micro conferences an average of 11 times and the simulation videos an average of six times during the experimental period. The differences between the viewing times of these videos can be explained by the fact that the first type of videos transfers more basic theoretical knowledge than the second type (simulation and interactive videos).

However, only one item related to the discussion forums had a mean score below 3 (2.90). The results of discussion forum usage also showed a very low degree of online interaction in view of the possibilities offered by the VLE. Similar to the findings of Gerdprasert et al. (2011), E-mail and discussion forums represent the least exploited and least valued online resources. Only 10 out of 21 students discussed via the VLE during the experimental period and the majority of messages exchanged (weekly average = 19) dealt with questions related to assessments and exams. Interaction in the forums was low even if the tutor initiated discussion topics. This can be explained by the fact that students prefer to wait for the face-to-face sessions to exchange and to expose their questions. Participants also noted the feeling of exhaustion caused by the extra time spent working online.

In summary, flipped classroom and the associated e-learning resources seem to be a real support for learning the emergency care course and the percentage of students who passed the summative exam in the first session was satisfactory. Certainly, the study did not show a statistically significant association between the number of pages viewed by students and their final exam scores. Nevertheless, students had certainly access to resources that enable them to meet the modular outcomes more easily than before the VLE was used.

LIMITATION

The number of students who participated in this study was limited and from a single training setting, which does not allow the generalization of the results. Nevertheless, this was the total number of nursing students registered in their second year during the academic year in question.

As this was a first experiment related to the emergency course, it was impossible to compare the results of this experiment with those of similar experiments. However, the adoption of this new approach for use in subsequent academic years may facilitate the comparison.

CONCLUSION

Learning analytics on VLE provide valuable insights on how students interact with online resources, enabling the identification of individual learning needs and preferences. These data support the development of targeted interventions, personalized learning paths, and adaptive feedback, particularly during face-to-face sessions.

The results reveal that a simple, easy-to-use, and engaging online learning environment has been developed to train nursing students. Flipped classroom is viewed by participants as an ideal method of training. All students would like the opportunity to participate in this type of course in the future. The educational resources available on the VLE seemed to contribute to a good learning experience for the students. Nevertheless, this VLE should be improved in terms of content and its next version should incorporate more self-assessment activities and interactive elements while encouraging students to participate in discussion forums. Furthermore, we feel that the present experience was an opportunity to improve our know-how in terms of designing and delivering interactive educational content and tutoring online. This process requires considerable time and effort.

The next version of the online course should capitalize on the advancements in VLEs made possible by AI. Future research should investigate advanced personalized learning mechanisms, particularly in the context of online MCQs, with an emphasis on real-time adaptability to learners' performance and needs.

REFERENCES

Abel, F., Bittencourt, I. I., Costa, E., Henze, N., Krause, D., & Vassileva, J. (2010). Recommendations in Online Discussion Forums for E-Learning Systems. *IEEE Transactions on Learning Technologies*, *3*(2), 165–176. DOI: 10.1109/TLT.2009.40

Afify, M. K. (2019). The influence of group size in the asynchronous online discussions on the development of critical thinking skills, and on improving students' performance in online discussion forum. *International Journal of Emerging Technologies in Learning (Online)*, *14*(5), 132.

Ahmed Mersal, F., & Ahmed Mersal, N. (2014). Effect of Blended Learning on Newly Nursing Student's Outcomes Regarding New Trends in Nursing Subject at Ain Shams University. *American Journal of Educational Research*, *2*(11), 1036–1043. DOI: 10.12691/education-2-11-6

Al-Huneidi, A. M., & Schreurs, J. (2012). Constructivism Based Blended Learning in Higher Education. [IJET]. *International Journal of Emerging Technologies in Learning*, *7*(1), 4–9. DOI: 10.3991/ijet.v7i1.1792

Assaad, A. (2016). Place et rôles de l'enseignant intervenant dans des dispositifs de formation universitaire à distance [The place and roles of teachers involved in university distance education programs] (Doctoral dissertation, Université de Lyon). Université de Lyon.

Atun, R., Kersnik, J., Švab, I., Majeed, A., Car, J., Al-Shorbaji, N., & Wheeler, E. (2015). eLearning for undergraduate health professional education: A systematic review informing a radical transformation of health workforce development. Imperial college.

Betihavas, V., Bridgman, H., Kornhaber, R., & Cross, M. (2016). The evidence for "flipping out": A systematic review of the flipped classroom in nursing education. *Nurse Education Today*, *38*, 15–21. DOI: 10.1016/j.nedt.2015.12.010 PMID: 26804940

Billings, D. M., & Halstead, J. A. (2012). Teaching in Nursing: A guide to the faculty. (4e éd.). Missouri: ELSEVIER Saunders.

Blackboard Inc. 2004. Blackboard United Kingdom. ≤https://www.blackboard.com/worldwide/gb/en/aboutbb.htm≥

Bloomfield, J., Roberts, J., & While, A. (2010). The effect of computer-assisted learning versus conventional teaching methods on the acquisition and retention of handwashing theory and skills in pre-qualification nursing students: A randomised controlled trial. *International Journal of Nursing Studies*, *47*(3), 287–294. DOI: 10.1016/j.ijnurstu.2009.08.003 PMID: 19762016

Bloomfield, J. G., & Jones, A. (2013). Using e-learning to support clinical skills acquisition: Exploring the experiences and perceptions of graduate first-year pre-registration nursing students — A mixed method study. *Nurse Education Today*, *33*(12), 1605–1611. DOI: 10.1016/j.nedt.2013.01.024 PMID: 23473860

Bober, M., Fasuga, R., & Šarmanová, J. (2007). Adaptive Mechanisms in Virtual Education Environment. In Fernandes, M. M. (Ed.), *ICEE2007 Coimbra*. University of Coimbra.

Brahimi, C., Steben, M., & Farley, C. (2008). Projet innovation en formation: Phase I: les technologies de l'information et de la communication (TIC) [Innovation project in training: Phase I: Information and communication technologies (ICT)]. Institut national de santé publique du Québec. Retrieved from http://collections.banq.qc.ca/ark:/52327/1927158

Bristol, T. J., & Zerwekh, J. (Eds.). (2011). *Essentials of e-learning for nurse educators*. F. A. Davis Company.

Chamberland, G., Lavoie, L., & Marquis, D. (1995). *20 Formules pédagogiques*. Presse de l'Université du Québec.

Charlin, B., Bordage, G., & Van Der Vleuten, C. (2003). Clinical reasoning assessment. [http://dx.doi.org/10.1051/pmed:2003015]. *Pédagogie Médicale*, *4*(1), 42–52. DOI: 10.1051/pmed:2003015

Charnet, C. (2019). *Comment réaliser une formation ou un enseignement numérique à distance? Guide pratique: former et se former* [How to design a digital distance training or teaching course? A practical guide: Training and self-training]. De Boeck Supérieur.

Chen, H.-Y., & Chuang, C.-H. (2012). The learning effectiveness of nursing students using online testing as an assistant tool: A cluster randomized controlled trial. *Nurse Education Today*, *32*(3), 208–213. DOI: 10.1016/j.nedt.2011.03.004 PMID: 21450377

Christopher, M. M., Thomas, J. A., & Tallent-Runnels, M. K. (2004). Raising the bar:Encouraging high level thinking in online discussion forums. *Roeper Review*, *26*(3), 166–171. DOI: 10.1080/02783190409554262

Collins, A., & Halverson, R. (2018). *Rethinking education in the age of technology: The digital revolution and schooling in America*. Teachers College Press.

Craig, G. P. (2015). *Evaluating discussion forums for undergraduate and graduate students*. Faculty Focus.

Critz, C. M., & Knight, D. (2013). Using the Flipped Classroom in Graduate Nursing Education. *Nurse Educator*, *38*(5), 210–213. DOI: 10.1097/NNE.0b013e3182a0e56a PMID: 23969751

Dehghanzadeh, S., & Jafaraghaie, F. (2018). Comparing the effects of traditional lecture and flipped classroom on nursing students' critical thinking disposition: A quasi-experimental study. *Nurse Education Today*, *71*, 151–156. DOI: 10.1016/j.nedt.2018.09.027 PMID: 30286373

dit Dariel, O. P. (2011). Exploring e-learning adoption in nurse education: A socio-cultural case study using Q and Bourdieu (Doctoral dissertation, University of Nottingham).

El-Sabagh, H. A. (2021). Adaptive e-learning environment based on learning styles and its impact on development students' engagement. *International Journal of Educational Technology in Higher Education*, *18*(1), 53. DOI: 10.1186/s41239-021-00289-4

Fadieieva, L. (2023). Adaptive learning: A cluster-based literature review (2011-2022). *Educational Technology Quarterly*, *2023*(3), 319–366. DOI: 10.55056/etq.613

Fontaine, G. (2016). Evaluation of the MOTIV@COEUR online training platform on brief motivational interventions with nurses in acute cardiovascular care. *Master's thesis* presented for the degree of Master of Science (M.Sc.) in Nursing Sciences, Expertise-Advice in Nursing Care. 159.

French National Authority for Health. (2015). Guide to the design of open and distance learning (FOAD) in the world of health. Evaluation and improvement of practices. France.

Gagnon, M.-P., Gagnon, J., Desmartis, M., & Njoya, M. (2013). The Impact of Blended Teaching on Knowledge, Satisfaction, and Self-Directed Learning in Nursing Undergraduates: A Randomized, Controlled Trial. *Nursing Education Perspectives*, *34*(6), 377–382. DOI: 10.5480/10-459 PMID: 24475598

Gerdprasert, S., Pruksacheva, T., Panijpan, B., & Ruenwongsa, P. (2011). An interactive web-based learning unit to facilitate and improve intrapartum nursing care of nursing students. *Nurse Education Today*, *31*(5), 531–535. DOI: 10.1016/j.nedt.2010.10.008 PMID: 21078535

Ghirardini, B. (2012). E-learning methodologies and good practices. A guide for designing and delivering e-learning solutions from the FAO eLearning Academy. Second Edition. Food and agriculture organization of the United Nations, Rome.

Gilboy, M. B., Heinerichs, S., & Pazzaglia, G. (2015). Enhancing Student Engagement Using the Flipped Classroom. *Journal of Nutrition Education and Behavior*, *47*(1), 109–114. DOI: 10.1016/j.jneb.2014.08.008 PMID: 25262529

Graf, S., Lin, F., & McGreal, R. (Eds.). (2011). *Intelligent and Adaptive Learning Systems: Technology Enhanced Support for Learners and Teachers: Technology Enhanced Support for Learners and Teachers*. IGI Global.

Green, S. M., Weaver, M., Voegeli, D., Fitzsimmons, D., Knowles, J., Harrison, M., & Shephard, K. (2006). The development and evaluation of the use of a virtual learning environment (Blackboard 5) to support the learning of pre-qualifying nursing students undertaking a human anatomy and physiology module. *Nurse Education Today*, *26*(5), 388–395. DOI: 10.1016/j.nedt.2005.11.008 PMID: 16414156

Guilbault, M., & Viau-Guay, A. (2017). *La classe inversée comme approche pédagogique en enseignement supérieur: état des connaissances scientifiques et recommandations* [The flipped classroom as a pedagogical approach in higher education: State of scientific knowledge and recommendations]. *Revue internationale de pédagogie de l'enseignement supérieur*, 33(1). Published online on March 6, 2017. Retrieved from https://journals.openedition.org/ripes/1193

Hansen, M. M. (2011). Are nursing students' clinical skills competency and self-confidence levels improved via video iPods? A randomized controlled pilot study. *Journal of Nursing Education and Practice*, *1*(1), 32. DOI: 10.5430/jnep.v1n1p32

Holenko, M., & Hoic-Bozic, N. (2008). Using Online Discussions in a Blended Learning Course. International Journal of Emerging Technologies in Learning (iJET), pp. 18-23, Available at: ≤https://online-journals.org/index.php/i-jet/article/view/630≥. doi:http://dx.doi.org/DOI: 10.3991/ijet.v3i0.630

Holland, A., Smith, F., McCrossan, G., Adamson, E., Watt, S., & Penny, K. (2013). Online video in clinical skills education of oral medication administration for undergraduate student nurses: A mixed methods, prospective cohort study. *Nurse Education Today*, *33*(6), 663–670. DOI: 10.1016/j.nedt.2012.01.006 PMID: 22341996

Honey, M., & Marshall, D. (2003, December). The impact of on-line multi-choice questions on undergraduate student nurses' learning. In *Proceedings of the 20th Annual Conference of the Australasian Society for Computers in Learning in Tertiary Education (ASCILITE)* (pp. 236-243).

Horiuchi, S., Yaju, Y., Koyo, M., Sakyo, Y., & Nakayama, K. (2009). Evaluation of a web-based graduate continuing nursing education program in Japan: A randomized controlled trial. *Nurse Education Today*, *29*(2), 140–149. DOI: 10.1016/j.nedt.2008.08.009 PMID: 18829141

Hsu, L.-L. (2011). Blended learning in ethics education: A survey of nursing students. *Nursing Ethics*, *18*(3), 418–430. DOI: 10.1177/0969733011398097 PMID: 21558117

Hsu, L.-L. (2012). Qualitative Assessment of a Blended Learning Intervention in an Undergraduate Nursing Course. *The Journal of Nursing Research*, *20*(4), 291–299. DOI: 10.1097/jnr.0b013e31827363bc PMID: 23154440

Jang, H. J., & Hong, S. Y. (2016). Effect of Blended Learning in Nursing Education. *International Journal of Multimedia and Ubiquitous Engineering*, *11*(5), 297–304. DOI: 10.14257/ijmue.2016.11.5.27

Katsaris, I., & Vidakis, N. (2021). Adaptive e-learning systems through learning styles: A review of the literature. *Advances in Mobile Learning Educational Research*, *1*(2), 124–145. DOI: 10.25082/AMLER.2021.02.007

Keefe, G., & Wharrad, H. J. (2012). Using e-learning to enhance nursing students' pain management education. *Nurse Education Today*, *32*(8), e66–e72. DOI: 10.1016/j.nedt.2012.03.018 PMID: 22513154

Kim, Y. M., Yoon, Y. S., Hong, H. C., & Min, A. (2019). Effects of a patient safety course using a flipped classroom approach among undergraduate nursing students: A quasi-experimental study. *Nurse Education Today*, *79*, 180–187. Advance online publication. DOI: 10.1016/j.nedt.2019.05.033 PMID: 31153088

Legros, D., de Pembroke, E. M., & Talbi, A. (2002). Les théories de l'apprentissage et les systèmes multimédias. [Learning theories and multimedia systems] In Legros, D., & Crinon, J. (Eds.), *Psychologie des apprentissages et multimédia* [Psychology of learning and multimedia]. (pp. 23–39). Armand Colin.

Lewis, C. E., Chen, D. C., & Relan, A. (2018). Implementation of a flipped classroom approach to promote active learning in the third-year surgery clerkship. *American Journal of Surgery*, *215*(2), 298–303. DOI: 10.1016/j.amjsurg.2017.08.050 PMID: 29169824

Li, C., He, J., Yuan, C., Chen, B., & Sun, Z. (2019). The effects of blended learning on knowledge, skills, and satisfaction in nursing students: A meta-analysis. *Nurse Education Today*, *82*, 51–57. Advance online publication. DOI: 10.1016/j.nedt.2019.08.004 PMID: 31437783

Li, Z., Tsai, M.-H., Tao, J., & Lorentz, C. (2014). Switching to blended learning: The impact on students' academic performance. *Journal of Nursing Education and Practice*, *4*(3). Advance online publication. DOI: 10.5430/jnep.v4n3p245

Liu, Q., Peng, W., Zhang, F., Hu, R., Li, Y., & Yan, W. (2016). The Effectiveness of Blended Learning in Health Professions: Systematic Review and Meta-Analysis. *Journal of Medical Internet Research*, *18*(1), e2. DOI: 10.2196/jmir.4807 PMID: 26729058

McLaughlin, J. E., Roth, M. T., Glatt, D. M., Gharkholonarehe, N., Davidson, C. A., Griffin, L. M., Esserman, D. A., & Mumper, R. J. (2014). The Flipped Classroom. *Academic Medicine*, *89*(2), 236–243. DOI: 10.1097/ACM.0000000000000086 PMID: 24270916

Missildine, K., Fountain, R., Summers, L., & Gosselin, K. (2013). Flipping the Classroom to Improve Student Performance and Satisfaction. Journal of Nursing Education, 52(10), 597 599. DOI: 10.3928/01484834-20130919-03

Nandi, D., Hamilton, M., & Harland, J. (2012). Evaluating the quality of interaction in asynchronous discussion forums in fully online courses. *Distance Education*, *33*(1), 5–30. DOI: 10.1080/01587919.2012.667957

Nandi, D., Hamilton, M., Harland, J., & Warburton, G. (2011). How active are students in online discussion forums? *Proceedings of the Thirteenth Australasian Computing Education Conference* - Volume 114. 125–134

Pangandaman HK (2018). Effects of Flipped Classroom Videos in the Return Demonstration Performance of Nursing Students. Sch J Appl Sci Res Vol: 1, Issu: 4 (55-58).

Park, E. O., & Park, J. H. (2017). Quasi-experimental study on the effectiveness of a flipped classroom for teaching adult health nursing: Flipped learning in adult health nursing. *Japan Journal of Nursing Science*, *15*(2), 125–134. DOI: 10.1111/jjns.12176 PMID: 28834418

Patanwala, A. E., Erstad, B. L., & Murphy, J. E. (2017). Student use of flipped classroom videos in a therapeutics course. *Currents in Pharmacy Teaching & Learning*, *9*(1), 50–54. DOI: 10.1016/j.cptl.2016.08.043 PMID: 29180154

Pelaccia, T. (2016). *Comment (mieux) former et évaluer les étudiants en médecine et en sciences de la santé* [How to better train and assess medical and health science students]. Edition De Boeck Supérieur.

Peraya, D. (2017). *Au centre des Mooc, les capsules vidéo: un renouveau de la télévision éducative?* [At the heart of MOOCs, video capsules: a renewal of educational television?]. Distances et médiations des savoirs, 17. Retrieved from https://journals.openedition.org/dms/1738

Perrier, C. (2014). L'apprentissage du raisonnement clinique infirmier par vignette clinique courte: Étude exploratoire [Learning nursing clinical reasoning through short clinical vignettes: An exploratory study]. *Recherche en Soins Infirmiers, 118*(3), 52–61. DOI: 10.3917/rsi.118.0052 PMID: 29383920

Rose, E., Claudius, I., Tabatabai, R., Kearl, L., Behar, S., & Jhun, P. (2016). The Flipped Classroom in Emergency Medicine Using Online Videos with Interpolated Questions. *The Journal of Emergency Medicine, 51*(3), 284–291.e1. DOI: 10.1016/j.jemermed.2016.05.033 PMID: 27381954

Rovai, A. P. (2007). Facilitating online discussions effectively. *The Internet and Higher Education, 10*(1), 77–88. DOI: 10.1016/j.iheduc.2006.10.001

Sachete, A. S., Gomez, R. S., Filho, A. C., & De Lima, J. V. (2024). Indicators of adaptive learning in virtual learning environments: Systematic literature review. *Revista Latinoamericana de Tecnología Educativa, 23*(2), 69–87. DOI: 10.17398/1695-288X.23.2.69

Sadhuwong, K., Koraneekij, P., & Natakuatoong, O. (2016). Effects of a Blended Learning Model Integrating Situated Multimedia Lessons and Cognitive Apprenticeship Method on the Clinical Reasoning Skills of Nursing Students. *Journal of Health Research, 30*, 6. DOI: 10.14456/jhr.2016.56

Schellens, T., & Valcke, M. (2006). Fostering knowledge construction in university students through asynchronous discussion groups. *Computers & Education, 46*(4), 349–370. DOI: 10.1016/j.compedu.2004.07.010

Scott, E., Soria, A., & Campo, M. (2017). Adaptive 3D Virtual Learning Environments—A Review of the Literature," in *IEEE Transactions on Learning Technologies*, vol. 10, no. 3, pp. 262-276. DOI: 10.1109/TLT.2016.2609910

Shorey, S., Kowitlawakul, Y., Devi, M. K., Chen, H.-C., Soong, S. K. A., & Ang, E. (2018). Blended learning pedagogy designed for communication module among undergraduate nursing students: A quasi-experimental study. *Nurse Education Today, 61*, 120–126. DOI: 10.1016/j.nedt.2017.11.011 PMID: 29197264

Shorey, S., Siew, A. L., & Ang, E. (2017). Experiences of nursing undergraduates on a redesigned blended communication module: A descriptive qualitative study. *Nurse Education Today*. Advance online publication. DOI: 10.1016/j.nedt.2017.11.01 PMID: 29190535

Singh, H. (2003). Building effective blended learning programs. *Educational Technology*, *43*(6), 51–54. Retrieved July 09, 2010, from https://www.bookstoread.com/framework/blended-learning.pdf

Smith, C. M., & McDonald, K. (2013). The Flipped Classroom for Professional Development: Part II. Making Podcasts and Videos. *Journal of Continuing Education in Nursing*, *44*(11), 486–487. DOI: 10.3928/00220124-20131025-93 PMID: 24199640

Smyth, S., Houghton, C., Cooney, A., & Casey, D. (2012). Students' experiences of blended learning across a range of postgraduate programmes. *Nurse Education Today*, *32*(4), 464–468. DOI: 10.1016/j.nedt.2011.05.014 PMID: 21645947

Sternberger, C. S. (2002). Embedding a Pedagogical Model in the Design of an Online Course. *Nurse Educator*, *27*(4), 170–173. DOI: 10.1097/00006223-200207000-00009 PMID: 12131813

Stone, R., Cooke, M., & Mitchell, M. (2019). Undergraduate nursing students' use of video technology in developing confidence in clinical skills for practice: A systematic integrative literature review. *Nurse Education Today*, *104230*. Advance online publication. DOI: 10.1016/j.nedt.2019.104230 PMID: 31689584

Sung, Y. H., Kwon, I. G., & Ryu, E. (2008). Blended learning on medication administration for new nurses: Integration of e-learning and face-to-face instruction in the classroom. *Nurse Education Today*, *28*(8), 943–952. DOI: 10.1016/j.nedt.2008.05.007 PMID: 18599162

Talaghzi, J., Bennane, A., Himmi, M., Bellafkih, M., & Benomar, A. (2020). Online AdaptiveLearning: A Review of Literature. *ACM Int. Conf. Proceeding Ser.*, pp. 115–120. DOI: DOI: 10.1145/3419604.3419759

Tan, C., Yue, W. G., & Fu, Y. (2017). Effectiveness of flipped classrooms in nursing education: Systematic review and meta-analysis. *Chinese Nursing Research*, *4*(4), 192–200. Advance online publication. DOI: 10.1016/j.cnre.2017.10.006

Thérèse, B., & Warnier, L. (2016). Evaluer les acquis des étudiants à l'aide de QCM. Louvain: Université catholique de Louvain. https://cdn.uclouvain.be/public/Exports%20reddot/ipm/documents/VADEMECUM_Mars_2016.pdf

UOttawa Teaching and Learning Support Service (SAEA). (2016). Quality Hybrid Course grid. UOttawa. https://saea.uottawa.ca/site/files/docs/SAEA/fonds-hybride/2017/SAEAAQGrille.pdf

Viel, C. C., Rodrigues, K. R. da H., Melo, E. L., Bueno, R., Pimentel, M. D. G. C., & Teixeira, C. A. C. (2014). Interaction with a Problem Solving Multi Video Lecture: Observing Students from Distance and Traditional Learning Courses. [IJET]. *International Journal of Emerging Technologies in Learning*, *9*(1), 39. DOI: 10.3991/ijet.v9i1.3358

Vygotskiĭ, L. S. (1987). *Mind in society: the development of higher psychological processes*. Harvard University Press.

Ward, M., Knowlton, M. C., & Laney, C. W. (2018). The flip side of traditional nursing education: A literature review. *Nurse Education in Practice*, *29*, 163–171. DOI: 10.1016/j.nepr.2018.01.003 PMID: 29414110

Wells-Beede, E. (2020). The Flipped Classroom in Nursing: The Nurse Educators' Experience. *Teaching and Learning in Nursing*, *15*(3), 168–174. DOI: 10.1016/j.teln.2020.02.002

Xu, Z. (2024). AI in education: Enhancing learning experiences and student outcomes. *Applied and Computational Engineering*, *51*(1), 104–111. DOI: 10.54254/2755-2721/51/20241187

Yang, Y. J., & Wu, C. (2009). An attribute-based ant colony system for adaptive learning object recommendation. *Expert Systems with Applications*, *36*(2), 3034–3047. DOI: 10.1016/j.eswa.2008.01.066

Zhu, L., Lian, Z., & Engström, M. (2019). Use of a flipped classroom in ophthalmology courses for nursing, dental and medical students: A quasi-experimental study using a mixed-methods approach. *Nurse Education Today*, *104262*. Advance online publication. DOI: 10.1016/j.nedt.2019.104262 PMID: 31759243

Chapter 11

Enhancing Business Communication Skills of BDIoT MA Students: A Longitudinal Exploration of Immersive Virtual Lab Integration

Youness Khatib
ENSAM, Morocco

Amine Khatib
Université du Littoral Côte d'Opale, France

Imane El Imadi
https://orcid.org/0000-0001-9076-5039
Faculty of Sciences Ben M'Sik, University Hassan II, Morocco

ABSTRACT

This longitudinal study explores the integration of immersive virtual labs to bridge the gap between language input and effective output for first-year Master students specializing in Big Data and Internet of Things (BDIoT) at ENSAM-CASA. Leveraging Computing and Modeling innovations, including artificial intelligence (AI), natural language processing (NLP), and the rise of the Metaverse, the study utilizes VirtualSpeech®, a leading platform in immersive language learning, to enhance students' Business English communication skills. The input-conversion-output model frames the approach, where immersive practice environments transform theoretical language input into practical, effective communication skills. In each academic year, we worked with 30 students, forming two distinct groups. Group A comprised first-year MA students from the 2022-2023 academic year, while Group

DOI: 10.4018/979-8-3373-0740-4.ch011

B had included their counterparts from the previous academic year (2021-2022).

1 INTRODUCTION:

In today's rapidly evolving educational landscape, innovations in Computing and Modeling are poised to revolutionize the teaching and learning of English for Specific Purposes (ESP), especially in university settings. As Moroccan universities continue to embrace digital transformation, the integration of advanced technologies offers significant potential for enhancing the ESP experience, especially for Masters (MA) students who require specialized language skills tailored to their fields. Computing and Modeling innovations are not limited to traditional digital tools. They encompass cutting-edge developments such as artificial intelligence (AI), natural language processing (NLP), and most notably, the rise of the Metaverse—a shared virtual environment that combines elements of both the physical and digital worlds. This transformation allows for a more immersive, interactive, and personalized learning experience, which is particularly beneficial for ESP, where contextual, real-world language use is essential.

This longitudinal study, spanning two academic years at ENSAM-CASA, embarks on a transformative journey by leveraging the immersive capabilities of VirtualSpeech® to enhance the English language skills, focusing on Business English, of first-year BDIoT MA students. VirtualSpeech®, a pioneering platform renowned for its immersive virtual language learning experiences, was selected as the foundational virtual environment for this experiment. The institution, recognizing the value of this innovative approach, acquired VR headsets and facilitated the enrollment of students in the VirtualSpeech platform. The decision to harness the power of VirtualSpeech underscores the commitment of ENSAM-CASA's management to advance the learning experience and provide students with cutting-edge tools.The core objective of this study has transitioned towards teaching English for Business to BDIoT MA students, capitalizing on the immersive learning environment offered by VirtualSpeech. While initially designed to enhance technical vocabulary, the experiment's newfound purpose extends to equipping students with essential language skills tailored to the workplace. Simultaneously, this initiative marks the beginning of a broader mission to design customized virtual material for English for Specific Purposes (ESP) tailored to the unique requirements of students in Engineering and Science higher education institutions. This research venture aims to redefine language education in technical fields, and by embracing VirtualSpeech, we anticipate a robust foundation to develop our own virtual materials, subsequently elevating ESP education within specialized disciplines. This journey exemplifies the institution's dedication to preparing students for the challenges of the digital age and the complexities of the modern workplace.

2 RELATED STUDIES

The integration of immersive virtual environments, such as the Metaverse, offers new opportunities for teaching English for Specific Purposes (ESP) to MA students by simulating professional contexts tailored to their needs. Scholars have increasingly explored the potential of these environments to enhance language learning by providing realistic, interactive settings for skill development.

Research on immersive simulations highlights the ways in which the Metaverse can facilitate language learning in environments that closely mirror real-world professional contexts. For instance, medical students benefit from virtual hospital simulations that enhance communication skills through patient interactions, case study discussions, and collaborative exercises, strengthening their ESP competencies (Aljuhani et al., 2019; Lavoie et al., 2024). In business-oriented ESP courses, students participate in virtual boardroom meetings or negotiation scenarios, gaining hands-on experience with business English in settings that simulate actual workplace tasks, thereby developing essential language and professional skills (McDonald, 2020; Predescu & Apostolakis, 2023).

The Metaverse also fosters collaborative learning spaces that function as virtual classrooms, where students from different regions work together and communicate using industry-specific English. This collaboration not only aids language acquisition but also develops vital cross-cultural communication skills, which are crucial for graduate students aiming to join international industries (García et al., 2023a; Turan & Avincan, 2022). Such settings are particularly beneficial for learners looking to navigate multicultural work environments where proficiency in language and cultural understanding is paramount (Makransky & Petersen, 2021; Stelios & Lyapunov, 2023). Moreover, virtual learning environments in the Metaverse increasingly incorporate AI-driven language assistance, offering students real-time feedback on aspects such as grammar, vocabulary, and context-specific usage. These AI tutors enhance learners' ability to use specialized language accurately and contextually, which is invaluable for students seeking precision in technical or field-specific communication (Johnson, 2023; Patel, 2022). Personalized learning paths are also made possible through machine learning algorithms that tailor content to meet individual needs by identifying gaps in students' knowledge—whether related to technical terminology or field-specific writing skills—thereby optimizing learning outcomes (Chen, 2022; García, 2023b).

The multimodal nature of the Metaverse, combining text, 3D models, videos, and real-time discussions, provides a rich learning experience, especially for graduate students. For example, engineering students can manipulate virtual models of machinery while discussing technical components in English—a process that strengthens both their technical knowledge and language proficiency (Anderson, 2022; Wang et al., 2023). This multisensory engagement not only deepens understanding but also helps learners retain information effectively. In addition to linguistic skills, ESP education within the Metaverse enables learners to acquire cultural and contextual knowledge, crucial for effective communication in international settings. The ability to experience professional environments across various cultural backdrops allows students to adapt their language use to align with different social and professional norms, enhancing their preparedness for global interactions (Johnson, 2023; Zhang & Li, 2023). Finally, the interactive and immersive qualities of the Metaverse contribute to heightened student engagement and motivation. Research shows that by situating learners in realistic scenarios, the Metaverse makes language learning dynamic and encourages students to apply their skills in contextually meaningful ways—promoting active participation and motivation to learn (García et al., 2023a; Patel, 2022). This engagement is instrumental in helping learners develop practical communication skills, ultimately making the learning experience both enjoyable and effective (Makransky & Petersen, 2021; McDonald, 2020).

Obviously, the growing body of literature underscores the Metaverse's potential to bridge the gap between theoretical language input and practical, effective output by providing learners with an engaging, cutting-edge, and contextually relevant platform for practicing ESP skills.

3 METHODOLOGY

This study adopted a quasi-experimental approach to investigate the effectiveness of immersive virtual labs in enhancing the English for Business communicative skills of students enrolled in the BDIoT Master (MA) program. The methodology was designed to compare two groups of students: Group A, which participated in immersive virtual lab-based learning, and Group B, which followed a traditional classroom approach using handouts and business textbooks.

3.1 Participants

The participants were divided into two distinct groups, each consisting of 30 students:

- **Group A** comprised first-year students from the 2022-2023 academic year. These students were newly enrolled in the BDIoT MA program and were exposed to the experimental condition, where immersive virtual labs were integrated into their English for Business course.
- **Group B** consisted of students from the previous academic year (2021-2022). These students represented the control group and were taught using traditional teaching methods, such as lectures, handouts, and a standard business English textbook.

3.2 Learning Conditions

In Group A, students participated in immersive virtual labs as part of their English for Business curriculum, where simulated professional environments enabled them to practice technical communication skills in realistic contexts. These virtual labs allowed students to articulate complex technical concepts in English, engage in professional discourse within a business-oriented immersive setting, and deliver presentations tailored to a professional business audience. The aim of these labs was to provide students with hands-on experiences that reflected real-world scenarios relevant to their field of study, promoting active learning and enhancing their ability to effectively communicate technical information.

Meanwhile, Group B followed a more traditional approach within the standard business English curriculum. Their learning activities included reading and analyzing materials from a business English textbook, completing written exercises, and discussing business concepts through handouts. Additionally, they participated in instructor-led classroom lectures that lacked the immersive, hands-on elements present in Group A's learning environment. The focus for Group B was to develop communicative competence using conventional materials and methods, similar to those typically used in English for Specific Purposes (ESP) courses aimed at business contexts.

3.3 Data Collection

To evaluate the impact of these differing approaches on English language proficiency, particularly in the realm of technical communication, both groups underwent the following data collection processes:

Pre- and Post-Assessments.

All students took a pre-assessment at the beginning of the study to establish a baseline for their language proficiency and technical communication skills.

After the intervention (immersive labs for Group A and traditional instruction for Group B), a post-assessment was conducted to measure any changes in language proficiency, with a focus on:

— Ability to communicate technical information clearly.
— Competency in professional discourse.
— Presentation skills in English.

These assessments were designed to evaluate reading, writing, speaking, and listening skills, with an emphasis on practical, business-related language tasks.

Interviews.

To complement the quantitative assessment, qualitative data were collected through semi-structured interviews with students from both groups. These interviews aimed to capture students' perceptions of their learning experiences, focusing on their engagement levels, perceived challenges, and perceived improvements in language proficiency.

For Group A, interviews explored how the immersive virtual labs influenced their learning experience, particularly in terms of increased engagement, practical application of language skills, and confidence in professional settings.

For Group B, interviews sought to understand the effectiveness of the traditional learning methods and their impact on students' language development.

3.4 Data Analysis

The study employed a mixed-methods approach, integrating both quantitative and qualitative data analysis techniques to thoroughly evaluate the effects of immersive virtual labs on language proficiency and technical communication. Quantitative analysis included descriptive statistics to compare pre- and post-assessment scores, providing insights into the overall improvement in language skills across both groups. To ensure these changes were statistically meaningful, inferential tests were conducted, examining the significance of differences in performance between students exposed to immersive labs and those in traditional settings. On the qualitative side, thematic analysis was used on interview data, identifying critical themes related to student engagement, practical applicability of language skills, and perceptions of each instructional method. These themes offered a nuanced understanding of how immersive labs may influence motivation, confidence, and the perceived usefulness of language learning in professional contexts. By comparing qualitative feedback between the two groups, the study also explored students' readiness to use English in real-world professional settings, highlighting distinct experiences shaped by each instructional approach. This mixed-methods framework allowed for a comprehensive evaluation, bridging the quantitative measures of language proficiency with in-depth qualitative insights into the learning process and outcomes.

3.5 Research Design Rationale

This research design facilitates a comparative analysis of language skill development between students using immersive virtual labs (Group A) and those following traditional classroom instruction (Group B). By adopting a quasi-experimental approach with pre- and post-assessments and qualitative interviews, the study offers valuable insights into the effectiveness of immersive virtual labs in enhancing the technical and professional communication skills of BDIoT MA students. The mixed-methods approach ensures that both objective proficiency changes and subjective student experiences are thoroughly examined, allowing for a nuanced understanding of the potential of immersive learning environments in ESP contexts.

4 EXPERIMENTAL FRAMEWORK

This longitudinal study aimed to enhance the business communication skills of first- year BDIoT MA students, particularly in Business English, by introducing immersive virtual labs through the VirtualSpeech platform. The immersive labs offered students interactive environments where they could practice and improve their communication skills in real-world business settings. Group A (2022-2023 cohort) received this intervention, while Group B (2021-2022 cohort) followed a traditional learning approach.

4.1 Needs Analysis

A comprehensive needs analysis was conducted in the first month of the course to understand the initial language proficiency and specific language needs of both Group A and Group B. This analysis involved a combination of checklists, questionnaires, interviews, simulations, and pre-tests, allowing for a detailed assessment of the students' strengths and weaknesses in both Business English proficiency and technical vocabulary mastery. The focus was on identifying gaps that would inform the design and implementation of the experimental intervention.

4.2 Needs Analysis Methods

The needs analysis for this study employed a range of methods to gain a comprehensive understanding of students' communication skills and learning requirements. Checklists were used to systematically monitor the frequency and accuracy of key communication skills, providing quantitative data on student performance. Questionnaires gathered self-reported data from students regarding their confidence levels and perceived proficiency in business communication, offering insights into their self-assessed skill levels.

Semi-structured interviews with students offered a more in-depth perspective, revealing specific challenges and areas where students felt they needed improvement. Additionally, simulations were conducted in virtual environments, featuring scenarios such as business meetings and customer support calls, to assess students' real-time communication skills within professional contexts. Finally, pre-tests were administered to measure both technical vocabulary knowledge and overall Business English proficiency, establishing a baseline to track progress and evaluate the impact of the instructional methods used.

Pre-Test Results.

Table 1 provides an overview of the pre-test results, highlighting the discrepancies in Business English proficiency and technical vocabulary mastery for both groups. The results show that while students in both Group A and Group B demonstrated strong technical vocabulary skills related to their field (Big Data and IoT), their business communication skills were significantly lacking.

Table 1. Needs Analysis Results – Pre-Test for Business Communication Proficiency and Technical Vocabulary Mastery

Communicative Events	Business English Proficiency (Group A)	Technical Vocabulary Mastery (Group A)	Business English Proficiency (Group B)	Technical Vocabulary Mastery (Group B)
Business Meeting Simulation	Low (e.g., Difficulty in introducing themselves and using business etiquette)	High (e.g., Correctly discussing BDIoT concepts)	Low (e.g., Difficulty in conducting negotiations and using business vocabulary)	High (e.g., Correctly using technical jargon related to BDIoT)
Email Writing (Business Proposal)	Low (e.g., Inappropriate tone and format)	High (e.g., Properly crafting technical emails)	Low (e.g., Difficulty in structuring business proposals)	High (e.g., Effective technical communication)
Customer Support Call Simulation	Low (e.g., Struggling to address customer queries in English)	High (e.g., Proficiently resolving technical issues)	Low (e.g., Difficulty in handling customer inquiries in English)	High (e.g., Expertly addressing technical concerns)

Analysis of Pre-Test Results.

The needs analysis, as summarized in Table 1, revealed distinct differences in students' communication abilities across technical and business contexts. Both Group A and Group B demonstrated strong technical vocabulary skills, showing proficiency in discussing BDIoT concepts and accurately using field-specific jargon. However, both groups struggled with Business English across a variety of communicative tasks essential for professional interactions. In business meeting simulations, students faced challenges with basic business etiquette, including formal introductions, which hindered their ability to navigate professional settings effectively. Similarly, in email writing tasks, many students were unable to craft formal business proposals, often displaying issues with tone and structure that diminished the professionalism of their messages. During customer support call simulations, students found it challenging to respond to customer queries in a concise and professional manner. These findings underscored a critical gap in students' business communication skills, highlighting the need for focused instructional intervention to strengthen their proficiency in Business English for practical, workplace-related scenarios.

4.3 Intervention: Immersive Virtual Labs

Based on the needs analysis, immersive virtual labs were introduced as a targeted intervention to improve the business communication skills of Group A. The VirtualSpeech platform was chosen for its ability to provide realistic, interactive environments where students could practice essential communication tasks. These virtual labs featured business meeting simulations, where students engaged in role- playing scenarios requiring them to conduct meetings, negotiate, and present technical information using Business English. Additionally, email writing exercises offered real- time feedback on structure, tone, and formatting, tailored to the demands of professional business correspondence. In customer support scenarios, students practiced resolving customer issues in English, honing both their technical language proficiency and customer interaction skills. In contrast, Group B followed a traditional curriculum that utilized textbook exercises, handouts, and classroom discussions.

4.4 Expected Outcomes and Rationale

The intervention was designed with the expectation that immersive virtual labs would address identified language gaps by offering hands-on experience, immersing students in real-world business scenarios that allow for the practical application of business communication skills. Immediate feedback was provided to offer students actionable insights into their performance, promoting rapid improvement in language use. Additionally, the immersive nature of the labs was anticipated to increase student engagement and motivation, resulting in improved learning outcomes compared to traditional methods.

4.5 Framework for Evaluation

The impact of the immersive virtual labs on Group A was evaluated through a structured framework that included post-tests and qualitative feedback gathered from student interviews. These results were then compared to those of Group B, who received instruction through traditional classroom methods. The evaluation framework was designed to assess two key areas: Business English Proficiency and Technical Vocabulary Mastery. Business English Proficiency focused on students' ability to communicate effectively in formal business contexts, encompassing skills such as conducting meetings, writing professional emails, and managing customer interactions with the appropriate tone and clarity. Technical Vocabulary Mastery measured students' ability to accurately and appropriately use industry-specific terminology within their communications. This dual focus allowed for a comprehensive assessment of both general communication skills and technical language use, providing insight into how well students were prepared for real-world business interactions. By comparing these results across both groups, the evaluation aimed to determine the effectiveness of immersive virtual labs relative to traditional learning methods in enhancing students' readiness for professional communication in business settings.

The next section will delve into the results of this experiment and discuss how the immersive virtual labs impacted the technical communication skills of Group A students, addressing their specific linguistic requirements for the business environment.

5 RESULTS AND ANALYSIS

This section presents the results of the experimental framework, focusing on how the immersive virtual labs impacted the Business English and technical communication skills of Group A students in comparison to Group B. By examining both quantitative and qualitative data, we analyze the effectiveness of the virtual labs in addressing the specific linguistic requirements of students in the business environment. The evaluation framework included pre- and post-tests, assessing Business English proficiency and technical vocabulary mastery, alongside qualitative insights gathered from student interviews. The results are structured to provide a clear comparative analysis between the two groups.

5.1 Quantitative Analysis: Pre- and Post-Test Results

The pre- and post-tests were designed to assess improvement in two main areas: Business English Proficiency and Technical Vocabulary Mastery. The results from Group A (immersive virtual labs) and Group B (traditional classroom) are summarized in Table 2 and Table 3.

Table 2. Business English Proficiency Score Comparison for Group A and Group B

Group	Pre-Test Mean Score	Post-Test Mean Score	Improvement (%)
Group A	55	82	+49.1%
Group B	54	65	+20.4%

Key Findings:

1. Group A demonstrated a significant improvement (+49.1%) in Business English proficiency, moving from an average score of 55 in the pre-test to 82 in the post-test. The improvement is attributable to the hands-on, immersive nature of

the virtual labs, which allowed students to practice real-world communication tasks (e.g., business meetings, emails, and customer support).

2. Group B, which followed a traditional classroom approach, saw only a moderate improvement (+20.4%), with a mean score increase from 54 to 65. The lack of interactive and practical exercises in a business context likely limited their progress.

Table 3. Technical Vocabulary Mastery Score Comparison for Group A and Group B

Group	Pre-Test Mean Score	Post-Test Mean Score	Improvement (%)
Group A	70	89	+27.1%
Group B	71	80	+12.7%

Key Findings:

3. Both groups started with a relatively high level of technical vocabulary mastery, as evidenced by pre-test scores around 70. This reflects the strong background of students in the technical aspects of their field (BDIoT).
4. However, Group A showed a greater improvement (+27.1%) in mastering technical vocabulary in business communication contexts, reaching a post-test score of 89. The immersive labs helped them apply technical terms effectively in various business settings, such as meetings and presentations.
5. Group B, on the other hand, showed a smaller improvement (+12.7%), indicating that while traditional methods helped reinforce technical vocabulary, they lacked the contextual application of these terms in real-world business communication.

5.2 Qualitative Analysis: Interview Insights

To gain deeper insights into the student experiences and the overall effectiveness of the immersive virtual labs, qualitative data were gathered through semi-structured interviews. Students from both groups were interviewed, and their feedback was analyzed using thematic analysis.

Key Themes from Group A (Immersive Virtual Labs):

Students in Group A, who participated in immersive virtual labs, highlighted several key themes regarding their experience. A notable outcome was an increased confidence in business communication, with many students reporting that practicing in simulated environments boosted their comfort level in professional settings. After participating in virtual boardroom scenarios, one student remarked, "*The virtual boardroom scenarios were incredibly helpful. It felt like I was really in a meeting.*

This made me more comfortable using formal business language." Another significant theme was improved real-world application of technical vocabulary. Students observed that the virtual labs enabled them to apply industry-specific terms effectively in diverse contexts, including emails, presentations, and customer support tasks. One participant reflected, "*I knew the technical words before, but using them in a real business conversation was challenging. The labs made it easier to incorporate these terms naturally.*" Lastly, students reported enhanced engagement and motivation, frequently attributing their heightened interest to the immersive, interactive nature of the virtual labs. Unlike traditional classroom settings, the virtual environment allowed them to visualize and participate in dynamic, realistic scenarios. One interviewee commented, "*It was fun, and I felt like I was learning something useful every time I completed a simulation.*"

This enthusiasm for the hands-on learning format underscores the labs' effectiveness in maintaining students' attention and encouraging active participation in their learning process.

Key Themes from Group B (Traditional Classroom):

Students in Group B, who followed the traditional classroom approach, highlighted several challenges they faced. One prominent theme was the limited contextual application of skills learned. Students found it difficult to translate textbook knowledge into effective business communication, expressing that, while they understood vocabulary and grammar rules, they struggled to apply these skills in real-world professional scenarios. As one student explained, "I understand the business terms, but it's hard to use them in real conversations or presentations. I feel like we need more practice speaking." Another key issue was a lack of engagement stemming from the passive nature of traditional learning methods. Many students described how reading handouts and completing textbook exercises felt disconnected from practical application, which affected their motivation. One participant shared, "It's hard to stay engaged when the lessons don't feel relevant to what we will actually need to do in a business setting."

This disconnect between classroom activities and real-world tasks underscored a broader need for interactive, applied learning experiences that traditional methods struggled to provide.

5.3 Comparative Analysis: Business Communication vs. Technical Vocabulary

The experimental intervention demonstrated a clear impact on the Business English proficiency of Group A, as evidenced by both the quantitative data and qualitative feedback. The immersive virtual labs enabled students to engage in practical, business- related tasks that fostered real-world communication skills, leading to a significant improvement in Business English proficiency. Conversely, while both groups showed improvement in technical vocabulary mastery, the more notable gains were seen in Group A, suggesting that the virtual lab environments helped students use technical jargon more effectively in business contexts.

Table 4. Comparative Improvement in Business Communication and Technical Vocabulary Mastery

Skill	Group A (Improvement %)	Group B (Improvement %)
Business English Proficiency	+49.1%	+20.4%
Technical Vocabulary Mastery	+27.1%	+12.7%

6 DISCUSSION

The results clearly demonstrate that immersive virtual labs offer a more effective method for improving Business English communication skills compared to traditional classroom-based methods. By providing students with realistic, interactive scenarios, the virtual labs allowed students to actively engage in business tasks that closely mimic the real-world challenges they will face in their professional careers. This hands-on, practical experience appears to have played a crucial role in boosting both language confidence and proficiency.

Moreover, the results underscore the importance of **contextual application** in learning technical vocabulary. While both groups had a strong foundation in technical language, only Group A benefited from learning how to apply these terms in business communication. This finding suggests that immersive, practice-oriented learning environments can help bridge the gap between **technical knowledge** and its practical use in professional settings.

6.1 Bridging the Gap Between Input and Effective Output in Language Learning

The findings of this study underscore the critical role of immersive, practice-oriented learning environments in transforming technical knowledge into practical communicative competence. While traditional language learning often emphasizes input, primarily through receptive skills (reading and listening), it is not sufficient by itself to develop effective output, which involves productive skills like speaking and writing. The gap between input and output must be bridged by a crucial Conversion/Practice Stage, where learners actively apply their knowledge in context.

In this context, the Metaverse and Virtual Reality (VR) emerge as powerful tools that provide the necessary immersive environments for this stage. By offering simulated real-world business scenarios, the Metaverse allows learners to practice their communication skills in interactive and dynamic ways. This process enhances their ability to transition from passive understanding (input) to active and effective communication (output).

Table 5. Stages in the Language Learning Process (Y. KHATIB)

Stage	Description	Skills Involved	Role in Communication Development
Stage1: Input	Learners receive language input via reading, listening, or watching.	Receptive skills (Reading, Listening)	Provides foundational knowledge of vocabulary, grammar, and structure.
Stage2: Conversion/ Practice	Learners engage in active practice through immersive activities like VR and Metaverse simulations.	Interactive practice (Simulations, Role-plays)	Critical for transitioning knowledge into practical, communicative skills.
Stage3: Output	Learners produce language, expressing ideas through speaking or writing.	Productive skills (Speaking, Writing)	Demonstrates language proficiency and effective communication in real-world contexts.

Key Insights:

Several key insights emerged from the analysis of both learning approaches. First, input alone is not enough; while receptive skills such as reading and listening are essential for language learning, they do not directly translate into effective communication skills. Simply consuming English content doesn't lead to proficiency in business communication, as students must be able to actively produce language in relevant contexts. The importance of the conversion/practice stage became apparent, as this is the point where learners integrate their knowledge and start applying it in realistic situations. Immersive virtual environments, like those offered in platforms such as the

Metaverse, play a vital role in facilitating this stage by allowing learners to participate in simulated business meetings, email writing, and professional discussions. These scenarios help bridge the gap between theory and real-world application. Finally, the effective output stage—where learners are able to produce contextually appropriate and professional language—is essential for business communication readiness. This stage is reached only through sufficient practice; without it, the gap between input and output persists, leaving learners unprepared for real-world interactions in a professional setting. The analysis emphasized that effective practice is critical for learners to achieve communicative competence in business contexts.

This three-stage framework highlights the transformative potential of immersive technology in education. The virtual labs, powered by the Metaverse, serve as the missing bridge between theoretical knowledge and practical application. Traditional classroom settings often lack this middle stage, focusing too much on input and expecting output without providing adequate practice opportunities. By contrast, VR and immersive technologies replicate the complexities of professional settings, allowing learners to develop not just technical vocabulary but also the communicative confidence required for business contexts. The results of our study demonstrate that immersive learning environments significantly enhance Business English proficiency by giving students the practice they need to engage in real-world professional tasks. This approach addresses a key gap in traditional ESP teaching and highlights the Metaverse as a crucial tool in fostering communicative competence for specific professional fields.

In summary, the Conversion/Practice Stage, enabled by immersive virtual labs, ensures that learners can bridge the gap between knowing English and effectively using English in professional, technical contexts.

7 CONCLUSION

This longitudinal study represents a significant advancement in equipping first-year Master's students specializing in Big Data and the Internet of Things (BDIoT) with essential workplace language skills, particularly in Business English. By introducing immersive virtual labs through the VirtualSpeech platform for Group A during the 2022-2023 academic year, the study yielded valuable insights and demonstrated tangible results, highlighting several key takeaways.

First, enhanced presentation skills emerged as a notable outcome. The immersive virtual labs helped Group A students develop their ability to address diverse audiences, articulate complex technical concepts, and use appropriate business terminology. This improved confidence in delivering presentations aligns well with the broader goal of preparing students for the modern workplace's demands. The labs also fostered business vocabulary and phrase acquisition, with Group A students demonstrating a richer vocabulary and greater competence in using essential business terms during

simulated interactions. This linguistic growth has directly contributed to their ability to communicate effectively in a professional context, enhancing both clarity and confidence. Additionally, participation in business meetings through the virtual environment allowed students to practice engagement in professional discussions, share opinions, and negotiate in English. This familiarity with professional discourse nuances has empowered them to interact more confidently in real-world business settings.

A comparative analysis between Group A and Group B underscored the impact of the immersive labs. Group A showed notable improvements in language proficiency, particularly in Business English, with their post-assessment scores exceeding those of Group B. Furthermore, Group A students demonstrated a stronger command of business vocabulary, along with higher engagement and participation in simulated scenarios, suggesting that the immersive labs effectively enhance business communication skills by addressing the specific linguistic demands of the workplace. Another critical insight was the role of immersive labs in addressing shyness and building confidence. The virtual environment provided a safe, supportive space for students to practice and refine their communication skills, which helped them overcome self-consciousness and increased their comfort in business contexts. Many students reported feeling more at ease and self-assured in these virtual settings, enabling them to practice without the pressures of a physical classroom. However, the study also identified challenges and areas for further development. For example, students found it challenging to simulate meetings with professionals and top management in ways that mirrored real-world complexities. This points to the need for further refinement of the labs to replicate advanced business scenarios more accurately, ensuring that students gain a comprehensive experience in Business English communication.

To sum up, Immersive Virtual Labs have significantly enhanced the Business English proficiency and technical communication skills of Group A students, addressing the specific linguistic requirements for the business environment. These results support the conclusion that immersive virtual learning environments are highly effective for teaching English for Specific Purposes (ESP), particularly in fields like BDIoT, where technical knowledge must be communicated in a business context.

REFERENCES

Aljuhani, K., Sandhu, K., & Li, X. (2019). Virtual labs in higher education: A systematic review. *Computers & Education*, *136*, 104–114. DOI: 10.1016/j.compedu.2019.03.006

Anderson, J. (2022). Engineering education and the Metaverse: The future of immersive learning. *Journal of Virtual Learning*, *18*(2), 77–91.

Bailenson, J. N. (2020). *Experience on demand: What virtual reality is, how it works, and what it can do*. W. W. Norton & Company.

Blake, R. J. (2013). *Brave new digital classroom: Technology and foreign language learning*. Georgetown University Press.

Chen, L. (2022). Personalized learning and artificial intelligence: Adaptive solutions in higher education. *Journal of Educational Technology Systems*, *51*(1), 5–22. DOI: 10.2190/AGAL-BAUK-RH89-3L2G

Craig, K., & Kay, L. (2023). Integrating VR in higher education: Systematic review on competency development and technological requirements. *Higher Learning Research Communications*, *12*(1), 45–63.

Dalgarno, B., Lee, M. J. W., Carlson, L., Gregory, S., & Tynan, B. (2011). An Australian and New Zealand scoping study on the use of 3D immersive virtual worlds in higher education. *Australasian Journal of Educational Technology*, *27*(3), 1–15. DOI: 10.14742/ajet.978

Fei, Y., Lavoie, D., & Chen, R. (2023). Immersive learning technologies in STEM: A review of VR and AR integration in higher education. *Journal of Educational Technology*, *44*(2), 33–57.

García, M. (2023). Personalized learning paths in AI-supported ESP platforms. *Journal of Language & Learning Technologies*, *41*(2), 101–115.

Garcia, M., López, S., & Rivas, T. (2023). AI-driven tools in virtual learning spaces: Impact on language proficiency. *Language Learning & Technology*, *27*(1), 33–50.

Ghazouani, M., Chafiq, N., Zaher, N., Azouazi, M., & Chakir, A. (2023). Merging big data with the Metaverse: A proposed architecture with multiple layers. *International Journal of Emerging Technologies in Learning*, *18*(6), 100–115.

Godwin-Jones, R. (2014). Language as communication, language as code: Second language acquisition in a digital age. *Language Learning & Technology*, *18*(1), 248–264.

Grgurovic, M., Law, T., & Devrim, D. (2012). Virtual reality for ESL/EFL reading and vocabulary learning. *Language Learning & Technology*, *16*(2), 3–11.

Hubbard, P. (2008). *Computer-assisted language learning: Critical concepts in linguistics*. Taylor & Francis.

Johnson, D. (2023). Real-time AI support in immersive ESP environments. *Journal of Computer Assisted Learning*, *39*(4), 392–406.

Lavoie, D., Stelios, A., & Mondragon Regalado, N. (2024). Immersive learning platforms: The role of VR in competency-based learning in higher education. *Frontiers in Education*, *9*, 734–754.

Makransky, G., & Petersen, G. B. (2021). Investigating the impact of VR on student engagement and retention in higher education. *Computers & Education*, *166*, 104129. DOI: 10.1016/j.compedu.2021.104129

McDonald, R. (2020). Virtual reality labs for remote learning: A new approach to science education. *Educational Technology Research and Development*, *68*, 1723–1737.

Miller, M., & Hegelheimer, V. (2006). The SIMs meet ESL: Integrating computer gaming into the language curriculum. *Computer Assisted Language Learning*, *19*(5), 456–489.

Patel, N. (2022). Artificial intelligence tutors for ESP learners in virtual environments. *Journal of Language and Technology*, *20*(3), 221–237.

Pelz, B. (2004). (My) three principles of effective online pedagogy. *Journal of Asynchronous Learning Networks*, *8*(3), 33–46.

Predescu, M., & Apostolakis, C. (2023). Immersive horizons: Exploring virtual reality's impact on higher education pedagogy and integration. *IEEE Conference on Education Technology*, 28(3), 184–193.

Salmon, G. (2004). *E-moderating: The key to online teaching and learning*. Routledge. DOI: 10.4324/9780203465424

Sari, R. P., Khasanah, U., & Pramudya, D. (2019). Developing student motivation through virtual labs in online learning environments. [iJET]. *International Journal of Emerging Technologies in Learning*, *14*(4), 120–136.

Stelios, A., & Lyapunov, V. (2023). Enhancing critical thinking skills through VR-based educational modules. *Journal of Applied Educational Research*, *15*(1), 89–110.

Thorne, S. L. (2008). Transcultural communication in open internet environments and massively multiplayer online games. In Matters, M. (Ed.), *Language, education and technology* (pp. 107–124). DOI: 10.1075/aals.3.17tho

Turan, Z., & Avincan, E. (2022). The role of virtual reality in enhancing practical skills in remote education. *Interactive Learning Environments, 30*(7), 1005–1021.

Wang, H., Lee, J., & Chang, M. (2023). Interactive 3D models for technical English learning in engineering. *International Journal of Educational Technology in Higher Education, 20*(1), 15. PMID: 36919042

Warschauer, M. (1997). Computer-mediated collaborative learning: Theory and practice. *Modern Language Journal, 81*(4), 470–481.

Warschauer, M., Shetzer, H., & Meloni, C. (2000). Internet for English teaching. *TESOL Journal, 9*(2), 7–11.

Zhang, Y., & Li, F. (2023). Virtual language training for cross-cultural business communication. *Business Communication Quarterly, 86*(2), 101–118.

Chapter 12
Application of Pythagoras Theorem From Heron'a Formula to Derive the Foci of an Ellipse for Cyber Nomads

Kathirvel Ayyaswamy
https://orcid.org/0000-0002-5347-9110
Department of Computer Science and Engineering, Saveetha Engineering College, Chennai, India

A. Anthony Raj
https://orcid.org/0000-0001-5417-4856
Panimalar Engineering College, India

Naren Kathirvel
https://orcid.org/0009-0003-7581-5482
Anand Institute of Higher Technology, India

G. Kuppuswami
https://orcid.org/0009-0007-9537-9736
Panimalar Engineering College, India

ABSTRACT

In this paper, we derived the Pythagoras theorem from Heron's formula. Also we provide the application of this result plays vital role to obtain foci of an ellipse. The foci of an ellipse are derived through a combination of geometric principles. While Heron's formula is useful for calculating areas of triangles, the primary derivation

DOI: 10.4018/979-8-3373-0740-4.ch012

of the foci comes from the Pythagorean theorem, which connects the semi-major and semi-minor axes of the ellipse. The relationship between the Pythagorean theorem, Heron's formula, and the foci of an ellipse is an interesting geometric application. By offering personalised, adaptable learning, instant feedback, and interactive experiences, AI and humanoid computing empower cyber nomads to stay engaged, progress at their own pace, and master subjects effectively. Technologies remove barriers of time and location, creating a learning environment that is as responsive and supportive as any traditional classroom. For cyber nomads, AI and humanoid computing represent a lifeline to continuous, high-quality education no matter where they are in the world.

1. INTRODUCTION AND PRELIMINARIES

Although Pythagoras introduced and popularised the theorem, there is sufficient evidence proving its existence in other civilizations, 1000 years before Pythagoras was born. The oldest known evidence dates back to between 20th to 16th Century B.C in the Old Babylonian Period (Kirubakaran and Kathirvel, 2014) .

The Pythagoras theorem which is also referred to as the Pythagorean theorem explains the relationship between the three sides of a right-angled triangle. According to the Pythagoras theorem, the square of the hypotenuse is equal to the sum of the squares of the other two sides of a triangle (Jolin, Theophilus and Kathirvel, 2025).

Heron's formula provides a quick way of computing the area of a triangle given the length of the sides. Heron was a mathematician from Authorz (Jolin, Theophilus and Kathirvel, 2025).. This study aims to determine the area of Belitung island by using Heron's theorem in spherical geometry.

This study uses Google Maps to find the distance between points that will be used in finding the area. The use of Heron's theorem in spherical geometry because the earth is likened to a sphere so that to determine its area one can use the area of a triangle. The first experiment divided Belitung Island into 5 triangles and the second experiment divided it into 45 triangles (Kathirvel et al, 2023c). Let us derive the Pythagoras theorem from Heron's formula, besides we connecting the length, breadth and foci of an ellipse.

2.PYTHAGOREAN THEOREM

The Pythagorean theorem gives a fundamental relationship between the lengths of the three sides of a right-angled triangle.

Suppose to meet socially what theorem people remember from high-school geometry. The chances are high that the reply would be the Pythagorean Theorem (Subramaniam, et al 2021). But if they are asked to state the theorem they may not be able to do so except, perhaps, to say that it concerns triangles and that the conclusion is $c^2 = a^2 + b^2$.

Figure 1. Diagram representing the fundamental Pythagorean Theorem.

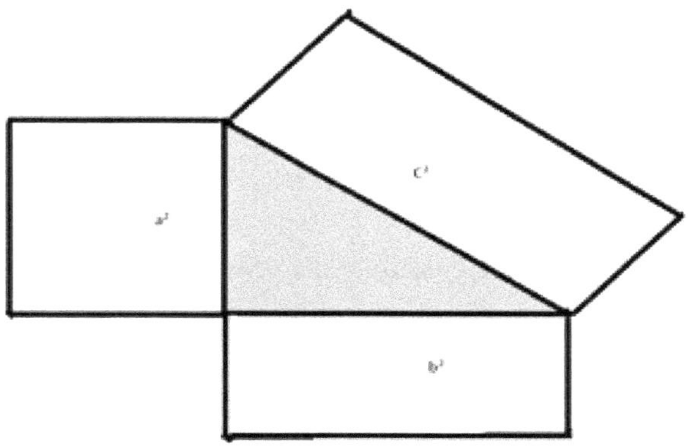

We make the case for which theorems of elementary Euclidean geometry should be called the "Pythagorean theorem for an arbitrary triangle" and the "Pythagorean theorem for a quadrilateral (Kathirvel et al, 2023b)." In making this presentation, we stress the use of the basic properties of triangles over use of the cosine formula (Subramaniam, et al 2021).

Heron's Formula: Heron's Formula is a well-known formula in geometry used to calculate the area of a triangle when the lengths of all three sides are known. It is particularly useful when you do not know the height of the triangle, but you do know the three side lengths. Here's how it works (Sundar and Kathirvel, 2020b),:

Heron's Formula for the Area of a Triangle

Let the three sides of a triangle be aaa, bbb, and ccc. The semi-perimeter sss of the triangle is defined (Sundar and Kathirvel, 2019), as:

Let the sides of the triangle be denoted by a, b and c, and let S denote the semi-perimeter, where S is defined by $S = (a + b + c) / 2$.

Area of $\triangle ABC = \sqrt{s(s-a)(s-b)(s-c)}$

Derivation of Heron's Formula

Heron's formula is derived from a more general expression for the area of a triangle, which is based on the circumradius and angles of the triangle. However, Heron's formula itself can be seen as a more convenient, practical method of finding the area when you know the side lengths (Kathirvel et al, 2023d).

Steps for Using Heron's Formula

1. Find the Semi-perimeter: First, calculate the semi-perimeter sss of the triangle:

$S = (a + b + c) / 2$

Heron's formula provides a way to find the area of a triangle when only the lengths of its sides are known. If a triangle has side lengths a, b, and c, the formula states that the area A of the triangle is:

$$A = \sqrt{s(s-a)(s-b)(s-c)}$$

where s is the semi-perimeter of the triangle, defined as: $S = (a + b + c) / 2$.

Derivation of Heron's Formula

To derive Heron's formula, let's start with a triangle where we know the lengths of its sides, but not the height. We'll use the following steps:

1.Set up the Semi-Perimeter and Area Formula:
Start by defining the semi-perimeter s of the triangle: $S = (a + b + c) / 2$.

2. Express the Area Using the Height:

For any triangle with base a and corresponding height h, the area A is given by:
$A = \frac{1}{2}ah$

But since we don't know the height h, we need to express h in terms of a, b, and c using trigonometry.

3. Use Trigonometry to Relate the Sides:

In a triangle with side lengths a, b, and c, we can use the cosine rule to express cos C, where C is the angle opposite side c:

$$\cos C = \frac{a^2 + b^2 - c^2}{2ab}$$

4. Express the Height in Terms of sin C:

Since $\text{Sin}C = \sqrt{1 - \cos^2 c}$, we can substitute cos C from the cosine rule:

$$\text{Sin}C = \sqrt{1 - \left(\frac{a^2 + b^2 - c^2}{2ab}\right)^2}$$

5. Find Area Using sin C:

The area A of the triangle can also be expressed as:

$$A = \frac{1}{2}ab\text{Sin}C$$

Substitute sin C from the previous step:

$$A = \frac{1}{2}ab\sqrt{1 - \left(\frac{a^2 + b^2 - c^2}{2ab}\right)^2}$$

6. Simplify Using Algebraic Identities:

Simplify the expression under the square root by expanding and rearranging terms. After several steps (Sujatha et al, 2023), you will arrive at:

$$A = \sqrt{s(s - a)(s - b)(s - c)}$$

Thus, we derive Heron's formula for the area of a triangle based on its side lengths a, b, and c .

3. APPLICATIONS OF HERON'S FORMULA

Heron's formula is useful in many areas of geometry and trigonometry, including:

- Surveying: To compute the area of a triangular plot of land when only the side lengths are known.
- Navigation: For calculating areas in navigation charts and geographical studies.
- Engineering: In structural analysis, where triangle-shaped components are common and their areas need to be computed.

It's a powerful and efficient tool for solving geometric problems involving triangles!

Remark.2

Although the formula bearing Heron's name was known to Archimedes several centuries earlier (Kathirvel et al, 2023a), however, the formula is called Heron's formula in honor of him since he gave an ingenious proof of the theorem in his work Metrica. Because Heron of Alexandria was also known as Hero, some texts refer to Heron's formula as Hero's formula.

Example 1.

Let's use Heron's formula to find the area of a triangle with side lengths 23 cm, 46 cm and 41 cm.

First, we need to find S:

$S = (23 + 41 + 46) / 2 = 55$

Now, plug S and the three sides into Heron's formula and simplify.

Area, $A = \sqrt{55(55 - 23)(55 - 41)(55 - 46)}$

$= \sqrt{55(32)(14)(9)}$

$= \sqrt{221760}$

$A \approx 470.9 \text{ cm}^2$.

So, the area of the triangle with side lengths 23 cm, 46 cm and 41 cm is 470.9 cm^2.

Example 2.

In $\triangle GHI$, g=11, h=24, and i=18. To obtain the area of the triangle,

Figure 2. Example to calculate the area of a triangle.

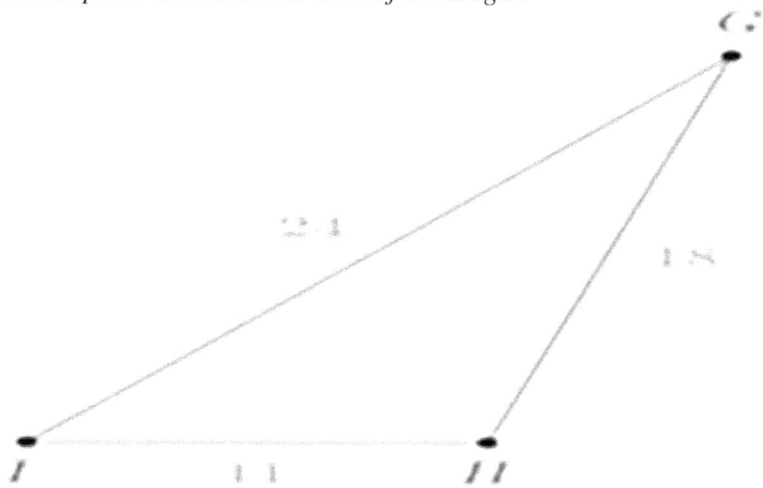

First, we've to find S:

$S = (11 + 24 + 18) / 2$

$= 26.5.$

Now, plug S and the three sides into Heron's Formula and simplify.

Area, $\sqrt{26.5(26.5 - 11)(26.5 - 24)(26.5 - 18)}$

$\sqrt{26.5(15.5)(2.5)(8.5)}$

$\sqrt{8728.44}$

.

Primary results

Result 1.1: Derivation of Pythagoras theorem from Heron's formula

Area of the triangle $= \frac{1}{2}ab$

Figure 3. Example tiangle.

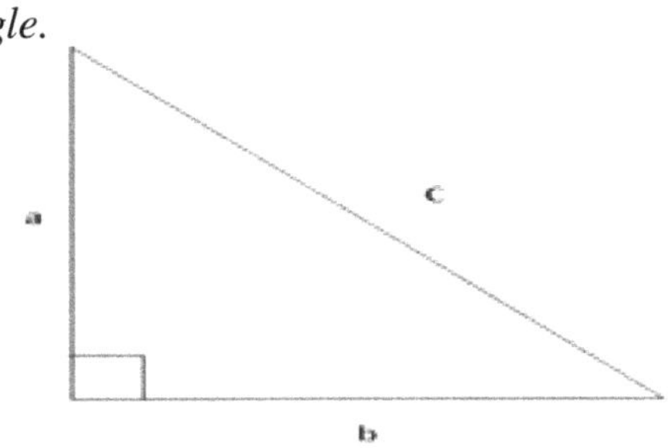

Again by Heron's formula,
Area of the triangle $\sqrt{s(s-a)(s-b)(s-c)}$

$$\sqrt{\left(\frac{a+b+c}{2}\right)\left(\frac{a+b+c}{2}-a\right)\left(\frac{a+b+c}{2}-b\right)\left(\frac{a+b+c}{2}-c\right)}$$

$\Rightarrow \frac{1}{2}ab = \sqrt{\left(\frac{a+b+c}{2}\right)\left(\frac{a+b+c-2a}{2}\right)\left(\frac{a-b+c}{2}\right)\left(\frac{a+b-c}{2}\right)} \Rightarrow a^2b^2 = \frac{4}{164}[(a+b+c)(-a+b+c)(a-b+c)(a+b-c)] \Rightarrow 4a^2b^2 = [-a^2+ab+ac-ab+b^2+bc-ac+bc+c^2][a^2+ab-ac-ab-b^2+bc+ac+bc-c^2]$

$= [-a^2+b^2+c^2+2bc][a^2-b^2-c^2+2bc]$

$\Rightarrow 4a^2b^2 = -a^4+a^2b^2+a^2c^2-2a^2bc+a^2b^2-b^4-b^2c^2+2b^3c+a^2c^2-b^2c^2-c^4+2bc^3+2a^2bc-2b^3c-2bc^3+4b^2c^2 \Rightarrow 2a^2b^2 = -a^4-b^4-b^2c^2-b^2c^2-c^4+4b^2c^2+2a^2c^2$

$$\Rightarrow a^4+b^4+c^4+2a^2b^2-2b^2c^2-2a^2c^2 = 0$$

$$\Rightarrow c^4-2(a^2+b^2)c^2+(a^2+b^2)^2 = 0$$

$$\Rightarrow [c^2-(a^2+b^2)]^2 = 0$$

$\Rightarrow c^2 - (a^2 + b^2) = 0$

$\Rightarrow c^2 = (a^2 + b^2)$

$\Rightarrow (a^2 + b^2) = c^2$

Hence the Pythagoras theorem is derived.

Result 1.2: Derivation for the relation between length, breadth and the distance between the foci of an ellipse

By the property of an ellipse,

$F_1A + F_2A = F_1C + F_2C$

Since the ellipse is symmetrical,

$F_1A + F_2A = 2F_1C [\because F_1C = F_2C]$

$\Rightarrow F_1A + F_1A + F_1F_2 = 2F_1C$

$\Rightarrow 2F_1A + f = 2F_1C$

$\Rightarrow 2\left(\frac{a}{2} - \frac{f}{2}\right) + f = 2F_1C$

$\Rightarrow a - f + f = 2F_1C$

$\Rightarrow a = 2F_1C$

$\Rightarrow F_1C = \frac{a}{2} \rightarrow (1)$

By Pythagoras theorem,

$F_1O^2 + O^2C = F_1C^2$

Applying equation (1)

Figure 4. Applying equation.

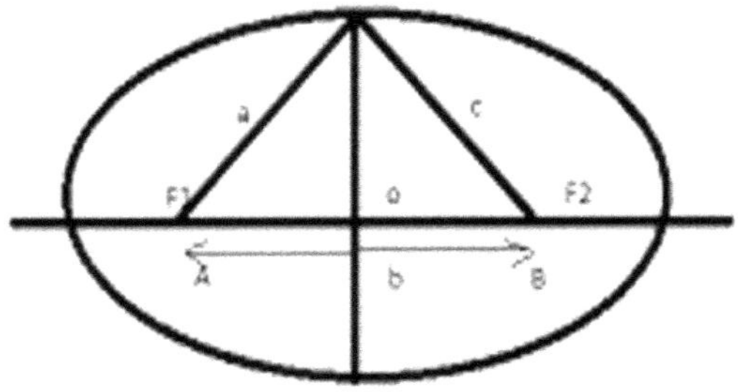

$$\Rightarrow \left(\frac{f}{2}\right)^2 + \left(\frac{b}{2}\right)^2 = \left(\frac{a}{2}\right)^2$$

$$\Rightarrow \frac{1}{4}[f^2 + b^2] = \frac{1}{4}a^2$$

$$\Rightarrow f^2 + b^2 = a^2$$

$$\Rightarrow b^2 = a^2 - f^2$$

$$\Rightarrow b = \sqrt{a^2 - f^2}$$

$$\Rightarrow f = \sqrt{a^2 - b^2}$$

In Computers and graphics design software like Blender (or) Auto CAD, to construct an ellipse, the program need the values of ‘a’ & ‘f’.

The user can calculate ‘f’ with a & b (length and breadth of an ellipse) using (Sangeetha & Kathirvel, 2019) formula$f = \sqrt{a^2 - b^2}$Then the Computer program will calculate the eccentricity $e = \frac{c}{a}$ or directly it constructs the ellipse. Hence the result is very useful in this field (K.Hamela and Dr.A.Kathirvel, ,2019a).

4. APPLICATIONS OF PYTHAGOREAN THEOREM

The AI algorithm to solve and teach the Pythagoras Theorem

To create an AI algorithm that can both solve and teach the Pythagorean Theorem, we should follow a few structured steps. This involves (1) understanding the mathematical principles, (2) designing a problem-solving approach, and (3) crafting an interactive teaching approach that breaks down the theorem for students.

1. Understanding the Pythagorean Theorem

The Pythagorean Theorem states: $a^2 + b^2 = c^2$

where a and b are the legs (perpendicular sides) of a right triangle, and c is the hypotenuse (the side opposite the right angle). This theorem applies only to right-angled triangles and is used to find a missing side length if the lengths of two sides are known (R. Sundar and Dr. A.Kathirvel, 2020a).

2. Problem-Solving Algorithm for Pythagorean Theorem

The AI needs to handle various types of problems:

1. Finding the Hypotenuse: Given a and b, find c.
2. Finding a Leg: Given c and one leg, find the other leg.

Here's how the algorithm can approach each case:

- Input: Take inputs a, b, and c (with one of them unknown).
- Determine Goal: Identify which variable is unknown.
- Apply Formula:
- If c (hypotenuse) is unknown, calculate $c^2 = (a^2 + b^2)$
- If a leg is unknown (say a, calculate $a = \sqrt{c^2 - b^2}$ or $b = \sqrt{c^2 - a^2}$.
- Output: Provide the calculated value.

3. Teaching the Pythagorean Theorem

To teach the theorem interactively, we could design a step-by-step instructional sequence, leveraging visuals and examples. Here's a potential AI approach:

Step-by-Step Instructional Design

1.Introduction:

- Explain what a right triangle is and highlight its parts: legs and hypotenuse.
- Introduce the Pythagorean Theorem formula with visual aids and basic examples.

2.Concept Reinforcement:

- Provide multiple right triangle examples with labeled side lengths.
- Visually demonstrate how a^2 and b^2 add up to equal c^2.

3. Interactive Practice:

- Present simple problems with feedback. For example:
- Problem 1: Given a = 3 and b = 4, find c.
- AI calculates c and explains each calculation step.
- Problem 2: Given c = 10 and b = 6, find a.
- The AI walks through isolating a, performing $a = \sqrt{c^2 - b^2}$, and taking the square root.

4. Common Mistakes and Tips:

- Address common mistakes, like misinterpreting which side is the hypotenuse.
- Reinforce the importance of confirming that the triangle is right-angled before using the theorem.

5.Quizzes and Feedback:

- Offer multiple-choice and open-ended questions for self-assessment.
- Provide immediate feedback on whether the answers are correct and detailed explanations if incorrect.

6. Advanced Applications:

- Introduce real-world problems, like finding distances on a coordinate plane.
- Extend to 3D problems, e.g., finding the diagonal in a rectangular prism using multiple applications of the theorem (Sundar and Kathirvel, 2020a).

This AI-based approach offers a comprehensive framework for solving and teaching the Pythagorean Theorem, with adaptability for various learning speeds and styles. It can be implemented as a rule-based system in simple cases, or with a more interactive UI using educational visuals and explanations if implemented in a web-based app.

5. THE AI ASSISTED PEDAGOGY TO TEACH THE THEOREM

Using AI-assisted pedagogy to teach the Pythagorean Theorem can make the learning experience interactive, personalized, and engaging for students. Here's a structured approach that integrates AI to enhance understanding through adaptive learning, visualization, and real-time feedback:

1. Adaptive Learning Pathways

An AI-driven system can adapt the lesson flow based on each student's pace and comprehension level. Here's how it works:

- Initial Assessment: The system starts with a brief diagnostic test to assess the student's existing knowledge of triangles and algebra.
- Personalized Pathway: Based on the assessment, the AI curates a learning path:
- For beginners, it includes foundational lessons on triangles and basic geometry.
- For advanced students, it may go straight to applying the theorem and solving more complex problems.

The AI adjusts the depth and pace of lessons, gradually introducing concepts like square roots and algebraic manipulation as needed.

2. Visual Demonstrations and Interactive Simulations

Understanding the Pythagorean Theorem is often easier with visual aids. The AI can generate custom animations and interactive tools to illustrate key concepts:

- Visual Proofs: The AI can show animated visual proofs, such as using squares built on each side of a triangle to demonstrate that$a^2 + b^2 = c^2$.
- Interactive Right Triangle Builder: Students can manipulate the lengths of two sides of a right triangle, observing real-time changes in the hypotenuse. The AI can guide the student through adjusting one side and recalculating, fostering an intuitive understanding of the relationship between the sides.

3.Step-by-Step Problem Solving with Immediate Feedback

AI can provide step-by-step instructions and immediate feedback on problem-solving:

- Guided Problem Solving: The system offers problems (e.g., finding a missing side) and walks students through each calculation. At each step, the AI checks their work, providing hints or corrections if they make an error.
- Error Recognition and Explanations: If a student makes a common mistake (like confusing the hypotenuse with a leg), the AI identifies it, explains the error, and reinforces the correct concept.

This instant feedback loop helps students grasp each step without feeling discouraged or confused.

4. Real-World Applications and Story-Based Scenarios

To make learning relevant, the AI can present real-world problems that require the Pythagorean Theorem:

- Contextual Scenarios: The AI generates scenarios like calculating the distance between two points in a city, determining the length of a ladder needed to reach a certain height, or finding the diagonal in a rectangular room (Kathirvel, A, 2024g).
- Interactive Storytelling: AI can use storytelling to keep students engaged. For instance, it might create a scenario where the student helps a character solve a problem by applying the theorem, adding an element of fun and purpose to learning.

5. Gamification and Challenges

AI can introduce gamified elements to boost engagement and motivation:

- Level-Based Learning: Students progress through levels by mastering concepts, from simple problems to complex applications (Kathirvel, and Naren, 2024h).
- Rewards and Achievements: The system offers rewards (badges, points, or certificates) for completing exercises correctly, reinforcing positive behavior.
- Peer Competition: In a classroom or online platform, AI can set up friendly competitions or challenges, encouraging students to apply their knowledge to beat scores or time records.

6. Cognitive Skills Assessment and Remediation

AI can continuously assess cognitive skills related to understanding the theorem and adapt the learning experience as necessary:

- Skill Tracking: The AI identifies specific skills each student struggles with, such as performing square root calculations or recognizing the right triangle.
- Remediation: If a student is struggling with a concept, the AI can bring in supplementary resources, like videos, extra practice problems, or simpler explanations, to strengthen weak areas.

7.Conversational and Socratic Teaching Style

With natural language processing capabilities, AI can engage students in a conversational learning process:

- Guided Questions: AI can use the Socratic method to prompt students with questions that lead them toward understanding, rather than simply providing answers.
- Clarifying Doubts: The AI acts as a virtual tutor, answering questions, clarifying doubts, and reinforcing learning in a way that's responsive to individual students' needs and inquiries.

8.Review and Mastery Checks

AI can ensure students truly understand the theorem by offering periodic mastery checks:

- Randomized Practice Sets: The AI generates unique sets of problems for students to solve, assessing whether they can apply the theorem independently.
- Cumulative Reviews: Regular quizzes and mini-tests are designed to review both recent and previous concepts, reinforcing long-term retention of the theorem and its applications.

9. Parental and Teacher Insights

For younger students, AI can provide teachers or parents with insights into a student's progress:

- Progress Reports: The AI shares reports on areas mastered and where the student needs more practice, helping teachers or parents provide additional support.

- Recommendations for Further Learning: The system can suggest extra activities, resources, or even fun projects, like building a model that uses the Pythagorean Theorem.

Summary

AI-assisted pedagogy for teaching the Pythagorean Theorem blends interactive learning, visual tools, and personalized guidance, which can help students not only understand but also appreciate the beauty and utility of this fundamental mathematical concept. The adaptability, real-time feedback, and engaging approaches ensure a rich learning experience tailored to each student's needs (Josh Kumar and Kathirvel, 2019).

6. FUTURE HUMANOID COMPUTING VIEW

Humanoid computing envisions a future where computers and digital systems interact with humans in ways that feel natural, intuitive, and human-like. It's more than just creating humanoid robots; it's about developing systems that understand, learn from, and collaborate with us, adapting to human emotions, language, gestures, and even our intentions. Here's an in-depth look at what humanoid computing could be and should be tomorrow:

1. Natural and Emotionally Intelligent Interaction
    - Today's Capabilities: Humanoid computing is already making strides in natural language processing, voice recognition, and facial expression analysis. These allow for more natural interactions, but emotional understanding is still limited.
    - Tomorrow's Vision: A future with emotionally intelligent AI could mean computers that detect subtle emotional cues, understand vocal intonations, or recognize nonverbal gestures like posture changes and facial expressions. For instance, an AI could notice when someone is frustrated and adjust its responses or simplify its explanations accordingly, providing a more empathetic and supportive interaction.
2. Physicality and Presence
    - Today's Robots and Avatars: Physical robots and digital avatars are increasingly mimicking human appearances and movements, often to enhance the way we interact with technology.
    - Tomorrow's Vision: In the future, humanoid computing might focus on improving the kinesthetic intelligence of these systems, allowing them to move with human-like fluidity and precision. These advancements

would be particularly impactful in areas like healthcare, caregiving, and education, where human warmth and physical presence are valuable. Humanoids that are capable of physically assisting the elderly, for example, or gently guiding children in educational tasks, could be highly beneficial.

3. Adaptable and Contextually Aware Systems
   - Current Context-Awareness: Today's systems can detect limited context, such as location, time, or basic user data. They adapt to us in surface-level ways, like customizing content based on our preferences.
   - Tomorrow's Vision: A truly humanoid computing system would be aware of nuanced, real-time context, including understanding the environment, social cues, and specific user histories. For instance, it might adjust the tone and complexity of its answers based on the user's background, recognize when it's in a quiet environment and respond softly, or even suggest a break if it senses fatigue. It could adapt in a way that feels as if it "knows" the person it's assisting, striking a balance between helpfulness and respect for privacy.
4. Augmenting Human Abilities
   - Current Augmentations: Digital assistants currently help by automating simple tasks, providing reminders, and improving productivity.
   - Tomorrow's Vision: Humanoid computing could enhance cognitive and physical abilities, operating as an extension of the human self. Imagine a personal AI that acts like a highly capable digital partner, helping individuals learn new skills, guiding creative projects, assisting with decision-making, and even supporting us in physical challenges via advanced exoskeletons or prosthetic interfaces. This could extend beyond the practical, offering cognitive companionship or assisting us in tasks we find difficult or monotonous (Ayyaswamy et al, 2024d).
5. Human-Like Learning and Memory
   - Current Limitations in Learning: Today's systems use machine learning to adapt to certain types of input, but they don't fully remember context or adjust based on long-term interactions with specific individuals (Naren et al, 2024e).
   - Tomorrow's Vision: Future humanoid computing systems could exhibit human-like learning and memory capabilities, recognizing patterns in long-term interactions and applying past experiences in new contexts. For example, an AI personal assistant might remember a user's habits over the years and anticipate needs, such as suggesting certain travel arrangements or reminding them of an annual event. This type of memory, however, would need to prioritize privacy and user control.

6. Collaborative Creativity and Problem Solving
   - Current AI Creativity: Current AI models can generate content, ideas, and basic solutions but often lack the ability to truly collaborate in a nuanced, back-and-forth human way.
   - Tomorrow's Vision: Imagine humanoid computing as an active partner in creative or complex tasks. In such a future, humanoid AIs could help scientists brainstorm research approaches, work alongside artists to create new forms of digital art, or aid entrepreneurs in identifying market trends by sharing insights and bouncing ideas in a conversational manner. The collaboration could feel like brainstorming with another person, with the AI offering innovative perspectives and insights.
7. Ethical and Social Intelligence
   - Current Ethical Awareness: Ethical considerations are programmed into systems, but they don't inherently "understand" morality or social norms.
   - Tomorrow's Vision: Humanoid computing systems could develop a form of ethical and social intelligence, programmed with nuanced moral frameworks. This could mean understanding when not to interrupt, balancing transparency with tact, and respecting cultural norms. In healthcare, for example, this might mean an AI that helps patients feel understood without intrusiveness, or in education, a teaching AI that knows how to encourage students while respecting their individuality (Kathirvel, and Srinivasan, 2011b).
8. Seamless Integration with Human Environments
   - Current Integration: Today, technology is embedded in everyday devices, but it still feels "separate" and often requires specific activation or input.
   - Tomorrow's Vision: In the future, humanoid computing should be seamlessly embedded within our environments, responding passively and proactively. This might mean computers that recognize (Ayyaswamy et al, 2024c) when they are needed and when they are not—like a personal assistant who becomes "invisible" when the user is focused on a personal task, or a humanoid home companion that only interacts when approached. The goal is for computing to be unobtrusive and as natural as any other part of our environment (Kathirvel, and Srinivasan, 2010).
9. Deep Personalization Balanced with Privacy
   - Current Personalization: Today's personalization focuses on data aggregation, which is sometimes invasive and doesn't always respect personal privacy.

- Tomorrow's Vision: Future humanoid computing should be able to provide a deeply personalized experience while offering complete user control over data and privacy. This means it would adapt to personal preferences without intrusive data mining, potentially using edge computing to process data on-device. For instance, a healthcare assistant could track fitness and wellness in a way that remains entirely private, or a personal AI could help organize work without sending information to external servers.

Summary

Humanoid computing, at its best, could evolve into a form of AI that not only mimics human behavior but actually enhances human life—working in partnership with us, intuitively understanding us, and seamlessly integrating into our environments. For humanoid computing to reach its full potential, it will need to develop both advanced social and ethical awareness, ensuring that technology remains aligned with human values and well-being.

In a classroom with "cyber nomad" students—those who are highly mobile, frequently changing locations, and often accessing classes online—AI and humanoid computing can play a transformative role in helping these students master subjects effectively and stay engaged despite their unique learning environment (Gobinath et al, 2024).

7. CASE SCENARIO: CYBER NOMAD STUDENTS IN A VIRTUAL CLASSROOM SETTING

Imagine a high school classroom where the majority of students are cyber nomads. They are spread across different time zones, frequently change physical locations due to travel or family obligations, and may not always have consistent access to real-time classes or live teacher support. These students often face challenges in maintaining a structured study schedule, staying motivated, and feeling connected to the classroom community.

Challenges for Cyber Nomad Students

1. Inconsistent Access to Live Classes: Due to time zones or internet limitations, students may miss live sessions or have limited access to real-time teacher interactions.
2. Difficulty in Following a Structured Learning Path: Frequent changes in environment can disrupt study routines, making it challenging to follow a sequential curriculum.

3. Limited Access to Timely Support: Without consistent access to teachers, students may struggle with clarifying doubts or receiving immediate feedback.
4. Feeling Isolated from the Classroom Community: Cyber nomads may feel disconnected from their classmates, impacting their motivation and sense of belonging.

How AI and Humanoid Computing Can Support Cyber Nomad Students

AI and humanoid computing can bridge these gaps by creating a flexible, responsive, and engaging learning environment tailored to the needs of cyber nomad students.

1. Personalized Learning Pathways and Virtual Assistants
   - Personalized Curriculum Adjustments: AI algorithms can analyze each student's progress, areas of strength, and gaps. Based on this data, it can provide personalized lesson sequences, allowing students to progress at their own pace.
   - 24/7 Virtual Teaching Assistants: An AI-driven virtual assistant, designed with humanoid computing principles, could serve as a tutor, answering questions, explaining concepts in multiple ways, and providing step-by-step problem-solving guidance. This ensures that students can get help regardless of their time zone.
   - Adaptive Scheduling: AI could adjust the timing and duration of lessons based on the student's current location, time zone, and daily availability, reducing the stress of maintaining a strict timetable.
2. Interactive and Engaging Content Through Humanoid AI
   - Realistic Virtual Avatars for Subject Support: Humanoid avatars resembling real teachers could be programmed with the educator's voice and mannerisms, offering a familiar and engaging teaching style for students. These avatars could guide students through lessons in an interactive way, making learning feel more personal and engaging.
   - Immersive 3D Learning Environments: For complex subjects like math and science, AI and humanoid computing can create interactive, virtual 3D environments where students manipulate objects and experiment within simulations. For instance, students could "walk around" a digital model of the solar system, interact with molecules in a chemistry lab, or visualize geometric concepts in a virtual space.
3. Real-Time Feedback and Continuous Assessment
   - Instant Feedback on Exercises and Assignments: AI algorithms can evaluate student submissions instantly, providing immediate feedback, detailed solutions, and suggestions for improvement. This gives stu-

dents continuous guidance and helps them understand mistakes right away (Hamela and Kathirvel, 2019b).

- Dynamic Progress Tracking: Humanoid AI assistants could offer personalized "progress reports" in a friendly (Sangeetha and Kathirvel, 2019), supportive manner, similar to a teacher's feedback. This feedback could highlight achievements, suggest areas for revision, and set tailored goals for the next steps.

4.Social Connection and Collaborative Learning

- Virtual Classmates and Study Groups: AI could create virtual "classmates" or enable avatar-based study groups, helping cyber nomad students engage in collaborative learning exercises. These virtual classmates could participate in discussions, practice problems (Hamela and Kathirvel, 2017), or simulate group projects, giving nomadic students a sense of peer interaction.
- Humanoid Teachers for Social Presence (Kirubakaran and Kathirvel, 2014): Virtual humanoid teachers or mentors could foster a social classroom experience. These avatars could run interactive class activities or discussions and encourage group participation. For example, a virtual teacher might initiate a debate, assign collaborative projects, or organize virtual "office hours" where students drop in for casual conversations (Sundar and Kathirvel, 2015).

5. On-the-Go Learning and Adaptive Resources

- Offline Learning Options: AI could offer downloadable, adaptive learning modules that allow students to continue studying even without internet access. These modules might include video lectures, interactive exercises, and practice tests that sync with the main platform once they reconnect (Kathirvel, Sudha and Devanai Sundaram (2009).
- Mobile-Friendly AI Tutors: AI-driven mobile applications tailored for nomadic lifestyles could deliver bite-sized learning sessions, vocabulary review, or math problem-solving practice. This flexibility allows students to study in small intervals, fitting learning into their travel schedules or intermittent online access.

6. Emotionally Intelligent Support and Motivation

- Emotion Recognition: Advanced humanoid AI could use emotion recognition to understand when students (Ayyaswamy et al, 2024b) are feeling frustrated, bored, or disengaged. It could respond by adjusting the lesson tone, suggesting a break, or even offering words of encouragement (Kathirvel A, and Maheswaran C P, 2024i).
- Goal Setting and Motivation Boosters: The AI assistant can track personal goals and milestones, periodically reminding students of their

progress and celebrating achievements. It could also incorporate motivational messages, reminders of long-term goals, or even mindfulness exercises to help students manage stress or fatigue (Kathirvel, 2025a & b).

7. Continuous Teacher Communication and Progress Insights

- Teacher Dashboards: AI can give teachers access to real-time insights into each cyber nomad student's performance, highlighting areas where students may need support and showing attendance or engagement patterns.
- AI-Guided Parent and Teacher Communication: AI could facilitate automated updates for parents and teachers, allowing them to monitor student progress and receive suggestions on how to provide additional support. This enables teachers to guide cyber nomad students without the need for constant, direct interaction.

Summary

With the right AI and humanoid computing tools, cyber nomad students can thrive in a flexible, adaptive learning environment that provides the support, interaction, and personalization they need. By leveraging real-time feedback, engaging content, social integration, and emotionally intelligent support, these technologies ensure that every student, no matter their location or time zone, has an engaging, efficient path to mastering the subject. This approach empowers cyber nomad students to stay connected to their learning goals and feel a true sense of belonging within a global classroom community.

For cyber nomads—individuals who frequently travel and rely on digital platforms for education or work—mastering a subject poses unique challenges. AI and humanoid computing can transform their learning experience by making education adaptive, accessible, and engaging, regardless of location or time zone. Here's how these technologies can help cyber nomads overcome their obstacles and achieve mastery(Kathirvel. A, Blesso Danny J, Shalem Preetham, Hinn Joe T O, Kennedy Roak C, and Immanuel Aldrin J, 2023):

8. CYBER NOMADS AND HOW COULD AI AND HUMANOID COMPUTING HELP THEM TO MASTER THE SUBJECT

1. Personalized, Adaptive Learning Pathways
    - Dynamic Content Adaptation: AI algorithms can create customized learning pathways that adapt to the cyber nomad's pace and knowledge level. For example, if a student shows strength in one topic but strug-

gles with another (Kathirvel. A, and Mavuri Shobitha, 2023), the AI can adjust, offering extra resources, simplified explanations, or targeted practice problems in weak areas (Kathirvel, and Srinivasan, 2011a).

- Self-Paced Learning Modules: AI-powered platforms can offer asynchronous lessons that allow cyber nomads to learn at their own pace. This feature is essential for those in different time zones who cannot always attend live classes, enabling them to progress according to their own schedule (Kathirvel andRajabushanam, 2011).

2. Humanoid AI Tutors for Real-Time Support
   - Virtual Teaching Assistants: Humanoid AI tutors can provide real-time, interactive support that feels personal and responsive. These digital assistants are available 24/7, enabling cyber nomads to ask questions, clarify doubts, or receive hints, regardless of when they're studying (Kathirvel. A, and Pavani Ale, 2023).
   - Conversational Learning: Through natural language processing, humanoid AI tutors can interact conversationally, allowing students to "talk through" problems, explore new concepts, and receive explanations in real-time. This approach helps recreate the benefits of face-to-face learning (Josh Kumar and Kathirvel, 2018), where students can work through ideas interactively.
3. Engaging, Immersive Learning Experiences
   - Virtual Reality and 3D Simulations: AI and humanoid computing can deliver immersive VR and 3D simulations for topics like anatomy, engineering (Mohana geetha et al, 2015), and architecture. For instance, a cyber nomad studying biology could virtually "explore" the human body in 3D, or an architecture (Suresh et al, 2015) student could "walk through" structures (Rithik, Kathirvel., and Naren (2024a). This flexibility lets them dive into complex subjects without physical resources.
   - Interactive Exercises and Labs: Humanoid AI can guide students through virtual experiments or simulations (Ayyaswamy et al, 2024a), making subjects more tangible and interactive. For example, AI can assist students in performing chemistry simulations or physics experiments virtually, ensuring a hands-on experience despite location limitations.
4. Instant Feedback and Continuous Assessment
   - Real-Time Feedback on Exercises: AI-driven learning platforms provide immediate feedback, helping students understand mistakes as they happen. Cyber nomads don't have to wait for instructor evaluations and can correct their approach instantly, promoting a continuous improvement mindset (Kathirvel, Subramaniam and Rajabushanam, 2011).

- Adaptive Assessment: AI systems can assess a student's performance over time and adjust difficulty levels accordingly. For example, if a cyber nomad consistently excels in basic exercises, the AI will offer more advanced problems, allowing them to progress naturally and avoid redundant practice.

5. Social and Collaborative Learning Across Time Zones
   - Virtual Study Groups and Peer Interaction: AI can create virtual study groups or match cyber nomads with peers for collaborative exercises and discussions. Humanoid avatars can facilitate these sessions, creating a social, classroom-like atmosphere that transcends physical limitations (Kathirvel, A, 2024e).
   - Project-Based Learning: For cyber nomads in project-driven courses, AI can facilitate collaborative work by tracking each member's contributions, syncing progress, and providing real-time updates. This setup makes it easy for nomads to engage in group work without the constraints of location or schedule(Kathirvel, A, 2024f)..
6. Humanoid AI for Motivation and Emotional Support
   - Emotion Recognition and Encouragement: Advanced humanoid computing can detect when a student is frustrated, tired, or disengaged and respond appropriately by adjusting lesson difficulty, suggesting a break, or offering motivational messages.
   - Personalized Goal-Setting and Progress Tracking: Humanoid AI assistants can help cyber nomads set personalized learning goals, track milestones, and celebrate small achievements. By fostering a sense of accomplishment and support, these systems help cyber nomads stay motivated and connected to their long-term goals.
7. Seamless Integration with Varied Learning Environments
   - Offline Access and Edge Computing: Recognizing that cyber nomads may have inconsistent internet access, AI-powered systems can offer offline modules or edge computing options, syncing data once connectivity is restored. This feature ensures that nomads can study in remote locations without interruption.
   - Mobile-Friendly Learning Tools: AI-driven mobile applications tailored for learning on the go can provide bite-sized lessons, flashcards, or problem-solving exercises, allowing cyber nomads to study during travel or in small time gaps.
8. Enhanced Teacher-Student Communication and Progress Monitoring
   - Teacher Dashboards with Insights: For students who are part of a larger course or program, AI systems can give teachers access to dashboards showing each cyber nomad's progress, strengths, and areas of difficulty.

This allows teachers to provide individualized support even when not directly connected.

- Automated Progress Updates: AI can generate automated reports for both students and teachers, summarizing achievements and challenges. These updates enable students to keep track of their development and allow teachers to step in as needed, even remotely.

Summary

By offering personalized, adaptable learning, instant feedback, and interactive experiences, AI and humanoid computing empower cyber nomads to stay engaged, progress at their own pace, and master subjects effectively. These technologies remove barriers of time and location, creating a learning environment that is as responsive and supportive as any traditional classroom. For cyber nomads, AI and humanoid computing represent a lifeline to continuous, high-quality education no matter where they are in the world.

9. CONCLUSION

All in all, I believe the Pythagoras Theorem has been influencing the way humans have been living since its discovery. It has helped make machines and tools many of which have roots derived from it. The theorem's simplicity and compact nature as well as its universality in theoretical and practical aspects of every sphere of life was a revolution to the way mankind thought and worked. Thereby, It has been historically acting as the seer of modern endeavour, helping us to develop many comforts . The foci of an ellipse are derived through a combination of geometric principles. While Heron's formula is useful for calculating areas of triangles, the primary derivation of the foci comes from the Pythagorean theorem, which connects the semi-major and semi-minor axes of the ellipse.

REFERENCES

Ayyaswamy, K. (2024). Enhancing Digital Technology Planning, Leadership, and Management to Transform Education. In Bhatia, M., & Mushtaq, M. T. (Eds.), *Navigating Innovative Technologies and Intelligent Systems in Modern Education* (pp. 1–9). IGI Global., DOI: 10.4018/979-8-3693-5370-7.ch001

Gobinath, V. M., Kathirvel, A., Rajesh Kanna, S. K., & Annamalai, K. (2024), "Chapter 5: Smart Technology in Management Industries: A Useful Perspective", Artificial Intelligence Applied to Industry 4.0, Wiley Publiser, USA, 1st Edition, July 2024, pp.93-106, , ISBN 978-1-394-21611-6DOI: 10.1002/9781394216147.ch5

Jolin, J. S., Theophilus, A., & Kathirvel, A. (2025)," Two factor mutual authentication with fingerprint and MAC Address Validation", International Journal of Communication Networks and Information Security, Vol. 16, No. 6, 2024, pp. 56 – 68. Publisher:Institute of Information Technology, Kohat University of Science and Technology, ISSN:2076-0930 E-ISSN:2073-607X, DoI:DOI: 10.5815/ijcnis.2024.06.05

Josh Kumar, J. M. S. P., Kathirvel, A., Kirubakaran, N., Sivaraman, P., & Subramaniam, M. (2015). A unified approach for detecting and eliminating selfish nodes in MANETs using TBUT. *EURASIP Journal on Wireless Communications and Networking*, *2015*, 1–11.

Kanagasundaram, H., & Ayyaswamy, K. (2019). Multi Objective ALO Based Energy Efficient and Secure Routing OLSR Protocol in MANET. *International Journal of Intelligent Engineering & Systems*, *12*(1).

Kanagasundaram, H., & Kathirvel, A. (2019). EIMO-ESOLSR: Energy efficient and security-based model for OLSR routing protocol in mobile ad-hoc network. *IET Communications*, *13*(5), 553–559.

Kathirvel, A. (2024e). Applications of Serverless Computing: Systematic Overview. In Aluvalu, R., & Maheswari, U. (Eds.), *Serverless Computing Concepts, Technology and Architecture* (Vol. 221-233). IGI Global., DOI: 10.4018/979-8-3693-1682-5.ch014

Kathirvel, A. (2024g). Innovation and Industry Application: IoT-Based Robotics Frontier of Automation in Industry Application. In Satishkumar, D., & Sivaraja, M. (Eds.), *Internet of Things and AI for Natural Disaster Management and Prediction* (pp. 83–105). IGI Global., DOI: 10.4018/979-8-3693-4284-8.ch004

Kathirvel, A., Das, D., Kirubakaran, S., Subramaniam, M., & Naveneethan, S. (2022). Based Mobile Bill Payment System Using Biometric Fingerprint. Recurrent Neural Networks: Concepts and Applications, 233.

Kathirvel, A., & Gandu, S. P. (2023, May). Systematic number plate detection using improved yolov5 detector. In 2023 2nd International Conference on Vision Towards Emerging Trends in Communication and Networking Technologies (ViTECoN) (pp. 1-6). IEEE.

Kathirvel, A., Gobinath, V. M., & Annamalai, K. (2024d), "Chapter 1: A Review on Additive Manufacturing in Industrial Environment", Advances in Pre- and Post-Additive Manufaturing Processes, Taylor & Francis Publiser, CRC Press, London, 1st Edition, May 2024, pp. 1-17, , ISBN 9781003428862. DOI:DOI: 10.1002/9781394216147.ch5

Kathirvel, A., Gobinath, V. M., Naren, A. K., & Maheswaran, C. P. (2025b). AI-based automated disease detection based on symptoms healthcare for pets and birds. In *AI and the Revival of Big Data* (pp. 311–345). IGI Global., DOI: 10.4018/979-8-3693-8472-5.ch014

Kathirvel, A., & Maheswaran, C. P. (2024i), "Chapter 8: Enhanced AI-Based Intrusion Detection and Response System for WSN", Artificial Intelligence for Intrusion Detection Systems, CRC Publiser/Chapman and Hall, New York, 1st Edition, 2023, ISBN 978-100096755-5, 978-103238665-2 DOI eBook ISBN 9781003346340DOI: 10.1201/9781003346340-8

Kathirvel, A., Maheswaran, C. P., Subramaniam, M., & Naren, A. K. (2023a), "Chapter 25: Quantum Computers Based on Distributed Computing Systems for the Next Generation: Overview and Applications", Quantum Computers Based on Distributed Computing Systems for the Next Generation, Handbook of Research on Quantum Computing for Smart Environments, IGI Global Publiser, Hershey, Pennsylvania, USA, March 2023. ISBN13: 9781668466971 ISBN10: 166846697X EISBN13: 9781668466988, DOI: DOI: 10.4018/978-1-6684-6697-1.ch025

Kathirvel, A., & Naren, A. K. (2024h). Diabetes and Pre-Diabetes Prediction by AI Using Tuned XGB Classifier. In Khang, A. (Ed.), *Medical Robotics and AI-Assisted Diagnostics for a High-Tech Healthcare Industry* (pp. 52–64). IGI Global., DOI: 10.4018/979-8-3693-2105-8.ch004

Kathirvel, A., Naren, A. K., & Gobinath, V. M and C. P. Maheswaran (2025a). "Chapter 3: Effective Leadership Strategies for Enhancing Student Success in Higher Education" In New Horizons in Leadership: Inclusive Explorations in Health, Technology, and Education, Hershey, PA: IGI Global, 2025, pp. 61–91. ISBN13: 9798369364376, EISBN13: 9798369364390, DOI: DOI: 10.4018/979-8-3693-6437-6.ch003

Kathirvel, A., Naren, A. K., & Santhoshi, B. (2024c). Business Intelligent and Blockchain in Entrepreneurship. In *Entrepreneurship Innovation and Education for Performance Improvement*. IGI Global., DOI: 10.4018/979-8-3693-7903-5.ch015

Kathirvel, A., Naren, A. K., & Subramanian, C. (2024b). Intelligent Serverless Computing Technology and Recent Trends: A Review. In *Driving Transformative Technology Trends with Cloud Computing*. IGI Global., DOI: 10.4018/979-8-3693-2869-9.ch002

Kathirvel, A., Navaneethan, S., & Subramaniam, M. (2023b). *EIDR Umpiring Security Models for Wireless Sensor Network", ARTIFICIAL INTELLIGENT TECHNIQUES FOR WIRELESS COMMUNICATION AND NETWORKING*. Scrivener Publishing, John Wiley & Sons., DOI: 10.1002/9781119821809.ch19

Kathirvel, A., Sabarinathan, C., Saravanan, N., & Ramesh, S. Meera, Karnavel K and Sudha D (2023d), "Chapter 9: Artificial Intelligence-Based Bill System: Fingerprint Mechanism", METHODS, IMPLEMENTATION, AND APPLICATION OF CYBER SECURITY INTELLIGENCE AND ANALYTICS, IGI Global Publiser, Hershey, Pennsylvania, USA ISBN13: 9781668439913 ISBN10: 1668439913 EISBN13: 9781668439937 DOI: 10.4018/978-1-6684-3991-3.ch009

Kathirvel, A., & Shobitha, M. (2023). Digital Assets Fair Estimation Using Artificial Intelligence. Institute of Electrical and Electronics Engineers Inc, 10.

Kathirvel, A., & Srinivasan, R. (2010). Enhanced triple umpiring system for security and performance improvement in wireless MANETS. *International Journal of Communication Networks and Information Security*, *2*(2), 77.

Kathirvel, A., & Srinivasan, R. (2011a). ETUS: An enhanced triple umpiring system for security and performance improvement of mobile ad hoc networks. *International Journal of Network Management*, *21*(5), 341–359.

Kathirvel, A., & Srinivasan, R. (2011b). ETUS: An enhanced triple umpiring system for security and performance improvement of mobile ad hoc networks. *International Journal of Network Management*, *21*(5), 341–359.

Kathirvel, A., Subramaniam, M., Navaneethan, S., & Sabarinath, C. (2021), "Improved IDR Response System for Sensor Network", Journal of Web Engineering, Vol. 20 1, 53–88, 2021. Publisher: © River Publishers, 15 Feb 2021, ISSN: 1540-9589 (Print Version). ISSN: 1544-5976 (Online Version), DOI: 10.13052/jwe1540-9589.2013

Kathirvel, A., Subramaniam, M., & Rajabushanam, C. (2011). Burglar detecting system for wireless mobile ad hoc network. *European Journal of Scientific Research*, *62*(1), 14–23.

Kathirvel, A., Sudha, R., & Devanai Sundaram, R. M. (2009), "A System of Tool for Identifying Ragas Using MIDI," IEEE Second International Conference on Computer and Electrical Engineering, Dubai, UAE, Vol. 2, 2009, pp. 644 – 647. Article number 53802592009 International Conference on Computer and Electrical Engineering, ICCEE 2009 28th– 30th December 2009 ISBN 978-076953925-6 DOI: https://ieeexplore.ieee.org/document/5380259DOI: 10.1109/ICCEE.2009.49

Kirubakaran, N., & Kathirvel, A. (2014). Performance improvement of security attacks in wireless mobile adhoc networks. *Asian Journal of Information Technology*, *13*(2), 68–76.

Koneri Chandrasekaran, S., Savarimuthu, P., Andi Elumalai, P., & Ayyaswamy, K. (2015). Primary path reservation using enhanced slot assignment in TDMA for session admission. *TheScientificWorldJournal*, *2015*(1), 405974.

Kumar, J., & Kathirvel, A. (2019). Analysis and ideas for improved routing in MANET.

Kumar, J. J., & Kathirvel, A. (2018). Optimum Power Management in Mobile Ad-Hoc Networks. *Journal of Engineering Science and Technology*, *13*(6), 1805–1815.

Mohana Geetha, D., Muthusundar, S. K., Subramaniam, M., & Ayyaswamy, K. (2015). Temporary redundant transmission mechanism for SCTP multihomed hosts. *TheScientificWorldJournal*, *2015*(1), 158697.

Naren, A. K., Kathirvel, A., & Santhoshi, B. (2024). " Chapter 5: Critical Approaches to Data Engineering Systems Innovation and Industry Application Using IoT" In Critical Approaches to Data Engineering Systems and Analysis, Hershey, PA: IGI Global, 2024.DoI: DOI: 10.4018/979-8-3693-2260-4.ch005

Pavani, A., & Kathirvel, A. (2023, April). Machine learning and deep learning algorithms for network data analytics function in 5G cellular networks. In *2023 International Conference on Inventive Computation Technologies (ICICT)* (pp. 28-33). IEEE.

Rajabhushanam, C., & Kathirvel, A. (2011). System of one to three umpire security system for wireless mobile ad hoc network. *Journal of Computational Science*, *7*(12), 1854.

Rithik, G., Kathirvel, A., & Naren, A. K. (2024a). The IoT of Robotics: The Frontier of Automation. In *Artificial Intelligence-Enabled Digital Twin for Smart Manufacturing, Wiley Publiser- Scrivener Publishing LLC, Online*. Print., DOI: 10.1002/9781394303601.ch13

Subramaniam, M., Kathirvel, A., Sabitha, E., & Anwar Basha, H. (2021), "Modified Firefly Algorithm and Fuzzy C-Mean Clustering Based Semantic Information Retrieval", Journal of Web Engineering, Vol. 20 1, 33–52, 2021. Publisher: © River Publishers, 15 Feb 2021, ISSN: 1540-9589 (Print Version). ISSN: 1544-5976 (Online Version), DOI: 10.13052/jwe1540-9589.2012

Sujatha, D., Subramaniam, M., & Kathirvel, A. (2023). *Class Level Multi-Feature Semantic Similarity Based Efficient Multimedia Big Data Retrieval", ARTIFICIAL INTELLIGENT TECHNIQUES FOR WIRELESS COMMUNICATION AND NETWORKING*. Scrivener Publishing, John Wiley & Sons., DOI: 10.1002/9781119821809.ch11

Sundar, R., & Kathirvel, A. (2015). Enhanced Trust Based Delegation for Load Balancing in Manets. *International Journal of Applied Engineering Research: IJAER*, *10*(92), 104–109.

Sundar, R., & Kathirvel, A. (2020a). Aggressively delivered mechanism over variable length density using a simulated annealing algorithm in mobile ad hoc network. *Transactions on Emerging Telecommunications Technologies*, *31*(12), e3863.

Sundar, R., & Kathirvel, A. (2020b). Enhanced cluster-based stable path for load balancing and reducing overhead using artificial bee colony in MANETs. *International Journal of Vehicle Information and Communication Systems*, *5*(1), 41–54.

Sundar, R., & Kathirvel, D. A. (2019). Efficient prior path failure recovery algorithm using channel aware routing in manet. *International Journal of Innovative Technology and Exploring Engineering*, *8*(5), 97–103.

Compilation of References

Abdul Jabbar, A. I., & Felicia, P. J. R. r. (2015). Gameplay engagement and learning in game-based learning. *Systematic Reviews*, *85*(4), 740–779.

Abel, F., Bittencourt, I. I., Costa, E., Henze, N., Krause, D., & Vassileva, J. (2010). Recommendations in Online Discussion Forums for E-Learning Systems. *IEEE Transactions on Learning Technologies*, *3*(2), 165–176. DOI: 10.1109/TLT.2009.40

Abramson, L. Y., Seligman, M. E., & Teasdale, J. D. (1978). Learned helplessness in humans: Critique and reformulation. *Journal of Abnormal Psychology*, *87*(1), 49–74. DOI: 10.1037/0021-843X.87.1.49 PMID: 649856

Adadi, A., & Berrada, M. (2018). Peeking inside the black-box: A survey on explainable artificial intelligence (XAI). *IEEE Access : Practical Innovations, Open Solutions*, *6*, 52138–52160. DOI: 10.1109/ACCESS.2018.2870052

Afify, M. K. (2019). The influence of group size in the asynchronous online discussions on the development of critical thinking skills, and on improving students' performance in online discussion forum. *International Journal of Emerging Technologies in Learning (Online)*, *14*(5), 132.

Age, I. L. (2018). L'influence D'une E-Évaluation Dynamique Sur L'engagement Cognitif D'étudiants En Contexte De Grand Groupe À L'université.

Agency for Healthcare Research and Quality. *Team Strategies & Tools to Enhance Performance & Patient Safety.* (2014). https://www.ahrq.gov/teamstepps-program/index.html

Ahmad, T. S. A. S., Abedin, N. F. Z., Ahmad, I., Paramasivam, S., & Mustapha, W. Z. W. (2022). Awareness and Attitudes of Undergraduate Students towards Plagiarism: Are There Any Differences between Genders? *Asian Journal of University Education*, *18*(3), 597–605.

Ahmed Mersal, F., & Ahmed Mersal, N. (2014). Effect of Blended Learning on Newly Nursing Student's Outcomes Regarding New Trends in Nursing Subject at Ain Shams University. *American Journal of Educational Research*, *2*(11), 1036–1043. DOI: 10.12691/education-2-11-6

Alamri, H., Lowell, V., Watson, W., & Watson, S. L. (2020). Using personalized learning as an instructional approach to motivate learners in online higher education: Learner self-determination and intrinsic motivation. *Journal of Research on Technology in Education*, *52*(3), 322–352. DOI: 10.1080/15391523.2020.1728449

Alasgarova, R., & Rzayev, J. (2024). The role of Artificial Intelligence in shaping high school students' motivation. [IJTES]. *International Journal of Technology in Education and Science*, *8*(2), 311–324. DOI: 10.46328/ijtes.553

Al-Huneidi, A. M., & Schreurs, J. (2012). Constructivism Based Blended Learning in Higher Education. [IJET]. *International Journal of Emerging Technologies in Learning*, *7*(1), 4–9. DOI: 10.3991/ijet.v7i1.1792

Alkaissi, H., & McFarlane, S. I. (2023). Artificial hallucinations in ChatGPT: Implications in scientific writing. *Cureus*, *15*(2), 1–4. DOI: 10.7759/cureus.35179 PMID: 36811129

Alves, S., Gosse, B., & Sprimont, P. (2010). Dimensions et conséquences de la satisfaction au travail des apprentis. *Revue internationale de psychosociologie, 16*(40), 161–180. https://doi.org/DOI: 10.3917/rips.040.0161

Amiel, T., & Reeves, T. C. (2008). Design-based research and educational technology: Rethinking technology and the research agenda. *Journal of Educational Technology & Society*, *11*(4), 29–40.

Andersen, B. L., Jørnø, R. L., & Nortvig, A.-M. J. C. E. T. (2021). Blending adaptive learning technology into nursing education: A scoping review. *14*(1), ep333.

Anderson, J. (2022). Engineering education and the Metaverse: The future of immersive learning. *Journal of Virtual Learning*, *18*(2), 77–91.

Anderson, L. W. (1988). Opportunity to learn. In Dunkin, M. J. (Ed.), *The International encyclopedia of teaching and teacher education* (pp. 368–372). Pergamon Press.

Anderson, T., & Shattuck, J. (2012). Design-based research: A decade of progress in education research? *Educational Researcher*, *41*(1), 16–25. DOI: 10.3102/0013189X11428813

Angelov, P. P., Soares, E. A., Jiang, R., Arnold, N. I., & Atkinson, P. M. (2021). Explainable artificial intelligence: An analytical review. *Wiley Interdisciplinary Reviews. Data Mining and Knowledge Discovery*, *11*(5), e1424. DOI: 10.1002/widm.1424

Appollis, J., & Sutcliffe, C. M. (2022). The use of social media such as WhatsApp, YouTube and Instagram in enhancing rather than impeding the learning of College students: An investigative case study. *Journal of Education and Social Sciences*, *22*(1), 1–11.

Assaad, A. (2016). Place et rôles de l'enseignant intervenant dans des dispositifs de formation universitaire à distance [The place and roles of teachers involved in university distance education programs] (Doctoral dissertation, Université de Lyon). Université de Lyon.

Attali, J. (2008). *Rapport de la Commission pour la libération de la croissance française* (245 p.). https://www.liberationdelacroissance.fr/files/rapports/rapportCLCF.pdf

Atun, R., Kersnik, J., Švab, I., Majeed, A., Car, J., Al-Shorbaji, N., & Wheeler, E. (2015). eLearning for undergraduate health professional education: A systematic review informing a radical transformation of health workforce development. Imperial college.

Aucancela, M., Briones, A. G., & Chamoso, P. (2023). *Educational Recommender Systems : A Systematic Literature Review*. 933-951. DOI: 10.22492/issn.2435-9467.2023.74

Ayyaswamy, K. (2024). Enhancing Digital Technology Planning, Leadership, and Management to Transform Education. In Bhatia, M., & Mushtaq, M. T. (Eds.), *Navigating Innovative Technologies and Intelligent Systems in Modern Education* (pp. 1–9). IGI Global., DOI: 10.4018/979-8-3693-5370-7.ch001

Badouch, M., & Boutaounte, M. (2023). Personalized Travel Recommendation Systems : A Study of Machine Learning Approaches in Tourism. *Journal of Artificial Intelligence. Machine Learning and Neural Network*, *33*(33), 35–45. DOI: 10.55529/jaimlnn.33.35.45

Baepler, P., Walker, J., Driessen, M. J. C., & education. (2014). It's not about seat time: Blending, flipping, and efficiency in active learning classrooms. *78*, 227-236.

Baeten, M., Kyndt, E., Struyven, K., & Dochy, F. (2010). Using student-centred learning environments to stimulate deep approaches to learning: Factors encouraging or discouraging their effectiveness. *Educational Research Review*, *5*(3), 243–260. DOI: 10.1016/j.edurev.2010.06.001

Bagot, F. (2006). Élitaire pour tous: Entretiens sur les classes préparatoires aux grandes

Baidada, M., Mansouri, K., & Poirier, F. (2021). Hybrid Filtering Recommendation System in an Educational Context : Experiment in Higher Education in Morocco. *International Journal of Web-Based Learning and Teaching Technologies*, *17*(1), 1–17. DOI: 10.4018/IJWLTT.294573

Bailenson, J. N. (2020). *Experience on demand: What virtual reality is, how it works, and what it can do*. W. W. Norton & Company.

Bailey, T. R. (2005). Paths to persistence: An analysis of research on program effectiveness at community colleges.

Balim, A. G. (2013). The effect of mind-mapping applications on upper primary students' success and inquiry-learning skills in science and environment education. *International Research in Geographical and Environmental Education*, *22*(4), 337–352. DOI: 10.1080/10382046.2013.826543

Bannan, B. (2009). The integrative learning design framework: An illustrated example from the domain of instructional technology. An introduction to educational design research, 53-73.

Bansal, H., & Khan, R. (2018). A review paper on human computer interaction. *International Journal of Advanced Research in Computer Science and Software Engineering*, *8*(4), 53. DOI: 10.23956/ijarcsse.v8i4.630

Baribeau, C. (2009). Analyse des données des entretiens de groupe. *Recherches Qualitatives*, *28*(1), 133–148. DOI: 10.7202/1085324ar

Baribeau, C., & Germain, M. (2010). L'entretien de groupe: Considérations théoriques et méthodologiques. *Recherches Qualitatives*, *29*(1), 28–49. DOI: 10.7202/1085131ar

Baron, G. (2008). Technologies de l'information et de la communication et indigènes numériques: quelle situation? https://hal.science/hal-00696420

Barr, R. B., & Tagg, J. (1995). From teaching to learning—A new paradigm for undergraduate education. Change: The magazine of higher learning, 27(6), 12-26.

Barr, R. B., & Tagg, J. (1995). From teaching to learning—A new paradigm for undergraduate education. Change: The magazine of higher learning, 27(6), 12-26.doi: . 10544672DOI: 10.1080/00091383.1995

Bearman, M., Nieminen, J. H., & Ajjawi, R. (2023). Designing assessment in a digital world: An organising framework. *Assessment & Evaluation in Higher Education*, *48*(3), 291–304. DOI: 10.1080/02602938.2022.2069674

Bedin, V., & Broussal, D. (2011). L'évaluation interactive des apprentissages dans l'enseignement supérieur: intérêt pédagogique et limites. Les dossiers des sciences de l'éducation, (26), 133-144.

Belfer, R., Kochmar, E., & Serban, I. V. (2022). Raising student completion rates with adaptive curriculum and contextual bandits. International Conference on Artificial Intelligence in Education, Bergmann, J. (2012). Flip your classroom: Reach every student in every class every day. DOI: 10.1007/978-3-031-11644-5_74

Ben Haman, O. (2021). The Moroccan education system, dilemma of language and think-tanks: The challenges of social development for the North African country. *Journal of North African Studies*, *26*(4), 709–732. DOI: 10.1080/13629387.2019.1711061

Ben Youssef, A., & Hadhri, W. (2009). Les dynamiques d'usage des TIC par les enseignants universitaires. *Reseaux (London)*, *155*(3), 23–54.

Benhamdi, S., Babouri, A., & Chiky, R. (2017). Système de recommandation personnalisé pour environnement e-Learning. Éducation et Technologies de l'Information, 22, 1455-1477. DOI DOI: 10.1007/s10639-016-9504-y

Benkrima, F. (2021). *Le développement de la compétence orale chez les étudiants pendant le confinement: Cas des étudiants de 3e année licence français à l'Université Kasdi Merbah Ouargla — Promotion 2019-2020*. http://dspace.univ-ouargla.dz/jspui/handle/123456789/28593

Benosman, M. (2016). *Learning-based adaptive control: An extremum seeking approach–theory and applications*. Butterworth-Heinemann.

Bernabé, E., & Dupont, P. (2001). *Le leadership pédagogique: Une approche managériale du style d'enseignement.*

Bernacki, M. L., Greene, M. J., & Lobczowski, N. G. J. E. P. R. (2021). A systematic review of research on personalized learning: Personalized by whom, to what, how, and for what purpose (s)?, *33*(4), 1675-1715.

Bernard, R. M., Borokhovski, E., & Tamim, R. M. (2018). The state of research on distance, online, and blended learning: Meta-analyses and qualitative systematic reviews. In *Handbook of distance education* (pp. 92–104). Routledge. DOI: 10.4324/9781315296135-8

Bernate, J. A. y Fonseca, I. P. (2023). Impacto de las Tecnologías de Información y Comunicación en la educación del siglo XXI: Revisión bibliométrica. Revistade ciencias sociales, 29(1), 227-242. https://doi.org/DOI: 10.31876/rcs.v29i1

Betihavas, V., Bridgman, H., Kornhaber, R., & Cross, M. (2016). The evidence for "flipping out": A systematic review of the flipped classroom in nursing education. *Nurse Education Today*, *38*, 15–21. DOI: 10.1016/j.nedt.2015.12.010 PMID: 26804940

Biggs, J., & Tang, C. (2011). Teaching for Quality Learning at University: What the Student Does. Open University Press (4e éd.). New-York: USA.

Billings, D. M., & Halstead, J. A. (2012). Teaching in Nursing: A guide to the faculty. (4e éd.). Missouri: ELSEVIER Saunders.

Blackboard Inc. 2004. Blackboard United Kingdom. ≤https://www.blackboard.com/worldwide/gb/en/aboutbb.htm≥

Blais, S. (2023). L'évaluation dynamique en mathématiques: des avantages et des limites de l'utilisation de cette approche auprès d'un élève du 2e cycle du primaire en difficulté d'apprentissage.

Blake, R. J. (2013). *Brave new digital classroom: Technology and foreign language learning*. Georgetown University Press.

Bloom, B. S. (1968). Learning for Mastery. Instruction and Curriculum. Regional Education Laboratory for the Carolinas and Virginia, Topical Papers and Reprints, Number 1. *Evaluation Comment, 1*(2). https://eric.ed.gov/?id=eD053419

Bloomfield, J. G., & Jones, A. (2013). Using e-learning to support clinical skills acquisition: Exploring the experiences and perceptions of graduate first-year pre-registration nursing students — A mixed method study. *Nurse Education Today*, *33*(12), 1605–1611. DOI: 10.1016/j.nedt.2013.01.024 PMID: 23473860

Bloomfield, J., Roberts, J., & While, A. (2010). The effect of computer-assisted learning versus conventional teaching methods on the acquisition and retention of handwashing theory and skills in pre-qualification nursing students: A randomised controlled trial. *International Journal of Nursing Studies*, *47*(3), 287–294. DOI: 10.1016/j.ijnurstu.2009.08.003 PMID: 19762016

Bober, M., Fasuga, R., & Šarmanová, J. (2007). Adaptive Mechanisms in Virtual Education Environment. In Fernandes, M. M. (Ed.), *ICEE2007 Coimbra*. University of Coimbra.

Boring, C. (2020). *Microlearning: An andragogical case study on knowledge retention, learner satisfaction, and behavior change*. Robert Morris University.

Boucher, C. (2015). La rétroaction: élément phare pour l'apprentissage de nos étudiants. Le tableau, 4(3).

Boud, D., & Molloy, E. (2013). Rethinking models of feedback for learning: The challenge of design. *Assessment & Evaluation in Higher Education*, *38*(6), 698–712. DOI: 10.1080/02602938.2012.691462

Boukhari, S., Sadiq, M., Radid, M., Naciri, A., & Chemsi, G. (2024). *Mind Maps and Artificial Intelligence: Towards an Active Understanding of Redox in Secondary School Students. Lecture Notes in Networks and Systems* (Vol. 862). Springer., DOI: 10.1007/978-3-031-71429-0_1

Brahimi, C., Steben, M., & Farley, C. (2008). Projet innovation en formation: Phase I: les technologies de l'information et de la communication (TIC) [Innovation project in training: Phase I: Information and communication technologies (ICT)]. Institut national de santé publique du Québec. Retrieved from http://collections.banq.qc.ca/ark:/52327/1927158

Brézillon, P. (2023). The Real-World Applications. In *Research on Modeling and Using Context Over 25 Years* (p. 5–18). Springer Nature Switzerland. DOI: 10.1007/978-3-031-39338-9_2

Bristol, T. J., & Zerwekh, J. (Eds.). (2011). *Essentials of e-learning for nurse educators*. F. A. Davis Company.

Brown, A. L. (1992). Design experiments: Theoretical and methodological challenges in creating complex interventions in classroom settings. *Journal of the Learning Sciences*, *2*(2), 141–178. DOI: 10.1207/s15327809jls0202_2

Brown-Chidsey, R., & Bickford, R. (2015). *Practical handbook of multi-tiered systems of support: Building academic and behavioral success in schools*. Guilford Publications.

Brown, P. C., Roediger, H. L.III, & McDaniel, M. A. (2014). *Make it stick: The science of successful learning*. Harvard University Press.

Burgsteiner, H., Kandlhofer, M., & Steinbauer, G. (2016, March). Irobot: Teaching the basics of artificial intelligence in high schools. *Proceedings of the AAAI Conference on Artificial Intelligence*, *30*(1) DOI: 10.1609/aaai.v30i1.9864

Burguete, E. (2021). Proposition d'une méthodologie de conception et d'évaluation d'un SPOC en microlearning. Adjectif: analyses et recherches sur les TICE, 2021(1).

Busemeyer, J. R., & Diederich, A. (2010). Cognitive modeling. *Sage (Atlanta, Ga.)*.

Buzan, T. (2024). *Mind map mastery: The complete guide to learning and using the most powerful thinking tool in the universe*. Jaico Publishing House.

Caballe, S., & Clariso, R. (2016). Formative assessment, learning data analytics and gamification. In *ICT education*. Morgan Kaufmann.

Cai, W., & Chen, Q. (2018). An experimental research of augmented reality technology from the perspective of mobile learning. *2018 IEEE International Conference on Teaching, Assessment, and Learning for Engineering (TALE)*.

Cai, Y., Ke, W., Cui, E., & Yu, F. (2022). A deep recommendation model of cross-grained sentiments of user reviews and ratings. *Information Processing & Management, 59*(2), 102842. DOI: 10.1016/j.ipm.2021.102842

Carli, R., & Calvaresi, D. (2024). The Wildcard XAI: from a Necessity, to a Resource, to a Dangerous Decoy. In Calvaresi, D., (Eds.), Lecture Notes in Computer Science: Vol. 14847. *Explainable and Transparent AI and Multi-Agent Systems. EXTRAAMAS 2024*. Springer., DOI: 10.1007/978-3-031-70074-3_13

Caro Dambreville, S. (2014). Mind maps: a paradigm shift in learning. Communication, technologies and development, (1).DOI: 10.4000/12746

Castillo-Merino, D., Serradell-López, E., & Vilaseca-Requena, J. (2009). Usage des technologies de l'information et de la communication dans l'enseignement supérieur. *Reseaux (London), 155*(3), 55–80. DOI: 10.3917/res.155.0055

Cecile, C. D. Q., & Richard, T. (2018). Étude De La Communication Interprofessionnelle Entre Medecins Et Infirmiers Exercant En Maisons De Sante Pluri-Professionnelles (Doctoral dissertation). file:///C:/Users/az/Downloads/THm_2018_CARNEIRO_DE_QUEIROZ_Cecile_et_TY_Richard%20(1).pdf

Celik, I., Dindar, M., Muukkonen, H., & Järvelä, S. (2022). The Promises and Challenges of Artificial Intelligence for Teachers: A Systematic Review of Research. *TechTrends, 66*(4), 616–630. DOI: 10.1007/s11528-022-00715-y

Chaiyo, Y., & Nokham, R. (2017, March). The effect of Kahoot, Quizizz and Google Forms on the student's perception in the classrooms response system. In 2017 International conference on digital arts, media and technology (ICDAMT) (pp. 178-182). IEEE.

Chamberland, G., Lavoie, L., & Marquis, D. (1995). *20 Formules pédagogiques*. Presse de l'Université du Québec.

Chan, C. K. Y., & Tsi, L. H. (2023). The AI revolution in education: Will AI replace or assist teachers in higher education? arXiv preprint arXiv:2305.01185. https://doi .org//arXiv.2305.01185DOI: 10.48550

Charlin, B., Bordage, G., & Van Der Vleuten, C. (2003). Clinical reasoning assessment. [http://dx.doi.org/10.1051/pmed:2003015]. *Pédagogie Médicale*, *4*(1), 42–52. DOI: 10.1051/pmed:2003015

Charnet, C. (2019). *Comment réaliser une formation ou un enseignement numérique à distance? Guide pratique: former et se former* [How to design a digital distance training or teaching course? A practical guide: Training and self-training]. De Boeck Supérieur.

Chatterjee, J., & Dethlefs, N. (2023). This new conversational AI model can be your friend, philosopher, and guide and even your worst enemy. Patterns, 4(1). DOI: 10.1016/j.patter.2022.100676

Chaushi, B. A., Selimi, B., Chaushi, A., & Apostolova, M. (2023, Jul). Explainable artificial intelligence in education: A comprehensive review. In *World Conference on Explainable Artificial Intelligence* (p. 48-71). Cham: Springer Nature Switzerland. DOI: 10.1007/978-3-031-44067-0_3

Chemsi, G., Sadiq, M., Radid, M., & Talbi, M. (2019). Formative E-assessment and behavioral commitment of students. *Case of the Faculty of Science Ben M'sik.*, *14*(12), 4.

Chen, D., & Xu, F. (2024). Design and implementation of machine learning algorithms in automatic grading of students' assignments. *Journal of Electrical Systems*, *20*(3s), 899–919. DOI: 10.52783/jes.1388

Cheng, I., Safont, L. V., & Basu, A. (2010). *Multimedia in education: Adaptive learning and testing*. World Scientific. DOI: 10.1142/7111

Chen, H.-Y., & Chuang, C.-H. (2012). The learning effectiveness of nursing students using online testing as an assistant tool: A cluster randomized controlled trial. *Nurse Education Today*, *32*(3), 208–213. DOI: 10.1016/j.nedt.2011.03.004 PMID: 21450377

Chen, L. (2022). Personalized learning and artificial intelligence: Adaptive solutions in higher education. *Journal of Educational Technology Systems*, *51*(1), 5–22. DOI: 10.2190/AGAL-BAUK-RH89-3L2G

Chiu, TKF, Moorhouse, BL, Chai, CS, & Ismailov, M. (2023). Soutien des enseignants et motivation des élèves à apprendre avec un chatbot basé sur l'intelligence artificielle (IA). Environnements d'apprentissage interactifs, 32 (7), 3240–3256. DOI: 10.1080/10494820.2023.2172044

Chiu, T. K. (2022). Applying the self-determination theory (SDT) to explain student engagement in online learning during the COVID-19 pandemic. *Journal of Research on Technology in Education, 54*(1), 14–30. DOI: 10.1080/15391523.2021.1891998

Choi, S.-M., Lee, D., Jang, K., Park, C., & Lee, S. (2023). Improving Data Sparsity in Recommender Systems Using Matrix Regeneration with Item Features. *Mathematics, 11*(2), 292. DOI: 10.3390/math11020292

Chopin, M. (2006). Temps d'enseignement et temps didactique: Approche didactique de la question du temps dans l'enseignement des mathématiques au cycle 3 de l'école élémentaire. *Carrefours de l'éducation, 21*(1), 53–71. https://doi.org/ DOI: 10.3917/cdle.021.0053

Christodoulou, A., & Angeli, C. (2022, June). Adaptive learning techniques for a personalized educational software in developing teachers' technological pedagogical content knowledge. In Frontiers in Education (Vol. 7, p. 789397). Frontiers Media SA. DOI: 10.3389/feduc.2022.789397

Christopher, M. M., Thomas, J. A., & Tallent-Runnels, M. K. (2004). Raising the bar:Encouraging high level thinking in online discussion forums. *Roeper Review, 26*(3), 166–171. DOI: 10.1080/02783190409554262

Chukwuere, J. E. (2024). *The Future of AI Chatbots in Higher Education*. Qeios., DOI: 10.32388/UE841K

Clark, R. C., & Mayer, R. E. (2023). *E-learning and the science of instruction: Proven guidelines for consumers and designers of multimedia learning*. john Wiley & sons.

Coates, H. B. (2008). Attracting, engaging and retaining: New conversations about learning.

Cohen, A., Doucède, G., Clouqueur, E., Debarge, V., Béhal, H., Rubod, C., & Hanssens, S. (2021). Utilisation de l'outil SAED : Évaluation de l'intérêt d'une formation courte sur la qualité de la communication entre soignants à court et à long terme. *Gynécologie, Obstétrique, Fertilité & Sénologie, 49*(11), 823–829. Advance online publication. DOI: 10.1016/j.gofs.2021.04.010 PMID: 33933673

Cohen, E. R., Feinglass, J., Barsuk, J. H., Barnard, C., O'Donnell, A., McGaghie, W. C., & Wayne, D. B. (2010). Cost Savings From Reduced Catheter-Related Bloodstream Infection After Simulation-Based Education for Residents in a Medical Intensive Care Unit. *Simulation in Healthcare, 5*(2), 98–102. DOI: 10.1097/SIH.0b013e3181bc8304 PMID: 20389233

Collins, A., & Halverson, R. (2018). *Rethinking education in the age of technology: The digital revolution and schooling in America*. Teachers College Press.

Collins, A., Joseph, D., & Bielaczyc, K. (2016). Design research: Theoretical and methodological issues. In *Design-based Research* (pp. 15–42). Psychology Press.

Cook, D. A., Hatala, R., Brydges, R., Zendejas, B., Szostek, J. H., Wang, A. T., Erwin, P. J., & Hamstra, S. J. (n.d.). *Technology-Enhanced Simulation for Health Professions Education*. 11.

Craig, G. P. (2015). *Evaluating discussion forums for undergraduate and graduate students*. Faculty Focus.

Craig, K., & Kay, L. (2023). Integrating VR in higher education: Systematic review on competency development and technological requirements. *Higher Learning Research Communications*, *12*(1), 45–63.

Crişan, C., Pavelea, A., & Ghimbuluţ, O. (2015). A need assessment on students' career guidance. *Procedia: Social and Behavioral Sciences*, *180*, 1022–1029.

Critz, C. M., & Knight, D. (2013). Using the Flipped Classroom in Graduate Nursing Education. *Nurse Educator*, *38*(5), 210–213. DOI: 10.1097/NNE.0b013e3182a0e56a PMID: 23969751

Cuban, L. (1993). *How Teachers Taught: Constancy and Change in American Classrooms, 1890-1990*. Teachers College Press.

Cuseo, J. (2007). *The Empirical Case Against Large Class Size: Adverse Effects on the Teaching*. Learning, and Retention of First-Year Students.

Dalgarno, B., Lee, M. J. W., Carlson, L., Gregory, S., & Tynan, B. (2011). An Australian and New Zealand scoping study on the use of 3D immersive virtual worlds in higher education. *Australasian Journal of Educational Technology*, *27*(3), 1–15. DOI: 10.14742/ajet.978

Darling-Hammond, L. (2006). Darling-, Linda. Constructing 21st-century teacher education. *Journal of Teacher Education*, *57*(3), 300–314. DOI: 10.1177/0022487105285962

Das, N. K., Sahoo, S., & Pati, L. (2021). Online learning: Challenges for education in rural and remote areas. suicide, 8(7). DOI: DOI: 10.17148/IARJSET.2021.8712

Dave, V. S., Zhang, B., Al Hasan, M., AlJadda, K., & Korayem, M. (2018). A Combined Representation Learning Approach for Better Job and Skill Recommendation. *Proceedings of the 27th ACM International Conference on Information and Knowledge Management*, 1997-2005. DOI: 10.1145/3269206.3272023

Davila, A., & Domínguez, M. (2010). Formats des groupes et types de discussion dans la recherche sociale qualitative. *Recherches Qualitatives*, *29*(1), 50–68. DOI: 10.7202/1085132ar

De Broeck, F., & Hausman, M. (2020). The potential of mind maps for assessment in times of pandemic. Assess. *International Journal of Research in Education and Training*, *1*, 85–96.

De Clercq, M. (2023). Les défis de l'enseignement supérieur: entre accessibilité, équité et réussite. *Diversité. Revue d'actualité et de réflexion sur l'action éducative*, (202), volume 1.

De Freitas, S. (2013). *Education in computer generated environments*. Routledge. DOI: 10.4324/9780203094709

De Gagne, J. C. J. I. j. o. e. r., & health, p. (2023). The state of artificial intelligence in nursing education: Past, present, and future directions. In (Vol. 20, pp. 4884): MDPI.

Deci, E. L., & Ryan, R. M. J. J. o. r. i. p. (1985). The general causality orientations scale: Self-determination in personality. *19*(2), 109-134.

Deci, E. L., & Ryan, R. M. J. P. i. (2000). The" what" and" why" of goal pursuits: Human needs and the self-determination of behavior. *11*(4), 227-268.

Deci, E. L. (1971). Effects of externally mediated rewards on intrinsic motivation. *Journal of Personality and Social Psychology*, *18*(1), 105–115. DOI: 10.1037/h0030644

Deci, E. L., & Ryan, R. M. (1985). *Intrinsic motivation and self-determination in human behavior*. Plenum. DOI: 10.1007/978-1-4899-2271-7

Deci, E. L., & Ryan, R. M. (2000). The" what" and" why" of goal pursuits: Human needs and the self-determination of behavior. *Psychological Inquiry*, *11*(4), 227–268. DOI: 10.1207/S15327965PLI1104_01

Dehghanzadeh, S., & Jafaraghaie, F. (2018). Comparing the effects of traditional lecture and flipped classroom on nursing students' critical thinking disposition: A quasi-experimental study. *Nurse Education Today*, *71*, 151–156. DOI: 10.1016/j.nedt.2018.09.027 PMID: 30286373

Dejours, R. (2017). Classes préparatoires. *Adolescence*, *35*(2), 361–370. DOI: 10.3917/ado.100.0361

Dhahri, M., & Khribi, M. K. (2021). *A REVIEW OF EDUCATIONAL RECOMMENDER SYSTEMS FOR TEACHERS*.

Dhananjaya, G. M., Goudar, R. H., Kulkarni, A. A., Rathod, V. N., & Hukkeri, G. S. (2024). A Digital Recommendation System for Personalized Learning to Enhance Online Education : A Review. *IEEE Access : Practical Innovations, Open Solutions, 12*, 34019–34041. DOI: 10.1109/ACCESS.2024.3369901

Dibble, M. (2023). *Schools ban ChatGPT amid fears of artificial intelligence-assisted cheating*. VOA News.

Dignum, V. (2021). The role and challenges of education for responsible AI. *London Review of Education, 19*(1), 1–11. DOI: 10.14324/LRE.19.1.01

Dillahunt, T. R., Israni, A., Lu, A. J., Cai, M., & Hsiao, J. C.-Y. (2021). Examining the Use of Online Platforms for Employment : A Survey of U.S. Job Seekers. *Proceedings of the 2021 CHI Conference on Human Factors in Computing Systems*, 1-23. DOI: 10.1145/3411764.3445350

Dimova, R., Stoyanova, R., & Doykov, I. (2018). Mixed-methods study of reported clinical cases of undesirable events, medical errors, and near misses in health care. *Journal of Evaluation in Clinical Practice, 24*(4), 752–757. DOI: 10.1111/jep.12970 PMID: 29947085

Dinsmore, D. L., & Alexander, P. A. (2012). A critical discussion of deep and surface processing: What it means, how it is measured, the role of context, and model specification. *Educational Psychology Review, 24*(4), 499–567. DOI: 10.1007/s10648-012-9198-7

dit Dariel, O. P. (2011). Exploring e-learning adoption in nurse education: A socio-cultural case study using Q and Bourdieu (Doctoral dissertation, University of Nottingham).

Djouad, T., Settouti, L. S., Prié, Y., Reffay, C. & Mille, A. Un Système à Base de Traces pour la modélisation et l'élaboration d'indicateurs d'activités éducatives individuelles et collectives. Mise à l'épreuve sur Moodle.

Doan, B. K. V. (2021). Quels motifs amènent des professeurs d'université à mettre en place des pratiques pédagogiques non magistrales dans le contexte de l'enseignement à de grands groupes?.

Doshi-Velez, F., & Kim, B. (2017). Towards a rigorous science of interpretable machine learning. *arXiv preprint arXiv:1702.08608.*

Drake, B. M., & Walz, A. (2018). Evolving business intelligence and data analytics in higher education. *New Directions for Institutional Research, 2018*(178), 39–52. DOI: 10.1002/ir.20266

Dube, B. (2020). Rural online learning in the context of COVID 19 in South Africa: Evoking an inclusive education approach. *Multidisciplinary Journal of Educational Research, 10*(2), 135–157. DOI: 10.17583/remie.2020.5607

Dwivedi, Y. K., Kshetri, N., Hughes, L., Slade, E. L., Jeyaraj, A., Kar, A. K., Baabdullah, A. M., Koohang, A., Raghavan, V., Ahuja, M., Albanna, H., Albashrawi, M. A., Al-Busaidi, A. S., Balakrishnan, J., Barlette, Y., Basu, S., Bose, I., Brooks, L., Buhalis, D., & Wright, R. (2023). Opinion paper: "So what if ChatGPT wrote it?" Multidisciplinary perspectives on opportunities, challenges and implications of generative conversational AI for research, practice and policy. *International Journal of Information Management, 71*, 1–63. DOI: 10.1016/j.ijinfomgt.2023.102642

Elmourabit, Z., Asmaâ Retbi, & Nour-Eddine El Faddouli. (2024). The Impact of Generative Artificial Intelligence on Education : A Comparative Study. *European Conference on E-Learning, 23*(1), 470-476. DOI: 10.34190/ecel.23.1.2975

Elsaadany, I. K., Gonzalez-Vargas, J. M., Moore, J. Z., & Miller, S. R. (2023). Progressive Medical Simulation: An Analysis of the Integration of Progressive and Personalized Learning in Central Line Simulators. *Proceedings of the Human Factors and Ergonomics Society Annual Meeting, 67*(1), 1868–1874. DOI: 10.1177/21695067231192713 PMID: 38450121

El-Sabagh, H. A. (2021). Adaptive e-learning environment based on learning styles and its impact on development students' engagement. *International Journal of Educational Technology in Higher Education, 18*(1), 53. DOI: 10.1186/s41239-021-00289-4

Endrizzi, L. (2012). *Les technologies numériques dans l'enseignement supérieur, entre défis et opportunités*. https://ens-lyon.hal.science/ensl-01651604

Ennadi, M. (2022, 1 septembre). L'apprentissage en ligne et l'expérience des étudiants universitaires à l'utilisation des TIC. *Revue de Management et Cultures*. https://revues.imist.ma/index.php/REMAC/article/view/34249/17561

Ernoult, M., & Talamoni, C. (2006). Le QCM: un outil pour la formation et l'évaluation. Bulletin vert de l'APMEP, (462).

Fadieieva, L. (2023). Adaptive learning: A cluster-based literature review (2011-2022). *Educational Technology Quarterly, 2023*(3), 319–366. DOI: 10.55056/etq.613

Faouzi, L., Gourja, B., Belarbi, N., & Nachit, M. B. (2019). Mind Map Recognition in a Graphical Representation: An Evaluative Approach. Doi:DOI: 10.19044/esj.2019.v15n23p76

Farrand, P., Fearzana, H., & Hennessy, E. (2002). The efficacy of the mind map study technique. *Medical Education*, *36*(5), 426–431. DOI: 10.1046/j.1365-2923.2002.01205.x PMID: 12028392

Farrell, T., & Rushby, N. (2016). Assessment and learning technologies: An overview. *British Journal of Educational Technology*, *47*(1), 106–120. DOI: 10.1111/bjet.12348

Fauré, L. (2017). Co-enseignement et développement professionnel des enseignants en agroéquipements de l'enseignement agricole (Doctoral dissertation, Université Toulouse le Mirail-Toulouse II).

Fayyaz, Z., Ebrahimian, M., Nawara, D., Ibrahim, A., & Kashef, R. (2020). Recommendation Systems : Algorithms, Challenges, Metrics, and Business Opportunities. *Applied Sciences (Basel, Switzerland)*, *10*(21), 7748. DOI: 10.3390/app10217748

Fei, Y., Lavoie, D., & Chen, R. (2023). Immersive learning technologies in STEM: A review of VR and AR integration in higher education. *Journal of Educational Technology*, *44*(2), 33–57.

Félix, E., Amadieu, F., & Broisin, J. (2024). Personal Characteristics and Explanations in Technology-Enhanced Environments: An Exploratory Study in Computer Science Education.

Felix, C. V. (2020). The Role of the Teacher and AI in Education. In Sengupta, E., Blessinger, P., & Makhanya, M. (Eds.), *International Perspectives on the Role of Technology in Humanizing Higher Education* (Vol. 33, pp. 33–48). Emerald Publishing Limited., DOI: 10.1108/S2055-364120200000033003

Figari, G. (1994). *Évaluer: quel référentiel?* De Boeck.

Fisher, R., Cavanagh, J., & Bowles, A. (2011). Assisting transition to university: Using assessment as a formative learning tool. *Assessment & Evaluation in Higher Education*, *36*(2), 225–237. DOI: 10.1080/02602930903308241

Fitria, T. N. (2022). Microlearning in teaching and learning process: A review. CENDEKIA: Jurnal Ilmu Sosial. *Bahasa Dan Pendidikan*, *2*(4), 114–135.

Fontaine, G. (2016). Evaluation of the MOTIV@COEUR online training platform on brief motivational interventions with nurses in acute cardiovascular care. *Master's thesis* presented for the degree of Master of Science (M.Sc.) in Nursing Sciences, Expertise-Advice in Nursing Care. 159.

Foreman, S. D. (2017). *The LMS guidebook: Learning management systems demystified*. Association for Talent Development.

Foronda, C., Liu, S., & Bauman, E. B. (2013). Evaluation of Simulation in Undergraduate Nurse Education: An Integrative Review. *Clinical Simulation in Nursing*, *9*(10), e409–e416. DOI: 10.1016/j.ecns.2012.11.003

Fréchette, S. (2008). Autorégulation de l'apprentissage de l'exercice du rôle de soutien à la motivation de l'élève au secondaire dans le cadre de la formation des enseignants (Doctoral dissertation, Université du Québec à Montréal).

Fredricks, J. A., Blumenfeld, P. C., & Paris, A. H. J. R. o. e. r. (2004). School engagement: Potential of the concept, state of the evidence. *74*(1), 59-109.

French National Authority for Health. (2015). Guide to the design of open and distance learning (FOAD) in the world of health. Evaluation and improvement of practices. France.

Frey, C. B., & Osborne, M. A. (2017). The future of employment: How susceptible are jobs to computerisation? *Technological Forecasting and Social Change*, *114*, 254–280. DOI: 10.1016/j.techfore.2016.08.019

Fui-Hoon Nah, F., Zheng, R., Cai, J., Siau, K., & Chen, L. (2023). IA générative et ChatGPT: Applications, défis et collaboration IA-humain. *Journal of Information Technology Case and Application Research*, *25*(3), 277–304. DOI: 10.1080/15228053.2023.2233814

Gaba, D. M. (2004). The future vision of simulation in health care. *BMJ Quality & Safety*, *13*(suppl 1), i2–i10. DOI: 10.1136/qshc.2004.009878 PMID: 15465951

Gagnon, M.-P., Gagnon, J., Desmartis, M., & Njoya, M. (2013). The Impact of Blended Teaching on Knowledge, Satisfaction, and Self-Directed Learning in Nursing Undergraduates: A Randomized, Controlled Trial. *Nursing Education Perspectives*, *34*(6), 377–382. DOI: 10.5480/10-459 PMID: 24475598

García, M. (2023). Personalized learning paths in AI-supported ESP platforms. *Journal of Language & Learning Technologies*, *41*(2), 101–115.

Garcia, M., López, S., & Rivas, T. (2023). AI-driven tools in virtual learning spaces: Impact on language proficiency. *Language Learning & Technology*, *27*(1), 33–50.

Gedrimiene, E., Celik, I., Kaasila, A., Mäkitalo, K., & Muukkonen, H. (2024). Artificial Intelligence (AI)-enhanced learning analytics (LA) for supporting Career decisions : Advantages and challenges from user perspective. *Education and Information Technologies*, *29*(1), 297–322. DOI: 10.1007/s10639-023-12277-4

Gegenfurtner, A., & Ebner, C. J. E. R. R. (2019). Webinars in higher education and professional training: A meta-analysis and systematic review of randomized controlled trials. *28*, 100293.

Gerdprasert, S., Pruksacheva, T., Panijpan, B., & Ruenwongsa, P. (2011). An interactive web-based learning unit to facilitate and improve intrapartum nursing care of nursing students. *Nurse Education Today*, *31*(5), 531–535. DOI: 10.1016/j.nedt.2010.10.008 PMID: 21078535

Ghazouani, M., Chafiq, N., Zaher, N., Azouazi, M., & Chakir, A. (2023). Merging big data with the Metaverse: A proposed architecture with multiple layers. *International Journal of Emerging Technologies in Learning*, *18*(6), 100–115.

Ghirardini, B. (2012). E-learning methodologies and good practices. A guide for designing and delivering e-learning solutions from the FAO eLearning Academy. Second Edition. Food and agriculture organization of the United Nations, Rome.

Gikandi, J. W., Morrow, D., & Davis, N. E. (2011). Online formative assessment in higher education: A review of the literature. *Computers & Education*, *57*(4), 2333–2351.

Gilboy, M. B., Heinerichs, S., & Pazzaglia, G. (2015). Enhancing Student Engagement Using the Flipped Classroom. *Journal of Nutrition Education and Behavior*, *47*(1), 109–114. DOI: 10.1016/j.jneb.2014.08.008 PMID: 25262529

Glazer, N. (2014). Formative plus Summative Assessment in Large Undergraduate Courses: Why Both? *International Journal on Teaching and Learning in Higher Education*, *26*(2), 276–286.

Gobinath, V. M., Kathirvel, A., Rajesh Kanna, S. K., & Annamalai, K. (2024), "Chapter 5: Smart Technology in Management Industries: A Useful Perspective", Artificial Intelligence Applied to Industry 4.0, Wiley Publiser, USA, 1st Edition, July 2024, pp.93-106, , ISBN 978-1-394-21611-6DOI: 10.1002/9781394216147.ch5

Godwin-Jones, R. (2014). Language as communication, language as code: Second language acquisition in a digital age. *Language Learning & Technology*, *18*(1), 248–264.

Gómez, S., Zervas, P., Sampson, D. G., & Fabregat, R. (2014). Context-aware adaptive and personalized mobile learning delivery supported by UoLmP. Journal of King Saud University-Computer and Information Sciences, 26(1), 47-61. DOI: 10.1016/j.rhum.2023.10.358

Gonzalez-Gonzalez, CS (2023). The impact of artificial intelligence on education: transforming the way we teach and learn. DOI: DOI: 10.25145/j.qurricul.2023.36.03

Govindan, S. N., Singh, H. K., Ling, L. W., Sekar, M. J. J. o. E., & Promotion, H. (2023). Effect of blended self-directed learning on nursing students: Quasi-experimental approach. *12*(1), 229.

Graf, S., Lin, F., & McGreal, R. (Eds.). (2011). *Intelligent and Adaptive Learning Systems: Technology Enhanced Support for Learners and Teachers: Technology Enhanced Support for Learners and Teachers*. IGI Global.

Grant, C. A., & Sleeter, C. E. (2012). *Doing multicultural education for achievement and equity*. Routledge. DOI: 10.4324/9780203831397

Grassini, S. (2023). Shaping the future of education: Exploring the potential and consequences of AI and ChatGPT in educational settings. *Education Sciences*, *13*(7), 692. DOI: 10.3390/educsci13070692

Greenberg, K. H. (2000). Inside professional practice: A collaborative, systems orientation to linking dynamic assessment and intervention. Dynamic assessment: Prevailing models and applications, 489-519.

Greene, B. A. (2015). Measuring cognitive engagement with self-report scales: Reflections from over 20 years of research. *Educational Psychologist*, *50*(1), 14–30. DOI: 10.1080/00461520.2014.989230

Greene, J. A., & Azevedo, R. (2010). The measurement of learners' self-regulated cognitive and metacognitive processes while using computer-based learning environments. *Educational Psychologist*, *45*(4), 203–209. DOI: 10.1080/00461520.2010.515935

Green, S. M., Weaver, M., Voegeli, D., Fitzsimmons, D., Knowles, J., Harrison, M., & Shephard, K. (2006). The development and evaluation of the use of a virtual learning environment (Blackboard 5) to support the learning of pre-qualifying nursing students undertaking a human anatomy and physiology module. *Nurse Education Today*, *26*(5), 388–395. DOI: 10.1016/j.nedt.2005.11.008 PMID: 16414156

Grgurovic, M., Law, T., & Devrim, D. (2012). Virtual reality for ESL/EFL reading and vocabulary learning. *Language Learning & Technology*, *16*(2), 3–11.

Guay, F., Vallerand, R. J., & Blanchard, C. (2000). On the assessment of situational intrinsic and extrinsic motivation:The situational motivation scale. *Motivation and Emotion*, *24*(3), 175–213. DOI: 10.1023/A:1005614228250

Guennoun, B., & Benjelloun, N. (2016). Regards des étudiants sur l'intégration des TIC dans l'enseignement supérieur scientifique. *Revue internationale des technologies en pédagogie universitaire, 13*(1), 61. https://doi.org/DOI: 10.18162/ritpu-2016-v13n1-05

Guilbault, M., & Viau-Guay, A. (2017). *La classe inversée comme approche pédagogique en enseignement supérieur: état des connaissances scientifiques et recommandations* [The flipped classroom as a pedagogical approach in higher education: State of scientific knowledge and recommendations]. *Revue internationale de pédagogie de l'enseignement supérieur*, 33(1). Published online on March 6, 2017. Retrieved from https://journals.openedition.org/ripes/1193

Guo, P. J., Kim, J., & Rubin, R. (2014). How video production affects student engagement: An empirical study of MOOC videos. Proceedings of the first ACM conference on Learning@ scale conference, Idrissi, W. E. M. E., Chemsi, G., Kababi, K. E., & Radid, M. (2022). The Impact of Serious Game on the Nursing Students' Learning, Behavioral Engagement, and Motivation. *17*(1), 18-35.

Haig, K. M., Sutton, S., & Whittington, J. (2006). SBAR: A Shared Mental Model for Improving Communication Between Clinicians. *Joint Commission Journal on Quality and Patient Safety*, *32*(3), 167–175. DOI: 10.1016/S1553-7250(06)32022-3 PMID: 16617948

Halder, S., & Argyropoulos, V. (2019). *Inclusion, equity and access for individuals with disabilities*. Springer. DOI: 10.1007/978-981-13-5962-0

Haleem, A., Javaid, M., Qadri, M. A., & Suman, R. (2022). Understanding the role of digital technologies in education: A review. Sustainable operations and computers, 3, 275-285.

Halimi, A. (2023). L'enseignement à distance dans l'université marocaine après la Covid-19: Cas de l'université Hassan II. Disponible sur https://revues.imist.ma/index.php/IAJESP/index

Hamdan, Y. (2022). L'innovation dans l'enseignement supérieur marocain au temps de la digitalisation: Bilan, défis et perspectives. *Revue Marocaine de Didactique et Pédagogie*, *2*(1).

Hansen, M. M. (2011). Are nursing students' clinical skills competency and self-confidence levels improved via video iPods? A randomized controlled pilot study. *Journal of Nursing Education and Practice*, *1*(1), 32. DOI: 10.5430/jnep.v1n1p32

Harter, S. (1981). Une nouvelle échelle d'auto-évaluation de l'orientation intrinsèque et extrinsèque en classe: Composantes motivationnelles et informationnelles. *Developmental Psychology*, *17*, 300–312. DOI: 10.1037/0012-1649.17.3.300

Hassan, M. M., Mirza, T., & Hussain, M. W. (2020). A critical review by teachers on the online teaching-learning during the COVID-19. *International Journal of Education and Management Engineering*, *10*(5), 17–27. DOI: 10.5815/ijeme.2020.05.03

Hastie, H., Lim, M. Y., Janarthanam, S., Deshmukh, A., Aylett, R., Foster, M. E., & Hall, L. (2016). I remember you! interaction with memory for an empathic virtual robotic tutor.

Haute Autorité de Santé (HAS). *SAED: Un guide pour faciliter la communication entre professionnels de santé*. (2014, October). Haute Autorité de Santé. https://www.has-sante.fr/jcms/c_1776178/fr/saed-un-guide-pour-faciliter-la-communication-entre-professionnels-de-sante

Henderson, R. W., & Landesman, E. M. (1993, February). The Interactive Videodisc System in the Zone of Proximal Development: Academic Motivation and Learning Outcomes in Precalculus. [Internet]. *Journal of Educational Computing Research*, *9*(1), 29–43. DOI: 10.2190/J53A-V7VT-22D0-VGEK

Hinkle, J. F. J. S. O. N. (2023). Personalization and Learning Outcome in a Nursing Pathophysiology and Pharmacology Course: Canvas© Mastery Adoption Pilot Study. *9*, 23779608231186030.

Holenko, M., & Hoic-Bozic, N. (2008). Using Online Discussions in a Blended Learning Course. International Journal of Emerging Technologies in Learning (iJET), pp. 18-23, Available at: <https://online-journals.org/index.php/i-jet/article/view/630>. doi:http://dx.doi.org/DOI: 10.3991/ijet.v3i0.630

Holland, A., Smith, F., McCrossan, G., Adamson, E., Watt, S., & Penny, K. (2013). Online video in clinical skills education of oral medication administration for undergraduate student nurses: A mixed methods, prospective cohort study. *Nurse Education Today*, *33*(6), 663–670. DOI: 10.1016/j.nedt.2012.01.006 PMID: 22341996

Honey, M., & Marshall, D. (2003, December). The impact of on-line multi-choice questions on undergraduate student nurses' learning. In *Proceedings of the 20th Annual Conference of the Australasian Society for Computers in Learning in Tertiary Education (ASCILITE)* (pp. 236-243).

Horiuchi, S., Yaju, Y., Koyo, M., Sakyo, Y., & Nakayama, K. (2009). Evaluation of a web-based graduate continuing nursing education program in Japan: A randomized controlled trial. *Nurse Education Today*, *29*(2), 140–149. DOI: 10.1016/j.nedt.2008.08.009 PMID: 18829141

Hsu, L.-L. (2011). Blended learning in ethics education: A survey of nursing students. *Nursing Ethics*, *18*(3), 418–430. DOI: 10.1177/0969733011398097 PMID: 21558117

Hsu, L.-L. (2012). Qualitative Assessment of a Blended Learning Intervention in an Undergraduate Nursing Course. *The Journal of Nursing Research*, *20*(4), 291–299. DOI: 10.1097/jnr.0b013e31827363bc PMID: 23154440

Hubbard, P. (2008). *Computer-assisted language learning: Critical concepts in linguistics*. Taylor & Francis.

Hudlicka, E. (2016). Virtual affective agents and therapeutic games. In *Artificial intelligence in behavioral and mental health care* (p. 81–115). Academic Press., DOI: 10.1016/B978-0-12-420248-1.00004-0

Hurst, R. A. (2024). Analysis of the Impact of Personalized Learning Paths in Mobile Learning Platforms on the Development of Self-Directed Learning Strategies Among Brazilian College Students. *Research and Advances in Education*, *3*(3), 9–14. DOI: 10.56397/RAE.2024.03.02

Iatrellis, O., Samaras, N., Dervenis, C., & Panagiotakopoulos, T. (2023, October). KONX: A Dynamic Approach for Explainable AI in Higher Education. In *Proceedings of the 7th International Conference on Algorithms, Computing and Systems* (p. 118-124). DOI: 10.1145/3631908.3631925

Iatrellis, O., Samaras, N., Kokkinos, K., & Panagiotakopoulos, T. (2024). Leveraging Generative AI for Sustainable Academic Advising : Enhancing Educational Practices through AI-Driven Recommendations. *Sustainability (Basel)*, *16*(17), 7829. DOI: 10.3390/su16177829

Idrizi, E. (2024, May). Exploring the Role of Explainable Artificial Intelligence (XAI) in Adaptive learning systems. In *Proceedings of the Cognitive Models and Artificial Intelligence Conference* (p. 100-105). DOI: 10.1145/3660853.3660877

Ilieva, G., Yankova, T., Klisarova-Belcheva, S., Dimitrov, A., Bratkov, M., & Angelov, D. (2023). Effects of generative chatbots in higher education. *Information (Basel)*, *14*(9), 492. DOI: 10.3390/info14090492

Iskender, A. (2023). Holy or unholy? Interview with open AI's ChatGPT. *European Journal of Tourism Research*, *34*(3414), 1–11. DOI: 10.54055/ejtr.v34i.3169

Jamal, A. (2023). The role of Artificial Intelligence (AI) in teacher education: Opportunities & challenges. *International Journal of Research and Analytical Reviews*, *10*(1), 140–146.

Jang, H. J., & Hong, S. Y. (2016). Effect of Blended Learning in Nursing Education. *International Journal of Multimedia and Ubiquitous Engineering*, *11*(5), 297–304. DOI: 10.14257/ijmue.2016.11.5.27

Jares, T. E., Wilcox, W., Cahalan, R., & Dickey, G. J. T. A. e. j. (2019). An examination of the effectiveness of online adaptive learning technologies. *29*(1).

Jarrahi, M. H. (2018). Artificial intelligence and the future of work: Human-AI symbiosis in organizational decision making. *Business Horizons, 61*(4), 577–586. DOI: 10.1016/j.bushor.2018.03.007

Jiao, H. (2015). Enhancing students' engagement in learning through a formative e-assessment tool that motivates students to take action on feedback. *Australasian Journal of Engineering Education, 20*(1), 9–18. DOI: 10.7158/D13-002.2015.20.1

Jin, S. et Peng, L. (2022). Perception en classe dans l'enseignement supérieur: impact des facteurs spatiaux sur la satisfaction des étudiants dans les cours magistral par rapport aux salles de classe d'apprentissage actif. Frontières en psychologie, 13, 941285

Johnson, D. W., & Johnson, R. T. J. E. r. (2009). An educational psychology success story: Social interdependence theory and cooperative learning. *38*(5), 365-379.

Johnson, L., Adams Becker, S., Cummins, M., Estrada, V., Freeman, A., & Hall, C. (2016). NMC Horizon Report: 2016 Higher Education Edition. Austin, Texas: The New Media Consortium. https://www.learntechlib.org/p/171478/

Johnson, D. (2023). Real-time AI support in immersive ESP environments. *Journal of Computer Assisted Learning, 39*(4), 392–406.

Jolin, J. S., Theophilus, A., & Kathirvel, A. (2025)," Two factor mutual authentication with fingerprint and MAC Address Validation", International Journal of Communication Networks and Information Security, Vol. 16, No. 6, 2024, pp. 56 – 68. Publisher:Institute of Information Technology, Kohat University of Science and Technology, ISSN:2076-0930 E-ISSN:2073-607X, DoI:DOI: 10.5815/ijcnis.2024.06.05

Josh Kumar, J. M. S. P., Kathirvel, A., Kirubakaran, N., Sivaraman, P., & Subramaniam, M. (2015). A unified approach for detecting and eliminating selfish nodes in MANETs using TBUT. *EURASIP Journal on Wireless Communications and Networking, 2015*, 1–11.

Jouquan, J., & Parent, F. (2013). *Les enjeux épistémologiques et méthodologiques de l'évaluation des pratiques professionnelles en santé. Parent F, Jouquan J. Penser la formation des professionnels de la santé. Une perspective intégrative*. De Boeck.

Jung, E., Kim, D., Yoon, M., Park, S., & Oakley, B. (2019). The influence of instructional design on learner control, sense of achievement, and perceived effectiveness in a supersize MOOC course. *Computers & Education, 128*, 377–388. DOI: 10.1016/j.compedu.2018.10.001

Ju, S. Y., & Adam, Z. (2018). Implementing Quizizz as game based learning in the Arabic classroom. *European Journal of Social Science Education and Research, 5*(1), 194–198. DOI: 10.26417/ejser.v12i1.p208-212

Kaaouachi, A. (2010). L'évaluation dans le système d'enseignement supérieur au Maroc: Bilan des réalisations, limites et principaux défis. Towards an Arab Higher Education Space: International Challenges and Societal Responsibilities, 409-422.

Kaaouachi, A. (2004). Evaluation des acquis des étudiants dans l'université marocaine. *Prospecfive Pédagogique*, *27*, 37–41.

Kaddouri, M., & Bouamri, A. (2010). Usage de plateformes d'enseignement à distance dans l'enseignement supérieur marocain: Avantages pédagogiques et difficultés d'appropriation. *Questions Vives*, *5*(14), 107–118. DOI: 10.4000/questionsvives.642

Kamal, N., Sarker, F., Rahman, A., Hossain, S., & Mamun, K. A. (2024). Recommender System in Academic Choices of Higher Education : A Systematic Review. *IEEE Access : Practical Innovations, Open Solutions*, *12*, 35475–35501. DOI: 10.1109/ACCESS.2024.3368058

Kanagasundaram, H., & Ayyaswamy, K. (2019). Multi Objective ALO Based Energy Efficient and Secure Routing OLSR Protocol in MANET. *International Journal of Intelligent Engineering & Systems*, *12*(1).

Kanagasundaram, H., & Kathirvel, A. (2019). EIMO-ESOLSR: Energy efficient and security-based model for OLSR routing protocol in mobile ad-hoc network. *IET Communications*, *13*(5), 553–559.

Kandlhofer, M., Steinbauer, G., Hirschmugl-Gaisch, S., & Huber, P. (2016, October). Artificial intelligence and computer science in education: From kindergarten to university. In 2016 IEEE frontiers in education conference (FIE) (p. 1-9). IEEE. DOI: DOI: 10.1109/FIE.2016.7757570

Karsenti, T. (2001). Pédagogies et nouvelles technologies: Former des enseignants pour le nouveau millénaire. Dans *Actes du IXe sommet de la Francophonie, Colloque Éthique et nouvelles Technologies, l'appropriation des savoirs en question* (Beyrouth, 24–28 septembre).

Karsenti, T. (2002). L'alphabétisation et les technologies de l'information à l'aube du nouveau millénaire: Nouvelle conception, nouvelles perspectives. *Canadian Journal for the Study of Adult Education*, *15*(2), 37–60. DOI: 10.56105/cjsae.v15i2.1916

Kasneci, E., Seßler, K., Küchemann, S., Bannert, M., Dementieva, D., Fischer, F., Gasser, U., Groh, G., Günnemann, S., Hüllermeier, E., Krusche, S., Kutyniok, G., Michaeli, T., Nerdel, C., Pfeffer, J., Poquet, O., Sailer, M., Schmidt, A., Seidel, T., & Kasneci, G. (2023). ChatGPT for good? On opportunities and challenges of large language models for education. *Learning and Individual Differences*, *103*, 102274. DOI: 10.1016/j.lindif.2023.102274

Kathirvel, A., & Gandu, S. P. (2023, May). Systematic number plate detection using improved yolov5 detector. In 2023 2nd International Conference on Vision Towards Emerging Trends in Communication and Networking Technologies (ViTECoN) (pp. 1-6). IEEE.

Kathirvel, A., & Maheswaran, C. P. (2024i), "Chapter 8: Enhanced AI-Based Intrusion Detection and Response System for WSN", Artificial Intelligence for Intrusion Detection Systems, CRC Publiser/Chapman and Hall, New York, 1st Edition, 2023, ISBN 978-100096755-5, 978-103238665-2 DOI eBook ISBN 9781003346340DOI: 10.1201/9781003346340-8

Kathirvel, A., & Shobitha, M. (2023). Digital Assets Fair Estimation Using Artificial Intelligence. Institute of Electrical and Electronics Engineers Inc, 10.

Kathirvel, A., Das, D., Kirubakaran, S., Subramaniam, M., & Naveneethan, S. (2022). Based Mobile Bill Payment System Using Biometric Fingerprint. Recurrent Neural Networks: Concepts and Applications, 233.

Kathirvel, A., Maheswaran, C. P., Subramaniam, M., & Naren, A. K. (2023a), "Chapter 25: Quantum Computers Based on Distributed Computing Systems for the Next Generation: Overview and Applications", Quantum Computers Based on Distributed Computing Systems for the Next Generation, Handbook of Research on Quantum Computing for Smart Environments, IGI Global Publiser, Hershey, Pennsylvania, USA, March 2023. ISBN13: 9781668466971 ISBN10: 166846697X EISBN13: 9781668466988, DOI: DOI: 10.4018/978-1-6684-6697-1.ch025

Kathirvel, A., Naren, A. K., & Gobinath, V. M and C. P. Maheswaran (2025a). "Chapter 3: Effective Leadership Strategies for Enhancing Student Success in Higher Education" In New Horizons in Leadership: Inclusive Explorations in Health, Technology, and Education, Hershey, PA: IGI Global, 2025, pp. 61–91. ISBN13: 9798369364376, EISBN13: 9798369364390, DOI: DOI: 10.4018/979-8-3693-6437-6.ch003

Kathirvel, A., Sabarinathan, C., Saravanan, N., & Ramesh, S. Meera, Karnavel K and Sudha D (2023d), "Chapter 9: Artificial Intelligence-Based Bill System: Fingerprint Mechanism", METHODS, IMPLEMENTATION, AND APPLICATION OF CYBER SECURITY INTELLIGENCE AND ANALYTICS, IGI Global Publiser, Hershey, Pennsylvania, USA ISBN13: 9781668439913 ISBN10: 1668439913 EISBN13: 9781668439937 DOI: 10.4018/978-1-6684-3991-3.ch009

Kathirvel, A., Subramaniam, M., Navaneethan, S., & Sabarinath, C. (2021), "Improved IDR Response System for Sensor Network", Journal of Web Engineering, Vol. 20 1, 53–88, 2021. Publisher: © River Publishers, 15 Feb 2021, ISSN: 1540-9589 (Print Version). ISSN: 1544-5976 (Online Version), DOI: 10.13052/jwe1540-9589.2013

Kathirvel, A., Sudha, R., & Devanai Sundaram, R. M. (2009), "A System of Tool for Identifying Ragas Using MIDI," IEEE Second International Conference on Computer and Electrical Engineering, Dubai, UAE, Vol. 2, 2009, pp. 644 – 647. Article number 53802592009 International Conference on Computer and Electrical Engineering, ICCEE 2009 28th– 30th December 2009 ISBN 978-076953925-6 DOI: https://ieeexplore.ieee.org/document/5380259DOI: 10.1109/ICCEE.2009.49

Kathirvel, A. (2024e). Applications of Serverless Computing: Systematic Overview. In Aluvalu, R., & Maheswari, U. (Eds.), *Serverless Computing Concepts, Technology and Architecture* (Vol. 221-233). IGI Global., DOI: 10.4018/979-8-3693-1682-5.ch014

Kathirvel, A. (2024g). Innovation and Industry Application: IoT-Based Robotics Frontier of Automation in Industry Application. In Satishkumar, D., & Sivaraja, M. (Eds.), *Internet of Things and AI for Natural Disaster Management and Prediction* (pp. 83–105). IGI Global., DOI: 10.4018/979-8-3693-4284-8.ch004

Kathirvel, A., Gobinath, V. M., Naren, A. K., & Maheswaran, C. P. (2025b). AI-based automated disease detection based on symptoms healthcare for pets and birds. In *AI and the Revival of Big Data* (pp. 311–345). IGI Global., DOI: 10.4018/979-8-3693-8472-5.ch014

Kathirvel, A., & Naren, A. K. (2024h). Diabetes and Pre-Diabetes Prediction by AI Using Tuned XGB Classifier. In Khang, A. (Ed.), *Medical Robotics and AI-Assisted Diagnostics for a High-Tech Healthcare Industry* (pp. 52–64). IGI Global., DOI: 10.4018/979-8-3693-2105-8.ch004

Kathirvel, A., Naren, A. K., & Santhoshi, B. (2024c). Business Intelligent and Blockchain in Entrepreneurship. In *Entrepreneurship Innovation and Education for Performance Improvement*. IGI Global., DOI: 10.4018/979-8-3693-7903-5.ch015

Kathirvel, A., Naren, A. K., & Subramanian, C. (2024b). Intelligent Serverless Computing Technology and Recent Trends: A Review. In *Driving Transformative Technology Trends with Cloud Computing*. IGI Global., DOI: 10.4018/979-8-3693-2869-9.ch002

Kathirvel, A., Navaneethan, S., & Subramaniam, M. (2023b). *EIDR Umpiring Security Models for Wireless Sensor Network", ARTIFICIAL INTELLIGENT TECHNIQUES FOR WIRELESS COMMUNICATION AND NETWORKING*. Scrivener Publishing, John Wiley & Sons., DOI: 10.1002/9781119821809.ch19

Kathirvel, A., & Srinivasan, R. (2010). Enhanced triple umpiring system for security and performance improvement in wireless MANETS. *International Journal of Communication Networks and Information Security*, *2*(2), 77.

Kathirvel, A., & Srinivasan, R. (2011a). ETUS: An enhanced triple umpiring system for security and performance improvement of mobile ad hoc networks. *International Journal of Network Management*, *21*(5), 341–359.

Kathirvel, A., Subramaniam, M., & Rajabushanam, C. (2011). Burglar detecting system for wireless mobile ad hoc network. *European Journal of Scientific Research*, *62*(1), 14–23.

Katsaris, I., & Vidakis, N. (2021). Adaptive e-learning systems through learning styles: A review of the literature. *Advances in Mobile Learning Educational Research*, *1*(2), 124–145. DOI: 10.25082/AMLER.2021.02.007

Kayalı, B., & Balat, Ş. (2024). Assessment, Evaluation, and Feedback in Online Education With Artificial Intelligence-Supported Tools. In *AI Algorithms and ChatGPT for Student Engagement in Online Learning* (p. 124–135). IGI Global. DOI: 10.4018/979-8-3693-4268-8.ch008

Keefe, G., & Wharrad, H. J. (2012). Using e-learning to enhance nursing students' pain management education. *Nurse Education Today*, *32*(8), e66–e72. DOI: 10.1016/j.nedt.2012.03.018 PMID: 22513154

Kerr, A. (2011). L'enseignement et l'apprentissage dans les classes nombreuses des universités ontariennes: Teaching and learning in large classes at Ontario universities: an exploratory study.

Khosravi, H., Shum, S. B., Chen, G., Conati, C., Tsai, Y., Kay, J., Knight, S., Martinez-Maldonado, R., Sadiq, S., & Gašević, D. (2022). Explainable Artificial Intelligence in education. *Computers and Education Artificial Intelligence*, *3*, 100074. DOI: 10.1016/j.caeai.2022.100074

Kiesler, C. A. (1971). The psychology of commitment: Experiments linking behavior to belief.

Kim, H. S., Kim, M. Y., Cho, M. K., & Jang, S. J. J. I. J. o. N. P. (2017). Effectiveness of applying flipped learning to clinical nursing practicums for nursing students in Korea: A randomized controlled trial. *23*(5), e12574.

Kim, P., Suh, E., & Song, D. (2015). Development of a design-based learning curriculum through design-based research for a technology-enabled science classroom. *Educational Technology Research and Development*, *63*(4), 575–602. DOI: 10.1007/s11423-015-9376-7

Kim, Y. M., Yoon, Y. S., Hong, H. C., & Min, A. (2019). Effects of a patient safety course using a flipped classroom approach among undergraduate nursing students: A quasi-experimental study. *Nurse Education Today*, *79*, 180–187. Advance online publication. DOI: 10.1016/j.nedt.2019.05.033 PMID: 31153088

Kirubakaran, N., & Kathirvel, A. (2014). Performance improvement of security attacks in wireless mobile adhoc networks. *Asian Journal of Information Technology*, *13*(2), 68–76.

Kiselev, P., Kiselev, B., Matsuta, V., Feshchenko, A., Bogdanovskaya, I., & Kosheleva, A. (2020). Career guidance based on machine learning : Social networks in professional identity construction. *Procedia Computer Science*, *169*, 158–163. DOI: 10.1016/j.procs.2020.02.128

Kizilcec, R. F., Pérez-Sanagustín, M., & Maldonado, J. J. (2017). Self-regulated learning strategies predict learner behavior and goal attainment in Massive Open Online Courses. *Computers & Education*, *104*, 18–33.

Kizilcec, R. F., Piech, C., & Schneider, E. (2013). Deconstructing disengagement: analyzing learner subpopulations in massive open online courses. *Proceedings of the third international conference on learning analytics and knowledge.*

Koneri Chandrasekaran, S., Savarimuthu, P., Andi Elumalai, P., & Ayyaswamy, K. (2015). Primary path reservation using enhanced slot assignment in TDMA for session admission. *TheScientificWorldJournal*, *2015*(1), 405974.

Kong, S. C., Cheung, W. M. Y., & Zhang, G. (2022). Evaluating artificial intelligence literacy courses for fostering conceptual learning, literacy and empowerment in university students: Refocusing to conceptual building. *Computers in Human Behavior Reports*, *7*, 100223. DOI: 10.1016/j.chbr.2022.100223

Kozanitis, A. (2021). Évaluation des apprentissages en formation à distance: les situations authentiques à la rescousse. Revue internationale des technologies en pédagogie universitaire, 18(1), 276-290.

Krajcik, J. S., Blumenfeld, P. C., Marx, R. W., Bass, K. M., Fredricks, J., & Soloway, E. (1998). Inquiry in project-based science classrooms: Initial attempts by middle school students. *Journal of the Learning Sciences*, *7*(3–4), 313–350. DOI: 10.1080/10508406.1998.9672057

Kuh, G. D., Cruce, T. M., Shoup, R., Kinzie, J., & Gonyea, R. M. (2008). Unmasking the effects of student engagement on first-year college grades and persistence. *The Journal of Higher Education*, *79*(5), 540–563. DOI: 10.1080/00221546.2008.11772116

Kuhlthau, C. C., & Maniotes, L. K. (2010). *Guided inquiry: Learning in the 21st century. Libraries Unlimited. Levy, J. C. (2015). Adaptive learning and the human condition*. Routledge.

Kumar, J., & Kathirvel, A. (2019). Analysis and ideas for improved routing in MANET.

Kumar, J. J., & Kathirvel, A. (2018). Optimum Power Management in Mobile Ad-Hoc Networks. *Journal of Engineering Science and Technology*, *13*(6), 1805–1815.

Kumawat, K. (2024). Explainable AI: Interpretable models for transparent decision-making. *International Journal of Food and Nutritional Science*, *9*(3). DOI: 10.48047/IJFANS/09/03/30

Labadze, L., Grigolia, M., & Machaidze, L. (2023). Role of AI chatbots in education: Systematic literature review. *International Journal of Educational Technology in Higher Education*, *20*(1), 56. DOI: 10.1186/s41239-023-00426-1

Ladage, C., & Audran, J. (2011). Questions et test en ligne sur des plateformes EIAH: Des pratiques rétrocognitives réinterrogées par l'analyse des traces. Conférence EIAH 2011 Environnements informatiques pour l'apprentissage humain, 381-393. https://hal.archives-ouvertes.fr/hal00611391/document

Laskar, M. T. R., Bari, M. S., Rahman, M., Bhuiyan, M. A. H., Joty, S., & Huang, J. X. (2023). A systematic study and comprehensive evaluation of ChatGPT on benchmark datasets. arXiv preprint arXiv:2305.18486. /arXiv.2305.18486DOI: 10.18653/v1/2023.findings-acl.29

Lavoie, D., Stelios, A., & Mondragon Regalado, N. (2024). Immersive learning platforms: The role of VR in competency-based learning in higher education. *Frontiers in Education*, *9*, 734–754.

Le Levier, C., Cluzel, F., Hadjeb, L., & Lemée, F. (2018). Transposition de la méthodologie SAED en formation aide-soignante. *L'Aide-Soignante*, *32*(202), 26–28. DOI: 10.1016/j.aidsoi.2018.10.009

Leduc, D., Kozanitis, A., & Lepage, I. (2018). L'engagement cognitif en contexte postsecondaire: Traduction, adaptation et validation d'une échelle de mesure. *McGill Journal of Education*, *53*(3). Advance online publication. DOI: 10.7202/1058412ar

Legros, D., de Pembroke, E. M., & Talbi, A. (2002). Les théories de l'apprentissage et les systèmes multimédias. [Learning theories and multimedia systems] In Legros, D., & Crinon, J. (Eds.), *Psychologie des apprentissages et multimédia* [Psychology of learning and multimedia]. (pp. 23–39). Armand Colin.

Leonard, M., Graham, S., & Bonacum, D. (2004). The human factor: The critical importance of effective teamwork and communication in providing safe care. *BMJ Quality & Safety*, *13*(suppl 1), i85–i90. DOI: 10.1136/qshc.2004.010033 PMID: 15465961

Lepage, I. (2018). L'influence d'une e-évaluation dynamique sur l'engagement cognitif d'étudiants en contexte de grand groupe à l'université.

Leung, C. (2007). Dynamic assessment: Assessment for and as teaching? *Language Assessment Quarterly*, *4*(3), 257–278. DOI: 10.1080/15434300701481127

Lewis, C. E., Chen, D. C., & Relan, A. (2018). Implementation of a flipped classroom approach to promote active learning in the third-year surgery clerkship. *American Journal of Surgery*, *215*(2), 298–303. DOI: 10.1016/j.amjsurg.2017.08.050 PMID: 29169824

Li, C., He, J., Yuan, C., Chen, B., & Sun, Z. (2019). The effects of blended learning on knowledge, skills, and satisfaction in nursing students: A meta-analysis. *Nurse Education Today*, *82*, 51–57. Advance online publication. DOI: 10.1016/j.nedt.2019.08.004 PMID: 31437783

Li, J., & Ye, Z. (2020). Course Recommendations in Online Education Based on Collaborative Filtering Recommendation Algorithm. *Complexity*, *2020*, 1–10. DOI: 10.1155/2020/8882813

Limonova, V., Santos, A., São Mamede, H., & Filipe, V. (2023). The research context of artificial intelligence and gamification to improve student engagement and attendance in higher education.

Lim, W. M., Gunasekara, A., Pallant, J. L., Pallant, J. I., & Pechenkina, E. (2023). Generative AI and the future of education: Ragnarök or reformation? A paradoxical perspective from management educators. *International Journal of Management Education, 21*(2), 100790. DOI: 10.1016/j.ijme.2023.100790

Lipton, Z. C. (2018). The mythos of model interpretability: In machine learning, the concept of interpretability is both important and slippery. *ACM Queue; Tomorrow's Computing Today, 16*(3), 31–57. DOI: 10.1145/3236386.3241340

Liriwati, F. Y. (2023). Transformasi Kurikulum. *Kecerdasan Buatan Untuk Membangun Pendidikan Yang Relevan di Masa Depan., 1*, 62–71.

Li, S., & Li, X. (2020). Collaborative Filtering Recommendation Algorithm Based on User Characteristics and User Interests. *Journal of Physics: Conference Series, 1616*(1), 012032. DOI: 10.1088/1742-6596/1616/1/012032

Lison, C., Bédard, D., Beaucher, C., & Trudelle, D. (2014). De l'innovation à un modèle de dynamique innovationnelle en enseignement supérieur. Revue internationale de pédagogie de l'enseignement supérieur, 30(30 (1)).

Lison, C. (2011). *Programmes innovants en formation des enseignants du secondaire: perceptions, conceptions et pratiques*. Université de Sherbrooke.

Liu, Q., & Khalil, M. (2024, May). Explainable AI in Learning Analytics: Improving Predictive Models and Advancing Transparency Trust. In *2024 IEEE Global Engineering Education Conference (EDUCON)* (p. 1-7). IEEE. DOI: 10.1109/EDUCON60312.2024.10578733

Liu, Q., Peng, W., Zhang, F., Hu, R., Li, Y., & Yan, W. (2016). The Effectiveness of Blended Learning in Health Professions: Systematic Review and Meta-Analysis. *Journal of Medical Internet Research, 18*(1), e2. DOI: 10.2196/jmir.4807 PMID: 26729058

Liu, R., Qiao, X., & Liu, Y. (2006). A paradigm shift of learner-centered teaching style: Reality or illusion? *Journal of Second Language Acquisition and Teaching, 13*, 77–91.

Liu, Y. (2023). Explainable artificial intelligence and its practical applications. *Applied and Computational Engineering, 4*(1), 755–759. DOI: 10.54254/2755-2721/4/2023419

Li, Z., Tsai, M.-H., Tao, J., & Lorentz, C. (2014). Switching to blended learning: The impact on students' academic performance. *Journal of Nursing Education and Practice, 4*(3). Advance online publication. DOI: 10.5430/jnep.v4n3p245

Lo, C. K. (2023). What is the impact of ChatGPT on education? A rapid review of the literature. *Education Sciences*, *13*(4), 410. DOI: 10.3390/educsci13040410

Long, D., & Magerko, B. (2020, April). What is AI literacy? Competencies and design considerations. In *Proceedings of the 2020 CHI conference on human factors in computing systems* (p. 1-16). DOI: 10.1145/3313831.3376727

Luckin, R., & Holmes, W. (2016). Intelligence unleashed: An argument for AI in education

Lu, H. (2020). Online learning: The meanings of student engagement. *Education Journal*, *9*(3), 73–79. DOI: 10.11648/j.edu.20200903.13

Lukpat, A. (2023). ChatGPT banned in New York City public schools over concerns about cheating, learning development. The Wall Street Journal.https://www.wsj.com/articles/chatgpt-banned-in-new-york-city-public-schools-over-concerns-about-cheating-learning-development-11673024059

Majumdar, R., Takami, K., & Ogata, H. (2023, July). Learning with Explainable AI-Recommendations at School: Extracting Patterns of Self-Directed Learning from Learning Logs. In *2023 IEEE International Conference on Advanced Learning Technologies (ICALT)* (p. 245-249). IEEE. DOI: 10.1109/ICALT58122.2023.00078

Makransky, G., & Petersen, G. B. (2021). Investigating the impact of VR on student engagement and retention in higher education. *Computers & Education*, *166*, 104129. DOI: 10.1016/j.compedu.2021.104129

Mandran, N., Prior, E., & Vermeulen, M. (2020). Comment outiller la méthode Design-Based-Research?.

Mandran, N., Planche, M., Marzin-Janvier, P., Vermeulen, M., Karoui, A., Ham, C. D., & Hoffmann, C. (2021). Comment construire un processus d'évaluation en EIAH fondé sur le Design-Based Research? *Sciences et Technologies de l'Information et de la Communication pour l'Éducation et la Formation*, *28*(1), 139–168.

Margaryan, A., Nicol, D., Littlejohn, A., & Trinder, K. (2008). Students' use of technologies to support formal and informal learning. In Luca, J., & Weippl, E. (Éds.), *Proceedings of World Conference on Educational Multimedia, Hypermedia and Telecommunications (ED-MEDIA) 2008* (pp. 4257–4266). Chesapeake, VA: Association for the Advancement of Computing in Education (AACE).

Martell, K. (2007). Assessing student learning: Are business schools making the grade? *Journal of Education for Business*, *82*(4), 189–195. DOI: 10.3200/JOEB.82.4.189-195

Martin, F., Chen, Y., Moore, R. L., Westine, C. D. J. E. T. R., & Development. (2020). Systematic review of adaptive learning research designs, context, strategies, and technologies from 2009 to 2018. *68*(4), 1903-1929.

Mastafi, M., & Bouhlou, H. (2016). Intégration des TIC dans l'enseignement supérieur marocain: réflexions et perspectives. Penser les TIC dans les universités du Maghreb.

Ma, W., Adesope, O. O., Nesbit, J. C., & Liu, Q. (2014). Intelligent tutoring systems and learning outcomes: A meta-analysis. *Journal of Educational Psychology*, *106*(4), 901–918. DOI: 10.1037/a0037123

McClelland, D. C. (1985). How motives, skills, and values determine what people do. *The American Psychologist*, *40*(7), 812–825. DOI: 10.1037/0003-066X.40.7.812

McDonald, R. (2020). Virtual reality labs for remote learning: A new approach to science education. *Educational Technology Research and Development*, *68*, 1723–1737.

McGaghie, W. C., Issenberg, S. B., Cohen, E. R., Barsuk, J. H., & Wayne, D. B. (2011). Does Simulation-Based Medical Education With Deliberate Practice Yield Better Results Than Traditional Clinical Education? A Meta-Analytic Comparative Review of the Evidence. *Academic Medicine*, *86*(6), 706–711. DOI: 10.1097/ACM.0b013e318217e119 PMID: 21512370

McGarr, O. (2009). A review of podcasting in higher education: Its influence on the traditional lecture. *Australasian Journal of Educational Technology*, *25*(3), 25. DOI: 10.14742/ajet.1136

McKeachie, W. J. (1978). *Teaching tips: A guidebook for the beginning college teacher*. DC Heath.

McKenney, S., & Reeves, T. (2018). *Conducting educational design research*. Routledge., DOI: 10.1145/2460296.2460330

McLaughlin, J. E., Roth, M. T., Glatt, D. M., Gharkholonarehe, N., Davidson, C. A., Griffin, L. M., Esserman, D. A., & Mumper, R. J. (2014). The Flipped Classroom. *Academic Medicine*, *89*(2), 236–243. DOI: 10.1097/ACM.0000000000000086 PMID: 24270916

McLeod, S., & Graber, J. (2018). *Harnessing technology for deeper learning: Solutions for creating the learning spaces students deserve*. Solution Tree Press.

Means, B., Toyama, Y., Murphy, R., Bakia, M., & Jones, K. (2009). Evaluation of evidence-based practices in online learning: A meta-analysis and review of online learning studies.

Messaoudi, A. (2024). The challenges of AI in education: from data protection to algorithmic biases. Mediations & mediatizations, (18), 148-160. DOI: 10.52358/mm.vi18.409

Michel-Villarreal, R., Vilalta-Perdomo, E., Salinas-Navarro, D. E., Thierry-Aguilera, R., & Gerardou, F. S. (2023). Challenges and opportunities of generative AI for higher education as explained by ChatGPT. *Education Sciences, 13*(9), 856. DOI: 10.3390/educsci13090856

Michiels, I. (2018). Etude de l'impact potentiel d'une formation par e-learning au Situation-Background-Assessment Recommendation (SBAR) auprès d'étudiants infirmiers (Master's thesis). https://luck.synhera.be/bitstream/handle/123456789/300/18%20mai-MICHIELS%20Isabelle-M2%20PASI-Me%20moire-1.pdf?sequence=1

Miller, M., & Hegelheimer, V. (2006). The SIMs meet ESL: Integrating computer gaming into the language curriculum. *Computer Assisted Language Learning, 19*(5), 456–489.

Miller, R. B., Greene, B. A., Montalvo, G. P., Ravindran, B., & Nichols, J. D. (1996). Engagement in academic work: The role of learning goals, future consequences, pleasing others, and perceived ability. *Contemporary Educational Psychology, 21*(4), 388–422. DOI: 10.1006/ceps.1996.0028 PMID: 8979871

Ministry of Higher Education, Scientific Research, and Innovation. (2025). *Official website of the Ministry of Higher Education, Scientific Research, and Innovation.* https://www.enssup.gov.ma/fr

Mirowsky, J. (2017). *Education, social status, and health.* Routledge. DOI: 10.4324/9781351328081

Missildine, K., Fountain, R., Summers, L., & Gosselin, K. (2013). Flipping the Classroom to Improve Student Performance and Satisfaction. Journal of Nursing Education, 52(10), 597 599. DOI: 10.3928/01484834-20130919-03

Mohamed, M. H., Khafagy, M. H., & Ibrahim, M. H. (2019). Recommender Systems Challenges and Solutions Survey. *2019 International Conference on Innovative Trends in Computer Engineering (ITCE)*, 149-155. DOI: 10.1109/ITCE.2019.8646645

Mohana Geetha, D., Muthusundar, S. K., Subramaniam, M., & Ayyaswamy, K. (2015). Temporary redundant transmission mechanism for SCTP multihomed hosts. *TheScientificWorldJournal, 2015*(1), 158697.

Moharm, K. (2019). A Framework for Adaptive Personalized E-learning Recommender Systems. *International Journal of Intelligent Information Systems*, *8*(1), 12. DOI: 10.11648/j.ijiis.20190801.13

Montiel-Ruiz, FJ and López Ruiz, M. (2023). L'intelligence artificielle comme ressource pédagogique dans une école groupée rurale. Revue interuniversitaire RiiTE de recherche en technologie éducative, (15), 28-40. DOI: 10.6018/riite.592031

Morgan, D. L. (1996). *Focus groups as qualitative research* (Vol. 16). Sage publications.

Morocho-Cayamcela, M. E., Lee, H., & Lim, W. (2019). Machine learning for 5G/B5G mobile and wireless communications: Potential, limitations, and future directions. *IEEE Access : Practical Innovations, Open Solutions*, *7*, 137184–137206. DOI: 10.1109/ACCESS.2019.2942390

Morris, M. R. (2023). Scientists' Perspectives on the Potential for Generative AI in their Fields. arXiv preprint arXiv:2304.01420.

Morroco, C. C., Walker, A., & Lewis, L. R. (2003). Access to a schoolwide thinking curriculum: Leadership challenges and solutions. *Journal of Special Education Leadership*, *1*(1), 5–14.

Moybeka, A. M., Syariatin, N., Tatipang, D. P., Mushthoza, D. A., Dewi, N. P. J. L., & Tineh, S. (2023). Artificial Intelligence and English classroom: The implications of AI toward EFL students' motivation. Edumaspul. *Jurnal Pendidikan*, *7*(2), 2444–2454.

Naciri, A., Hajji, M. E., Radid, M., Kharbach, A., & Chemsi, G. J. E. J. o. G. M. (2022). Exploring Student Motivation and Performance in the Flipped Classroom: A Case Study of Nursing Students. *19*(3).

Nandi, D., Hamilton, M., & Harland, J. (2012). Evaluating the quality of interaction in asynchronous discussion forums in fully online courses. *Distance Education*, *33*(1), 5–30. DOI: 10.1080/01587919.2012.667957

Nandi, D., Hamilton, M., Harland, J., & Warburton, G. (2011). How active are students in online discussion forums? *Proceedings of the Thirteenth Australasian Computing Education Conference* - Volume 114. 125–134

Naren, A. K., Kathirvel, A., & Santhoshi, B. (2024). "Chapter 5: Critical Approaches to Data Engineering Systems Innovation and Industry Application Using IoT" In Critical Approaches to Data Engineering Systems and Analysis, Hershey, PA: IGI Global, 2024.DoI: DOI: 10.4018/979-8-3693-2260-4.ch005

Neugebauer, S. R., Galloway, E. P., & Dobbs, C. L. (2023). *Reimagining language instruction: New approaches to promoting equity*. Teachers College Press.

Newman, A., Bryant, G., Stokes, P., & Squeo, T. (2013). Learning to adapt: Understanding the adaptive learning supplier landscape. Tyton Partners white paper

Ng, D. T. K., Leung, J. K. L., Chu, K. W. S., & Qiao, M. S. (2021). AI literacy: Definition, teaching, evaluation and ethical issues. *Proceedings of the Association for Information Science and Technology*, *58*(1), 504–509. DOI: 10.1002/pra2.487

Nguyen, A., Kremantzis, M., Essien, A., Petrounias, I., & Hosseini, S. (2024). Enhancing student engagement through artificial intelligence (AI): Understanding the basics, opportunities, and challenges. *Journal of University Teaching & Learning Practice*, *21*(06). DOI: 10.53761/caraaq92

Nguyen, T. P. V., Lee, Y. F., Le, T. H., Nguyen, H. B. N. J. I. J. I., & Technology, E. (2023). Applying a Formative Assessment Model for a Blended Learning Environment to Promote Students'. *Engagement and Motivation.*, *13*(11), 1735–1740.

Nicol, D. J., & Macfarlane-Dick, D. J. S. i. h. e. (2006). Formative assessment and self-regulated learning: A model and seven principles of good feedback practice. *31*(2), 199-218.

Nieminen, J. H., Bearman, M., & Ajjawi, R. (2023). Designing the digital in authentic assessment: Is it fit for purpose? *Assessment & Evaluation in Higher Education*, *48*(4), 529–543.

Nortvig, A.-M., Petersen, A. K., & Balle, S. H. J. E. J. o. E.-l. (2018). A literature review of the factors influencing e-learning and blended learning in relation to learning outcome, student satisfaction and engagement. *16*(1), pp46-55-pp46-55.

Ntoutsi, E., Fafalios, P., Gadiraju, U., Iosifidis, V., Nejdl, W., Vidal, M. E., Ruggieri, S., Turini, F., Papadopoulos, S., Krasanakis, E., Kompatsiaris, I., Kinder-Kurlanda, K., Wagner, C., Karimi, F., Fernandez, M., Alani, H., Berendt, B., Kruegel, T., Heinze, C., & Staab, S. (2020). Bias in data-driven artificial intelligence systems—An introductory survey. *Wiley Interdisciplinary Reviews. Data Mining and Knowledge Discovery*, *10*(3), e1356. DOI: 10.1002/widm.1356

Nunnally, J. C. (1978). *Théorie psychométrique (2e édition)*. Jossey-Bass.

Ogata, H., Flanagan, B., Takami, K., Dai, Y., Nakamoto, R., & Takii, K. (2024). EXAIT: Educational eXplainable artificial intelligent tools for personalized learning. *Research and Practice in Technology Enhanced Learning*, 19.

Oliveira, M. (s. d.). *Intelligence artificielle appliquée au processus de recrutement—Les perceptions des recruteurs.*

Oulmaati, K., Ezzahri, S., & Samadi, K. (2017). Usage des TIC et apprentissages des étudiants inscrits en études islamiques à l'Université Abdelmalek Essaadi. *Revue internationale des technologies en pédagogie universitaire, 14*(1), 40. https://doi.org/DOI: 10.18162/ritpu-2017-v14n1-03

Ouoba, N. E. (2024). L'intégration des outils d'intelligence artificielle dans l'enseignement supérieur: perceptions, usages et défis. *Les Cahiers de l'ACAREF, 4.*

Ouzzani, M., Hammady, H., Fedorowicz, Z., & Elmagarmid, A. (2016). Rayyan—A web and mobile app for systematic reviews. *Systematic Reviews*, *5*(1), 1–10. DOI: 10.1186/s13643-016-0384-4 PMID: 27919275

Ozverir, I., Osam, U. V., & Herrington, J. (2017). Investigating the effects of authentic activities on foreign language learning: A design-based research approach. *Journal of Educational Technology & Society*, *20*(4), 261–274.

Page, M. J., McKenzie, J. E., Bossuyt, P. M., Boutron, I., Hoffmann, T. C., Mulrow, C. D., Shamseer, L., Tetzlaff, J. M., Akl, E. A., Brennan, S. E., Chou, R., Glanville, J., Grimshaw, J. M., Hróbjartsson, A., Lalu, M. M., Li, T., Loder, E. W., Mayo-Wilson, E., McDonald, S., & Moher, D. (2021). The PRISMA 2020 statement: An updated guideline for reporting systematic reviews. *BMJ (Clinical Research Ed.)*, *372*(71), n71. Advance online publication. DOI: 10.1136/bmj.n71 PMID: 33782057

Panagiotidis, P., Krystalli, P., & Arvanitis, P. (2018). Technology as a motivational factor in foreign language learning. *European Journal of Education*, *6*(1), 69–84. DOI: 10.2478/ejed-2023-0007

Pangandaman HK (2018). Effects of Flipped Classroom Videos in the Return Demonstration Performance of Nursing Students. Sch J Appl Sci Res Vol: 1, Issu: 4 (55-58).

Pappas, I. O., Giannakos, M. N., & Mikalef, P. J. J. o. C. i. H. E. (2017). Investigating students' use and adoption of with-video assignments: lessons learnt for video-based open educational resources. *29*, 160-177.

Parent, S. (2014). De la motivation à l'engagement: un processus multidimensionnel lié à la réussite de vos étudiants. Pédagogie collégiale vol. 27, no 3, printemps 2014.

Park, E. O., & Park, J. H. (2017). Quasi-experimental study on the effectiveness of a flipped classroom for teaching adult health nursing: Flipped learning in adult health nursing. *Japan Journal of Nursing Science*, *15*(2), 125–134. DOI: 10.1111/jjns.12176 PMID: 28834418

Patanwala, A. E., Erstad, B. L., & Murphy, J. E. (2017). Student use of flipped classroom videos in a therapeutics course. *Currents in Pharmacy Teaching & Learning*, *9*(1), 50–54. DOI: 10.1016/j.cptl.2016.08.043 PMID: 29180154

Patel, D., Patel, F., & Chauhan, U. (2023). Recommendation Systems : Types, Applications, and Challenges. *International Journal of Computing and Digital Systems*, *13*(1), 851–868. DOI: 10.12785/ijcds/130168

Patel, N. (2022). Artificial intelligence tutors for ESP learners in virtual environments. *Journal of Language and Technology*, *20*(3), 221–237.

Patmanthara, S., Febiharsa, D., & Dwiyanto, F. A. (2019, October). Social media as a learning media: A comparative analysis of Youtube, WhatsApp, Facebook and Instagram utillization. In *2019 International Conference on Electrical, Electronics and Information Engineering (ICEEIE)* (Vol. 6, p. 183-186). IEEE. DOI: DOI: 10.1109/ICEEIE47180.2019.8981441

Pavani, A., & Kathirvel, A. (2023, April). Machine learning and deep learning algorithms for network data analytics function in 5G cellular networks. In *2023 International Conference on Inventive Computation Technologies (ICICT)* (pp. 28-33). IEEE.

Pavlik, J. V. (2023). Collaborating With ChatGPT: Considering the Implications of Generative Artificial.Intelligence for Journalism and Media Education. Journalism & Mass Communication Educator, 107769582211495–. DOI: 10.1177/10776958221149577

Pease, B. (2021). *Undoing privilege: Unearned advantage and systemic injustice in an unequal world*. Bloomsbury Publishing.

Pelaccia, T. (2016). *Comment (mieux) former et évaluer les étudiants en médecine et en sciences de la santé* [How to better train and assess medical and health science students]. Edition De Boeck Supérieur.

Pelz, B. (2004). (My) three principles of effective online pedagogy. *Journal of Asynchronous Learning Networks*, *8*(3), 33–46.

Peraya, D. (2017). *Au centre des Mooc, les capsules vidéo: un renouveau de la télévision éducative?* [At the heart of MOOCs, video capsules: a renewal of educational television?]. Distances et médiations des savoirs, 17. Retrieved from https://journals.openedition.org/dms/1738

Peraya, D. (2019a). Entre l'enseignement et la recherche, quelle place pour les Learning Analytics ? Distances et médiations des savoirs, 27, 1-4. DOI: 10.4000/dms.4080

Peraya, D. (2019b). Les Learning Analytics, entre fantasmes et réalités. Distances et médiations des savoirs, 28, 1-3. DOI: 10.4000/dms.4599

Perrier, C. (2014). L'apprentissage du raisonnement clinique infirmier par vignette clinique courte: Étude exploratoire [Learning nursing clinical reasoning through short clinical vignettes: An exploratory study]. *Recherche en Soins Infirmiers*, *118*(3), 52–61. DOI: 10.3917/rsi.118.0052 PMID: 29383920

Peters, G. A., & Peters, B. J. (2007). *Medical Error and Patient Safety: Human Factors in Medicine*. CRC Press., DOI: 10.1201/9781420064797

Pierrot, L. (2019). Les LA: Des réponses et des promesses. Distances et médiations des savoirs, 26, 1-7. DOI: 10.4000/dms.3764

Pintrich, P. R. (2004). A conceptual framework for assessing motivation and self-regulated learning in college students. *Educational Psychology Review*, *16*(4), 385–407. DOI: 10.1007/s10648-004-0006-x

Pintrich, P. R., & De Groot, E. V. (1990). Motivational and self regulated learning components of classroom academic performance. *Journal of Educational Psychology*, *82*(1), 33–40. DOI: 10.1037/0022-0663.82.1.33

Pintrinch, P. R., & Schunk, D. H. (2002). *Motivation in education : theory, research, and applications*. Merrill Prentice Hall.

Pirot, L., & De Ketele, J. (2002). L'engagement académique de l'étudiant comme facteur de réussite à l'université: Étude exploratoire menée dans deux facultés contrastées. *Revue des Sciences de l'Education*, *26*(2), 367–394. DOI: 10.7202/000127ar

Plass, J. L., & Pawar, S. (2020). Toward a taxonomy of adaptivity for learning. *Journal of Research on Technology in Education*, *52*(3), 275–300. DOI: 10.1080/15391523.2020.1719943

Poellhuber, B., & Roy, N. (2019). Quelques réflexions en lien avec l'analytique de l'apprentissage. Distances et médiations des savoirs, 26, 1-9. DOI: 10.4000/dms.3745

Pollock, J. E. (2012). *Feedback: The hinge that joins teaching and learning*. Corwin Press.

Popenici, S. A. D., & Kerr, S. (2017). Exploring the impact of artificial intelligence on teaching and learning in higher education. *Research and Practice in Technology Enhanced Learning*, *12*(1), 22–13. DOI: 10.1186/s41039-017-0062-8 PMID: 30595727

Pratama, M. P., Sampelolo, R., & Lura, H. (2023). Revolutionizing education: harnessing the power of artificial intelligence for personalized learning. Klasikal: Journal of education, language teaching and science, 5(2), 350-357. DOI: 10.52208/klasikal.v5i2.877

Predescu, M., & Apostolakis, C. (2023). Immersive horizons: Exploring virtual reality's impact on higher education pedagogy and integration. *IEEE Conference on Education Technology*, 28(3), 184–193.

Prensky, M. (2003). *Digital game-based learning. Computers in entertainment*. Paragon House.

Price, A. M., Perkins, K. K., Holmes, N. G., & Wieman, C. E. (2019). How and why do high school teachers use PhET interactive simulations? In *2017 Physics Education Research Conference Proceedings*. https://doi.org/DOI: 10.1119/perc.2018.pr.Price

Rachha, A., & Seyam, M. (2023). Explainable AI in education: Current trends, challenges, and opportunities. *SoutheastCon*, *2023*, 232–239. DOI: 10.1109/SoutheastCon51012.2023.10115140

Ragnedda, M., & Muschert, G. W. (2013). *The digital divide*. Routledge. DOI: 10.4324/9780203069769

Rahayu, I. S. D., & Purnawarman, P. (2019, June). The use of Quizizz in improving students' grammar understanding through self-assessment. In *Eleventh Conference on Applied Linguistics (CONAPLIN 2018)* (pp. 102-106). Atlantis Press.

Rahman, M. M., & Watanobe, Y. (2023). ChatGPT for education and research: Opportunities, threats, and strategies. *Applied Sciences (Basel, Switzerland)*, *13*(9), 5783. DOI: 10.3390/app13095783

Rajabhushanam, C., & Kathirvel, A. (2011). System of one to three umpire security system for wireless mobile ad hoc network. *Journal of Computational Science*, *7*(12), 1854.

Ranoliya, B. R., Raghuwanshi, N., & Singh, S. (2017). Chatbot for university related FAQs. In *2017 International Conference on Advances in Computing, Communications and Informatics (ICACCI)* (pp. 1525–1530). Udupi. DOI: 10.1109/ICACCI.2017.8126057

Rathod, V. N., Goudar, R. H., Kulkarni, A., M, D. G., & Hukkeri, G. S. (2024). A Survey on E-Learning Recommendation Systems for Autistic People. *IEEE Access : Practical Innovations, Open Solutions*, *12*, 11723–11732. DOI: 10.1109/ACCESS.2024.3355589

Reddy, K. S. V., Reddy, M. A., Kaur, V., & Kaur, G. (2022). Career Guidance System Using Ensemble Learning. SSRN *Electronic Journal*. DOI: 10.2139/ssrn.4157249

Reeve, J., & Jang, H. (2006). What teachers say and do to support students' autonomy during a learning activity. *Journal of Educational Psychology*, *98*(1), 209.

Reeves, T. C. (2000). Enhancing the worth of instructional technology research through "design experiments" and other development research strategies. International perspectives on instructional technology research for the 21st century, 27(1), 1-15.

Renz, A., & Vladova, G. (2021). Reinvigorating the Discourse on Human- Centered Artificial Intelligence in Educational Technologies. 11(5).

Reverdy, C. (2013). *Des projets pour mieux apprendre?*https://hal.science/hal-01657236

Ribeiro, M. T., Singh, S., & Guestrin, C. (2016). Model-agnostic interpretability of machine learning. *arXiv preprint arXiv:1606.05386.*

Richards, D., & Dignum, V. (2019). Supporting and challenging learners through pedagogical agents: Addressing ethical issues through designing for values. *British Journal of Educational Technology*, *50*(6), 2885–2901. DOI: 10.1111/bjet.12863

Rickabaugh, J. (2016). *Tapping the power of personalized learning: A roadmap for school leaders*. ASCD.

Ricketts, C., & Wilks, S. (2002). *Improving student performance through computer-based assessment: Insights from recent research*. Assessment & Evaluation in Higher.

Rienties, B., Simonsen, H. K., Herodotou, C., & Levy, J. (2020). Defining the Boundaries Between Artificial Intelligence in Education, Computer- Supported Collaborative Learning, Educational Data Mining, and Learning Analytics: A Need for Coherence. 1–5. DOI: 10.3389/feduc.2020.00128

Riesenberg, L. A., Leisch, J., & Cunningham, J. M. (2010). Nursing Handoffs: A Systematic Review of the Literature. *The American Journal of Nursing*, *110*(4), 24–34. DOI: 10.1097/01.NAJ.0000370154.79857.09 PMID: 20335686

Rithik, G., Kathirvel, A., & Naren, A. K. (2024a). The IoT of Robotics: The Frontier of Automation. In *Artificial Intelligence-Enabled Digital Twin for Smart Manufacturing, Wiley Publiser- Scrivener Publishing LLC, Online*. Print., DOI: 10.1002/9781394303601.ch13

Rogers, P. L. (2001). Traditions to transformations: The forced evolution of higher education. *AACE Journal*, *9*(1), 47–60.

Roll, I., & Wylie, R. (2016). Evolution and Revolution in Artificial Intelligence in Education. *International Journal of Artificial Intelligence in Education*, *26*(2), 582–599. DOI: 10.1007/s40593-016-0110-3

Romero, M. (2019). Analyser les apprentissages à partir des traces: Des opportunités aux enjeux éthiques. Distances et médiations des savoirs, 26, 1-6. DOI: 10.4000/dms.3754

Rose, E., Claudius, I., Tabatabai, R., Kearl, L., Behar, S., & Jhun, P. (2016). The Flipped Classroom in Emergency Medicine Using Online Videos with Interpolated Questions. *The Journal of Emergency Medicine*, *51*(3), 284–291.e1. DOI: 10.1016/j.jemermed.2016.05.033 PMID: 27381954

Rovai, A. P. (2007). Facilitating online discussions effectively. *The Internet and Higher Education*, *10*(1), 77–88. DOI: 10.1016/j.iheduc.2006.10.001

Rubio-Arraez, S. (2022). Improving academic performance through the combination of canvas and blackboard learn platforms in master's degree students. In *EDULEARN22 Proceedings* (pp. 8856-8862). IATED.

Ruiz Miranda, E. (2023). La révolution de l'intelligence artificielle dans l'éducation: une revue ChatGPT. Revue d'études et de recherches en psychologie et en éducation (REIPE), 10 (1), 156-160. DOI: 10.17979/reipe.2023.10.1.9594

Ryan, R. M., & Deci, E. L. J. C. e. p. (2020). Intrinsic and extrinsic motivation from a self-determination theory perspective: Definitions, theory, practices, and future directions. *61*, 101860.

Ryan, R. M., & Deci, E. L. (2022). Self-determination theory. In *Encyclopedia of quality of life and well-being research* (pp. 1–7). Springer. DOI: 10.1007/978-3-319-69909-7_2630-2

Saba, F., & Shearer, R. L. (2017). *Transactional distance and adaptive learning: Planning for the future of higher education*. Routledge. DOI: 10.4324/9780203731819

Sachete, A. S., Gomez, R. S., Filho, A. C., & De Lima, J. V. (2024). Indicators of adaptive learning in virtual learning environments: Systematic literature review. *Revista Latinoamericana de Tecnología Educativa*, *23*(2), 69–87. DOI: 10.17398/1695-288X.23.2.69

Sacré, M., Toczek, M. C., Policard, F., Serres, G., Paulet, C., Petit, S., ... & Lafontaine, D. (2020). L'efficacité d'un dispositif d'enseignement hybride en fonction des caractéristiques des étudiants. Revue internationale des technologies en pédagogie universitaire, 17(2), 9-29.

Sadhuwong, K., Koraneekij, P., & Natakuatoong, O. (2016). Effects of a Blended Learning Model Integrating Situated Multimedia Lessons and Cognitive Apprenticeship Method on the Clinical Reasoning Skills of Nursing Students. *Journal of Health Research, 30*, 6. DOI: 10.14456/jhr.2016.56

Saeed, W., & Omlin, C. (2023). Explainable AI (XAI): A systematic meta-survey of current challenges and future opportunities. *Knowledge-Based Systems, 263*, 110273. DOI: 10.1016/j.knosys.2023.110273

Sahni, J. J. J. o. E.-l., & Education, H. (2019). Does blended learning enhance student engagement? Evidence from higher education. *2019*(2019), 1-14.

Salmon, G. (2004). *E-moderating: The key to online teaching and learning*. Routledge. DOI: 10.4324/9780203465424

Sanchez, É., & Monod-Ansaldi, R. (2015). Recherche collaborative orientée par la conception: Un paradigme méthodologique pour prendre en compte la complexité des situations d'enseignement-apprentissage. Éducation et didactique, 2, 73-94.

Sari, R. P., Khasanah, U., & Pramudya, D. (2019). Developing student motivation through virtual labs in online learning environments. [iJET]. *International Journal of Emerging Technologies in Learning, 14*(4), 120–136.

Saunders, G., & Klemming, F. (2003). Integrating technology into a traditional learning environment: Reasons for and risks of success. *Active Learning in Higher Education, 4*(1), 74–86. DOI: 10.1177/1469787403004001006

Schellens, T., & Valcke, M. (2006). Fostering knowledge construction in university students through asynchronous discussion groups. *Computers & Education, 46*(4), 349–370. DOI: 10.1016/j.compedu.2004.07.010

Schiff, D. (2021). Out of the laboratory and into the classroom: The future of artificial intelligence in education. *AI & Society, 36*(1), 331–348. DOI: 10.1007/s00146-020-01033-8 PMID: 32836908

Schmid, R., & Petko, D. (2019). Does the use of educational technology in personalized learning environments correlate with self-reported digital skills and beliefs of secondary-school students?. Computers & education, 136, 75-86.19.03.006 DOI: DOI: 10.1016/j.compedu.2019.03.006

Scott, E., Soria, A., & Campo, M. (2017). Adaptive 3D Virtual Learning Environments—A Review of the Literature," in *IEEE Transactions on Learning Technologies*, vol. 10, no. 3, pp. 262-276. DOI: 10.1109/TLT.2016.2609910

Seo, K., Dodson, S., Harandi, N. M., Roberson, N., Fels, S., Roll, I. J. C., & Education. (2021). Active learning with online video: The impact of learning context on engagement. *165*, 104132.

Sheldon, KM, Ryan, R., & Reis, HT (1996). Qu'est-ce qui fait une bonne journée ? Compétence et autonomie dans la journée et chez la personne. Bulletin de psychologie sociale et de personnalité, 22 (12), 1270-1279. DOI: 10.1177/01461672962212007

Shi, Y., Yang, H., Dou, Y., & Zeng, Y. (2023). Effects of mind mapping-based instruction on student cognitive learning outcomes: A meta-analysis. *Asia Pacific Education Review*, *24*(3), 303–317. DOI: 10.1007/s12564-022-09746-9

Shorey, S., Kowitlawakul, Y., Devi, M. K., Chen, H.-C., Soong, S. K. A., & Ang, E. (2018). Blended learning pedagogy designed for communication module among undergraduate nursing students: A quasi-experimental study. *Nurse Education Today*, *61*, 120–126. DOI: 10.1016/j.nedt.2017.11.011 PMID: 29197264

Shorey, S., Siew, A. L., & Ang, E. (2017). Experiences of nursing undergraduates on a redesigned blended communication module: A descriptive qualitative study. *Nurse Education Today*. Advance online publication. DOI: 10.1016/j.nedt.2017.11.01 PMID: 29190535

Siau, K., & Wang, W. (2020). Artificial intelligence (AI) ethics: Ethics of AI and ethical AI. *Journal of Database Management*, *31*(2), 74–87. DOI: 10.4018/JDM.2020040105

Sidir, M., & Benchenna, A. (2008). Du recours aux TICE en temps de crise? Le cas des universités marocaines. *Distances Et Savoirs*, *6*(2), 211–236. DOI: 10.3166/ds.6.211-236

Siemens, G., & Baker, R. (2012). Learning analytics and educational data mining: Towards communication and collaboration. *Proceedings of the 2nd International Conference on Learning Analytics and Knowledge*, 252-254. DOI: 10.1145/2330601.2330661

Singhal, A., Pratap, P., Dixit, K. K., & Kathuria, K. (2024, Mar). Advancements in Explainable AI: Bridging the Gap Between Model Complexity and Interpretability. In *2024 2nd International Conference on Disruptive Technologies (ICDT)* (pp. 675-680). IEEE.

Singh, H. (2003). Building effective blended learning programs. *Educational Technology*, *43*(6), 51–54. Retrieved July 09, 2010, from https://www.bookstoread.com/framework/blended-learning.pdf

Singh, H., & Miah, S. J. (2020). Smart education literature: A theoretical analysis. *Education and Information Technologies, 25*(4), 3299–3328. DOI: 10.1007/s10639-020-10116-4

Siron, J. L., Bertrand, A., Kostine, M., Lichaud, O., Berard, E., Mehsen, N., & Germain, P. (2023). Evaluating artificial intelligence: 30 open-ended questions for ChatGPT. *Journal of Rheumatism, 90*, A240.

Smith, D., Cleak, H., & Vreugdenhil, A. J. A. s. w. (2015). "What are they really doing?" An exploration of student learning activities in field placement. *68*(4), 515-531.

Smith, C. M., & McDonald, K. (2013). The Flipped Classroom for Professional Development: Part II. Making Podcasts and Videos. *Journal of Continuing Education in Nursing, 44*(11), 486–487. DOI: 10.3928/00220124-20131025-93 PMID: 24199640

Smyth, S., Houghton, C., Cooney, A., & Casey, D. (2012). Students' experiences of blended learning across a range of postgraduate programmes. *Nurse Education Today, 32*(4), 464–468. DOI: 10.1016/j.nedt.2011.05.014 PMID: 21645947

Sowan, A. K., & Jenkins, L. S. J. I. j. o. m. i. (2013). Designing, delivering and evaluating a distance learning nursing course responsive to students needs. *82*(6), 553-564.

Srinivasa, K. G., & Kurni, M. (2021). *A beginner's guide to learning analytics*. Springer.

Steinbauer, G., Kandlhofer, M., Chklovski, T., Heintz, F., & Koenig, S. (2021). A differentiated discussion about AI education K-12. *Kunstliche Intelligenz, 35*(2), 131–137. DOI: 10.1007/s13218-021-00724-8 PMID: 34007103

Stelios, A., & Lyapunov, V. (2023). Enhancing critical thinking skills through VR-based educational modules. *Journal of Applied Educational Research, 15*(1), 89–110.

Sternberger, C. S. (2002). Embedding a Pedagogical Model in the Design of an Online Course. *Nurse Educator, 27*(4), 170–173. DOI: 10.1097/00006223-200207000-00009 PMID: 12131813

Stokel-Walker, C. (2022). AI bot ChatGPT writes smart essays-should academics worry? *Nature*. Advance online publication. DOI: 10.1038/d41586-022-04397-7 PMID: 36494443

Stone, R., Cooke, M., & Mitchell, M. (2019). Undergraduate nursing students' use of video technology in developing confidence in clinical skills for practice: A systematic integrative literature review. *Nurse Education Today, 104230.* Advance online publication. DOI: 10.1016/j.nedt.2019.104230 PMID: 31689584

Su, J., Ng, DTK et Chu, SKW (2023). L'intelligence artificielle (IA) dans l'éducation de la petite enfance: défis et opportunités. Ordinateurs et éducation: intelligence artificielle, 4, 100124. DOI: 10.1016/j.caeai.2023.100124

Subramaniam, M., Kathirvel, A., Sabitha, E., & Anwar Basha, H. (2021), "Modified Firefly Algorithm and Fuzzy C-Mean Clustering Based Semantic Information Retrieval", Journal of Web Engineering, Vol. 20 1, 33–52, 2021. Publisher: © River Publishers, 15 Feb 2021, ISSN: 1540-9589 (Print Version). ISSN: 1544-5976 (Online Version), DOI: 10.13052/jwe1540-9589.2012

Su, J., & Zhong, Y. (2022). Artificial intelligence (AI) in early childhood education: Curriculum design and future directions. *Computers and Education: Artificial Intelligence*, *3*, 100072. DOI: 10.1016/j.caeai.2022.100072

Sujatha, D., Subramaniam, M., & Kathirvel, A. (2023). *Class Level Multi-Feature Semantic Similarity Based Efficient Multimedia Big Data Retrieval", ARTIFICIAL INTELLIGENT TECHNIQUES FOR WIRELESS COMMUNICATION AND NETWORKING*. Scrivener Publishing, John Wiley & Sons., DOI: 10.1002/9781119821809.ch11

Sundar, R., & Kathirvel, A. (2015). Enhanced Trust Based Delegation for Load Balancing in Manets. *International Journal of Applied Engineering Research: IJAER*, *10*(92), 104–109.

Sundar, R., & Kathirvel, A. (2020a). Aggressively delivered mechanism over variable length density using a simulated annealing algorithm in mobile ad hoc network. *Transactions on Emerging Telecommunications Technologies*, *31*(12), e3863.

Sundar, R., & Kathirvel, A. (2020b). Enhanced cluster-based stable path for load balancing and reducing overhead using artificial bee colony in MANETs. *International Journal of Vehicle Information and Communication Systems*, *5*(1), 41–54.

Sundar, R., & Kathirvel, D. A. (2019). Efficient prior path failure recovery algorithm using channel aware routing in manet. *International Journal of Innovative Technology and Exploring Engineering*, *8*(5), 97–103.

Sung, Y. H., Kwon, I. G., & Ryu, E. (2008). Blended learning on medication administration for new nurses: Integration of e-learning and face-to-face instruction in the classroom. *Nurse Education Today, 28*(8), 943–952. DOI: 10.1016/j.nedt.2008.05.007 PMID: 18599162

Susarla, A., Gopal, R., Thatcher, J. B., & Sarker, S. (2023). The Janus effect of generative AI: Charting the path for responsible conduct of scholarly activities in information systems. *Information Systems Research, 34*(2), 1–10. DOI: 10.1287/isre.2023.ed.v34.n2

Tadlaoui, M., Sehaba, K., & George, S. (2015). Recommendation of Learning Resources based on Social Relations: *Proceedings of the 7th International Conference on Computer Supported Education*, 425-432. DOI: 10.5220/0005452304250432

Talaghzi, J., Bennane, A., Himmi, M., Bellafkih, M., & Benomar, A. (2020). Online AdaptiveLearning: A Review of Literature. *ACM Int. Conf. Proceeding Ser.*, pp. 115–120. DOI: DOI: 10.1145/3419604.3419759

Talbot, L. (2009). *L'évaluation formative: comment évaluer pour remédier aux difficultés d'apprentissage*. Armand Colin.

Tan, C., Yue, W. G., & Fu, Y. (2017). Effectiveness of flipped classrooms in nursing education: Systematic review and meta-analysis. *Chinese Nursing Research, 4*(4), 192–200. Advance online publication. DOI: 10.1016/j.cnre.2017.10.006

Tardif, J. (2015). La construction des connaissances. 2, Les pratiques pédagogiques. v. 11, no 3, mars 1998, p. 4-9 Pédagogie collégiale.

Terzopoulos, G., & Satratzemi, M. (2019). Voice Assistants and Artificial Intelligence in Education. *Proceedings of the 9th Balkan Conference on Informatics*, 1–6. DOI: 10.1145/3351556.3351588

Thérèse, B., & Warnier, L. (2016). Evaluer les acquis des étudiants à l'aide de QCM. Louvain: Université catholique de Louvain. https://cdn.uclouvain.be/public/Exports%20reddot/ipm/documents/VADEMECUM_Mars_2016.pdf

Thomas, J. A., Wadsworth, D., Jin, Y., Clarke, J., Page, R., Thunders, M. J. H. E. R., & Development. (2017). Engagement with online self-tests as a predictor of student success. *36*(5), 1061-1071.

Thomas, C. M., Bertram, E., & Johnson, D. (2009). The SBAR Communication Technique: Teaching Nursing Students Professional Communication Skills. *Nurse Educator, 34*(4), 176–180. DOI: 10.1097/NNE.0b013e3181aaba54 PMID: 19574858

Thomas, K. M., O'Bannon, B. W., & Bolton, N. (2013). Cell phones in the classroom: Teachers' perspectives of inclusion, benefits, and barriers. *Computers in the Schools*, *30*(4), 295–308.

Thorne, S. L. (2008). Transcultural communication in open internet environments and massively multiplayer online games. In Matters, M. (Ed.), *Language, education and technology* (pp. 107–124). DOI: 10.1075/aals.3.17tho

Thorp, H. H. (2023). ChatGPT is fun, but not an author. Science. *Science*, *379*(6630), 313. DOI: 10.1126/science.adg7879 PMID: 36701446

Timmis, S., Broadfoot, P., Sutherland, R. et Oldfield, A. (2016). Repenser l'évaluation à l'ère numérique: opportunités, défis et risques. Journal britannique de recherche pédagogique, 42 (3), 454-476.

Timmis, S., Broadfoot, P., Sutherland, R., & Oldfield, A. (2016). Rethinking assessment in a digital age: Opportunities, challenges and risks. *British Educational Research Journal*, *42*(3), 454–476. DOI: 10.1002/berj.3215

Timms, M. J. (2016). Letting Artificial Intelligence in Education Out of the Box: Educational Cobots and Smart Classrooms. *International Journal of Artificial Intelligence in Education*, *26*(2), 701–712. DOI: 10.1007/s40593-016-0095-y

Tubaro, P. (2019). Les Learning Analytics vus par la sociologie. Distances et médiations des savoirs, 28, 1-8. DOI: 10.4000/dms.4608

Tuomi, I. (2018). The Impact of Artificial Intelligence on Learning, Teaching, and Education, JRC Science for Policy Report, European Joint Research Centre. https://publications.jrc.ec.europa.eu/repository/bitstream/JRC113226/jrc113226_jrcb4_the_impact_of_artificial_intelligence_on_learning_final_2.pdf

Turan, Z., & Avincan, E. (2022). The role of virtual reality in enhancing practical skills in remote education. *Interactive Learning Environments*, *30*(7), 1005–1021.

UOttawa Teaching and Learning Support Service (SAEA). (2016). Quality Hybrid Course grid. UOttawa. https://saea.uottawa.ca/site/files/docs/SAEA/fonds-hybride/2017/SAEAAQGrille.pdf

Urdaneta-Ponte, M. C., Mendez-Zorrilla, A., & Oleagordia-Ruiz, I. (2021). Recommendation Systems for Education : Systematic Review. *Electronics (Basel)*, *10*(14), 1611. DOI: 10.3390/electronics10141611

Valentine, A., Gemin, B., Vashaw, L., Watson, J., Harrington, C., & LeBlanc, E. (2021). Digital learning in rural K–12 settings: A survey of challenges and progress in the United States. Research Anthology on Developing Effective Online Learning Courses, 1987-2019. DOI: DOI: 10.4018/978-1-7998-8047-9.ch099

Vallerand, R. J. (1997). Toward a hierarchical model of intrinsic and extrinsic motivation. In Zanna, M. P. (Ed.), (pp. 271–360). Advances in experimental social psychology. Academic Press. DOI: 10.1016/S0065-2601(08)60019-2

Van Dis, E. A., Bollen, J., Zuidema, W., van Rooij, R., & Bockting, C. L. (2023). ChatGPT: Five priorities for research. *Nature*, *614*(7947), 224–226. DOI: 10.1038/d41586-023-00288-7 PMID: 36737653

Vanderhoven, E., Schellens, T., Vanderlinde, R., & Valcke, M. (2016). Developing educational materials about risks on social network sites: A design based research approach. *Educational Technology Research and Development*, *64*(3), 459–480. DOI: 10.1007/s11423-015-9415-4

VanLehn, K. (2006). The behavior of tutoring systems. *International Journal of Artificial Intelligence in Education*, *16*(3), 227–265.

Varsamidou, A. (2024). The pedagogical value of mind maps in the FLE classroom: How to integrate them into didactic scenarios to develop and assess language skills. *Journal of Languages and Translation*, *4*(2), 14–24. DOI: 10.70204/jlt.v4i2.375

Verlot, M., & Suijs, S. (2000). L'apprentissage pragmatique de l'interculturel. *Diversité*, *120*(1), 111–125.

Viau, R. (2009). *La motivation à apprendre en milieu scolaire*. Erpi.

Viel, C. C., Rodrigues, K. R. da H., Melo, E. L., Bueno, R., Pimentel, M. D. G. C., & Teixeira, C. A. C. (2014). Interaction with a Problem Solving Multi Video Lecture: Observing Students from Distance and Traditional Learning Courses. [IJET]. *International Journal of Emerging Technologies in Learning*, *9*(1), 39. DOI: 10.3991/ijet.v9i1.3358

Vujadinovic, N. (2020). Communication and Public Relations in Healthcare. In *Health Information Management: Empowering Public Health* (pp. 42–51). IOS Press. https://doi.org/DOI: 10.3233/SHTI200664

Vygotskiĭ, L. S. (1987). *Mind in society: the development of higher psychological processes*. Harvard University Press.

Vytasek, J. M., Patzak, A., & Winne, P. H. (2020). Analytics for student engagement. *Machine learning paradigms: Advances in Learning Analytics*, 23-48.

Walckiers, M., & De Praetere, T. (2004). L'apprentissage collaboratif en ligne, huit avantages qui en font un must. *Distances Et Savoirs*, *2*(1), 53–75. DOI: 10.3166/ds.2.53-75

Walkington, C., & Bernacki, M. L. (2020). Appraising research on personalized learning: Definitions, theoretical alignment, advancements, and future directions. *Journal of Research on Technology in Education*, *52*(3), 235–252. DOI: 10.1080/15391523.2020.1747757

Wang, F. H. (2024, Jun). On the Effect of Explainable AI on Programming Learning: A Case Study of using Gradient Integration Technology. In *CS & IT Conference Proceedings* (Vol. 14, No. 12). CS & IT Conference Proceedings. DOI: 10.5121/csit.2024.141202

Wang, F., & Hannafin, M. J. (2005). Design-based research and technology-enhanced learning environments. *Educational Technology Research and Development*, *53*(4), 5–23. DOI: 10.1007/BF02504682

Wang, H., Lee, J., & Chang, M. (2023). Interactive 3D models for technical English learning in engineering. *International Journal of Educational Technology in Higher Education*, *20*(1), 15. PMID: 36919042

Ward, M., Knowlton, M. C., & Laney, C. W. (2018). The flip side of traditional nursing education: A literature review. *Nurse Education in Practice*, *29*, 163–171. DOI: 10.1016/j.nepr.2018.01.003 PMID: 29414110

Warschauer, M. (1997). Computer-mediated collaborative learning: Theory and practice. *Modern Language Journal*, *81*(4), 470–481.

Warschauer, M., Shetzer, H., & Meloni, C. (2000). Internet for English teaching. *TESOL Journal*, *9*(2), 7–11.

Watson, W. R., Watson, S. L., & Reigeluth, C. M. (2012). A systemic integration of technology for new-paradigm education. *Educational Technology*, *52*, 25–29.

Wells-Beede, E. (2020). The Flipped Classroom in Nursing: The Nurse Educators' Experience. *Teaching and Learning in Nursing*, *15*(3), 168–174. DOI: 10.1016/j.teln.2020.02.002

Welser, H. T., Khan, M. L., & Dickard, M. (2019). Digital remediation: Social support and online learning communities can help offset rural digital inequality. *Information Communication and Society*, *22*(5), 717–723. DOI: 10.1080/1369118X.2019.1566485

Wenger, E. (2014). *Artificial intelligence and tutoring systems: Computational and cognitive approaches to the communication of knowledge*. Morgan Kaufmann.

Westman, S., Kauttonen, J., Klemetti, A., Korhonen, N., Manninen, M., Mononen, A., Niittymäki, S., & Paananen, H. (2021). Artificial Intelligence for Career Guidance – Current Requirements and Prospects for the Future. *IAFOR Journal of Education*, *9*(4), 43–62. DOI: 10.22492/ije.9.4.03

Williams, D. A. J. J. o. R. (2017). Exploring the issues of adult students with brain injuries in the online learning environment. *83*(3), 53-61.

Williamson, B. (2017). Big data in education: The digital future of learning, policy and practice. *Sage (Atlanta, Ga.)*. Advance online publication. DOI: 10.4135/9781529714920

Wogu, I. A. P., Misra, S., Olu-Owolabi, E. F., Assibong, P. A., & Udoh, O. D. (2018). Artificial Intelligence, Artificial Teachers and the Fate of Learners in the 21st Century Education Sector: Implications for Theory and Practice. *International Journal of Pure and Applied Mathematics*, *119*(16), 2245–2259.

Wu, L., Shah, S., Choi, S., Tiwari, M., & Posse, C. (2014). The browsemaps: Collaborative filtering at LinkedIn. RSWeb@ RecSys, 1271.

Xu, G., Jia, G., Shi, L., & Zhang, Z. (2021). Personalized Course Recommendation System Fusing with Knowledge Graph and Collaborative Filtering. *Computational Intelligence and Neuroscience*, *2021*(1), 9590502. DOI: 10.1155/2021/9590502 PMID: 34616447

Xu, Z. (2024). AI in education: Enhancing learning experiences and student outcomes. *Applied and Computational Engineering*, *51*(1), 104–111. DOI: 10.54254/2755-2721/51/20241187

Yang, T. (2017, June). The mind map, a didactic tool to aid memorization for lexicon teaching/learning. In RJC2017-20èmes Rencontres des jeunes chercheurs en Sciences du Langage

Yang, T. (2024). Impact of Artificial Intelligence Software on English Learning Motivation and Achievement. In SHS Web of Conferences (Vol. 193, p. 02011). EDP Sciences. DOI: 10.1051/shsconf/202419302011

Yang, Y. J., & Wu, C. (2009). An attribute-based ant colony system for adaptive learning object recommendation. *Expert Systems with Applications*, *36*(2), 3034–3047. DOI: 10.1016/j.eswa.2008.01.066

Youssef, L., Chemsi, G., & Radid, M. (2023). The Effect of Group Size on Students' Cognitive and Behavioral Engagement. *International Journal of Emerging Technologies in Learning*, *18*(15).

Zalte, S. M. (2023). Revolutionizing education: Leveraging ai-ml technologies to enhance teaching and learning outcomes. 12(12), 679–688. https://doi.org/DOI: 10.48047/ecb/2023.12.si12.058

Zayet, T. M. A., Ismail, M. A., Almadi, S. H. S., Zawia, J. M. H., & Mohamad Nor, A. (2023). What is needed to build a personalized recommender system for K-12 students' E-Learning? Recommendations for future systems and a conceptual framework. *Education and Information Technologies*, *28*(6), 7487–7508. DOI: 10.1007/s10639-022-11489-4 PMID: 36532791

Zhang, Q., Lu, J., & Jin, Y. (2021). Artificial intelligence in recommender systems. *Complex & Intelligent Systems*, *7*(1), 439–457. DOI: 10.1007/s40747-020-00212-w

Zhang, Y., & Li, F. (2023). Virtual language training for cross-cultural business communication. *Business Communication Quarterly*, *86*(2), 101–118.

Zhao, F. (2019). Using Quizizz to integrate fun multiplayer activity in the accounting classroom. *International Journal of Higher Education*, *8*(1), 37–43. DOI: 10.5430/ijhe.v8n1p37

Zheng, L., Bhagat, K. K., Zhen, Y., Zhang, X. J. J. o. E. T., & Society. (2020). The effectiveness of the flipped classroom on students' learning achievement and learning motivation. *23*(1), 1-15.

Zhu, Z. T., Yu, M. H., & Riezebos, P. (2016). A research framework of smart education. *Smart learning environments, 3*, 1-17.

Zhu, L., Lian, Z., & Engström, M. (2019). Use of a flipped classroom in ophthalmology courses for nursing, dental and medical students: A quasi-experimental study using a mixed-methods approach. *Nurse Education Today*, *104262*. Advance online publication. DOI: 10.1016/j.nedt.2019.104262 PMID: 31759243

Zimmerman, B. J., & Labuhn, A. S. (2012). Self-regulation of learning: Process approaches to personal development.

Zimmerman, B. J., & Martinez-Pons, M. (1988). Construct validation of a strategy model of student self-regulated learning. *Journal of Educational Psychology*, *80*(3), 284–290. DOI: 10.1037/0022-0663.80.3.284

Zotou, M., Tambouris, E., Tarabanis, K. J. E. T. R., & Development. (2020). Data-driven problem based learning: Enhancing problem based learning with learning analytics. *68*(6), 3393-3424.

Zouaoui, M. (2006). L'enseignement supérieur depuis l'indépendance: la dégradation de la qualité était-elle inéluctable? In *Cinquante ans de développement humain au Maroc et perspectives 2025* (pp. 159–195).

Zwarenstein, M., Goldman, J., & Reeves, S. (2009). Interprofessional collaboration: Effects of practice-based interventions on professional practice and healthcare outcomes. *The Cochrane Library*. Advance online publication. DOI: 10.1002/14651858.CD000072.pub2 PMID: 19588316

Видавництво, П. А. І. С. (2021, avril). Expérience d'utilisation de Google Classroom dans le processus d'étude des étudiants francophones à l'Académie de médecine de Dnipropetrovsk. *The DSMU Repository*. https://repo.dma.dp.ua/7211/

About The Contributors

Assia Benabid is an academic based at the Faculty of Sciences Ben M'Sick, Casablanca, Morocco, and has contributed significantly to educational research. Her work primarily focuses on addressing issues in higher education, including university dropout rates and improving language competencies among science students. One of her notable studies explores the phenomenon of university dropout in Morocco, identifying causes such as the language barrier in higher education and inadequate guidance for students. This research, conducted at the Faculty of Sciences Ben M'Sick, involved surveying undergraduate students and highlighted the need for better support systems to reduce dropout rates(NVEO). Additionally, Benabid has also contributed to improving scientific writing among Moroccan postgraduate students. She emphasizes the importance of a structured writing process to help students develop linguistic competence in French, particularly in the context of science education(EU Journal). These works demonstrate her commitment to enhancing education and student success in Morocco.

Ghizlane Chemsi has a PhD in Educational Technology. She is a Professor at the Faculty of Sciences at Ben M'Sick, Hassan II University of Casablanca, Morocco. She operates in several fields of educational sciences, including educational technologies, assessment, and engineering of assessments. She is a member of the Observatory of Research in Didactics and University Pedagogy (ORDIPU), the Association for the Development of Evaluation Methodologies in Education (ADMEE)-Morocco, and the Multidisciplinary Laboratory in Sciences and Information Communication and Education Technology (LAPSTICE) (E-mail: g.chemsi@gmail.com).

***

A K Naren, scholar, Anand Institue of Higher Technology,, chennai

Omar Abidi - Professor at the Higher Institute of Health Professions and Techniques of Casablanca. Morocco. Deputy Director in charge of Scientific Research, Continuing Education and Cooperation.

Mounir Arai - Professor at the Higher Institute of Health Professions and Techniques of Casablanca. Morocco. Doctor in Health sciences.

Kathirvel Ayyaswamy, acquired, B.E.(CSE), M.E. (CSE) from Crescent Engineering College affiliated to University of Madras and Ph. D (CSE.) from Anna University. He is currently working as Professor, Dept of Computer Science and Engineering, Saveetha Engineering College, Chennai. He is a studious researcher by himself, completed 18 sponsored research projects worth of Rs 103 lakhs and published more than 110 articles in journals and conferences. 6 research scholars have completed Ph. D and 3 under progress under his guidance. He is working as scientific and editorial board member of many journals. He has reviewed dozens of papers in many journals. He has author of 19 books. His research interests are protocol development for wireless ad hoc networks, security in ad hoc network, data communication and networks, mobile computing, wireless networks, WSN and DTN. He is a Life member of the ISTE (India), IACSIT (Singapore), Life Member IAENG (Hong Kong), Member ICST (Europe), IAES, etc. He has given a number of guest lecturers/expert talks and seminars, workshops and symposiums.

Mohamed Badouch is a computer engineer and PhD student in artificial intelligence at Ibn Zohr University in Agadir, Morocco, with over 7 years of professional experience. He is also a part-time professor in computer science at Chouaib Doukkali University, where he prepares and teaches modules on Machine Learning, Deep Learning, and Object-Oriented Programming. Mohamed has actively participated in numerous international conferences, presenting his work on recommendation systems and machine learning. His notable contributions include presentations on hotel recommendation systems using Deep Learning, comparative analysis of machine learning algorithms, and intelligent recommendations. In addition to his conference activities, he has published several scientific articles in Scopus-indexed journals, covering topics such as e-commerce recommendation systems and tourism. Mohamed is also a member of the organizing committee of several international conferences and a reviewer for scientific journals. His teaching and research activities are complemented by ongoing academic training in scientific writing and artificial intelligence.

Ghizlane Chemsi has a PhD in Educational Technology. She is a Professor at the Faculty of Sciences at Ben M'Sick, Hassan II University of Casablanca, Morocco. She operates in several fields of educational sciences, including educational technologies, assessment, and engineering of assessments. She is a member of the Observatory of Research in Didactics and University Pedagogy (ORDIPU), the Association for the Development of Evaluation Methodologies in Education (ADMEE)-Morocco, and the Multidisciplinary Laboratory in Sciences and Information Communication and Education Technology (LAPSTICE) (E-mail: g.chemsi@gmail.com).

Wissam El Machtani El Idrissi, Professor at the Higher Institute of Health Professions and Techniques * Doctor in educational sciences * Master's degree in paramedical sciences

G.B.Hema Latha is a experienced faculty professional with 23 years of teaching experience with diverse set of academic qualifications like Ph.D in (Computer Science), M.Phil in (Computer Science),M.Tech in (Information Technology & Engineering) &MCA. Published and presented research Paper in national and international conference and journals like web of Science.Her areas of research interest are image processing and Green computing. She is also member of Board of studies, as subject expert in various colleges.

Rachid Gouifrane - Professor at the Higher Institute of Health Professions and Techniques of Casablanca. Morocco. Doctor in educational sciences.

Youssef Laaziz is a PhD student in the Laboratory of Physical Chemistry of Materials at the Faculty of Sciences Ben M'Sick (LCPM), Hassan II University of Casablanca, Morocco. He is a researcher in the field of education and training. Additionally, he serves as a pedagogical inspector of primary education at the Ministry of National Education, Preschool, and Sports (E-mail: youssef.laaziz-etu@ etu.univh2c.ma).

Halima Lajane - Professor at the Higher Institute of Health Professions and Techniques of Casablanca. Morocco. Doctor in educational sciences.

Abderrahmane Lamiri - Professor at the Higher Institute of Health Professions and Techniques of Casablanca. Morocco. Doctor in educational sciences.

Amina Lhbibani - Professor at the Higher Institute of Health Professions and Techniques of Casablanca. Morocco. Doctor in educational sciences.

Hasna Mahmoud, I am a PhD researcher in Computer Science at the Faculty of Sciences University Ibn Zohr:. I graduated with a Master's degree in Big Data and

Artificial Intelligence from the Faculty of Taroudant in 2023. My research centers on advancements in Artificial Intelligence.

Mohsen Mahmoudi-Dehaki is currently an Assistant Professor in Teaching English as a Foreign Language (TEFL) at the Islamic Azad University of Najafabad, Iran. With more than ten years of experience in educating both undergraduate and postgraduate students, he has gained recognition as a distinguished educator and researcher. His scholarly work has been extensively published in various national and international journals, enhancing his standing in the academic community. In addition to his teaching responsibilities, Dr. Mahmoudi-Dehaki actively participates as a peer reviewer for several reputable scientific journals, which upholds rigorous academic standards. He has received notable accolades, such as winning first place in the English Writing Award in Iran, a prestigious honor awarded to university students across state institutions. His research paper titled "COVID-19 Lingo or Covidipedia" has attracted considerable attention, amassing over 70,000 visits and becoming the most viewed article in Iranian scientific journals. This achievement highlights his substantial influence within the academic sector. Dr. Mahmoudi-Dehaki's research and teaching interests encompass a wide array of innovative areas within applied linguistics, including psycho/cognitive/neurocognitive/sociocultural aspects and clinical linguistics. He also possesses expertise in educational technology, educational psychology, and psychometrics, showcasing his diverse knowledge across interdisciplinary fields related to education and linguistics.

Maria Mazouri - Professor at the Higher Institute of Health Professions and Techniques of Casablanca. Morocco. Doctor in private law.

Aziz Naciri: is a PhD in Educational Technology at Faculty of Sciences Ben M'Sik, University Hassan II of Casablanca, Morocco, B.P 7955 Sidi Othmane. He is a Lecturer and coordinator of the option: "social worker" at the Higher Institute of Nursing and Health Techniques of Laayoune, Morocco.

Nasim Nasr-Esfahani, PhD, is an Assistant Professor of TEFL at the Islamic Azad University of Isfahan (Khorasgan), Iran. She earned her PhD in TEFL at the Islamic Azad University of Isfahan, Khorasgan. She has over two decades of experience teaching undergraduate and postgraduate students in Iran. Her publications have appeared in leading international journals, such as the Australian Journal of Teacher Education. She serves as a reviewer and article editor of RELP Journal. Her areas of research and teaching interests are dynamic and evolving and span language education, generative artificial intelligence (GenAI) in education, critical thinking skills, oral and written communication skills, student engagement, advancing equity in education, brain-based teaching and learning, neurolinguistics, psycholinguistics as well as teaching and research methodologies.

Rabia Qaisar - Professor at the Higher Institute of Health Professions and Techniques of Casablanca. Morocco. Doctor in educational sciences.

Mohamed Radid has a PhD in Physical Chemistry. He is currently the Vice Dean of the Faculty of Sciences at Ben M'Sick, Hassan II University of Casablanca, Morocco, a position he has held since 2014. He is a member of the Observatory of Research in Didactics and University Pedagogy (ORDIPU) and a member of the Board of Directors of the Association for the Development of Evaluation Methodologies in Education (ADMEE)-Europe. He is an expert in the fields of teaching and research on educational technologies assessment, engineering of assessment, chemistry didactics, and university pedagogy (E-mail: m.radid@gmail .com)

Mohamed Radid has a PhD in Physical Chemistry. He is currently the Vice Dean of the Faculty of Sciences at Ben M'Sick, Hassan II University of Casablanca, Morocco, a position he has held since 2014. He is a member of the Observatory of Research in Didactics and University Pedagogy (ORDIPU) and a member of the Board of Directors of the Association for the Development of Evaluation Methodologies in Education (ADMEE)-Europe. He is an expert in the fields of teaching and research on educational technologies assessment, engineering of assessment, chemistry didactics, and university pedagogy (E-mail: m.radid@gmail .com).

Index

A

B

C

D

E

P

Q

S

V

X

www.ingramcontent.com/pod-product-compliance
Ingram Content Group UK Ltd.
Pitfield, Milton Keynes, MK11 3LW, UK
UKHW050948290926
15470UKWH00005B/1710

9 798337 307404